FOUNDATIONS
OF HUMAN BEHAVIOR

FOUNDATIONS
OF HUMAN BEHAVIOR

Louis Kaplan

Harper & Row, Publishers, New York, Evanston, and London

F-R

TO MY WIFE, SALLY,

AND OUR SONS, PAUL AND STEVEN

CONTENTS

PREFACE   xi

PART I. BEHAVIOR AND ADJUSTMENT

1. The Adjustment Process   3

Problems of adjustment in modern society. The
meaning of adjustment. Criteria of adjustment. Varieties of adjustive behavior.

2. Psychobiological Origins of Human Behavior   20
Facts and theories of heredity. Factors modifying the
influence of heredity. Brain function and behavior.
Glandular and metabolic influences on behavior. Social influences on biological functioning.

3. The Growth Process   44
Normal stages of growth. Some basic principles of
growth. Dynamics of growth. Need satisfactions
and personality development.

4. Psychological Forces in the Home   70
Role of the mother. Influence of the father in the
home. Patterns of parent-child interaction. Disciplinary practices in the family. Psychological effects
of a child's position in the family.

5. Cultural Influences on Behavior 97
Interaction of family and culture. Social-class influences on adjustment.

PART II. ATTAINING MATURITY

6. The Self Concept 123
Emergence of the self concept. Self concept and behavior. Changes in the self.

7. Emotional Development 149
Nature of emotions. Differentiation of emotional behavior. Emotional maturity.

8. Development and Decline of Human Abilities 171
Physical and motor development. Intelligence and mental activity. Age and productivity. Factors which affect the use of abilities.

PART III. PSYCHOLOGICAL STRESS AND
ADJUSTMENT TO STRESS

9. Psychological Stress 199
Some sources of psychological stress. Acute and chronic stress. Somatic reactions to psychological stress. Anxiety as a response to stress. Patterns of reaction to stress. Stress tolerance.

10. Coping with Anxiety 224
Classification of defense mechanisms. Mechanisms of deception. Mechanisms of substitution. Mechanisms of avoidance. The function of adjustment mechanisms.

11. The Deterioration of Adjustment 246
Symptoms of maladjustment. Personality deviations.

12. Severe Disorders of Behavior 267
The neuroses. The psychoses. Origins of the psychoses.

PART IV. READJUSTMENT AND THE PREVENTION OF MALADJUSTMENT

13. **Therapy and Readjustment** 299
Somatic therapies. Psychological therapies.

14. **Mental Hygiene** 323
Primary prevention. Secondary prevention. Mental-hygiene programs. Effects of mental-hygiene programs on prevention of maladjustment.

INDEX OF NAMES 349
INDEX OF SUBJECTS 357

PREFACE

The study of human adjustment extends into the fields of psychology, psychiatry, biology, medicine, sociology, education, physiology, mental hygiene, and other sciences and social sciences which have to do with human behavior. How to merge these various streams of knowledge into a meaningful whole which is neither too superficial nor too cluttered with detail is a matter of conjecture.

Problems of adjustment usually are approached in one of two ways. The first is to deal with specific life situations, such as dating, sexual relationships, vocational choice, and the like, hoping to derive principles of behavior from a discussion of these basic problems. Another approach is to present research findings and generally accepted concepts about human behavior, and leave it to the instructor and his students to make the personal applications.

The author has chosen the second of these alternatives, partly because the increased sophistication of the modern college student enables him to handle research findings intelligently, and partly because the discussion of specific problems has, in his experience, proved more entertaining than enlightening. Therefore, this textbook does not propose to teach the student how to achieve happiness, how to resolve his personal conflicts, or how to attain a perfect state of adjustment. Instead, it draws upon hundreds of references from many disciplines and tries to present a clear, systematic description of what is known about the process of adjustment, on the assumption that such knowledge will aid the individual to understand himself and gain insight into the behavior of others.

The underlying purpose of this book is to trace the course of normal adjustment and describe the factors which are instrumental in shaping human behavior. We take the position that the human organism is born with certain capacities and characteristics which are influenced by heredity and by his biophysical makeup. As he grows, he evolves a personality and a concept of himself which are strongly influenced by the environmental forces he encounters. The process of adjustment is one of attaining a reasonable balance between a variety of forces within the individual and a variety of demands in the environment. No one achieves a perfect balance of these forces, or a completely stable one. No one achieves complete mastery of himself or of his environment. The best an individual can hope for is to meet life's requirements and demands with as much understanding as he can acquire.

This basic theme is expanded upon in the four parts of this textbook. Part I outlines present knowledge of the interrelationships between physiological, psychological, and social processes, as they form the foundations of behavior. Part II deals with the dynamics of behavior and the basic forces underlying the development of adjustment. Part III describes the major stresses encountered in life and how adjustment may deteriorate under the impact of stress. Part IV is concerned with means of regaining satisfactory adjustment and with the prevention of maladjustment.

Since this is intended to be a brief book, each of these subjects is treated concisely and with a minimum of descriptive material. References are provided at the close of each chapter not only to document the content of the chapter but also to provide the student with resources for probing more deeply into the subject.

L.K.

PART I BEHAVIOR AND ADJUSTMENT

Chapter 1　　The
Adjustment Process

As we move toward the twenty-first century on a wave of accelerating technological and scientific development, it becomes increasingly important to ask what is happening to man's ability to cope with the new environment he is creating. Many students of human behavior are seriously concerned with this question. They see evidence of widespread emotional instability and anxiety; so widespread that some have labeled this the "age of anxiety" (38).

Other generations have faced threat, peril, and anxiety, but there is something different about the tensions which confront us today. Current emotional stresses are more subtle, more intangible, and more pervasive. They provide no easy targets to attack, no savages to conquer, no plagues to fight, no places to hide. Instead, man is faced with an increasingly complex world, which taxes his adjustive capacities and makes it difficult for him to order his environment and achieve a sense of harmony with it.

These facts make it imperative for the educated person to know something about the stresses and strains of modern living and to become acquainted with the dynamics of human behavior and adjustment. He needs to know these things so that he can live his own life more intelligently and exert a wholesome influence on the lives of others.

We begin our study by reviewing some of the evidence on maladjustment so that the extent of this problem may be appreciated. Thereafter, we shall present an organized compilation of fact and theory regarding the dynamics of human behavior. However, it should be noted at the outset that this book does not offer a prescription for living, nor provide recipes for attaining success. It deals with fundamental facts and principles which have been shown to be important if people are to develop their full potentialities and reach a reasonable level of emotional stability and personal adequacy. Such knowledge will not guarantee better adjustment, since many factors interfere with an individual's ability to utilize his intellect in meeting the problems of life. However, without some understanding of the process of adjustment a person is limited in the extent to which he can comprehend, modify, or adjust to, the factors which are instrumental in shaping his pattern of living (25).

PROBLEMS OF ADJUSTMENT IN MODERN SOCIETY

There is little question that psychological disorders and disturbed interpersonal relationships have become one of the commanding problems of our age. They affect more people than any other single human disease or disability, and the rigors of modern life appear to be producing maladjusted individuals at a faster rate than facilities and personnel to care for them can be provided.

The formidable effects of maladjustment in our society are reflected in a variety of statistics on personal and social disorganization. A few of these data are cited below to reveal some conditions which no society can afford to ignore.

Mental Illness

Each year almost a million people receive treatment in mental hospitals, while another half million are treated in clinics and by private therapists. The number of new admissions to mental hospitals and clinics continues to rise, and the end is not in sight (15, 23). It is estimated that mental illness is costing the nation about 3 billion dollars per year in direct medical care, hospitalization, and loss of income (4). However, these figures may be minimal since the true incidence of mental illness is not known. Various studies indicate that about 10 or 12 percent of the population are so seriously disturbed emotionally that they would benefit from professional treatment. Some authorities place this figure even higher, at 60 to 80 percent of the population (18, 33). Of course, the statistics on emotional disturbance depend upon varying criteria used to identify these disorders. Yet, despite the inexactness of these studies, there is little doubt that psychopathology is more widespread in the general population than the ordinary citizen realizes.

Juvenile Delinquency

Antisocial conduct among youngsters increased steadily for a decade after World War II, exceeding the rate of growth for this age group in the population. In 1961, for the first time in recent history, delinquency cases were somewhat under the rate of increase for the child population (35). The number of children in public institutions for delinquents has likewise been on the increase. It has been estimated that more money is spent each year on the apprehension, conviction, and control of delinquents than for the support of the public schools (28).

Nor do these official statistics tell the whole story of antisocial conduct among minors. There are many youngsters whose behavior is just as asocial as those brought into court, but who manage to avoid detection, or are handled informally by the police or by social agencies. The incidence of hidden delinquency may be higher than the number of juveniles handled by police and courts (26).

Wasted Talents

From 18 to 50 percent of our talented high school youth do not go on to college. Inadequate motivation, influenced by family, community, and other social forces, underlies the failure of these students to realize their full potential. Able young people are leaving school early to take jobs beneath their ability and, when seen in later life, reflect feelings of frustration and dissatisfaction (15, 16, 20, 34).

There is also a great waste of talent among college students.

More than half of all students who enter college do not remain long enough to earn a degree. The reason given by these college dropouts is commonly that of inability to maintain academic standards. However, this scholastic failure frequently has been found associated with apathy, depression, excessive anxiety, compulsive behavior, obsessive thinking, physical symptoms of emotional origin, and other behavior indicative of inadequate adjustment. In one major university it was found that 15 to 20 percent of each graduating class requested help for handicapping emotional problems at some time during their college career (29). Severe psychoses, including suicide, occur in colleges and universities at the average rate of about two per thousand students per year (3).

The loss of capable people who do not make the most of their endowments because of incomplete education is skimming potential leadership from our country. Health officers in colleges and universities feel that the severity, if not the extent, of this problem is increasing in magnitude. Maladjustment, lack of motivation, general purposelessness, and aimless drifting are real problems in institutions of higher education. Yet, these factors are receiving relatively little attention from those responsible for the education of youth (29).

Other Evidence of Emotional Disturbance

The data on alcoholism, drug addiction, suicide, broken marriages, and crime further document the seriousness of emotional disturbances in our society. Conservative estimates point to the existence of 3 or 4 million alcoholics or problem drinkers in the nation (7). No one knows how many users of narcotics there are, but hospital records and police files indicate the existence of at least 1 addict per 3000 population, and most officials feel that this is an inadequate estimate of the problem (2). Marriages broken by legal divorce affect more than a million men, women, and children each year. Desertion and separation, the extent of which is unknown, increase greatly the number of broken homes and the attendant human misery (36). Each year some 300,000 people attempt suicide, and about 1 in 5 is successful. Suicide ranks eleventh among the causes of death and is twelve times greater than the loss of life in aircraft accidents (10, 21). Since 1950, crime has increased almost four times as fast as the population has grown. Over 7 million people in the nation have criminal records (37).

Taken together, these facts on maladjustment point to the existence of economic, social, and personal suffering on a substantial scale. Yet, the average citizen considers himself in good mental health. A national survey involving interviews with a random sample of adults found that one-third of this group rated themselves as very happy, and more than half reported themselves pretty happy, despite the fact that one-fourth of the people interviewed had at one time sought professional help for emotional troubles (9).

THE MEANING OF ADJUSTMENT

The most effective way to attack a public health problem of major proportions is to introduce preventive measures on an equally broad scale. The prevention of maladjustment requires an understanding of the basic factors involved in the adjustment process and how behavior is influenced by the various forces one encounters from birth through maturity. We shall begin to develop these understandings by exploring the meaning of adjustment.

Adjustment as a Process

Adjustment is commonly conceived to be a vague state of well-being or happiness. Needless to say, this popular notion is not consistent with what is known about human behavior. The human organism is a living, reacting being which is constantly striving to achieve a balance between his internal demands and the requirements of his environment. Since there is virtually continuous fluctuation of internal psychological forces and external conditions, adjustment must be an active system of behavior. It is not a condition, but a process in which changing forces call forth adaptive reactions which have certain elements of consistency that lend stability to behavior. We might call these stabilizing elements personality or character, using a loose definition of these terms (12, 19).

Other Concepts of Adjustment

There are other ways of viewing the process of adjustment, each of which has some merit but is not in itself complete. For example, we speak of the necessity for adjusting to a new climate, or a new school, or a new employer, implying that there are conditions which an individual cannot alter and to which he must accommodate. The mental hygienist takes a more personal view of the adjustment process and speaks of the need for a person's adjusting to himself, understanding his strengths and weaknesses, facing up to reality, and achieving a harmony within himself. Much emphasis is placed on the achievement of self-acceptance, on freedom from internal conflict, on self-realization, and on developing a unifying set of values which give life purpose and meaning (27).

There is also a social aspect of adjustment which requires the individual to achieve a reasonable compromise between his drive for self-realization and the demands of society. The culture exerts powerful influences for conformity and offers to conforming individuals its security and support. However, this subordination of individuality to the group may become an escape from adjustment. The person who compromises his self-integrity for the sake of becoming exactly like others submerges himself in the group instead of building his own internal strengths. These people can survive only in an environment which provides a steady, safe existence. They cannot tolerate the uncertainty and challenge of competitive life (6). On the other hand, the individual who disengages himself from society may be equally out of balance with his environment. A necessary component of human adjustment is the selective development of one's potentialities along culturally appropriate lines.

These interpretations of the adjustment process illustrate that adjustment is not a condition of happiness or contentment which can be earned and, once earned, retained for life, like a college degree. It is a dynamic process that has many facets. Rather than try to distill a common core of meaning from the various interpretations that have been made, we shall accept the fact that adjustment is a multidimensional process and discuss some criteria for evaluating its effectiveness.

CRITERIA OF ADJUSTMENT

Although the need for multiple criteria of adjustment is recognized, a consensus has not been reached regarding the particular array of criteria which is most valid. The trouble is that standards of adjustive behavior vary with time, place, culture, circumstances, and the characteristics of the individual. There is no single life style which is best for all people, but many life styles of varying form. The behavior of a soldier in combat will be very different from that of a teacher in a classroom, yet each may be entirely appropriate under the existing circumstances (14).

Despite these variations, a number of proposals have been made regarding the main attributes of positive adjustment (1, 14, 32). From these we have selected five criteria which seem to encompass what most authorities would agree constitutes the basic core of adjustment.

A Unifying Outlook on Life

The well-adjusted person has a set of values which provide a focus to his behavior. These values include material goals such as a home or car, spiritual goals, social goals, and numerous attitudes and other motivating forces that give meaning to life and provide direction and order to behavior. With firmly held values and goals a person can withstand temporary hardships and deprivations and so order his life that he deals effectively with changing environmental conditions. Whether this be called one's philosophy, or mind-set, or whatever, each of us needs a unifying cognitive outlook on life to strive purposefully toward conscious goals.

Realistic Self-Perception

The well-adjusted person not only needs to know what he wants out of life but must be capable of making intelligent plans to achieve his ends. He must be able to view himself realistically, appraising his abilities and setting a level of aspiration within reasonable limits. He does not attempt to obscure his weaknesses but takes them into account, and if he cannot overcome them, learns to live with them. He knows what he is capable of doing, pursues his goals to the best of his ability, and accepts the inevitable compromises and substitutions which must be made.

This sounds like a reasonable expectation, but many people encounter serious frustration because they do not have a realistic perception of themselves. In our schools are thousands of students of good intellectual ability who are underachieving academically because they have a low self-concept. Many reading difficulties have been traced to a similar lack of confidence in one's abilities. Parents often put severe pressures on children to accomplish more than the youngsters are capable of doing, because, unknowingly, they are trying to satisfy their own unfulfilled aspirations through the lives of the children. When people can accept the truth about themselves, they can do something about their problems, but when self-perceptions are obscured by psychological subterfuge, they create many adjustment difficulties.

Emotional Maturity

The adjusted person is capable of regulating his emotional behavior so that he is neither devoid of emotions nor overwhelmed by them. He can vary his emotional expression in accordance with the requirements of the situation while maintaining the basic core of his personality. That is, a person is not expected to behave at church as he would at a party, but neither is he expected to undergo radical changes in his personality.

The emotionally mature person is one who can be depended upon by others. He is self-assured, can give and accept affection, and has an inner security which is not easily shaken by emotional stress. Of course, everyone gets upset once in a while. In fact, if a person did not react emotionally to certain situations, we would suspect that something were wrong with him. Emotional maturity requires regulated emotional expression, and reactions that are appropriate and socially approved, but it does not exclude temporary upsets resulting from a crisis situation, so long as the individual regains his equilibrium when the crisis has passed.

Social Sensitivity

The adjusted person is capable of establishing satisfying contacts with other people. He feels comfortable in the presence of others and does not try to use people for his own ends. His outlook on life is socially oriented rather than exclusively self-seeking in nature. He has the capacity to visualize himself as he appears in the eyes of others, and is capable of adapting his behavior so that he may merit social approval. He is not too different from other people, nor is he entirely a conformist. The achievement of satisfying social relationships does not require a person to be an extrovert, but it does require a sensitivity to the welfare of others so that through their reactions his own sense of well-being is enhanced.

Dynamic Equilibrium

The final criterion of adjustment which we shall consider relates to the balance which must be maintained between the inner forces of behavior and the outer forces of environment. Since these forces are constantly shifting, the individual who has a rigid set of habits and attitudes may lack the flexibility necessary for adapting to changing conditions. On the other hand, he must be sufficiently well integrated to withstand stresses and strains without being pushed off balance. What we are speaking of here is a quality of inner resourcefulness which enables a person to achieve a harmony with his environment. This is the "give-and-take" characteristic of a dynamic equilibrium that permits one to adjust to changing conditions while maintaining his personal stability and integration.

VARIETIES OF ADJUSTIVE BEHAVIOR

These criteria of adjustment may make it appear that no one could possibly achieve such a well-regulated existence. This is another way of saying that none of us is perfectly adjusted at all times. Adjustment cannot be classified precisely as good or bad, normal or abnormal, but must be evaluated along a continuing scale ranging from behavior which is essentially normal to behavior which is completely beyond the bounds of normality.

Adjustment and Normality

Normality encompasses a range of behavior in which the criteria of adjustment mentioned above play a prominent part. A normal person is able to get along with other people; he has synchronized his aspirations with reality; he has adequate self-esteem and self-confidence, an abiding set of values, and maintains a relatively even emotional tone. But he is by no means perfect. Even the most effective individual has within him some areas of sensitivity or some unresolved emotional experiences that can cause him to behave irrationally under certain trying conditions. Normal people occasionally feel anxious, hostile, aggressive, inferior, or afraid. They may shy away from facing problems or responsibilities, or behave in other ways which at the moment are maladaptive. At some time or other, most normal people experience headaches, insomnia, nervousness, and other physical symptoms of anxiety. If prolonged, such reactions may lead to personality disorders. The saving quality of normality is the ability of the individual to overcome these nervous states when his problems are solved or when he reaches a compromise with them. It is this long-term emotional balance, rather than the temporary upsets in equilibrium, by which we judge the normality of behavior.

Maladjusted Behavior. There are varying degrees of maladjustment ranging from behavior which is just beyond the bounds of normality to conditions of complete incapacitation. Considering maladjustment along a scale from mild to severe, at the extreme end of the scale would be the psychoses, which are ailments so severe that the individual should be under professional care. At the opposite end would be the character or personality disorders. These are not entirely abnormal, but people afflicted by them display patterns of thinking, feeling, and acting that are sufficiently distorted to cause them considerable difficulty. Between these extremes are the neuroses or psychoneuroses, ailments involving a variety of distressing symptoms which make people unhappy, nervous, hypersensitive, and prone to exaggerated emotional reactions (8).

While maladjustment may be classified along this theoretical scale, it must be noted that people do not stay in their categories very well. There is much overlapping of behavior, sometimes veering toward one end of the scale, sometimes toward the opposite end, and at times crossing over into the range of normality. This, of course, causes a great deal of difficulty for the diagnosticians who must often use general descriptions of maladjustment to encompass this shift in symptoms. For instance, the term "transient situational personality disturbance" has been coined to cover a class of disorders for which no specific label could be found. We shall go into this problem more thoroughly in a later chapter when we deal with behavior deviations.

The Relativity of Normalcy. As has been shown, the difference between normal and abnormal adjustment is a quantitative difference—one of degree. The line between the normal and the maladjusted is a thin one, across which many people seesaw for temporary periods at various times during their lives. No person is completely adjusted; he is adjusted only to a degree. Nor are seriously disturbed people entirely maladjusted at all times and in all respects. Normal individuals carry within them the potentialities for poor adjustment which under extreme circumstances can be activated and lead to irrational behavior. The maladjusted person, except in cases where behavior is frozen into unalterable patterns of reaction dominated by unconscious processes, has the potentiality for learning another way of life and the hope of achieving a normal existence (16).

Adaptation and Adjustment

Another way of interpreting the quality of behavior is to distinguish between adaptive and adjustive behavior. Adaptive behavior leads to the immediate reduction of tension. Whether it is adjustive depends upon whether this relief facilitates or impedes future adjustment. For example, the student who is tense over an impending examination may relieve his anxiety by playing tennis. If this adaptive behavior relaxes him so that he can return to his studies refreshed, it may lead to adjustive behavior because he is facing his problems. If he continues to find escape through one activity after another, then his basic anxiety is not affected and he is not adjusting to the situation.

People may persist for years in adaptive behavior which brings immediate rewards but does not contribute to long-term satisfaction. They have little tolerance for emotional stress and use any available means to secure relief. The adjusted person, on the other hand, is capable of delaying immediate relief of anxiety in favor of behavior patterns which build toward more constructive and lasting rewards. How people develop this capacity to forego attractive short-term rewards for more enduring satisfactions is one of the major themes in the study of adjustment.

Adjustment and Anxiety

The concept of adjustment as a dynamic interaction of individual and environment, with relative standards for judging adequacy or normality, obviously does not suggest a constant state of equanimity. The adjusted person feels reasonably secure and has learned to live with most of the problems he could not resolve. However, he is not entirely at peace with himself or his world. One must not confuse adjustment with tranquility. Tranquility often results in stagnation and loss of vitality. In this sense it is just as destructive to adjustment as the opposing condition of severe anxiety.

Moderate anxiety is a normal aspect of life. In fact, it is essential for effective living because it stimulates people to attack their problems. Without pressures, incentives, and some frustration, people would not be motivated to exert themselves. Complacent people lose the emotional stimulus needed to develop will power or to acquire the capacity and resiliency needed to face difficulties and recover from setbacks. They do not learn to deal adequately with powerful emotions and are more prone to breakdowns under severe stress. This has been one of the problems encountered in the use of tranquilizing drugs. Too many people are willing to exchange contentment for individual striving. By swallowing a pill they obscure their anxieties and disguise their problems. This helps them endure life, but removes the impetus for constructive behavior and permits the build-up of serious emotional problems (31).

The Development of Adjustment

We have described some aspects of behavior as they relate to the process of adjustment. Now let us put these together into an overview of how adjustment emerges in the course of human development.

The human organism is born with certain capacities and characteristics which are influenced by his heredity, his biological, chemical, and physical make-up, and by forces which affect him before, during, and after birth. Once he enters this world, environmental forces begin to impinge on the individual, and he must strive to satisfy his basic needs and drives within the framework of cultural requirements. Through the interaction of the forces within and outside him, the individual develops a set of habit patterns, values, outlooks, and behavior characteristics which become part of his unique personality.

The process of adjustment is not one of merely fitting into established patterns of living. Adjustment requires individual effort and attainment. Parents cannot hand it down to their children. Each individual must become a person in his own right by attaining a reasonable balance among all the forces which affect him. Since there is a continuous emergence of new requirements within and without the individual, he must exert constant effort to maintain an equilibrium among these forces.

This process of adjustment is never ended while life goes on. No one achieves complete mastery of himself or his environment. There is no perfect adjustment, no complete state of well-being, happiness, or satisfaction. The best an individual can hope for is to meet life's requirements as well as he can and attain a degree of relative emotional well-being which, while short of perfection, enables him to function within the broad range of normality. A major function of education is to acquaint the young adult with the facts and principles relating to the process of human adjustment. While such knowledge is no guarantee of achieving better adjustment, an understanding of the dynamics of human behavior can be instrumental in helping an individual shape his pattern of life in a mature and intelligent way.

SUMMARY

Psychological disorders and disturbed personal relationships have become a public health problem of major proportions. Each year about a million and a half people in this country receive treatment for some form of mental illness, and this represents only a small proportion of those who need such treatment. Statistics on juvenile delinquency, crime, wasted talents, alcoholism, narcotics addiction, divorce, and suicide add to this picture of a society with serious problems of human adjustment.

If we are to make progress toward preventing maladjustment, our people need to be concerned with enhancing the quality of living within their own little worlds and in the nation as a whole. This process must begin with improving our understanding of how behavior, and the factors which influence behavior, may affect the adjustment process. College students preparing for leadership roles in their communities are particularly in need of such insights, so that they may order their own lives more effectively and exert a positive influence on the lives of others.

Adjustment has been described as a dynamic process which requires individual effort and attainment. Society may assist the individual by reducing the stresses which tax his adaptive capacities, but it is the individual himself who must develop his effectiveness as a human being. While no one can expect to attain a perfect state of adjustment, most people can acquire enough understanding of themselves and of others to function within the broad limits of normality. To do this, a person needs a unifying set of values, realistic self-perceptions, a reasonable level of emotional maturity, social sensitivity, and a flexible pattern of behavior that will enable him to adapt to change. These qualities can be expected to emerge in the process of growth and development if conditions are favorable and if the individual applies his intelligence to shaping his own life.

REFERENCES

1. Allport, G. W., "Personality: Normal and Abnormal," *Personality and Social Encounter,* Beacon Press, 1960, pp. 155–168.
2. Ausubel, D. P., "Controversial Issues in the Management of Drug Addiction: Legalization, Ambulatory Treatment and the British System," *Ment. Hyg.,* October, 1960, 44:535–544.
3. Farnsworth, D. L., *Student Values and Mental Health,* Paper presented at the Association for Higher Education, Cleveland, June 30, 1954, 10 pp., mimeographed.
4. Fein, R., *Economics of Mental Illness,* Basic Books, 1958.
5. Ford Foundation, *Mental Health,* 477 Madison Avenue, New York, May, 1958.
6. Fromm, E., *Escape from Freedom,* Farrar, Straus & Cudahy, 1941.
7. Ginsburg, S. W., "The Neuroses," *Mental Health in the United States, Ann. Amer. Acad. Polit. Soc. Sci.,* March, 1953, 286:55–64.
8. Green, J., "Psychosomatic Disturbances as a Form of Substituted Behavior," *J. Psychosom. Res.,* 1957, 2:85–96.
9. Gurin, G., *et al., Americans View Their Mental Health,* Basic Books, 1960.
10. Hirsh, J., "Suicide," *Ment. Hyg.,* October, 1960, 44:496–502.
11. Hughes, C. C., *et al., People of Cove and Woodlot,* Basic Books, 1960.
12. Hunt, J. McV., "Experience and the Development of Motivation: Some Reinterpretations," *Child Develpm.,* September, 1960, 31:489–504.
13. Jacobs, P. E., *Changing Values in College,* Harper & Row, 1957.
14. Jahoda, M., *Current Concepts of Positive Mental Health,* Basic Books, 1958.
15. Joint Commission on Mental Illness and Health, *Action for Mental Health,* Basic Books, 1960.

16. Kubie, L. S., "Social Forces and the Neurotic Process," in Leighton, A. H., *et al.* (Eds.), *Explorations in Social Psychiatry,* Basic Books, 1957.

17. Leighton, A. H., *My Name is Legion,* Basic Books, 1959.

18. Leighton, D. C., "The Distribution of Psychiatric Symptoms in a Small Town," *Amer. J. Psychiat.,* March, 1956, 112:716–723.

19. Lindemann, E., "Mental Health—Fundamental to a Dynamic Epidemiology of Health," in Galdston, I., (Ed.), *The Epidemiology of Health,* New York Academy of Medicine, 1953.

20. Little, J. K., "A State-wide Inquiry into: (a) Decisions of Youth About Education Beyond High School, (b) Factors Which Influence These Decisions," U.S. Office of Education, *Cooperative Research Program, Project No. 247,* November, 1958.

21. Metropolitan Life Insurance Company, "The Frequency of Suicide," *Statist. Bull.,* December, 1960, 41:9–10.

22. National Association for Mental Health, *Facts About Mental Illness,* 10 Columbus Circle, New York, 4 pp., undated.

23. National Institute of Mental Health, *Mental Health Statistics, Current Reports,* Series MHB–H–7, Bethesda, Md., January, 1963.

24. Norman, V. B., "Psychiatric Clinic Outpatients in the U.S., 1959," *Ment. Hyg.,* July, 1962, 46:321–343.

25. Peck, B., *Effect of Self-Observation upon Self-Awareness: An Exploratory Study,* Unpublished Doctoral Thesis, University of Maryland, 1957.

26. Perlman, I. R., "Delinquency Prevention: The Size of the Problem," U.S. Children's Bureau, *Juvenile Delinquency Facts, Facets,* No. 4, 1960.

27. Rogers, C. R., *On Becoming A Person,* Houghton Mifflin, 1961.

28. Rowland, R. L., and Perlman, I. R., "Statistics on Public Institutions for Delinquent Children, 1958," U.S. Children's Bureau, *Statistical Series,* No. 59, 1960.

29. Rust, R. M., and Davie, J. S., "The Personal Problems of College Students," *Ment. Hyg.,* April, 1961, 45:247–257.

30. Sawry, J. M., and Telford, C. W., *Dynamics of Mental Health,* Allyn & Bacon, 1963.

31. Schmideberg, M., "Tolerance in Upbringing and Its Abuses," *Intern. J. soc. Psychiat.,* Autumn, 1959, 5:123–130.

32. Smith, M. B., "Mental Health Reconsidered: A Special Case

of the Problems and Values in Psychology," *Amer. Psychologist,* 1961, **16**:299–306.

33. Srole, L., *et al., Mental Health in the Metropolis: The Midtown Manhattan Study,* Vol. I, McGraw-Hill—Blakiston, 1962.

34. Stroup, F., "An Investigation of Factors Related to Educational Discontinuance of College Ability High School Seniors," U.S. Office of Education, *Cooperative Research Program, Project No. 008,* November, 1958.

35. U.S. Children's Bureau, *Juvenile Court Statistics, 1961,* Statistical Series No. 69, 1962.

36. U.S. Department of Health, Education and Welfare, Office of the Secretary, *Health, Education and Welfare Trends,* GPO, 1960.

37. U.S. Department of Justice, Federal Bureau of Investigation, "Crime in the United States," *Uniform Crime Reports, 1959,* GPO, 1960.

38. Wheelis, A., *The Quest for Identity,* Norton, 1958.

Chapter 2 Psychobiological Origins of Human Behavior

Many theories about the origins of human behavior have been advanced over the years. At one time the explanation for differing forms of behavior was sought in the structure of the brain. Normal people were assumed to have intact brains, disturbed people defective brains. However, despite the dissection of literally thousands of human brains, no evidence could be found to support this theory. The brain structure of a deceased criminal could not be distinguished from that of a judge; nor could the brain of a man who was insane at the time of death be differentiated from that of a normal person who had died of heart disease. After much futile effort this line of investigation was discontinued, to be followed by newer theories which arose, gathered adherents, then also faded away as they became untenable.

Currently, the psychobiological approach to the study of human behavior is receiving major emphasis. Scientists using modern devices are peering into hitherto inaccessible aspects of life. The electron microscope has revealed the once invisible virus and genes whose existence had been merely suspected. Electrodes implanted deep in the brain have enabled physiologists to chart the processes going on in this living tissue. Chemists using radioactive isotopes are discovering new things about metabolism, glandular action, and chemical changes in the body. These biological and physiological facts are just beginning to find their way into interpretations of human behavior.

In the years ahead, we may expect textbooks dealing with the psychological aspects of human behavior to be increasingly concerned with the facts which are now being learned about heredity, modifiers of heredity, brain functioning, glandular and metabolic influences on behavior, social influences on biological functioning, and the interrelation of these factors as they affect personality development.

FACTS AND THEORIES OF HEREDITY

Scientists have learned a great deal about the transmission of physical characteristics through genetic channels. There is little dispute over the fact that we inherit patterns for growth and change, certain skills and abilities, and constitutional traits like intelligence, physical appearance, and sensitivity. But whether personality characteristics and behavior patterns are transmitted genetically along the family tree is still a moot question. Research has neither been able to prove nor disprove that a pattern of adjustment or maladjustment may be laid down at the time of conception. Consequently, as we examine past and current thinking about the influence of heredity on behavior, we encounter much speculation based on empirical observation.

Heredity, Body Build, and Behavior

Among the more interesting and persistent of the speculations on heredity and behavior is the theory of body types. A strong belief has persisted over the years that people may be classified into certain types on the basis of inherited body build and that each type will have its characteristic forms of temperament and behavior. Thus we speak of the fat-jolly type, the thin-nervous type, the muscular-athletic type, implying that each type has genetically endowed characteristics which shape the body, temperament, and behavior.

This theory dates back to ancient times when Hippocrates assumed that the four humors of the body--black bile, yellow bile, mucus, and blood—were passed on in various proportions from parents to children. Thus an individual might develop a melancholic, choleric, phlegmatic, or sanguine temperament, depending upon the humors which had been transmitted to him.

Since the days of Hippocrates, many other classifications of body build and temperament have been developed. These have added to our language, if not to our understanding of behavior and adjustment. In the nineteenth century, Lombroso, an Italian criminologist, studied prison inmates and described the criminal type as men with receding chins, cleft palates, large ears, and generally irregular and unattractive features. The rogue's gallery of a modern police department lends little support to this description of a criminal type. Later, Kretschmer, a German psychiatrist, introduced the terms, *pyknic*—the fat, good-natured, easy-going individual; *asthenic*—the tall, thin, sensitive type; *athletic*—the muscular type, and *dysplastic*—a category for those who did not fit into any of the others. Each type was said to result from internal chemical reactions caused by the brain and glands.

There have been many other classifications associating body build with intelligence, with introversion and extroversion, and with tendencies to develop various types of emotional ailments. The most exhaustive study of body types was made in recent years by Sheldon (48). He classified individuals as *ectomorphs* —lean and lanky types who tend to be highly sensitive, introspective, and self-conscious; *mesomorphs*—the rugged, athletic extrovert type; and *endomorphs*—the relaxed, polite, sociable, complacent fat man. This classification is broken down further into various combinations and cross-types of these three basic categories.

Sheldon's somatotypes have been both supported and criticized by other investigators. Page and his associates administered the Minnesota Multiphasic Personality Inventory to persons classified by physique categories and found no distinguishing temperament characteristics among them (36). On the other hand, studies conducted in Sweden, while not confirming the specific relationships between temperament and physique described by Sheldon, showed some definite relations between body build and susceptibility to persuasion. The athletic type was most gullible and easiest to influence; the tall, slender types were appreciably harder to persuade, while the short, stocky type proved to be the most independent minded and least susceptible to persuasion (14).

Parnell (37) recently adapted Sheldon's classification to a fat, muscular, and linear scale and studied the relationship between body type and emotional disturbance. He claimed to find a highly significant tendency for mental disturbances to occur more often in persons having a build made up of more fat than muscles. Men with a higher proportion of muscle to fat tended to be most healthy. Among women under thirty, the disposition to breakdowns was significantly greater among the lean types than the fat types.

Efforts to relate behavior to body types continue today in various forms. For example, physicians describe the typical candidate for a stomach ulcer as a high-strung, driving, aggressive, energetic man of above average intelligence who is eager to get ahead. He works long hours, gets insufficient rest, probably gulps his food, and may drink or smoke too much. He is thin, sometimes nervous, and inclined to be short-tempered and easily upset (54). The candidate for heart trouble is the junior executive striving for the top, or the frustrated white-collar worker. He is inclined to be short, stocky, muscular, large-boned, tending to baldness, and often an athlete with a vigorous, ambitious, aggressive personality (11).

Observation leads us to believe that there is some empirical relationship between body build and personality characteristics. However, this relationship is not necessarily genetically decided. A person's physique may determine whether he engages in athletics, develops feelings of self-consciousness, or becomes socially acceptable. By limiting the possibilities for experience, body build may predispose an individual to develop certain characteristics. Whether this predisposition actually results in the types of behavior associated with certain body builds depends upon the opportunities open to the individual. The chubby child is not genetically destined to become the jolly fat man, nor the underweight child the lean thinker. The determining conditions that regulate the final outcome of behavior lie in the interactions of the genetic system with the physical and social environment.

Sources of Evidence on Heredity

Much of what is known about inheritance is derived from studies of insects, plants, and animals whose breeding and environment can be controlled rigidly. It has been proven that physical characteristics can be transmitted through the genes in plants and animals. Temperament in animals has likewise been linked to inheritance. Experimenters have mated albino rats with nervous and excitable Norway rats and produced colonies in which the albinos are nervous and the Norways docile. Neither chemical, structural, nor environmental differences could account for the transmission of these temperament characteristics. Similarly, it has been demonstrated that controlled breeding can produce dogs and sheep that are susceptible to neurosis, and others that are sluggish, passive, and imperturbable.

The evidence regarding human beings is much less conclusive. People have a long life span; they cannot be mated experimentally, and their diets, habits, and living conditions are not subject to experimental control. Moreover, the thousands of genes contained in each of the 23 chromosomes received from the father and the 23 contributed by the mother make possible over eight million combinations which provide a tremendous range of biological differences among individuals. Therefore, our knowledge is less precise on human than on animal heredity. Unable to study human beings in the laboratory, scientists had to derive most of their data on human inheritance from studies of twins. Modern biochemical analysis has added another dimension to these investigations which may have even greater significance than the traditional studies of human genetics.

Studies of Twins

Much of the early data which supported heredity as a determining force in behavior was derived from studies of monozygotic (identical) and dizygotic (fraternal) twins. These studies traced the development of twins from birth to maturity and demonstrated the similarity of behavior among them. The studies of Rosanoff (44) and Kallmann (24, 25) are cited here to illustrate the approach and findings of twin studies.

Rosanoff and his associates studied 137 monozygotic twins over a period of years and found that almost 87 percent developed the same type of behavior patterns in later years. That is, if one of the twins was involved in behavior difficulties, the other was similarly affected. This was interpreted to mean that both twins had inherited factors which caused similar behavior to emerge. This study reported the fact that in 13 percent of the twins there was no similarity in their behavior. Moreover, about 42 percent of the same-sex dizygotic twins showed similar behavior. Since the genetic relationship between dizygotic twins is no closer than that of siblings, how this high incidence of similar behavior could be caused by heredity is not explained.

Similarly, Kallmann has made extensive studies of the heredity transmission of various types of psychoses. In one instance he found that if a child in the family had schizophrenia, a half-brother or sister had a 7 percent chance of developing this ailment; a fraternal twin a 14.5 percent chance, while in identical twins, if one had schizophrenia there was an 86.2 percent chance that the other would have it also (25).

In his study of manic-depressive types of psychoses, Kallmann found that while the expectancy rate of this illness in the general population is somewhat less than one-half of one percent, it appeared in 26.3 percent of fraternal twins and in 95.7 percent of identical twins if one of the twins developed this ailment (24).

These, and similar studies, have been interpreted to mean that the genes outweigh all other forces in determining the course of human behavior (10). However, such studies have been questioned because they deal with a very select group of people. Their subjects are taken from child guidance clinics, school clinics, neurological clinics, special classes for problem children, juvenile courts, correctional institutions, criminal courts, prisons, and mental hospitals. These people are hardly representative of the general population. Normal people have not been used as controls to test these findings, and too often only the concordant or positive findings are reported, with no explanation offered on how to account for the twins in the general population whose behavior patterns differ from those under study (5, 51).

Biochemical Research

Perhaps the greatest weakness of the twin studies is that they are primarily descriptive and offer no explanation of how the genes affect behavior. Biochemical research is beginning to provide some answers to this question. Genes have been revealed to carry protein molecules which may be the underlying cause of disturbed behavior. Specific diseases, such as a type of mental retardation resulting from inability of the body to tolerate galactose, a natural sugar, and inadequate metabolism of phenylalanine, a common constituent of protein foods, have been traced to a genetic lack of certain essential enzymes. Other studies are under way to pinpoint the specific mode of action of genes. Once this information is available, it may be possible to alter physiological processes that produce adverse effects in the body by making changes in the action of the genes (9, 17, 41).

Another focus of research is on the number and alignment of genes within the chromosomes. Evidence points to the possibility that the mysterious condition known as *Mongolism*, in which a child is born with severe mental retardation and with distinctive physical features such as an enlarged tongue, almond eyes, and characteristically shaped head and face, may actually be due to an upset in the normal number of chromosomes in the body. When this error occurs, the fertilized egg has an extra chromosome which is believed to be the determinant of Mongolism (5).

The chemical structure of the gene itself has been analyzed and found to consist of giant protein molecules arranged in long chains whose links are combined in various ways. These molecules are coiled strands of a highly complex substance known as DNA (deoxyribonucleic acid), which is believed to be an elemental form of life found in cell nuclei of all higher organisms (16). As scientists unravel this basic hereditary material and learn how various linkages and patterns of chemicals function, they hope to discover how hereditary characteristics are transmitted. The discovery and synthesis of basic protein molecules has been accomplished and may some day lead to new interpretations of the origins and character of human nature. Eventually, science may be able to explain the healthy organism in terms of its molecular arrangements, and the sick organism in terms of defects in these arrangements (41).

FACTORS MODIFYING THE INFLUENCE OF HEREDITY

There are various physical and physiological factors which can influence the manner in which genes perform their functions. Biologists have demonstrated that one-eyed fish may be produced by increasing the magnesium content of the water in which the fertilized egg develops. Other experiments have shown that by varying temperature, light, nutrients, and other factors, inherited characteristics can be modified in the laboratory in many ways. Nature illustrates this same phenomenon in the beehive. Whether an egg becomes a queen or a worker depends on its nutrition as well as its inheritance. Eggs nurtured on royal jelly become queens, while others with similar genetic endowment but supplied different nutrients become workers.

In humans, too, the embryonic roots of behavior may stem from conditions which exist after conception but which appear so early in life that they seem to have genetic origins. While heredity has an undisputed effect on the origins of growth and the emergence of behavior, there are conditions which regulate the final outcome of genetic influence.

Prenatal Influence on Human Behavior

The intrauterine development of the embryo and fetus may be affected by various chemicals, diseases, and physical factors. Oxygen deprivation, leading to a condition known as anoxia, can do permanent and irreversible damage to the brain of the growing organism. This was demonstrated in one instance by keeping infant monkeys inside the intact amniotic sac, removed surgically from the mother, until severe respiratory distress was evidenced. The sac was then opened and the infant resuscitated. The baby monkey showed all the classical signs of cerebral palsy and brain damage. By the sixty-seventh day of life, the infant monkey had not learned to feed itself, an accomplishment achieved by normal monkeys in twelve days (9).

Oxygen deprivation in human infants may have similar results. Anoxia can result from delayed birth, from RH blood-type incompatibilities, from circulatory impairment in the placental attachment of the uterus, or from conditions where the umbilical cord becomes wrapped around the neck of the fetus (57). In later life, infant anoxia may lead to considerable variation in disposition, quarrelsomeness, hypermotility, fluctuation in ability to concentrate, and a variety of behavioral and learning defects (35, 45).

The pacing of growth is determined by genetic factors if the chemical composition of the maternal blood stream is within normal limits. Under some conditions, foreign substances, or deficiencies of natural substances, affect the embryo and fetus and alter the course of growth. Several drugs, chemicals, and other materials are capable of permeating the amniotic membrane and distorting the growth process. The most common of these are narcotics, toxins, poisons such as lead and alcohol, X rays and radiation. Some infectious diseases like epidemic encephalitis, syphilis, and German measles can attack and permanently injure the brain of the fetus. So, too, can vitamin and hormone deficiencies and severe malnutrition (3, 22). Some infants whose mothers were treated with steroid hormones for threatened abortion have shown partial sexual reversal; girl babies became masculinized in utero, and boy babies feminized (12).

Many other factors may upset the timing and integration of neurological development. Oxygen deprivation during the first two weeks after conception may result in an incompletely formed skull or a hairlip. Various neurological handicaps, perceptual distortions, a lowered threshold for anxiety, and intellectual and social dysfunctions have been attributed to defects in maturation before birth. This is particularly true of prematurely born infants who suffer a variety of physical disorders that have pronounced effects on behavior (38).

Some prenatal conditions do not interfere with the growth process but somehow affect the activity of the fetus. It is known that babies differ greatly from one another, even during the first few weeks of life. Some are active, highly sensitive to stimulation, nervous, and high-strung. Others are quite placid and relatively unaggressive. There is a natural tendency to ascribe these basic differences in behavior to inherited factors. However, it is also possible that other factors may be involved. A chronically overemotional mother may stimulate fetal activity by discharging excess epinephrine into the blood stream. Even external stimuli like blaring radios, the vibration of household appliances, the roar of trains or airplanes, or violent movement of the mother may cause hyperactivity in the fetus (8:111). Because of these early environmental influences on growth and development, we cannot with certainty ascribe behavior to heredity alone. Good heredity in a poor intrauterine environment, or poor heredity in a good intrauterine environment, may be equally potent in affecting later behavior.

Birth Trauma and Postnatal Influences

The birth process and environmental influences after birth are additional factors to be considered in determining the origins of behavior.

Injury to the covering of the brain or to the brain substance is a matter of highest importance in the etiology of behavior difficulties. During birth the skull is pounded, maltreated, and squeezed. When cerebral tissue is damaged, inhibitory brain mechanisms whose function it is to control or regulate behavior are impaired or destroyed. The cerebral tissue of boys seems to be more vulnerable to birth trauma than that of girls, which may in part account for the higher incidence of delinquency and criminality in males (44).

Birth trauma, sedative drugs, and drugs used to induce labor may produce cerebral damage which is not detected at birth but becomes manifest in later life. Childhood schizophrenia is twice as common among children who experienced trauma at birth as it is among those whose births were normal (55). It is quite probable that many children who are classified as behavior problems in school may have sustained subtle brain damage during the birth process which shows up years later as hyperactivity, short attention span, poor impulse control, inability to concentrate, and erratic academic progress.

The character of life after birth may in a large measure determine the early response patterns of children. This is most obvious where children are born with hampering conditions such as defective sensory organs. The physical and social environments, which normally take on meanings through the sense organs, may produce frustration rather than satisfaction, accounting for the restricted personality development often found among children who are born blind, deaf, or neurologically damaged.

Equally important, but less obvious, are the effects of inadequate mother-child relationships in early life. If something happens to the affectional ties between mother and child, permanent damage may be done to the psychological development of the child. In extreme cases where inadequate mothering exists during the first few months of life, infants have been noted to withdraw from social stimulation and even develop autistic reactions which resemble a form of childhood psychosis. When children do not receive the kind of mothering that is normal and natural for human beings, it is difficult for them to develop the personality structure of normal people (15, 46:30). Further evidence of familial influences on behavior will be presented in a later chapter.

BRAIN FUNCTION AND BEHAVIOR

To understand the origins of human behavior, a knowledge of some of the fundamental processes of the brain is essential. The brain is the primary organ of the mind, the latter being a symbol which represents various mental processes. The billions of nerve cells in the brain operate as a signal center for receiving and sending impulses through which thought, judgment, perception and other mental activities are influenced. Earlier investigators lacked the instruments necessary for studying brain activity with precision and failed to make the connection between brain activity and behavior. With modern techniques, scientists have traced the transmission of electrical impulses along various nerve pathways in the brain and have identified electrical and chemical influences on brain activity which are significant factors in behavior.

Electrocortical Activity

There is considerable evidence that the brain generates and transmits electrical energy and that this electrical activity is related to various types of behavior. By the use of an electroencephalograph (EEG), the electrical impulses emanating from the surface of the brain can be picked up and inscribed on sensitized paper. The brain waves of a healthy person so produced are readily distinguishable from those of an epileptic or a brain-injured individual. The effects of fatigue, drugs, chemicals, and infections are also reflected in the graphs produced by the electroencephalograph (18).

The usefulness of this instrument has been limited by its inability to penetrate below the surface of the brain. Therefore, scientists developed a new instrument, the electrograph, which has the capacity for probing into the deeper recesses of the brain. This process involves the implantation of fine electrodes deep inside brain tissue. These electrodes not only pick up impulses but can stimulate the internal brain structures.

Most deep electrography research has been done on animals. The results in several instances have been quite dramatic. In one study, electrodes were implanted in the brain stem of monkeys. Months of prolonged electrical stimulation, which produced an effect similar to jangled nerves, resulted in the development of peptic ulcers similar to those of the human variety (52).

In another experiment, electrodes were inserted into the hypothalamus area of cats. With the current off, the cat would permit a rat to rove around its cage and crawl trustingly between its paws. When a switch was snapped, sending a small electric current into the electrodes, the cat was transformed into a snarling, savage beast, charging the rat with teeth and claws. When the current was cut off, the cat instantly reverted to its previous mild state and permitted the rat to crawl around unmolested (1).

The few studies made of human reactions to electrodes implanted in the brain have been done with psychotic patients. In one group of disturbed patients, it was noted that as emotional disturbances increased, the brain waves emanating from the underside of the temporal lobe took on a resemblance to those often seen in epilepsy. There was nothing in the patients' external environment to produce this action. The brain waves and the acute emotional disturbance seemed to develop out of something within the brain (17, 39). This interpretation was supported by another study in which electrical stimulation of the temporal lobe areas of the brain evoked emotional reactions such as feelings of fear, sadness, fright, and terror, when nothing in the environment was present to produce such reactions (56).

Chemical Influences on Brain Function

While electrographic studies have shown that behavior changes are associated with alteration of brain impulse patterns, they have not explained how these alterations occur. The chemical environment of the brain cells may be involved in this process. The neurons of the brain usually are well protected by large glial cells which fill the spaces between nerve cells and sheathe the capillaries that supply blood to the brain. These glia are thought to provide the blood-brain barrier that makes nerve cells extraordinarily resistant to toxic agents circulating in the blood (23).

However, the blood-brain barrier is not perfect, and certain chemicals may permeate through to the brain cells. This was first discovered by the observation that striking behavior changes occurred when people ate certain plants like the peyote cactus or a species of Mexican mushroom. Scientists then extracted the active ingredients from these plants, deriving

Psilocybin from the mushroom and mescaline from the cactus. In the laboratory they synthesized a close relative of these compounds, called lysergic acid diethylamide (LSD-25). When these drugs are injected into normal persons, they produce many of the symptoms of psychosis, including compulsive thought and speech, intense visual imagery, feelings of unreality, rapid shift of emotions, a peculiar restlessness and furtiveness, elaborate hallucinations, and language changes (20, 53).

It has recently been discovered that compounds occurring normally in the body may under certain conditions be converted to substances that have effects on the brain similar to the above-mentioned chemicals, producing hallucinations and other perceptual and emotional disturbances. One of these substances is tryptamine, one of the many amines occuring naturally in the body. When detoxification by the liver and elimination by the kidneys does not occur rapidly enough, tryptamine and its intermediary metabolites may cause behavioral disturbances. These findings suggest that variations in brain chemistry may be a major determinant of the variation in adaptive behavior occurring among normal individuals (34).

Effects of Sensory Deprivation on Cortical Activity

Normal brain functioning depends not only on a healthy structure and optimum physiological balance but also upon continuing sensory stimulation. Reports of brainwashing in the Korean War indicated that people who were completely cut off from environmental stimulation underwent some unusual changes in behavior. This led to experimental studies of this phenomenon. D. O. Hebb (19) of McGill University was one of the early investigators in this field. He offered college students $20 per day to remain quietly on a comfortable bed in an isolated cubicle, arising only for meals and toileting. The visual perception of these students was restricted by a translucent plastic visor which admitted light but did not permit vision. Auditory perceptions were muffled by a U-shaped foam-rubber pillow covering the ears, and by the continuous hum of an air conditioner and a fan which masked small sounds. The sense of touch was restricted by cotton gloves and long cardboard cuffs extending beyond the fingertips which permitted free movement but limited tactual perception.

Most of the volunteer students had planned to think about their studies and get a good rest during the experiment. But nearly all reported that they were unable to think clearly for any length of time. Several days of isolation caused many of them to have visions and hallucinations. These pictures became so vivid that they interfered with sleep. Some of the students heard people talking, one heard a music box playing constantly, others had varied bizarre feelings and sensations. Electroencephalograms showed the frequencies in the region of the principal brain rhythm to have slowed down in these subjects. These reactions disappeared a few days after the isolation ended.

Similar effects were achieved in other experiments. In one instance, medical and dental students were confined to a tank-type respirator (iron lung), in which they were fed automatically, completely immobilized, and shut off from all stimuli. Only 5 out of the original 30 who started the experiment were able to last the full 36 hours for which it was planned. In another experiment, normal subjects were deprived of sensory stimulation by immersing them completely in a tank of tepid water, leaving exposed only a blacked-out headgear through which they could breathe. Psychotic-like symptoms were produced in only a few hours (50).

Investigators are not sure just what happens to the brain during sensory deprivation. One theory is that lack of stimulation causes a depletion of ribonucleic acid (RNA) and essential proteins in the neurons. Lack of these substances causes the nerve cells to become incapable of carrying on their normal transmission of electrical impulses (23). Whatever the cause may be, experiments on sensory deprivation have shown that the human brain is dependent on varied and continuing sensory input. An unchanging environment and a monotonous, nonstimulating existence may cause the brain to discharge its electrical potential inwardly in the form of illusions and hallucinations. This may account for the visions reported by aviators during long flights and by truck drivers on long hauls.

Similar mental and emotional distress may occur in patients kept in the dark after cataract operations, in persons with severe hearing impairment, in polio victims confined to respirators, in prisoners kept in solitary confinement, and in refugees handicapped by language difficulties. Sufficiently prolonged deprivation of sensory stimuli can produce mental abnormalities and symptoms which resemble the effects of LSD, mescaline, or true psychoses (27, 58).

GLANDULAR AND METABOLIC INFLUENCES ON BEHAVIOR

If the genes establish the rough outline of behavior, and the brain is the administrator of mental and motor activity, the endocrine glands may be considered the regulators or pacemakers of the growth process. The hormones secreted by endocrine glands are carried to specific target organs in the body, where they stimulate or depress physiological processes in a selective way. So essential are these endocrine glands that their removal produces death or serious physiological malfunction if they are not replaced by hormones or other compensating treatment (21).

While the effects of the endocrine glands on the body as a whole have been well charted, the action of endocrines, hormones, and enzymes on the nervous system and on psychological functions has hardly been explored. Psychoendocrine research is now under way along two primary lines: one deals with the nervous excitation of glandular activity, the other with endocrine effects on metabolic processes that affect behavior.

Nervous Excitation of Endocrine Activity

It is known that endocrine malfunction can cause significant behavioral changes. Underactivity of the thyroid gland, for example, is associated with sluggishness, apathy, and low energy level, while overfunctioning of this gland causes the individual to be excessively active, irritable, and excitable. If the thymus gland, which ordinarily disappears around puberty, continues to be active, immaturity in sexual and emotional characteristics may result. Under-activity of the adrenals is associated with a tendency to become easily fatigued, while excessive adrenal activity induces a highly tense physical state. The imperfect function of other endocrine glands may likewise produce significant mental and emotional changes in the individual.

It now appears that this process may work in reverse and that external stimuli transmitted along neural pathways can trigger the release of endocrine products. This was demonstrated in an experiment with twenty-two anxiety-prone patients in a general hospital. The patients were subjected to interviews that deliberately probed into personal problems which were known to be disturbing to them. Blood tests were taken before and after each interview to detect changes in the plasma level of hydrocortisone, a product of the adrenal glands. It was found that the more upset the patient became, the greater the increase in hydrocortisone in his blood (40). Psychological stress may thus have a direct effect on endocrine function. Electroshock and insulin shock are thought to produce changes in behavior through similar action on the endocrine glands.

The Endocrines and Metabolism

There is a delicate chemical balance in the body which determines whether behavior will be normal or abnormal. A deficiency of some substances, such as glucose or oxygen, immediately brings about a dulling of perception and judgment, and in some cases produces depressive reactions, anxiety, and neurotic symptoms (31). A deficiency of certain vitamins may produce symptoms of fear, apprehension, irritability, depression, hostility, poor memory, and inability to make social adjustments. Numerous other examples could be cited where chemical imbalance results in psychological dysfunction.

The endocrines have been suspected of playing a fundamental role in maintaining the chemical balance of the body. The mechanism through which they do it is not yet clearly defined. It is believed that endocrine products serve a catalytic function and that enzymes are involved in this process. Some endocrine products are known to promote metabolism, while others, called antimetabolites, have the function of neutralizing the effects of certain metabolic products at the proper time. This mechanism has been explored in the case of one critical brain chemical called serotonin. A small amount of this hormone-like agent has a tonic effect on the nervous system, but unless neutralized at the proper time by other glandular products or enzymes, it can build up to a point where disturbing mental effects result (28).

It will be a while before research provides definite information on the complex interaction of glandular and chemical products in the body, and how they affect behavior. But the evidence to date indicates that an intimate relationship exists among these factors and that the course of behavior is dependent upon the individual's total biological and psychological functioning (2, 43).

SOCIAL INFLUENCES ON
BIOLOGICAL FUNCTIONING

Man is a social as well as a biological organism, and it is often difficult to distinguish the relative importance of psychobiological and social forces in influencing behavior. Physiological reactions to stress, for example, are quite closely linked to life styles. Some people consistently develop an upset stomach when exposed to anxiety; or they get an attack of diarrhea, or asthma, or some other reaction affecting a particular organ. Seldom will a physician find anything organically wrong with the organ affected. The physical response serves the individual in a symbolic form and somehow reflects the effects of his social experiences.

Or, to use another illustration of the close tie between social and biological functioning, studies of peptic ulcers show that these ailments often result from social isolation. One study of peptic ulcer among 45 men found that in 43 cases the symptoms started after the patient was isolated from his protective social relationships. This included isolation or separation from a cooperative community, from a team of workers, a circle of professional men, the family, or even from the protection of a superior. Evidently, human beings need supportive interpersonal relationships to maintain their physiological equilibrium. This may explain why there is a higher incidence of ulcer in cities with their loose social structure than in primitive tribes, why ulcer rates were higher among rear-echelon troops than among front-line troops during the last war, and why ulcer rates decreased in prisoner of war camps and increased after the liberation of prisoners (42).

Vulnerability to emotional disorders as well as to physical disorders is affected by the nature of an individual's social interactions. As mentioned previously, the drug called LSD can produce many symptoms of emotional disorder in normal people. The nature of the symptoms produced seems to depend in some measure upon the social conditions prevailing at the time the drug is administered. When given to individuals in isolation from others, symptoms of anxiety and depression are most prominent, while individuals in groups of two or more who receive the drug are more likely to display elation than depression (49). Even the severity of mental disturbances, or whether a person develops a tendency toward psychotic reactions, is heavily influenced by his social environment and how it affects his life (6).

In subsequent chapters we shall delve more deeply into the social influences which affect behavior and adjustment. This brief presentation is inserted here to avoid the implication that psychobiological forces are prepotent in determining the course of human adjustment. Gardner Murphy (33) expressed this precaution well when he said the following:

The genes are enormously important, but they do not call the shots. They do not punch the IBM cards; they do not sort us out and throw us into bins, where we can be counted or measured. Neither do the environmental contexts about us predetermine the slots, the grooves, through which we must glide. Rather, there is a strange, delicate process, hardly understood at all, by which certain latent potentialities within the genes are drawn out, molded, shaped as glass is shaped by the individual glass-blower, and in the same way, though we less frequently think of it this way, that the social forces are drawn upon, channeled and funneled into the living system in such a way as to accelerate or retard, magnify or minimize what the genes are trying to say.

SUMMARY

We bring into this world with our genetic inheritance a complete or incomplete nervous system, a normal or disturbed metabolism, a whole complex of physical structures and physiological activities, a biochemical system, and a variety of susceptibilities and constitutional vulnerabilites which are not yet clearly defined.

How this inheritance affects adjustment as growth progresses depends upon a host of other factors. Prenatal conditions, including the oxygen supply to the fetus, drugs, chemicals, diseases, and radiation may modify genetic influences adversely. Birth trauma and a variety of chemical, endocrine, metabolic, sensory, and social influences occurring after birth may also affect the pattern of growth of the human organism. So closely interrelated are these psychological, social, physiological, and environmental influences that they make it impossible to distinguish clearly the specific origins of behavior. Psychological and physiological responses are inseparable parts of a unitary process of adaptation. Working together, these various forces shape our individuality and make each of us a little different from everyone else.

Many of the factors which affect human behavior are beyond the control of the individual or the people who influence his life. But some of these factors can be modified so that significant improvement in adjustment takes place as the organism grows up under more favorable conditions. The remainder of this book is devoted to those aspects of human development which have to do with adjustment and which offer some possibility of altering the course of behavior.

REFERENCES

1. "Agonistic Is the Word for Fighting Feline," *Med. News,* June 22, 1960, **6**:16.
2. Batt, J. C., "Some Endocrine Considerations in Psychiatry," *Intern. Rec. Med.,* March, 1960, **173**:149–158.

3. Bender, L., "Genetic Data in Evaluation and Management of Disordered Behavior in Children," *Dis. nerv. System,* February, 1960, 21:57–64.

4. Bercel, N. A., *et al.,* "Model Psychoses Induced by LSD–25 in Normals," *Arch. Neurol. & Psychiat.,* June, 1956, 75:588–611.

5. Böök, J. A., "Genetical Etiology in Mental Illness," *Milbank Mem. Fund quart.,* July, 1960, 38:193–212.

6. Clausen, J. A., and Kohn, M. L., "The Ecological Approach in Social Psychiatry," *Amer. J. Sociol.,* September, 1954, 40:140–151.

7. Cobb, S., "Some Chemical Changes in Behavior Accompanying Endocrine Disorders," *J. nerv. & ment. Dis.,* February, 1960, 130:97–106.

8. Cole, L. E., *Human Behavior,* World, 1953.

9. "Current Research Relating to Children at the National Institutes of Health," Special report presented at the 25th Anniversary Meeting of the Society for Research in Child Development, reprinted from *Child Develpm.,* March, 1960, 31:209–214.

10. Felix, R. H., "New Scientific Developments in the Mental Health Field," *Soc. Serv. Rev.,* June, 1957, 31:123–134.

11. Friedman, M., and Rosenman, R. H., "Association of Specific Overt Behavior Patterns with Blood and Cardiovascular Findings," *J. Amer. Med. Ass.,* March 21, 1959, 169:1286–1296.

12. Garn, S. M., "Growth and Development," in Eli Ginzberg (Ed.), *The Nation's Children, 2. Development and Education,* Columbia, 1960, pp. 24–42.

13. Geiger, R. S., "Effects of LSD–25, Serotonin and Sera from Schizophrenic Patients on Adult Mammalian Brain Cultures," *J. Neuropsychiat.,* April, 1960, 1:185–190.

14. Gibson, J. E., "Your Looks Give You Away," *Today's Hlth.,* July, 1960, 38:6–7.

15. Goldstein, K., "Abnormal Conditions in Infancy," *J. nerv. ment. Dis.,* June, 1959, 128:538–557.

16. Golomb, S. W., "Genetic Coding," *Engng. & Sci.,* April, 1962, 25:9–14.

17. Goodman, H. O., and Herndon, C. N., "Genetic Factors in the Etiology of Mental Retardation," *Intern. Rec. Med.,* February, 1959, 172:61–74.

18. Gottleib, J. S., *et al.,* "Primary Behavior Disorders and Psychopathic Personality, II. The Inheritance of Electrocortical Activity," *Amer. J. Psychiat.,* 1947, 103:813.

19. Hebb, D. O., "The Motivating Effects of Exteroceptive Stimulation," *Amer. Psychologist,* 1958, 13:109–113.
20. Hoch, P. H., "Experimental Psychiatry: The Hallucinogenic Drugs," *State of Mind,* January, 1958, Vol. 2.
21. Houssay, B. A., "The Status of Endocrinology in 1985," *What's New* (Abbott Labs.), 25th Anniversary Issue, 1960, No. 220, pp. 36–37.
22. Hurder, W. P., "A Decade of Biological Research: Implications for Mental Retardations," *Proceedings of Two Conferences on Research Opportunities in Mental Retardation in Pennsylvania,* The Woods Schools, Langhorne, 1962, pp. 13–24.
23. Hyden, H., "Satellite Cells in the Nervous System," *Scient. Amer.,* December, 1961, 205:62–70.
24. Kallmann, F. J., *Heredity in Health and Mental Disorder,* Norton, 1953.
25. Kallmann, F. J., and Baroff, G. S., "Abnormalities in Behavior (in the Light of Psychogenetic Studies)," *Ann. Rev. Psychol.* 1955, 6:297–326.
26. Knobloch, H., and Pasamanick, B., "Environmental Factors Affecting Human Development Before and After Birth," *Pediat.,* August, 1960, 26:210.
27. Krasner, L., "Reinforcement, Verbal Behavior and Psychotherapy," *Amer. J. Orthopsychiat.,* July, 1963, 33:601–613.
28. Lund, F. H., "The Cause of Mental Illness," *Educ.,* March, 1962, 82:432–437.
29. Malitz, S., *et al.,* "Some Observations on Psilocybin, a New Hallucinogen, in Volunteer Subjects," *Comprehensive Psychiat.,* February, 1960, 1:8–17.
30. Marrazzi, A. S., "The Action of Psychotogens and a Neurophysiological Theory of Hallucination," *Amer. J. Psychiat.,* April, 1960, 116:911–914.
31. "Mental Symptoms Caused by Low Blood Sugar," *Calif. ment. Hlth. News,* September, 1958, p. 13.
32. Murphy, G., *Human Potentialities,* Basic Books, 1958.
33. Murphy, G., "New Vistas in Personality Research," *Personnel & Guidance J.,* October, 1961, 40:114–122.
34. National Institute of Mental Health, *Highlights of Progress in Mental Health Research, 1961,* Public Health Service Publication No. 919, Bethesda, Md., 1962.
35. Oettinger, L., Jr., *Medical Management of Behavior Disorders,* multilithed, St. Lukes Hospital, Pasadena, Calif., undated.

36. Page, H., *et. al.,* "An Empirical Study of the Relationship of Four Classes of Body Habitus to Responses on the MMPI," *Psychol. Reps.,* 1955, **5**:159–167.

37. Parnell, R. W., "Physique and Mental Breakdown in Young Adults," *Brit. Med. J.,* June 29, 1957, **1**:1485–1490.

38. Pasamanick, B., and Knobloch, H., "Epidemiologic Studies on the Complications of Pregnancy and the Birth Process," in Gerald Caplan (Ed.), *Prevention of Mental Disorders in Children,* Basic Books, 1961, pp. 74–94.

39. "Pavlovians Stress Electrical Study," *Med. News,* November 9, 1960, **6**:2.

40. Persky, H., *et al.,* "Relation of Emotional Responses and Changes in Plasma Hydrocortisone Level After Stressful Interview," *Arch. Neurol. Psychiat.,* April, 1958, **79**:434–447.

41. Pfeiffer, J., "The New Biology: The Role of Nucleic Acids in Medicine," *Med. News,* Special Supplement, May 11, 1960.

42. Pflanz, M., *et al.,* "Socio-Psychological Aspects of Peptic Ulcer," *J. psychosom. Res.,* February, 1956, **1**:68–74.

43. Reiss, M., "Endocrine Concomitants of Certain Physical Psychiatric Treatments," *Intern. Rec. Med.,* July, 1956, **169**:431–438.

44. Rosanoff, A. J., *et al.,* "The Etiology of Child Behavior Difficulties, Juvenile Delinquency, and Adult Criminality with Special Reference to Their Occurrence in Twins," *Psychiatric Monographs,* State of California, Department of Institutions, Sacramento, January, 1941.

45. Rosenfeld, G. B., and Bradley, C., "Childhood Behavior Sequelae of Asphyxia in Infancy—With Special Reference to Pertussis and Asphyxia Neonatorum," *Pediatrics,* July, 1948, **3**:74–84.

46. Sarason, S. B., *et al., Anxiety in Elementary School Children,* John Wiley & Sons, 1960.

47. Shagass, C., and Kerenyi, A. B., "Neurophysiologic Studies of Personality," *J. nerv. ment. Dis.,* February, 1958, **126**:141–147.

48. Sheldon, W. H., *et al., Varieties of Delinquent Youth: An Introduction to Constitutional Psychiatry,* Harper & Row, 1949.

49. Slater, P. E., *et al.,* "The Effect of Group Administration upon Symptom Formation Under LSD," *J. nerv. ment. Dis.,* April–June, 1957, **125**:312–315.

50. Solomon, P., "Sensory Deprivation: Its Meaning and Significance," *State of Mind,* November, 1958, **29**:1–5.

51. Stromgren, E., "Genetics and Mental Health," *Child.*, March-April, 1958, 5:49–54.

52. "The Story of Tranquilizers," *Today's Hlth.*, November, 1960, 38:32–33.

53. Unger, S. M., "Mescaline, LSD, Psilocybin, and Personality Change," *Psychiat.*, May, 1963, 26:111–125.

54. Vath, W. R., "Peptic Ulcers: Still a Medical Mystery," *Today's Hlth.*, September, 1960, 38:28–29.

55. Vorster, D., "An Investigation into the Part Played by Organic Factors in Childhood Schizophrenia," *J. ment. Sci.*, April, 1960, 106:494–522.

56. Weil, A. A., "Ictal Depressions and Anxiety in Temporal Lobe Disorders," *Report to the 111th Annual Meeting, The American Psychiatric Association*, Atlantic City, May 9–13, 1955.

57. Wortis, J., "Differential Diagnosis of Mental Retardation," in E. M. Bower and J. H. Rothstein (Eds.), *Diagnostic Problems in Mental Retardation, Bull. Calif. State Dep. Educ.*, Sacramento, August, 1958, 27:3–14.

58. Ziskind, E., "Isolation Stress in Medical and Mental Illness," *J. Amer. Med. Ass.*, November 15, 1958, 168:1427–1431.

Chapter 3   The Growth Process

In the previous chapter we referred to some of the forces that have an affect on the psychobiological factors which influence behavior. We shall now examine in greater detail the effects of the growth process and the requirements that are made on the developing human organism as he grows from childhood to maturity.

The life cycle may be divided into the periods of childhood, puberty, adolescence, early adulthood, middle age, and old age. Each stage makes certain demands on the adjustive capacities of the individual and provides experiences which contribute to the formation of his personality. While there are marked differences among individuals in terms of the rate and manner with which they pass through each stage of development, most normal people follow much the same course of growth and encounter similar problems of maturation and adjustment.

NORMAL STAGES OF GROWTH

As children pass through various stages of growth, their behavior undergoes many changes. In some periods of development, children are cooperative, predictable, and nice to have around. In other stages they are exasperating, irrational, and difficult to understand. Although such inconsistent behavior may be disturbing to adults, it is nonetheless a normal part of growing up.

To interpret the strivings of normal children as they pass through the developmental sequence from infancy to maturity, we shall describe, in capsule form, five stages of growth: the preschool period, early and middle childhood, the puberty years, the adolescent period, and the period beyond adolescence. There are no sharp divisions between these stages, for growth is continuous, with one stage merging into another like colors in the spectrum. Furthermore, there will be many individual deviations from the behavior descriptions provided, since the force of individuality is so strong that no two persons are exactly alike at a given age. However, authorities have found that these individual variations occur around a central theme, and for any selected stage it is possible to sketch a portrait which roughly delineates the behavior characteristics typical of the age (25:60).

The Preschool Child

Physically, the child's growth is as rapid from birth to five years of age as it is from five to fifteen years. During these five years he grows from a helpless, dependent infant to an active, noisy, vigorous child. This growth is uneven. The large muscles mature rapidly but are not completely under voluntary control. Consequently, the five-year old can run, skip, dance, climb, and jump, but is rather awkward and inefficient in his movements and often spills things or knocks them over when he reaches beyond arm's length (2).

The social and psychological development of the child during this period is swift and stormy. The progression from bassinet to crib, to high chair, to playpen, to backyard, to sidewalk, and finally to kindergarten takes place in just a few calendar years but is an epoch in social and psychological growth. This is a period of humanization during which the abjectly dependent infant becomes the self-assured, conforming citizen of the five-year-old world. The precipitous, pell-mell growth from helpless infancy to the chattering, roaming, adventurous zestfulness of the young child inevitably is accompanied by some thwarting and emotional outbursts. On the whole, however, these first few years of life can be expected to produce a child who has established basic attitudes toward himself and others, has developed reasonable control over his behavior, and is prepared to loosen his hold on the home and start the journey toward becoming a part of the wider social world (25:247).

Early and Middle Childhood

Development moves along at a fairly even pace between the age of six and the onset of puberty. The growth of bones, muscles, and nervous tissue marks the most dramatic physical change occurring in this period. Soon after he enters school, the child goes through a stage where the long bones of arms and legs grow rapidly, giving him a tall, thin appearance, as contrasted with his stocky, rounded figure of earlier years. As the large muscles of the legs, back, arms, shoulders, and wrist develop, children have an organic need for physical activity. They learn skills easily and practice them enthusiastically. Their increased strength and resistance to fatigue makes it possible for them to climb, swing, run, and play for a long period of time. This inexhaustible energy, usually accompanied by much shouting, often brings them into conflict with adults.

The nervous system reaches its maximum rate of development at age ten. At twelve the brain attains mature size. These neurological changes lead to the development of imagination and interests which are at a higher level of maturation than the muscular dexterity available to the child to carry out his projects. As a result, the child often gets into trouble by starting things which he is not physically able to complete (29).

The social behavior of the child during this period of life progresses from the small, loosely organized, quarrelsome play-groups of the six-year-old to cooperative team activities of the twelve-year-old. After the eighth year, group life takes on a new meaning and significance. The drive for emancipation from the family begins, and youngsters develop an engrossing interest in, and conformity to, the activities and standards of their age mates (53). When this stage appears, new attitudes toward adult authority emerge. At about the age of nine, boys and girls may show a disregard for adult standards, fight against previously accepted routines, question the decisions of their parents, and compare their rules and regulations with those which prevail in other homes (6). They learn a whole new set of techniques for controlling their parents and become quite skillful in knowing when to ignore, flatter, wheedle, cry, or act like little angels (48).

These struggles have an effect on the child's emotional life. His rebelling against people for whom he has a deep emotional attachment produces strains which may be expressed through psychological and physical symptoms such as restlessness, facial tics, nail-biting, skin-chewing, scratching, or the return of outgrown habit patterns (47, 53). Many youngsters of this age cease to be responsible, compliant children and become talkative, noisy, daring individualists who flaunt their courage and are willing to try anything. They are amazingly self-dependent and often openly hostile toward the adults they love best.

Despite these characteristics, parents and teachers find much satisfaction in children of elementary-school age. Their bustling activity, enthusiasm, spirit of helpfulness, eagerness to learn, inquisitiveness, and underlying need for adult support are wholesome qualities which outweigh the less desirable aspects of their behavior.

The Puberty Years

Between late childhood and early adolescence is a period in which growth changes are rapid and dramatic. These are the years of puberty or preadolescence, a time when old personality patterns are loosened in order to make room for what the child is to become (47).

This period is ushered in by a growth spurt which occurs between the ages of 10 and 14 for girls, and between 12 and 16 for boys. There are dramatic increases in height and weight, accompanied by other significant physiological changes. The cartilage framework of the nose develops, causing the nose to become larger and assume a distinct shape. At about this same time the hands and feet reach maximum size. These temporary anatomical exaggerations of nose, hands, and feet cause the youngster much concern.

Changes in the visceral organs influence the child's physiological capacities. The heart increases in size just before and during puberty. Arteries, however, grow less rapidly, causing the heart to pump blood into an opening only one-fifth as wide as itself. As a result, strenuous exercise may cause faintness, dizziness, heart strain, or enlargement of the heart (29). The digestive tract becomes mature at puberty, resulting in an enormous but often uncertain appetite. Also, the gonads in boys and girls increase in weight about four times as fast as the body as a whole, resulting in accelerated hormonal activity (37).

These and other physical changes of puberty introduce a number of disturbing influences in children's lives. Youngsters who had been playing together for years suddenly begin to notice differences in each other. The girl who enters puberty early loses her childhood interests, begins to dress more maturely, uses makeup, and becomes interested in boys. This creates a gap between her and friends who are still in the late childhood stage of growth. The boy who matures early may gain considerable status in his group, because his size, strength, and competency in group games are important determiners of prestige. Late-maturing boys, on the other hand, may develop anxiety over their size and physical ability (20, 27).

Adjusting to new physical proportions is a major problem for these youngsters who find it hard to realize how radically their bodies are changing. They may knock things over and appear clumsy or awkward because the 24-inch arm they were accustomed to has suddenly grown to 25 inches. They may not know what to do with their hands, and often suffer embarrassment over a new pair of shoes which looks so much larger than their old ones. There is considerable sensitivity over skin blemishes, developing breasts, increased weight, and other external manifestations of growth.

The child's energy output is another source of concern to him and his parents. Growth is taking place so rapidly that the preadolescent may seem lazy. Often this is due to physical fatigue; so much energy is required for growth that the youngster is too tired to exert himself. Because his actions contrast so sharply with his alert, energetic behavior of preceding years, the sporadic lassitude of preadolescence may cause considerable anxiety in the family (30).

School work may be noticeably affected during the puberty years. Data derived from the Harvard Growth Studies show evidence of a definite break in the mental-age growth curve among children going through puberty changes. Very little advance in mental age was noted during this period. Restlessness, lack of initiative, learning and behavioral difficulties are familiar concomitants of the disturbed physiological functioning which occurs during puberty (6, 14).

Depressed and negativistic states seem to be sufficiently common among preadolescents to constitute a typical characteristic. Girls enter this phase somewhere between the ages of 11 and 13. It may last for two to six months and generally ends with the onset of menstruation. Boys go through this stage somewhere between the ages of 13 and 15, completing it when the secondary sex characteristics appear. During this period boys and girls carry a chip on their shoulder. They are critical of home, parents, and society in general. They tend to be suspicious, unfriendly, and sensitive, and spend a great deal of time reading, daydreaming, or just moping around, feeling sorry for themselves (29, 47). Obviously, the puberty period is one which may try the patience of parents and teachers. These youngsters need the support, understanding, and respect of adults, but they also need to be left alone so that they can experiment with a variety of personality patterns and gain some insight into who they are.

The Adolescent Period

Adolescence usually is considered as the period extending from puberty to the late teens or early twenties. We have described the puberty years as a separate phase of growth in order to emphasize the critical changes which occur during this period. Therefore, our discussion of adolescence will be confined to the postpuberty years, when the child's growth is decelerating and most of his major physical development has been completed.

Many unsolved problems are carried over from the puberty

years and continue to produce emotional distress in adolescence. Included here are frequent changes of mood, sensitivity over physical appearance, and many old fears which crop up and press more vividly than ever before.

Normal adolescents worry constantly about these old problems and many new ones. School achievement looms as one of their chief worries (44). Although intellectual abilities are on the rise during this period, large numbers of high school youngsters say they cannot concentrate on their studies (18, 49). Confusion about religion, feelings of inadequacy, anxiety over social status, and problems of vocation, sex, and money are also common concerns of the typical adolescent.

These problems contribute to the unintegrated, diffusely anxious personality patterns found so often among adolescents. The emotions of adolescents are of such depth and intensity that they must not be treated lightly by adults. Frequently, a series of neurotic symptoms arises, beginning usually with difficulties involving concentration, sleep, and appetite, then progressing to minor depressive swings, strong tendencies toward introversion and fantasy, and sometimes hypochondria. These reactions occur so commonly that they may be regarded as a normal adolescent syndrome (22, 33, 43).

Closely associated with these emotional reactions, and contributing directly to them, are the adolescent's need to reform his ego and re-establish his sense of selfhood. Out of the disorganization of the puberty years he must reweave the pattern of his life into an adult image. This does not come about rapidly or easily, for the adolescent has many major conflicts to solve. Prominent among these is the conflict between himself and his family. Before he can become an individual in his own right he must alter his position in the family from that of a child to that of an equal with adults and a superior to younger brothers and sisters. Adolescents undertake this quest for independence with varying degrees of intensity. Some teen-agers overreact to adult authority and reject their family and the ethical, moral, or religious concepts which were taught them. Sometimes they even defy the dictates of their own conscience, since it, too, was shaped by adults (7).

Actually, most adolescents do not want to cast off their parents. Despite their protestations, many adolescents are not prepared to relinquish their dependency. Complete independence frightens them, intensifies their current feelings of inadequacy, and makes them feel rejected. Many of the teen-ager's outbursts are not so much against parents as they are a cover-up against these feelings of doubt and inadequacy. What they are seeking is not absolute freedom but a relationship which permits them to love and receive love from their parents without clinging to them as children. Once they attain recognition as equals, they are prepared to accept parental guidance and attention, if it is offered with consideration and respect.

Status in social groups is of paramount importance to adolescents. Group loyalties are particularly strong among boys. Girls are less likely to participate in large group activities and more inclined to break up into small cliques or sets composed of six to twelve favored individuals (37, 54). Heterosexual relations assume a new significance in the middle teens, particularly for boys. This is a romantic period, with a succession of crushes, hero worship, and falling in and out of love. Relationships between the sexes do not run smoothly because of oversensitivity, self-consciousness, and fear of being rejected or rebuffed.

In summary, the adolescent may be moody, confused, or oversensitive, with good cause. He is faced with the tremendous task of reconstructing his childhood self-image into an adult pattern. This entails clarifying his masculine or feminine role, coming to terms with social requirements, and revising his many childhood beliefs and fantasies in accordance with his real potentialities and limitations. The adolescent is experiencing a period of insecurity, accentuated by drives and desires which he feels intensely but does not completely understand. He wants to be accepted and loved but is afraid of showing this desire or demonstrating affection for others. He needs adult guidance but rebels against it and demands freedom and independence which he cannot assume. He has high ideals, a strong sense of morality, and great hopes in the opportunities which lie before him. Yet, he is anxious over his own abilities and unsure of his values and goals (17).

It is clear that these are difficult problems for a youngster to handle. It takes time to put the scattered pieces of a previously established identity into place on a new level of maturity. However, by the time they are in their late teens, most normal adolescents manage to reconcile their various conflicts and arrive at a reasonable state of integration (24, 55).

Beyond Adolescence. The periods of adulthood, middle age, and old age make up two-thirds or more of the total life span. Although maturation slows down during this period, the individual is confronted with adjustment problems fully as important as those which he experienced in earlier stages of life.

Adulthood

There is no precise point at which adolescence ends and adulthood begins. Arbitrarily, the age of 20 or 21 has been selected as the beginning of young adulthood, and the age of 45 as its end. There are great individual variations within these age boundaries. Many adolescents are physically and psychologically adults while legally classified as juveniles; and many persons who are adults legally are psychologically hardly more mature than adolescents. Some people are old at 45; others are just beginning their most productive years.

Up to about the age of 28, young adulthood is a period of transition marked by greater mobility and change than in any other age group. Young adults move from economic dependence to self-support, from being at home to starting a home of their own. They change jobs, develop new attitudes, and engage in a variety of temporary and shifting social relationships. This change and mobility has serious consequences for some young adults. This is reflected in social statistics which show that most divorces occur during this period of life, that young adults make up a majority of state and federal prisoners, and that the majority of schizophrenics admitted to mental hospitals for the first time are from this age group (51). However, most people manage to resolve the problems of this period and move on toward maturity. The normal young adult achieves a reasonable autonomy from his parents and develops his own patterns of living. He acquires a sense of identity, develops a meaningful interpretation of his past, present, and future, and establishes his place in society. As these adjustments are made, he grows into a mature, responsible adult citizen (19, 23).

Middle Age

The period of middle age is defined roughly as extending from about 45 to 65 years of age. In women it begins with the physiological changes which initiate the menopause or change of life. Restlessness, depression, anxiety, and a variety of neural, vascular, and emotional reactions are quite common during the menopause.

Men do not go through an analogous physiological upheaval but have a somewhat equivalent period of life termed the male climacteric. Some changes in endocrine function may take place during this period, but the primary symptoms are psychological rather than physical. Increased anxiety, irritability, and decline in sexual desire are commonly noted in the male at this time.

Both men and women show increased concern about health and physical appearance during the middle years. Their efforts to stay in shape or retain their youth through exercise, cosmetics, and diets are common subjects of cartoons and jokes. The admission that one is not the man or woman he used to be is difficult to make, and it is quite common for normal people to fight against this realization just as long as possible.

The middle years may find the family in its best economic position but in a changed atmosphere. Life for the male is usually active; he has work associations, hobbies, and interests. For the woman more serious adjustments are required as children leave the home. She may experience a gap in her life which she seeks to fill through club and community activities or by returning to work. The working wife is no longer a novelty. Since World War II, it has become common for girls to marry early, leave the work force to raise a family, then return to work between the ages of 35 and 54. Thus, the modern American woman develops two careers—one in the home and one in the business world (16).

As the period of middle age draws to a close, the interests of both men and women change and become more narrowed.

There is a tendency for them to become settled in their ways and resist things that are new or different. For some there comes a period of disillusionment and depression when they have to face the reality that youthful dreams are not to be attained. Frustrated ambitions may make more acute the change in life patterns which this period brings on.

Old Age

The period of old age is identified as the years from about 65 on. Rather rapid physical deterioration may occur in these later years. Chronic disabilities and diseases are quite prevalent, physical activity is reduced, and there is an increasing tendency toward solitary, passing-the-time type of activities. Variations in sleep patterns is particularly evident. There is a reduction in the number of hours slept, an increase in the time taken to get off to sleep, and a greater tendency toward frequent waking at night. The alteration of sleep patterns with age is more marked in women, usually appearing during middle age and accompanied by nervousness, rapid heartbeat, headaches, and other physical symptoms (41).

The psychological changes of this period may be more disturbing than the physical changes. Retirement from active employment can make life acutely empty for a man who has not planned for retirement and who has no compensating interests. Loneliness and the wretched feeling of being no longer needed may cause the once active man to become crotchety, complaining, irritable, depressed, and to disengage himself emotionally from his surroundings and become increasingly preoccupied with himself (8). Women may follow a similar path of emotional restriction, and since they tend to outlive men, some of them do so in their waning years. However, it is often easier for a woman to maintain a more youthful and active outlook on life by continuing with the club and community activities that formed an important part of her life during the middle years (42).

It is quite common, although not universal, for old age to terminate in senility. Senility consists of a sequence of deterioration which begins with extensive reminiscing and preoccupation with the past. This is followed by a period of forgetfulness; then the person begins to talk aloud to himself a great deal. Later, the tie with reality may be broken; the senile person stares into space, dozes frequently, confuses familiar faces, and often accuses people of neglecting him. Finally, there is a period of regression to childhood during which the individual may cry and moan, and become unable to take care of his basic physiological needs (36).

The rate of an old person's decline may be affected by his health and the amount of social interaction and intellectual stimulation he experiences. It has been said that a man ages as he has lived. Satisfactions achieved in later years are built upon the capabilities, interests, and potentials developed in the earlier years of life. With proper planning, the declining years of many of our older citizens need not be years of deterioration and gloomy vegetation (2). Many governmental and volunteer agencies have recognized this fact and taken constructive steps to improve the welfare of older citizens. Indeed, when it became obvious that the number of people 65 years of age and over in the nation was increasing about twice as rapidly as the population as a whole, the spotlight of research was trained on the later years. The science of gerontology arose to deal with problems of the aged; housing centers for "senior citizens" have become common features over the nation, and many agencies are providing counseling and recreational services for older people to help them develop new interests and engage in an active life. These efforts hold forth a promise of useful, happy lives for old people who might otherwise succumb to apathy and boredom (45, 46).

SOME BASIC PRINCIPLES OF GROWTH

Now that we have viewed the broad panorama of growth, certain basic principles of development need to be emphasized. It is obvious that the growth of children is not a smooth and pleasant process. Childhood consists of a series of recurrent crises. As the child grows older, he is constantly changing internally, and society is constantly changing its demands upon him.

Consequently, normal children are not free of adjustment prob-lems. The nature of development is such that few children mature without encountering some physical, mental, or emo-tional distress (9).

Individual Variations in Growth

Children follow an essentially similar, but not identical, sequence of growth. There is no universal, detailed timetable for human development. A child meets the requirements of development, maturation, and socialization at his own rate of progress, to attain the functional capacities and personality which are uniquely his own.

Because of this individual variation, the number of years a child has lived provides only a rough indication of his level of development. In every age group there will be some children ahead of their peers in terms of physical, mental, social, and emotional development, and there will be others who lag behind. For example, in a typical eighth grade where children are within a few months of the same chronological age, it can be expected that the range of achievement on a test in arith-metic fundamentals will extend from fifth-grade to twelfth-grade ability (12). These differences, in varying degrees, apply to other areas of development and become more accentuated as growth progresses.

Spurts and Plateaus in Growth

Growth is continuous but does not proceed in a straight upward direction. At times, a child's development goes on at a rapid rate; at other times, his growth seems to be at a stand-still, and sometimes he may even appear to slip backward in his rate of maturing. The path of development consists of steep places where growth is difficult, interspersed with plateaus where the child moves along smoothly.

This irregularity of growth has its emotional concomitants. When growth is most rapid, or when it slows down noticeably, emotional problems are accentuated. At these times, children may be irritable or show frequent up- and downswings in mood. Spurts in growth often are accompanied by a tendency to go all out in the use of a new skill or capacity. Children become intensely absorbed in a new mode of behavior or phase of development. As time passes, this fascination for the new power loses its novelty, and the new behavior becomes a part of the broad pattern of development (31).

Growth and Behavior

Growth is not necessarily accompanied by an improvement of behavior. Often, as a child matures, changes occur which create new problems or accentuate old ones. Also, a child never completely leaves one phase of growth when he enters another. He retains older ways of behaving, even though they may be obscured by new mannerisms and affectations. Much of the child is contained in the adolescent, and much of the infant in the child (11).

While children tend to cling to old patterns of behavior as they grow, they also undergo a developmental revision of habits. At every stage of growth, children will show forms of behavior which they will change or abandon in due time. It is difficult to predict which characteristics will remain with children as they mature, and which will be revised or discarded. Because a certain form of behavior is strongly entrenched at one stage of growth does not mean that it will carry over to a later stage. Yet, this is always a possibility, and what we see in a child at a particular time is often a precursor of things to come (21).

Developmental Tasks

Part of growing up consists of developing the skills, under-standings, feelings, attitudes, and modes of behavior appropriate to each new stage of development. As a child's physical and psychological capacities mature, he is confronted with new expectations and new demands. These are crucial life problems, termed developmental tasks, arising partly from the pressure of cultural processes and partly from the individual's own desires, aspirations, motives, and values.

Many of the common developmental tasks of childhood have been described in preceding pages. They range from learn-ing sex differences and sexual modesty in early childhood to achieving socially responsible behavior in adolescence. Havighurst (26) has suggested a series of life tasks which confront children at various stages of growth. Erikson (19) has a somewhat similar series of growth hurdles, described as eight stages in the life cycle of man. Individuals will vary in terms of the ease and speed with which these tasks are accomplished. However, society does not countenance too much deviation from the time limits within which various developmental lessons must be learned. Moreover, failure to learn the lessons of one period may impede growth by making it difficult or even impossible to learn these tasks at a later period. For instance, the child who does not learn to distinguish right from wrong during the period when conscience is being formed may have great difficulty in doing so later. In the case of psychopaths this task may never be accomplished. Similarly, the adolescent who is too severely dominated by his parents as he tries to achieve the developmental task of independence may not grow up psychologically (27). Life is a sequence of growth crises. Under favorable conditions, the accomplishment of each developmental task builds strength for the next and leads to the formation of a normal personality.

Growth and Behavior in Adulthood

Adults too, are confronted with developmental tasks—certain periods at which decisions have to be made and actions taken. These have not been as clearly defined as they have been for children, but they do exist. There are times in life when it is most propitious for an individual to secure an education, marry, choose a vocation, select a home, and meet other problems of life. If this action is taken too early or too late, conflict or frustration may ensue. However, there is much latitude in making these choices, because the period of adulthood extends over many more years of the total life span than does the period of childhood.

DYNAMICS OF GROWTH

Our discussion of growth and adjustment has been largely in terms of symptomatic or observable characteristics. To understand more fully the development of human behavior, we must look beyond overt action into the inner life of the individual and examine the psychological forces which motivate him. Merely observing what people do adds little to an understanding of human motivation. What is more important is an interpretation of why they do certain things. This leads us to a consideration of the motivating forces which provide energy and direction to our efforts toward adjustment.

The Basic Human Needs

Behavior may be viewed as arising from certain urges, desires, wishes, or drives which collectively we shall call the basic human needs. These needs create a tension or disequilibrium within the individual, and to relieve this tension he strives for certain goals and satisfactions. When these ends are attained, the stress is removed and the individual is in harmony with himself and his environment.

Psychologists are far from agreeing upon what constitutes the basic human needs. In general, there is concurrence that these needs may be divided into two categories: (1) the biological or organic needs which every individual must satisfy to preserve his organic integrity and (2) the psychosocial needs which are vital to the person's psychological and social well-being. These needs are present in everyone and generally are regarded as the primary internal motivating forces of behavior (39).

The Biological Needs. Because we are living organisms, there are certain basic needs which we must satisfy to preserve our physical integrity. We need food, water, air, chemicals, and vitamins in order to sustain life; we need to adjust to temperature differences, exercise to maintain muscle tonus, and rest when fatigued. When any of our normal functions are impeded, distressing tensions arise which motivate the individual toward relieving these tensions. The action undertaken to restore physiological equilibrium has been called homeostasis. It is an imperative and often automatic process, set in motion whenever organic equilibrium is disturbed (35).

The organic needs are primary and must be satisfied before the individual can go on to other concerns (40). However, additional forms of motivation are needed if the individual is to rise above the level of animal satisfactions and become a human being. During the first few weeks of infancy, organic needs are the predominant motivating forces for behavior. When the infant is fed and made comfortable, he will either sleep or rest contentedly. At no other time in life does the satisfaction of organic needs lead to such a state of adjustment. As the child grows up in a culture, he soon becomes influenced by the expectations and rewards of other human beings. He learns to want or need certain satisfactions which are psychosocial rather than organic in nature. As he attempts to satisfy these wants and needs, he in turn becomes a civilized human being and grows into socialized maturity.

The Psychosocial Needs. The psychological and social satisfactions we seek are learned in the process of growing up in a social environment. As growth progresses, the individual develops a need for interpersonal satisfactions, for group status, and for self-realization. These needs become just as vital to him as the organic needs which first motivated his behavior. The extent to which he satisfies them and the manner in which he does so may help him build a useful life, or may create such tensions that he is incapable of functioning adequately in society.

THE NEED FOR INTERPERSONAL SATISFACTIONS. The normal human being needs to be loved and to have willing recipients of his love. The satisfaction of this need makes a person feel secure and enables him to face life's problems with a basic inner strength.

The need for interpersonal satisfaction is quite obvious in the young child. At first, his affectional needs are all one-sided. He receives love but has no way to return it. As he grows older, he must have someone who will accept his love. By giving his love to someone who wants it, he develops an outgoing attitude that will help him build wholesome relationships with other people (9). One of the characteristics frequently found among delinquents is the absence of wholesome love relationships in the home. Out of this frigid environment come feelings of distrust. Not only does the delinquent lack affection for others, he frequently dislikes himself.

THE NEED FOR GROUP STATUS.   Growing out of the need for love and affection is the need to belong among people. At first it is a need to belong to one's family; then the social radius widens to the gang, team, school, or larger social group. Eventually, in the normal course of events, this quest for a sense of belonging leads the individual back to the family as a parent.

There are two aspects to this need for group status. One is to merge into an association larger than ourselves and thus to feel that others are like us and that we are like others. In this way, the group strengthens the individual. The second aspect of this process is that while belonging to a group, each person needs to be recognized for his individual importance. The person who becomes so completely submerged into a group that he loses his own identity may feel just as isolated as one who is excluded from a group.

The need for group status is one of the most powerful motivating forces affecting human behavior. This influence is most evident in the adolescent for whom the values of the group, rather than those of the individual or his parents, are often the determiners of what he learns, how he dresses, or how he acts (32).

As maturity is approached, group influences on individual behavior may be less pronounced, but they still continue to have a strong effect on how we act. Studies of adults have shown that the group can, and often does, affect the way individuals think, what they do, and even what they eat. It has been demonstrated experimentally that few adults have the courage to stand alone against a group. More often, individuals quietly go along with majority opinion, even when the majority is known to be wrong. This occurs with sufficient frequency in everyday life to be a familiar pattern of behavior (5, 15).

The phenomenon of group contagion is another illustration of the effects of the group on individuals. Emotions tend to fan through a group and arouse behavior which is not typical for the individuals involved. This is why people seem to go through a metamorphosis at conventions, athletic events, riots, or election campaigns and act in a manner which is quite different from their usual pattern of behavior. Even what we eat and how much is affected by whether we are alone or in a group. This is true of animals as well as humans (1, 52).

NEED FOR SELF-REALIZATION. The drive to become an individual is also a motivating force in behavior and enables a person to maintain his identity while gaining support and strength from a group. There is within each of us a need to build an ego, to develop a sense of self-esteem and self-adequacy, and to become what we are capable of becoming. The toddler who learns to walk has a compelling urge to use this power, and will no longer be satisfied to sit quietly in his mother's lap. Children struggle for independence from their parents because they must become individuals if they are to lead a normal life. Adults strive for recognition and for a sense of accomplishment. Each of us pursues self-initiated and self-directed activities which give us a sense of competence as a person (52).

At times, this drive toward self-realization, or self-actualization, may become so dominant that it takes precedence over other basic needs. For example, the athlete may ignore a painful injury or endure intense physical discomfort in order to achieve recognition. The scientist may go without food or sleep while in the midst of a crucial project. Once aroused and properly channeled, this drive for self-realization mobilizes an individual's energies and stimulates him toward becoming an effective human being (13:129).

Factors Influencing the Satisfaction of Needs

The process of satisfying one's basic needs is not entirely under the control of the individual. Social pressures, the influence of maturity, and one's range of experiences are some of the forces which determine when and how our needs may be satisfied.

Social Pressure. Every social group sets up the patterns into which its members are cast. The individuals in these groups must satisfy their needs according to cultural imperatives, partly because they know nothing beyond what the culture teaches, and partly because to differ radically from the group would result in rejection.

The fact that different cultures permit different forms of need satisfactions emphasizes the precaution that we must not interpret the behavior of others in terms of our own standards. Even within our own culture a given type of behavior will be accepted by one group and rejected by another. In some groups it is a mark of acceptance to be law abiding and honest. In others, one must defy authority in order to maintain his standing in the group. Thus, individual behavior is interpreted not only in terms of what an individual is after, but also in terms of what the group makes him go after in order to gain recognition (32, 50).

Maturity and Behavior. A normal person is expected to seek those satisfactions which are appropriate for his level of growth, and to seek them in a manner suited to his stage of development. Growing toward maturity is a process of learning to seek appropriate need satisfactions in a manner suited to a particular level of development. Society does not readily tolerate any great departure from the forms of behavior expected at each level of maturity. A child is expected to act like a child, and an adult like an adult. If people deviate too radically from the roles they are expected to play, they are viewed with suspicion. The extent to which a person is able to use progressively more mature means for obtaining need satisfactions is a measure of his growth toward psychological maturity.

Range of Experience. A third factor which influences the manner in which needs are satisfied is one's range of awareness and experience. In seeking outlets for the psychological or emotional pressures arising out of our needs, we do not always select the best course of action. We act in terms of what we know or are aware of. Our goals are selected from what is attainable in our environment (9:28). Many people are content to live in a restricted, secure, comfortable environment and derive satisfactions from a rather limited selection of opportunities. However, it is becoming more difficult to live this simple life because modern media of communication are expanding our horizons, making us dissatisfied with things which previously met our needs quite adequately.

Much of our modern advertising capitalizes upon the tendency for people to alter their goals as their horizons are expanded. People are made dissatisfied with their old cars or hats, so that they will buy new ones. The charms of other lands are displayed, so that we will want to travel. A college education is held out as the golden ladder to success, and many young people eagerly forsake the security of their homes to reach for this symbol of status and opportunity.

Perhaps it is a wholesome thing to create unrest, spurring people toward higher goals. Certainly the progress of civilization depends upon creating new horizons. However, this progress may also be the root of anxiety. The person who must constantly seek new conquests may be caught up in a whirl of unrest. Because nothing satisfies him for very long, life becomes a progression of constantly striving for ever changing goals. The ladder of success must end somewhere. One of the biggest problems of life is to decide for ourselves when to be satisfied with our achievements.

NEED SATISFACTIONS AND PERSONALITY DEVELOPMENT

If personality can be defined broadly as the skills and abilities of an individual, his effect on other people, and his conception of himself, then we must consider learning as a major influence on personality development (4:65). In the process of satisfying his basic needs, the individual finds that certain modes of behavior bring him more satisfaction and success than others. He tends to repeat these satisfying patterns of behavior until self-perpetuating, habitual modes of response are developed. Essentially, this is the basic conditioning process used in training animals. However, in humans, more than conditioning is involved. Satisfying experiences lead to the development of a mental frame of reference through which the individual builds a conception of himself and establishes relationships with other people. He acquires beliefs, expectations, attitudes, and motivations through which he perceives the world and reacts to it. This frame of reference is so important to individual stability that it tends to operate like a polarizing crystal, admitting those perceptions which fit into it and excluding those which contradict it (13:119).

This process of selective behavior begins early in life. As the child gains awareness of his own abilities, as he reacts to the

conditions in his home, school, and community, and as he satisfies his needs in response to internal and external demands, his
behavior patterns are established. These behavior patterns are
likely to be perpetuated into adulthood as important personality
characteristics of the individual (21). While changes do occur
as a result of later life experience, the central core of personality
is thought to remain relatively unchanged and has a potent
influence on the adjustment of the individual at more mature
levels (52).

Thus, the manner in which our needs are satisfied and the
experiences encountered in this process are fundamental factors
in personality formation. This makes it important for each
person to set conscious, reasonable goals for himself and to
develop appropriate techniques for attaining them. It would
be a significant contribution to humanity if we could define
these goals and describe the techniques which would lead to the
satisfactory adjustment of each individual. But these are things
which each person must learn for himself. What works for one
may not work for another because of the very different net-
works of inheritance, experiences, feelings, desires, and habit
patterns which are woven into our personalities. There are
some facts and principles to guide us in this process, and these
will be considered in later chapters; however, they can do no
more than point a direction. The road to maturity is often
rough and rocky, and each of us, at times, needs a helping hand
and sympathetic understanding as he copes with his individual
life requirements.

SUMMARY

Given an average inheritance and home environment, normal middle-class children can be expected to go through characteristic stages of growth. The preschool child develops the
physical and psychological abilities required for adapting to
social life outside the home. In his elementary-school years, the
youngster becomes a bigger and better child, learning to adjust
to other children, exercising his growing capacities, and developing self-reliance.

In the puberty years the child goes through a metamorphosis, emerging from this period with a changed body and a fluid personality which is no longer cemented by childhood bonds. Adolescence is the period of reforming personality in a new matrix. The early teens are disturbing years for the youngster, as he tries on new faces and experiments with new feelings and roles.

Beyond adolescence lies two-thirds or more of the life span. Physical maturation slows down, then ceases, but change continues and new adjustment problems confront the individual as he moves through the stages of adulthood, middle age, and old age.

From birth to senescence, growth follows certain broad patterns, but individual variations occur around the central path. At each stage of life, people must cope with the developmental tasks of the period. They inherit and otherwise acquire common basic needs which create tensions and motivate them to action. As an individual attempts to reduce these tensions, he develops action patterns which shape his personality.

While we live in a social world and must satisfy our needs in relation to the needs of other people, each individual builds his own private world as he moves through the life cycle. He develops a sensitivity to, and an interest in, the selected portions of the external world which fit his own frame of reference. Thus, growth and adjustment have individual as well as social components which are inextricably interwoven. The human species has a predictable life cycle, but the human individual is a unique product of the combined influences of inner and outer determinants of life.

REFERENCES

1. Allee, W. C., *The Social Life of Animals,* Beacon Press, 1958.
2. American Medical Association, "A New Concept of Aging," *J. Amer. Med. Ass.,* April 6, 1963, **184**:68–71.
3. American Medical Association, "Aging and Calcium Metabolism Linked in Research," *J. Amer. Med. Ass.,* December 29, 1962, **182**:32.
4. Anderson, J. E., "The Development of Behavior and Personality," in Eli Ginzberg (Ed.), *The Nation's Children, 2: Development and Education,* Columbia, 1960, pp. 43–69.

5. Asch, S. E., "Studies of Independence and Conformity: I. A Minority of One Against a Unanimous Majority," *Psychol. Monogr.* Vol. 70, Whole No. 416, American Psychological Association, 1956.

6. Blair, A. W., and Burton, W. H., *Growth and Development of the Preadolescent,* Appleton-Century-Crofts, 1951.

7. Bower, E. M., *et al.,* "High School Students Who Later Become Schizophrenic," *Bull. Calif. State Dep. Educ.,* Sacramento, August, 1960, Vol. 29, No. 8.

8. Braceland, F. J., "Feelings of Loneliness," *The Third Annual Forum on Human Relations,* Hartford, Conn., October 25, 1961, Connecticut Mutual Life Insurance Co., 1961, pp. 1–7.

9. Caplan, G., *Concepts of Mental Health and Consultation: Their Application in Public Health Social Work,* U S. Children's Bureau, 1959.

10. Chesrow, E. J., *et al.,* "A New Antiapathy Agent for Geriatric Patients," *Geriatrics,* November, 1960, 15:767–772.

11. Chess, S., *et al.,* "Implications of a Longitudinal Study of Child Development for Child Psychiatry," *Amer. J. Psychiat.,* November, 1960, 117:434–441.

12. Clark, W. W., "Identifying Difficulties in Learning Arithmetic," *Educ. Bull.,* No. 9, California Test Bureau, Monterey, 1961.

13. Coleman, J. C., *Personality Dynamics and Effective Behavior,* Scott, Foresman, 1960.

14. Cornell, E. L., and Armstrong, C. M., "Patterns of Mental Growth and Factors Related to Their Classification, ' *Research Relating to Children,* Bulletin II, Supplement 2, 1954, U.S. Children's Bureau, pp. 22–23.

15. Crutchfield, R. S., "Conformity and Character," *Amer. Psychologist,* May, 1955, 10:191–198.

16. Davis, K., "The Early Marriage Trend," *What's New,* Fall, 1958, Abbott Laboratories, No. 207.

17. Douvan, E., "Independence and Identity in Adolescence," *Child.,* September–October, 1957, 4:186–190.

18. Elias, L. J., *High School Youth Look at Their Problems,* State College of Washington, Pullman, 1949.

19. Erikson, E. H., "Youth and the Life Cycle," *Child.,* March–April, 1960, 7:43–49.

20. Faust, M. S., "Developmental Maturity as a Determinant in Prestige of Adolescent Girls," *Child Develpm.,* March, 1960, 31:173–184.

21. Fels Research Institute for the Study of Human Development, *Report for Period 1954–1959,* Yellow Springs, Ohio, May, 1960.
22. Fleege, U. H., *Self-Revelation of the Adolescent Boy,* Bruce, 1945.
23. Funkenstein, D. H., "The Student in a Changing Society," *Current Issues in Higher Education,* Association for Higher Education, Washington, March, 1960, pp. 160–164.
24. Gallagher, J. R., "Clinic for Adolescents," *Children,* September–October, 1954, 1:165–170.
25. Gesell, A., and Ilg, F. L., *Infant and Child in the Culture of Today,* Harper & Row, 1943.
26. Havighurst, R. J., *Developmental Tasks and Education,* Longmans, 1952.
27. Heffernan, H., and Smith, M., "The Young Adolescent," *Calif. J. elem. Educ.,* November, 1959, 28:69–79.
28. Hunt, J. McV., "Experience and the Development of Motivation: Some Reinterpretations," *Child Develpm.,* September, 1960, 31:489–504.
29. Hurlock, E. B., *Child Development,* McGraw-Hill, 1956.
30. Jenkins, C. G., Schacter, H., and Bauer, W. W., *These Are Your Children,* Scott, Foresman, 1953.
31. Jersild, A. T., *Child Psychology,* Prentice-Hall, 1960.
32. Josselyn, I. M., "Pyschological Changes in Adolescence," *Child.,* March–April, 1959, 6:43–47.
33. Knoebler, M., *Self-Revelation of the Adolescent Girl,* Bruce, 1936.
34. Kubie, L. S., "Are We Educating for Maturity?" *National Educ. Ass. J.,* January, 1959, 48:58–63.
35. Kubie, L. S., "Instincts and Homeostasis," *Psychosom. Med.,* January, 1948, 10:15–30.
36. Leeds, M., "Senile Recession: A Clinical Entity?" *J. Amer. Geriat. Soc.,* February, 1960, 8:122–131.
37. Lemkau, P. V., *Mental Hygiene in Public Health,* McGraw-Hill, 1949.
38. Lewin, K., "Group Discussion and Social Change," in E. E. Maccoby, *et al.* (Eds.), *Readings in Social Psychology,* Holt, Rinehart and Winston, 1958, pp. 197–211.
39. Lucas, C. M., and Horrocks, J. E., "An Experimental Approach to the Analysis of Adolescent Needs," *Child Develpm.,* September, 1960, 31:479–487.
40. Maslow, A. H., *Motivation and Personality,* Harper & Row, 1954.

41. McGhie, A., and Russell, S. M., "The Subjective Assessment of Normal Sleep Patterns," *J. ment. Sci.*, September, 1962, **108**: 642–654.

42. Metropolitan Life Insurance Co., "Trends in Survival at the Older Ages," *Statist. Bull.*, September, 1960, Vol. 41.

43. Murray, J. M., *Normal Personality Development*, National Committee for Mental Hygiene, 1949.

44. Patterson, F., *et al.*, *The Adolescent Citizen*, Free Press, 1960.

45. Population Reference Bureau, Inc., "New Emphasis on the Elderly," *Population Profile*, February 26, 1962.

46. President's Council on Aging, *The Older American*, GPO, 1963.

47. Redl, F., *Preadolescents, What Makes Them Tick?*, The Child Study Association of America, New York, 1959.

48. Redl, F., and Wattenberg, W. W., *Mental Hygiene in Teaching*, Harcourt, Brace & World, 1959.

49. Remmers, H. H., and Radler, D. H., *The American Teenager*, Bobbs-Merrill, 1957.

50. Schlesinger, L., "Why Do We Feel As We Do?", *Adult Leadership*, February, 1957, **5**:242–244.

51. Selznick, G. J., and Larkins, J., *What Is Known About Young Adults*, Survey Research Center, University of California, Berkeley, 1961, Mimeographed.

52. Sontag, L. W., "Dynamics of Personality Formation," *Pers.*, April, 1951, **1**:119–130.

53. Spock, B. M., "The School-Age Child. Some Behavioral, Anthropological and Physical Implications of the Latency Period," in F. J. Braceland (Ed.), *Abstracts and Reviews of Selected Literature in Psychiatry, Neurology, and Their Allied Fields*, The Institute of Living, Hartford, Conn., February, 1955, Series XXIII, p. 51.

54. U.S. Children's Bureau, *The Adolescent in Your Family*, Publication No. 347, 1954.

55. Zeller, W. W., "Attitudes Toward Adolescents," in *Society Challenges the Individual*, Report of the Mental Health Lectures in Hartford, Conn., March, 1962, Connecticut Mutual Life Insurance Co., 1962, pp. 12–19.

Chapter 4   Psychological
Forces in the Home

The home is a psychological laboratory within which human nature takes shape. It is the source of our most intimate and lasting impressions because here behavior is formed while the human personality is still plastic and readily molded. While later experience will modify the patterns of behavior established in the home, it will never erase them. The basic foundations of personality and adjustment are laid down during the early years of life when the child's world consists largely of his experiences within the family circle, and subsequent experience can do no more than build upon this foundation.

In this chapter we shall examine some of the dynamics of family life, including the roles of the mother and the father, the nature of parent-child interactions, the effects of disciplinary practices in the home, and the psychological implications of sibling relationships.

ROLE OF THE MOTHER

As adults look back upon their lives, the great majority say that their mothers were the greatest influence upon their personality development. The need of a young child for his mother cannot be exaggerated. Basic behavioral tendencies are formed during the preverbal stages of life when the mother is almost the only human contact the infant has. In subsequent years, the growing child remains dependent on the psychological and physical care he receives from his mother. So complex and vital are the relationships established between mother and child that it would be impossible to describe all the aspects of this process. We shall, therefore, limit our discussion to the effects of maternal deprivation and point out what can happen when a child does not receive adequate mothering during the early years of life.

Maternal Deprivation in Infancy

The seeds of adjustment are sown early in infancy, beginning with the physical comfort derived by the infant from his mother. When deprived of the physical and psychological satisfactions normally provided by the mother or a mother substitute, infants react in a manner which demonstrates that something vital has been denied to them. These reactions include physical symptoms, such as eczema, respiratory infections, colic, refusal to eat, and excessive crying (18). In cases of extended maternal deprivation, a psychological reaction known as infantile autism may occur. This is a form of childhood psychosis in which the child does not learn to speak, behaves oddly, has the appearance of being mentally defective, and does not develop a normal personality (22).

The mother does not necessarily have to be absent from the home to produce such effects on infants. Developmental retardation occurs among infants living with mothers who are not psychologically able to provide them with the necessary stimulation. These reactions have been known to occur in families where parents profess affection for their children but leave them in the care of a disinterested person while they busy themselves with their own affairs (23, 40).

Studies have been made of young children placed in institutions where they received no substitute mothering, which show that there are identifiable stages in the deterioration of behavior resulting from maternal deprivation. When first separated from their mothers, children react by crying, shaking the crib, throwing themselves about, and clinging to adults when picked up. After this initial stage of protest comes a despair reaction. Activity diminishes, the children cry only intermittently, make no demands on adults, and appear to be in a state of mournful waiting. Later, the children withdraw from social interaction; they become absorbed in their toys and develop peculiar mannerisms such as body rigidity, continued rocking, abnormal movement of the hands, and a fixed, half-smiling facial expression. When picked up, they may cringe, struggle, or shriek as if terrified by people (7, 41).

Subsequent Effects of Maternal Deprivation. Follow-up studies indicate that many of these early behavioral changes among infants who have had inadequate mothering are irreversible and have lasting effects on personality and adjustment. Goldfarb (19) studied a group of institutionalized children who were placed in foster homes at about the age of three years after having spent most of their lives separated from their mothers. When they reached school age, these youngsters proved difficult to manage. They disregarded school rules, accepted academic failure complacently, were destructive, stubborn, given to severe temper outbursts, and could not get along with other children. In general, these children presented a picture of warped personalities who could form no genuine attachments to anyone. They displayed retaliatory and aggressive behavior, and did not develop a conscience like ordinary children. There is also evidence that children who had been separated from their mothers early in life show a high incidence of personal and social pathology as adults. Broken marriages, poor work records, and criminal activity occurred with higher frequency among this group than among a comparable group which had not experienced maternal deprivation (14).

These studies of the effects of maternal deprivation emphasize the significance of infancy and early childhood in personality formation and adjustment. They show that a lack of affection during the early years of life leave an imprint on the child which is never completely erased. Although the process of deterioration can be aborted if a warm, loving adult is provided as a substitute mother, its effects cannot be entirely reversed. Children who have experienced maternal deprivation in infancy tend to display a relatively high incidence of nervous mannerisms, anxiety, and insecurity in later life (37, 38).

INFLUENCE OF THE FATHER IN THE HOME

Most of the studies that have been made on parental influences in the home have been focused on mothers. By comparison, information on the role of fathers is scant indeed. This does not necessarily mean that fathers are not important in influencing the behavior of children. The paucity of information may be due to the fact that mothers are more accessible for study. The research that has been done indicates that the father has an important role to play in maintaining the stability of the family group and in supporting the role of the mother. He also has a significant influence on the psychological development of boys and girls, and this influence becomes increasingly important as children grow older, reaching a peak during the puberty and adolescent stages (35:120).

The Father's Role in the Family

Probably if a father were with his children constantly and took care of them from earliest infancy, he would have a more vital and direct effect on the dynamics of the family. This was observed to happen in a family where the father assumed responsibility for his first-born child, cared for his nightly feedings, ministered to him when he was sick, rocked him, burped him, and generally was always present to make the child comfortable. Later in life when this child was ill or hurt, no one but his father could comfort him. This case suggests that the father's role may be thrust upon him by economic necessity rather than by psychological forces.

The father's personality and attitude toward child rearing also influences the role he plays in the family. If the father is a mild, unaggressive person who lets mother hold the reins, his masculine influence may have little effect on children. If the father goes to the other extreme and is a tyrant whose decisions have more weight than those of all other family members combined, he can hardly help having noticeable effects on his children. Given a relatively normal father who participates democratically in the affairs of the home and has a reasonable amount of time to spend with his family, there appear to be certain significant influences which he can exert on children.

First, he presents to children patterns of emotional response and social action associated with the aggressiveness, leadership, and objectivity which prevail in the world outside the home.

Second, he is of major importance in the sex typing of boys (32). The personal contacts which the child makes with members of his immediate environment influence the patterning of his personality. Boys need male identification figures for the development of a masculine personality and to derive an understanding of how men should behave. Through this process of identification the boy becomes masculine in his interests, habits, motives, and desires, and develops the characteristics which will enable him to assume the functions of a normal male adult. Not only does the father set a pattern by which the boy may structure his own masculinity, but he also helps the child conform to the demands of reality, serves to broaden his interests, and stimulates the development of qualities of leadership, discipline, authority, and self-direction which are conducive to the normal emancipation of the boy from home (9).

Third, a father is important in the sex typing of girls. The girl needs early contact with her father in order to gain an understanding of how men behave and how she should behave toward them. This helps to clarify her own femininity in relation to masculine modes of activity. Lacking the contact with desirable masculine patterns of conduct during childhood, girls may have difficulty in forming normal attachments with men in later life. The father provides the girl with the masculine protection and security usually associated with the male parent, and also acts as an agent through which the child makes a transition from the normal, homosexual stage of development to a secure and wholesome adjustment to the masculine sex (31).

Influence of the Father During Adolescence

A father means different things to children at different stages of development. The young child sees him as a big, strong person who can do anything and who represents power, strength, and security. To the growing boy he becomes a model and an answerer of questions. When children reach adolescence, fathers have an even more important function to perform. Teen-age boys have a great need for a man to look up to. If the father is a person who can be admired, and if he has a secure relationship with his son, the boy is better prepared to accept the responsibilities of manhood. The maleness of his father's interests helps the boy to build interests that will make him acceptable to his peers and frees him from the constant association with women which is the lot of the great majority of American boys (30).

It has been noted that where a father is missing at this stage of life, boys attach themselves to other male figures in their environment to satisfy their desire to be influenced by a person corresponding to the father. In this manner, teachers, scout leaders, recreation directors, and even imaginary and fictional males may become more important in the child's life than the real father if he is seldom seen.

The adolescent girl likewise needs a close relationship with her father. Girls in their teens are building an image of the man they would like to marry. They need to measure the boys they meet against an ideal marriage partner and depend greatly on the father or a father figure to provide a standard. The girl whose father is absent from the home builds dreams around him and produces an idealized standard of a husband which is sometimes difficult to fulfill (17).

Undesirable Father-Child Relationships

Where father-child relationships are unpleasant or unsatisfactory, the effects on children become evident early in life. Studies of nursery-school children show that youngsters in such homes are lacking in rivalry toward other children, have passive, colorless personalities, are often isolates, and exert little influence over other children (39).

Unsatisfactory father-child relationships have been found to be significantly associated with sex delinquency in girls. One study of 29 unwed mothers found them to have had highly disturbed relationships with their fathers. The girls had little concept of the roles of a father, husband, or man in the domestic or social world. These feelings were coupled with the lack of a close emotional bond with either parent. This led to compensating activity in an effort to find love, usually from a man (12).

The effects of poor father relationships among adolescent boys was impressively described in Kimball's study of educational failure among adolescent boys of superior intelligence (24). These boys had IQ's ranging from 125 to 139, but their scholastic achievement was very low. Their underlying difficulty was found to be poor father-son relationships, and identification with the mother. In almost every case the father expected too much of his son, set high goals for him, and was a strong disciplinarian. There were no warm interpersonal feelings between the boys and their fathers. The boys were forced to inhibit the direct expression of hostility felt toward the father, and instead expressed their feelings through indifference toward school achievement, sulking, and passive rebellion. They turned to their mothers for emotional support. This identification with the mother made it difficult for them to form friendly associations with a masculine figure. Particular difficulty was experienced in getting along with masculine authority figures.

These observations have been confirmed in other studies. When a boy is rejected by his father, he may have trouble adjusting to be a man, or he may develop feminine mannerisms as a reaction against his father's influence. Such boys also may be slow in learning masculine roles and may lack interest in sports and other motor activities (10, 29).

Effects of the Father's Absence

In families where the father is absent from the home or where he plays no vital role in the family, children may display a number of behavioral difficulties. The reactions of preschool children to the father's absence is dependent largely upon the attitude of the mother. If she is antagonistic or contemptuous toward the husband, the children show a great deal of aggression toward him. If the mother is affectionate toward the absent father, children picture him as an ideal person who is kind to everyone (2). Preschool boys react differently to the father's absence than do preschool girls. Sears (45) found that boys become less aggressive when the father is away from home, while the aggression of girls remains about the same. This was explained on the basis that the father is an important influence in setting the behavior patterns of boys, and tends to impose more rigid controls on them than on girls. Thus, when the father is away, pressure on the boy is released and he experiences less thwarting so has less need to be aggressive. This might be the reason why some children are more difficult to control when their fathers are at home than when they are away.

Among older children there are more distinct sex differences in reaction to the father's absence. Beginning among school-age youngsters and increasing in importance as children reach the 9- to 12-year-old stage, boys, especially, need their fathers to help them develop masculine forms of behavior. It has been noted that boys who are constantly with their mothers may develop effeminate characteristics and interests which become a source of disturbance during the teen-age period. Sometimes these boys retain effeminate voices long after their vocal chords are capable of forming the deeper male sounds.

For these reasons, the mother who is left alone to raise her children must make efforts to see that they have opportunities for close association with an adult who can serve as a father figure. The family friend or relative who can offer intimate companionship to a fatherless child performs an important service. Many youth agencies have assumed this responsibility by securing the help of fathers who devote their time to scout, club, and athletic activities (48).

The Authoritarian Father

In some families the father assumes the role of a dictatorial, authoritarian figure who dominates the household. He is the final court of appeal, the administrator of punishment, and the bestower of rewards. The dictatorial father may love his children, worry about them, and give them presents on occasion, but he can never unbend lest he reveal his own limitations and impair his reputation as a wise, powerful, infallible being. This type of family pattern is more common in foreign cultures than it is in America (43:15–40).

Anthropologists believe that the dictatorial father breeds people who suppress their sentiments and have a strong dependence on authority. The social consequences of such relationships is a mass respect for an authority figure, which makes some nations particularly susceptible to the leadership of dictators or demagogues. Although many Americans would like to see the father exercise more authority in the family, we are perhaps fortunate that the typical American father is not treated with greater awe. The democratic participation of the father in the family tempers the American's attitude toward people in authority (21:297–99).

PATTERNS OF PARENT-CHILD INTERACTION

The interpersonal relations of mother, father, and children establish a psychological climate in the home which affects all the members of the family. So close are these relationships that when one person becomes emotionally disturbed the psychological equilibrium of the entire family may be upset. This is particularly true when a parent is so affected. When parents are emotionally disturbed, it can be expected that three-fourths of the children coming from these households will have personal or interpersonal problems of adjustment (36). Moreover, the ideas, attitudes, and feelings resulting from such unfortunate home experiences continue to affect the child long after the original conditions have been removed (30).

In the normal household may be found many patterns of human relationship which have differing influences on the adjustment of children. Bossard (5) describes nineteen types of parent-child relationships, ranging from excessive affection to complete rejection. Since it is impractical to describe all of them here, four of the most commonly encountered types of interaction have been selected for emphasis. These are the patterns of rejection, overprotection, domination, and overindulgence. While there is often much overlapping of these categories, each is encountered with sufficient frequency to merit individual attention.

Rejection

One of the ironies of life is that some people who want children cannot have them, while others who have children do not want them. Parents may reject their children in many ways.

Sometimes it is done openly and brutally, as in cases where infants are abandoned or where children are beaten or starved. More often, rejecting parents do not deliberately set out to make their children feel unwanted, but the end result is the same. We see this happening in families where children are sent out on a round of boarding schools, military schools, and summer camps, with only an occasional stay at home; or where the care and training of children is turned over to nurses, servants, or relatives who provide the child with everything except the parental love he craves.

Few children are deceived by the form which rejection takes or the explanations offered for it. They sense the emotional undertones, the lack of intimate response, the frustration of their need to be loved, and in one way or another react to these feelings. Some children learn that it does no good to fight against feelings of being unwanted and accept the situation passively, often with deep-seated feelings of worthlessness and defeat. Others react through hostility and aggressiveness and become attention-seeking, hostile, hyperactive, rebellious children who want acceptance but whose behavior only succeeds in making them outlaws (47:45).

Most rejected children have been hurt and want to hurt back. They need love and attention, but their hostility to people makes it difficult to approach them. They drift into groups where the members find in each other, and in their common struggle against society, more acceptance, security, and satisfaction than is offered anywhere else. The rejected child also tends to become a rejecting child. He may reject himself, his parents, and society, and develop into a bitter, hostile individual.

Overprotection

The child who has everything done for him may become a plastic personality with no will of his own. Usually, he is an obedient and docile child. Adults call him a "good" child because he is polite, neat, gentle, respectful, and all that a parent wants him to be. However, such a youngster does not make friends easily and may grow up to be a lonely, isolated person.

It is difficult for parents to realize when they are overprotecting their children, because usually their motives are sincere, or they are acting in response to unconscious forces. Parents who develop an anxious, possessive, dependent attachment to their children seldom are aware that they are making the youngsters more yielding and submissive than is good for them. Often this overprotection is an unconscious effort to disguise the basic rejection which a parent feels for his child. By being solicitous of him, the parent avoids the necessity of facing the fact that he really did not want this child.

The ill effects of overprotection must not be interpreted to mean that children do not need parental protection. On the contrary, children must have the assurance that, while parents may at times disapprove of their behavior, they will not cut off their love because of it. Parents who protect a child in this way do not keep him from growing up by wrapping him in a protective blanket of oversolicitude. They support and love him, but also help him grow toward self-reliance and independence.

Domination

Some parents rule their children with an iron hand, in a belief that high standards must be set for a child and that he must be disciplined to work toward them. Parental domination of this type is usually characterized by attitudes of perfectionism and overambition. The perfectionism is expressed through insistence on absolute obedience, scrupulous cleanliness, and other rigid rules of living. Over-ambition for the child may take the form of pressing him to read early, to bring home high grades from school, to play the piano or violin, or do the many other things ambitious parents can invent.

Many children submit to the demands of their parents and offer no overt opposition. If their capacities come anywhere near meeting the expectations held out for them, they may internalize the drive and pressure of the parents and achieve considerable success in school and professional life. They usually have more difficulty with personal and social adjustment, because they tend to be tense, perfectionistic, worrisome people who are unable to relax and must go on striving for one success after another.

Children of average or less than average capacity who are forced to strive for goals beyond their reach are caught between forces which provide no alternative but escape. The standards set for them are beyond their abilities to achieve, yet if they do not attain them they are denied parental approval. This is referred to as a "double-bind" situation because there is no way for the victim to resolve it. The usual response of a child in such circumstances is to adopt tactics that will stall off unpleasant scenes, often cheating or lying to achieve this end.

Some children do not knuckle under to their parents; they take so much pressure, then rebel. This revolt may come at any time but often is seen at the periods of preadolescence and adolescence when psychological forces normally reduce the influence of parents over children (13).

There are many other variations of behavior seen among dominated children. Often they experience an intense conflict between the conscience built up under the strict control of parents and the desire to be free of home influences. This conflict breeds anxiety, doubt, and guilt, which at times causes these youngsters to react against their home upbringing. Such behavior has been observed among children who develop an aversion to religion because they had so large a dose of it at home that they can no longer tolerate the restrictions and moral punishment with which it has become associated.

Thus, the child of domineering, overambitious parents may turn out to be a driving, energetic, perfectionistic person; a meek, fearful person; or a rebel, a neurotic, or a cheat. Or, if he survives the pressures of growing up, he may become a relatively normal individual. In any case, a child whose parents plan his life and try to fit him into it, regardless of his abilities and interests, will face many difficult problems of adjustment (16).

Overindulgence

The typical "spoiled child" is one who has been overindulged or given too much of everything. This child usually has his own way at home. Parents submit to him and seem unable to assert their will against his. This indulgence may produce youngsters who are eccentric, undisciplined, aggressive, negativistic, infantile, or worse (44).

Levy's classical studies (27) of mothers who made excessive

concessions to their children illustrate what can happen. These children ate what they chose and when they chose. They left the table when they were ready, went to bed when they felt like it, threw their clothes around, told their mothers to shut up, struck them, spat at them, and went into a rage whenever they were opposed in any way.

In school these children had an unstable history. To their teachers and schoolmates they were bullies, show-offs, and nuisances. They did not profit from a succession of experiences which would have caused normal children to change their ways. When seen in adult life, they were still making exaggerated demands on the world and interested only in satisfying their immediate desires.

Not all of Levy's subjects became such tyrants. Some of them encountered schoolmates and teachers who would not tolerate their demanding, egocentric behavior. Their tendency to show off was tempered to an innocuous clowning; their fighting and bullying converted into an aggressive form of leadership; and their demanding ways developed into persuasive powers. Hence, the spoiled child need not become a lost child if he is treated with understanding and firmness.

The conclusion to be derived from these descriptions of parent-child interactions is that genuine parental love, untainted by overprotection, excessive coercion, indulgence, or other actions that curb a child's normal growth tendencies, are the foundations of good family life. As a child grows up in a consistent atmosphere of acceptance and self-direction, he learns to be independent, becomes sensitive to the welfare of other people, and develops the capacity to operate effectively within a framework of social regulations.

DISCIPLINARY PRACTICES IN THE FAMILY

The manner in which parents relate to children will determine the type of discipline that prevails in the family. However, parents are also affected by the advice of others, by their own experiences as children, and by the theories of child development which are in vogue at the time. Since many children have been brought up in accordance with the professional advice offered to parents, it is interesting to note how this advice has varied from generation to generation.

During the twentieth century, three theories of child development have had a major influence on how parents managed their children. In the 1920s the teachings of John B. Watson were popular. His psychological advice appeared at a time when conditioning was relied upon heavily for explaining the manner in which behavior was shaped. Watson's advice to parents was that they must not spoil the child by encouraging too much emotional dependence:

There is a sensible way of treating children. Treat them as though they were young adults. Let your behavior always be objective and kindly firm. Never hug and kiss them, never let them sit in your lap. If you must, kiss them once on the forehead when they say good night. Shake hands with them in the morning. Give them a pat on the head if they have made an extraordinary good job of a difficult task. Try it out. In a week's time you will find how easy it is to be perfectly objective with your child and at the same time kindly. You will be utterly ashamed of the mawkish, sentimental way you have been handling it (51:87).

We shall probably never know how many neurotic adults resulted from this pattern of child rearing. The generation that followed adopted a more humanitarian approach to child management. Under the influence of pediatricians, psychologists, and psychoanalysts, parents were encouraged to adapt their disciplinary procedures to fit in with the child's natural pattern of growth. They were urged to be considerate and tolerant; not to force the child to become socialized too soon but to wait until he was ready so as not to inhibit or distort his growth potential. What the child needed was an ample supply of love and affection while the maturation process was forming him into a self-disciplined person (11). Such advice was condemned by many as advocating a policy of permissiveness which provided no controls and allowed children to dominate the household.

Today, it is generally accepted that every child needs limits and controls if he is to grow normally and internalize his parents' code of behavior. On the other hand, excessive coercion is condemned as a practice which creates feelings of guilt in parents and hostility in children. The evidence on hand indicates that the effective way to produce children of mature, rational, self-disciplined morality is through a combination of love and controls which are consistent but neither too lenient nor too severe (35).

Beyond these general guidelines, it is difficult to discover a specific formula for managing children which will work well under all circumstances. Families differ as individuals differ. Some parents can spank their children with excellent results for both parents and offspring. Other parents create an emotional crisis whenever they punish their children. The *act* of discipline, it appears, is less important than the *atmosphere* in which it is applied.

A democratic home is considered to be the best kind of atmosphere for children to learn acceptable modes of conduct, because here they are involved in making decisions about their behavior. This does not mean that children vote on every rule or act. It implies a home in which human beings with all their frailties live together naturally on an experimental, cooperative basis. Since people, young and old, are not perfect, some disharmony in the home is to be expected. Sometimes parents will lose their patience and use their children as a target for the release of personal annoyances, or do other unwise things which in a less secure emotional climate would have serious consequences for children. Rivalry between siblings can be expected and, in fact, is desirable because children must meet conflict sooner or later, and there is no better place in which to learn how to cope with it constructively than in the protected environment of a home.

The stabilizing elements of the democratic home are the basic attitudes and feelings which bind together the members of the family. Beneath the surface interplay of family members in a normal home lies a foundation of love and mutual trust. Given these conditions and an appropriate balance of freedom and direction, the specific type of disciplinary practices used to manage children are of secondary importance. Parents may experiment with a variety of procedures and feel assured that, if the climate of the home is favorable, they will do little damage to children (11, 25).

It must be pointed out, however, that the type of child behavior that can be expected in a democratic home requires some adjustment on the part of parents. Children in these homes are active, outgoing, noisy youngsters who are not easy to control. But they are also intellectually alert, more realistic in their thinking, more mature in their judgment on ethical questions, more self-reliant, and have better emotional control and a greater sense of responsibility than children raised in nondemocratic homes (3, 26). The implication here is that parents who want their children to become secure, adjusted people may have to put up with some personal inconvenience during the growing years. These children really live in their homes; they resist being manipulated and insist upon having a voice in family affairs. They ask questions, want to know reasons for things, express their emotions and viewpoints, and in many other ways demonstrate that life is something to be understood through experimentation. Parents who can guide and channel this experimentation, and tolerate its effects, can expect children to assume responsibility for their own behavior and learn how to work in harmony with others.

PSYCHOLOGICAL EFFECTS OF A CHILD'S POSITION IN THE FAMILY

A great deal of importance is attached to the ordinal position of children in the family. Whether a youngster is an only child or the first, last, or middle child in a family has considerable influence on his home environment and how he reacts to it.

Despite the significance of a child's order of birth, it is difficult to ascribe a precise psychological role to children on the basis of this factor alone. So many other things play a part in shaping the home atmosphere that in any given instance they may overshadow the influence of the child's position in the family. The state of the family finances, the age of parents, where the family lives, the age range between children, and the sex of children are but a few of the factors which may influence the psychological climate of the home. Any one of these can result in quite a different home environment for children, independent of their order of birth.

Nevertheless, enough clinical evidence has been accumulated to make some fairly dependable generalizations about how children born at various times may be influenced by the environment they encounter in a normal family situation. It is helpful to keep these generalizations in mind as an aid to understanding the development of human behavior, even though the characteristics described are not invariably true.

The Older Child

The first-born child enjoys certain relations with his parents which differ from those experienced by children who come along later. Usually, parents are excited and proud over their first offspring. He occupies the center of the stage, and although they may make mistakes by expecting too much of him in one way and too little in another, there is an exciting freshness about his accomplishments which is not quite duplicated with later-born children.

Because the first child is older, bigger, and stronger, for a while at least, his life is one of firsts. He is first to cross the street alone, first to go to school, first to ride a bike, first to wear new clothes. He becomes the pioneer, the pathfinder, and the trail blazer in the family. Accompanying his position of leadership in the family are certain responsibilities which he must assume. The older child is often expected to set an example for younger children, to take care of them, resist the temptations to which they succumb, and in general to demonstrate a level of maturity commensurate with his privileges (33).

However, by the time the older child becomes secure in his position as the center of attraction within the family, several things happen to disrupt his security. For one thing, the passage of time usually brings a change in the parents' attitude toward children. The Fels Research Institute (26) noted that the child-centeredness of the home declines sharply from age two to five.

Parents tend to be very solicitous toward the child for the first two years, then their attention declines to a moderate level, even before a second child arrives.

The arrival of a second child often introduces a real crisis in the life of the first-born. Dethronement by a new arrival causes the older child to react in several ways. If the first-born is still very young, he may show his disturbance through changes in his eating or toilet habits, by crying, or by temper tantrums. If the first child is about school age when he is supplanted by a younger sibling, quite commonly he may express his resentment through various anxiety symptoms, including nightmares, nail biting, thumb sucking, restless sleep, stammering, enuresis, excessive shyness, neurotic vomiting, negativism, or fantasies. These may persist as long as they are effective in attracting attention, or until other means are found to comfort the child (4).

With the passing of time, feelings of displacement and jealousy may be reflected in the child's social activities. He may have a chip on his shoulder, lack a sense of humor, and act more maturely than is characteristic of his age. He may reflect a lack of security by seeking to be in a position of authority among his peers and by failing to recognize the rights of others. Such feelings may carry over into adult life. Even the choice of a marriage partner may be influenced by the unfulfilled strivings of the first-born child. It has been noted that the first-born son often tends to seek a wife who will make him feel important, someone whom he can take care of and dominate. This has been interpreted as a manifestation of the older child's unconscious desire to maintain his status of being first in the family. In his choice of a vocation the first-born seems to gravitate toward positions of authority in which he will have responsibility for others. He is likely to seek executive positions or other authoritative pursuits such as police work, teaching, or nursing (46).

The resentment of the oldest child toward displacement and his hostility toward competitors may bring him into conflict with society. The studies of Harris (20), Rouman (42), and Brockway (8) disclosed that first-born children tend to have more adjustment problems and poorer relations with playmates than do other children in the family. They have more troubles associated with eating, elimination, and sleeping, and show more evidence of fear and tension. There is also some evidence that a relatively high proportion of first-born children have trouble with the law and are involved in suicide attempts (34, 49).

In summary, the first-born child has a tendency towards extremes. He may develop strong leadership qualities and become a dominating personality with a great capacity for handling responsibility. On the other hand, there is the chance that his struggles for supremacy in and out of the family may lead him into personal and social difficulties.

In-Between Children

Middle children are said to have the least enviable position in the family. They have neither the priority of the first-born nor the novelty of the last-born. Parents find it hard to recapture with the second child the excitement of their eldest's first events. They do not start off at as high a level of child-centeredness as prevailed with the first, but their interest in the second child remains stable for a longer period (26). Yet, parents are likely to be less tolerant of the behavior of a middle child and tend to be more definite and prescriptive about the things he can or cannot do.

The in-between child must contend not only with the changed attitude of parents but more significantly, perhaps, with the personalities of older and younger children in the family. The middle child is wedged in among the other siblings. Always in front of him is the older child with whom he never catches up—the brother or sister who is bigger and stronger, with greater freedom of action and with constant priority on material things and experiences. Always behind him is the baby of the family whose claim for attention cannot be disputed and with whom he cannot compete. Thus, the problems of living may impose a great strain on the intermediate child (6).

How the in-between child reacts to this squeeze will depend

upon the characteristics of the other children. For instance, if the first child is particularly competent and successful, the second child may not have the ability to struggle against him. If the accomplishments of the first-born are not impressive, the second child may tend to be especially ambitious and develop a drive to overcome and surpass the first-born. In any event, the second-born child tends to be somewhat of a revolutionary in that he would like to see the power in the family change hands, whether he takes any overt action to do so or not (46).

The Youngest Child

The last-born child, because he is the baby and never really gives up this title, enjoys certain advantages. The parents, having now had considerable experience with children, are much more prepared for this child. They may be able to give him material things and cultural advantages which could not be provided for the older children. Other children in the family may also contribute to the welfare of the baby. They may fight his battles, intercede for him with the parents, make contacts for him outside the home, and steer him through his school and social experiences.

Life can become relatively easy for the youngest of the family with all these advantages to help him along. There are, however, some factors in his life which may not have an entirely wholesome influence on his personality development. For one thing, parents may unconsciously be unwilling to let him grow up. They find it hard to end the good times they have had with him, or to give up the close physical contact he has permitted and which children tend to resist as they grow older.

Parents may have difficulty handling the youngster's insistence for independence. If they give in to him, the older children may resent his having the special privileges which they were denied. Also, the young one may develop undesirable characteristics of domineering others and expecting to have his own way.

Where the baby of the family is coddled and given little opportunity to develop his own powers, he may become a pleasant, likable, dependent person who goes through life leaning on others and feeling that things will work out well and someone will always help him. Discipline may break down with him because he uses his sweetness, affability, and ingratiating smile to control his parents. He may expect and demand much of others and never give much of himself in return. Or he may learn to enjoy being the center of attention and go to any lengths to remain so.

On the other hand, the fact that the younger child is always surrounded by larger and older individuals may result in a feeling of physical and mental inferiority. To overcome such feelings, the child may become a rebel and try to compensate for his feelings of smallness by surpassing the others in some accomplishment, by choosing a vocation different from what is expected of him, or by emphasizing his distinctness from the rest of the family through asocial or nonconforming behavior (46).

Interaction of Siblings

When children live with other children of their own relative age and status, they have experiences which cannot be duplicated outside the home. One such experience is that of reality structuring. There is a natural tendency for children to create a world of make-believe—a tendency which movies and television have no doubt encouraged. The presence of other children in the family provides a safe-guard against spending too much time in a private world of fantasy. The intrusion of a brother or sister quickly crowds out imaginary companions and forces the child to react in terms of reality. Even when children engage in fantasy-play together, the presence and activity of several youngsters keep reality in its place and imagination separated from it.

Living with other children also provides a relief from the unnatural environment created by adults. Children cannot compete with adults nor match their accomplishments, nor join into their activities on a plane of equality. In their own little world, children understand each other, their interests and problems are common, they speak the same language and have the same kinds of experiences. Being able to talk things over intimately, frankly, late at night, or while at play, has great therapeutic value for children (4).

Children also provide each other with opportunities for emotional release. They pass along their humiliations and frustrations from the older to the younger in a sort of pecking order. The older brother or sister takes out on his younger siblings the hurts, disappointments, and frustrations experienced at the hands of adults or older children. "What the nine-year-olds endure from the eleven-year-olds they tend to wreak on the seven-year-olds" (4:111). While this may be a difficult experience for the youngest in the group, it nevertheless appears to be a universal healing process among children.

Of course, the benefits which children derive from each other are not without some disturbing aspects. Wherever there are children living together there will be conflict. Parents usually are annoyed by the squabbles and noise of children in conflict, and sometimes someone gets hurt. Yet even conflict is an essential part of sibling relations. It is one of the ways in which children learn to take turns, to limit their impulses in the presence of others, and to appreciate the rights of others. In a large measure, these are lessons which children can learn only from other children. Although this learning might at times appear to be distressingly painful, experiments with animals have shown that it is a vital part of the socialization process and, without this opportunity for natural interaction, social adjustment is seriously impaired (1).

The Only Child

The development of the only child in a family takes on particular significance in view of the lessons which children learn from growing up with brothers and sisters in the home. Popular opinion suggests that the only child is likely to be self-centered because of failure to learn give and take from siblings. It is also said that he is more mature and serious-minded than the average child, and that too much adult attention makes him precocious, and therefore unpopular with children.

The research both supports and contradicts these commonly

held beliefs. This is not unexpected, since many factors influence the effects of being a sole son or daughter. For instance, a child may be an only child because his sibling died, or because his parents married late in life, or were divorced early, or for a large variety of reasons, each of which would influence the emotional atmosphere surrounding the child. Also, how the only child is treated in the family conditions his personality development. Some parents make a conscientious effort to find companions for their children, sending them to camp, nursery schools, and other places where they can be with youngsters their own age. Other parents baby their child, protect him from social contacts, or force him to grow up too fast. This is why a study of one group of only children may reveal these youngsters to be well adjusted while another study, using a different sample, finds them to be more maladjusted than other children.

Strauss's analysis (46) of numerous case studies of only children suggests that the only child has the same role as the first-born, except that he is never dethroned. This role may make it difficult for him to face competition when he enters school. Never having had to share, or fight for anything at home, he tries to re-create this situation in the classroom. As he encounters resistance from his peers, he may become aggressive and display social immaturity, or he may adopt a passive, acquiescent form of behavior.

The personal feelings of only children, Strauss found, often were associated with a sense of detachment, a feeling of being apart from things or not belonging among children. The only child is not likely to be a joiner. When he does participate in group activity he may seek a small group where he can be a "big frog in a little pond." He is more at ease with adults than age-mates, and therefore may prefer to be left alone to work by himself rather than join in with other children. Not having learned the basic lessons of human relationships during early childhood, the only child may become the lonely child who does not know how to relate himself to peers at any age. In adult life the individualistic personal feelings of the only child may influence him to seek a vocation requiring a minimum of contact with other people. He may be intolerant of opposition, noncooperative, and impatient in his human relations at work and at home. The incidence of neuroses and character and behavior disorders has been found to be higher among only children than among the normal child population. This may indicate that only children are subjected to stresses which are not experienced by children who grow up with siblings (50).

SUMMARY

The dynamics of human interaction in the home provide children with experiences which lay the foundation for later adjustment. The influence of parents on children is particularly important. Well-adjusted parents who fulfill their roles properly and provide children with the physical and psychological support they need will contribute to normal personality development. Children who are deprived of a mother's affection early in life, who do not receive the full benefits of a father's guidance, who are disciplined inconsistently or unwisely, or are subjected to excessive rejection, overprotection, domination, or indulgence are prone to have a difficult time with the adjustment process.

The interaction among children in the family is also a significant aspect of the home atmosphere. Siblings have an important influence on one another, and the ordinal position of a child in the family has much to do with the kinds of psychological experiences he will have.

All these forces exerting their influence on children early in life and over a period of years make the home a psychological laboratory in which the seeds of adjustment are planted and nourished.

REFERENCES

1. American Medical Association, "Monkeys Thrive on Their Mothers' Love," *J. Amer. Med. Ass.,* February 16, 1963, **183**:43.
2. Bach, G. R., "Father-Fantasies and Father-Typing in Father-Separated Children," *Child Develpm.,* 1946, **17**:63–80.

3. Blood, R. O., Jr., "Some Differential Child-Rearing Philosophies, Practices, and Their Consequences: A Study of the Attitudes and Experiences of 'Traditional' and 'Developmental' Middle-Class Parents," *Research Relating to Children,* Supplement No. 4, U.S. Children's Bureau, April, 1951, p. 102.

4. Bossard, J .H. S., *The Sociology of Child Development,* Harper & Row, 1954.

5. Bossard, J. H. S., and Boll, E. S., *Family Situations,* University of Pennsylvania Press, 1943.

6. Bossard, J. H. S., and Boll, E. S., *The Sociology of Child Development,* Harper & Row, 1960.

7. Bowlby, J., "Separation Anxiety," *Intern. J. Psychoanal.,* March–June, 1960, 41:89–113.

8. Brockway, I. V., "An Investigation of the Home Backgrounds of Some Problem Children," *Research Relating to Children,* Bulletin II, Supplement 1, U.S. Children's Bureau, 1954, p. 51.

9. Bronfenbrenner, U., "The Changing American Child—A Speculative Analysis," *J. soc. Issues,* 1961, 17:6–18.

10. Browning, C. J., *Differential Social Relationships and Personality Factors of Parents and Boys in Two Delinquent Groups and One Non-Delinquent Group,* Unpublished Doctoral Dissertation, University of Southern California, Los Angeles, 1954.

11. Caldwell, B. M., and Richmond, J. B., "The Impact of Theories of Child Development," *Child.* March–April, 1962, 9:73–78.

12. Cattell, J. B., "Psychodynamic and Clinical Observations in a Group of Unmarried Mothers," *Amer. J. Psychiat.,* November, 1954, 111:337–342.

13. Chorost, S. B., *Parental Child-Rearing Attitudes and Their Correlates in Adolescent Aggression,* Unpublished Doctoral Dissertation, University of Texas, 1960.

14. Earle, A. M., and Earle, B. V., "Early Maternal Deprivation and Later Psychiatric Illness," *Amer. J. Orthopsychiat.,* January, 1961, 31:181–186.

15. Ehrenwald, J., "Neurosis in the Family," *Arch. gen. Psychiat.,* September, 1960, 3:232–242.

16. Elder, G. H., Jr., *Family Structure and the Transmission of Values and Norms in the Process of Child-Rearing,* Unpublished Doctoral Dissertation, University of North Carolina, 1961.

17. Faegre, M. L., *The Adolescent in Your Family,* U.S. Children's Bureau, Publication No. 347, 1954.

18. Garner, A. M., and Wenar, C., *The Mother-Child Interaction in Psychosomatic Disorder,* University of Illinois Press, 1959.
19. Goldfarb, W., "Psychological Privation in Infancy and Subsequent Adjustment," *Amer. J. Orthopsychiat.,* April, 1945, **15**: 247–255.
20. Hariss, D. B., "Parents and War-Born Children," *Child.,* July–August, 1954, 1:153–155.
21. Honigmann, J. J., *Culture and Personality,* Harper & Row, 1954.
22. Jervis, G. A., "Factors in Mental Retardation," *Child.,* November–December, 1954, 1:207–211.
23. Kanner, L., "Problems of Nosology and Psychodynamics of Early Infantile Autism," *Amer. J. Orthopsychiat.,* July, 1949, 19:416–426.
24. Kimball, B., "Case Studies in Educational Failure During Adolescence," *Amer. J. Orthopsychiat.,* April, 1953, 23:406–412.
25. Landis, P. H., "The Families That Produce Adjusted Adolescents," *Clearing House,* May, 1955, **29**:537–540.
26. Lasko, J. K., "Parent-Child Relationships," *Amer. J. Orthopsychiat.,* April, 1952, **22**:300–304.
27. Levy, D. M., *Maternal Overprotection,* Columbia, 1943.
28. Lidz, T., "Schizophrenia and the Family," *Psychiat.,* February, 1958, **21**:21–27.
29. Lidz, T., *et al.,* "The Role of the Father in the Environment of the Schizophrenic Patient," *Amer. J. Psychiat.,* August, 1956, **113**:126–132.
30. McCord, W., "The Familial Genesis of Psychoses," *Psychiat.,* February, 1962, **25**:60–71.
31. Merloo, J. A. M., "The Father Cuts the Cord," *Amer. J. Psychother.,* July, 1956, **10**:471–480.
32. Mussen, P., and Rutherford, E., "Parent-Child Relations and Parental Personality in Relation to Young Children's Sex-Role Preferences," *Child Develpm.,* September, 1963, **34**:589–607.
33. Neiser, E., *The Eldest Child,* Harper & Row, 1957.
34. O'Kelly, E., "Some Observations on Relationships Between Delinquent Girls and Their Parents," *Brit. J. med. Psychol.,* 1955, **28**:59–66.
35. Peck, R. F., *et al., The Psychology of Character Development,* Wiley, 1960.
36. Phillips, E. L., "Parent-Child Similarities in Personality Disturbances," *J. clin. Psychol.,* April, 1951, **7**:188–190.
37. Pringle, M. L. K., and Bossio, V., "Early, Prolonged Separa-

tion and Emotional Maladjustment," *J. Child Psychol. Psychiat.,* January, 1960, 1:37–48.

38. Prugh, D. G., *et al.,* "Deprivation of Maternal Care—A Reassessment of Its Effects," *World Health Organization, Public Health Paper No. 14,* International Documents Service, Columbia, 1962.

39. Radke, M. J., "The Relation of Parental Authority to Childrens' Behavior and Attitudes," *Monographs,* No. 22, University of Minnesota, Institute of Child Welfare, 1946.

40. Richmond, J. B., and Lipton, E. L., "Studies on Mental Health With Specific Implications for Pediatricians," in G. Caplan (Ed.), *Prevention of Mental Disorders in Children,* Basic Books, 1961, pp. 95–121.

41. Roudinesco, J., "Severe Maternal Deprivation and Personality Development in Childhood," *Understanding the Child,* October, 1952, 21:104–108.

42. Rouman, J., "Why They Misbehave," *California Parent-Teacher,* December, 1954, 31:14–15.

43. Schaffner, B., *Fatherland,* Columbia, 1948.

44. Schmideberg, M., "Tolerance in Upbringing and Its Abuses," *Intern. J. soc. Psychiat.,* Autumn, 1959, 5:123–130.

45. Sears, R. R., *et al.,* "Effects of Father Separation on Preschool Children's Doll Play Aggression," *Child Develpm.,* 1946, 17:219–243.

46. Straus, B. V., "The Dynamics of Ordinal Position Effects," *Quart. J. Child Behav.,* 1951, 3:133–146.

47. Symonds, P. M., *The Psychology of Parent-Child Relationships,* Appleton-Century-Crofts, 1939.

48. Tasch, R. J., "The Role of the Father in the Family," *J. Exp. Educ.,* 1952, 20:319–361.

49. Toolan, J. M., "Suicide and Suicidal Attempts in Children and Adolescents," *Amer. J. Psychiat.,* February, 1962, 118:719–724.

50. Vogel, W., and Lauterbach, C. G., "Sibling Patterns and Social Adjustment Among Normal and Psychiatrically Disturbed Soldiers," *J. consult. Psychol.,* June, 1963, 27:236–242.

51. Watson, J. B., *Psychological Care of Infant and Child,* Norton, 1928, p. 87.

Chapter 5   Cultural

Influences on Behavior

Man lives within a culture which establishes a great edifice into which each generation is born and from which it derives its values, customs, and practices. This culture is both visible and invisible. It consists of the predominant social patterns of a society, its institutions, objects, ideas, beliefs, knowledge, attitudes, sentiments, symbols, and other forces which fashion its members into a common image.

We have a common culture in America, but close examination reveals much diversity within it. Our culture is made up of a number of subcultures which are based upon differences in religion, occupation, education, racial and ethnic characteristics, wealth, geographic location, national origins, and other factors. From these subcultures emerge people whose values and life patterns are sufficiently different that it sometimes becomes difficult for members of one cultural group to understand, accept, or even communicate effectively with the members of other groups.

While cultural differences within this nation are not as extreme as those which exist between nations, they do exert important influences on the development of human behavior. To illustrate the effects of the common culture, we shall describe some of the ways that modern family life has changed in accordance with cultural imperatives. The influence of the subculture will be demonstrated by considering the effects of socioeconomic or social-class status in our society.

INTERACTION OF FAMILY AND CULTURE

Although we have been talking about the family as if it were a common entity, actually there is no single family type which is truly representative of our society. Families vary for many reasons: the carry over of Old-World cultural patterns by emigrants, economic status, the number and kinds of relatives in the household, and the authority lines in the home, to mention just a few. On the other hand, the cementing agents of our society have established enough similarity among the various types of families to justify selecting a model which roughly represents the average American family. This is the common family pattern of middle-class society, consisting of a father, mother, and two to four children. While we cannot encompass all American families in this simplified description, it is sufficiently accurate to serve as a frame of reference in which to discuss the interaction of family and culture (22).

The Nuclear Family Unit

The typical American family has undergone considerable change in the last half-century or so. For one thing, it has become a nuclear family—a small, independent unit, economically and socially, bound by rather loose ties to other relatives who do not live in the same house. The community ties of this nuclear family are superficial and tenuous because of its high rate of geographic and social mobility. Friendship patterns with others in the community are easily established, easily uprooted, and easily re-formed in a new situation. In metropolitan areas, one family in five moves each year. It is estimated that about twelve million children move from one house to another, or from one area to another, each year. For most of them this means a change in friends, schools, and familiar surroundings (34).

The significance of the small, mobile American family of today can best be appreciated by comparing it with family patterns in other societies, or with earlier rural families in this country. The communal family structure was once common in America and is still the prevailing pattern in the rest of the world. Here children are casually shared by relatives. Nieces, nephews, and cousins are treated the same as sons and daughters. The relatives discipline, feed, and care for each other's children as readily and efficiently as they care for their own. Authority lines in the home are definite and firm; the old people are the rulers, and the males are dominant. Respect and obedience to adults is bred into the children and seldom questioned. The whole family structure is bound together by economic need and is part of a social structure designed to perpetuate existing standards of life in the community.

The American nuclear family has less cohesiveness. It lacks the closeness that comes from working together toward a common goal. Family members, not dependent on one another as they once were, are tied together rather loosely with few shared responsibilities. Today, the home is more of a rendezvous for family members than a pivot around which life goes on. Extrafamilial interests in the school, neighborhood, business, or community often exert a greater pull on family members than ties that hold them within the home. This outer-directedness of the American home creates adjustment problems which are not found in the extended family systems of other cultures (10, 65).

Disruption of Family Units

The break-up of family units by death, divorce, separation, and other disruptive forces impinges on the modern family with considerable severity. When the family consisted of many children living together with parents, grandparents, and other relatives, the loss of one member of the household did not imperil the entire family structure. Today, the family is in a more precarious position because it is built on a very narrow platform of family members. The child has few persons to rely on for support, and when one is taken from him there is an unfilled gap in his life. This makes the parents' relationship to the child more intense than would be the case if there were additional relatives in the home to provide a broader base of emotional support (31:289). About 13 percent of the nation's children are living with either one parent or have no parents at all, and the number of broken families has been rising gradually during the past few decades (34). The result is that millions of children, many of them very young, are growing up in an incomplete home environment. While personal disorganization is not an inevitable outcome of the loss of a parent, a disrupted home adds to the stress of living and is a critical factor in the adjustment difficulties experienced by many youngsters (2).

Working Mothers

When women left home during World War II to work in defense industries, it was viewed as a temporary situation which would end with the war. But it has not ended and, in fact, has become a way of life for millions of families. There are now more than three times as many women working away from home than there were during the war period, and many of them leave young children behind when they go off to work (65).

The absence of the mother from the home may have varied effects on children, depending on why the woman works, the nature of her job, the age of the children, and who is available in the home to care for them. Not all children of working mothers suffer from neglect. Mothers who enjoy their jobs and do not really have to work seem to have few problems with their children. Those who work out of a sense of duty and are not satisfied with their jobs have more difficulty with their children. However, regardless of the mother's attitude toward her work, there is always the possibility that a woman who must both work and run a home may be too fractionated and emotionally enervated to give children all the affection and attention they need. Children may feel rejected, their discipline sporadic and haphazard, and parental guidance not always available when it is needed (27, 50).

The effects on a young child, particularly up to the age of three, may be especially disturbing if the mother does not provide a familiar, loving, comfortable person to take her place while she is at work. Working away from home may also have an unwholesome influence on the mother herself. She is often unduly tired, impatient, and irritable with the children and with her husband, creating friction in the household. For these reasons, a mother should weigh carefully the consequences of taking employment outside the home unless it is really essential from the point of view of finances or of her own morale.

Early Marriages

The age of marriage has tended to drop in all industrial societies in recent years, creating some unanticipated changes in patterns of family living. In 1962, about 40 percent of all brides were teen-agers, and over half of the teen-age wives become mothers while still in their teens. One consequence of this early marriage pattern is that the time span of each generation has been shortened. If the present rate of early marriages continues, more women will marry in the eighteenth year than in any other, and more will have their first child in the nineteenth year than in any other. This would make the 38-year-old grandmother commonplace (56).

In the earlier years of this nation's history, when life expectancy at birth was only about 40 years, early marriage and early childbearing were a necessity. With life expectancy now in excess of 70 years, the woman who has her last baby before she is 30 has a long life ahead of her and often is not prepared for it.

Many early marriages are made to get away from home and away from parental authority. This catapults young people into adult responsibility before they have acquired the ability to handle it. The young bride spends her late adolescent years preoccupied with marriage and children, and loses the opportunity to develop the skills and competencies she will need later if she wishes to enter the labor force. The young husband is firmly tied to a job which he does not dare leave, and spends the early years of adulthood, when his potential is at its peak, imprisoned by family responsibilities which deny him the opportunity to develop his abilities and prepare for the future (15). This premature imposition of family responsibility prevents young people from developing their talents and restricts their opportunities in life. It is little wonder that many of them experience frustration and disillusionment with their marriage. These early marriages are three times more likely to end in divorce than are those in which husbands and wives are 4 or 5 years older, and the rate of separation among teen-age mates is even higher. Moreover, as mentioned previously, it is doubtful whether teen-agers just out of school or still in school are ready to guide the maturation and education of children in this complex culture (55).

Effects of Urbanization and Mass Communication

Many of the cultural influences on families and individuals described above are the by-products of the urbanization of society. About two thirds of the nation's children live in large metropolitan areas where there is very little of the cooperative type of family enterprise common to agrarian society. Children of the city home have little responsible work to do within the home and tend to move outside for their recreation, work, and social activities. This movement out of the home not only removes them from the close observation of parents but also acquaints them with the ways of the world at a very tender age. The result is that children discover cultural conflicts and inconsistencies before they have the maturity to interpret them (34, 65).

In addition, mass media of communication, notably movies, radio, television, magazines, and newspapers, have been instrumental in bringing the outside world directly into the home. They complicate home relationships by challenging the standards and child-rearing practices of parents, introducing different moral values, and even suggesting to children the patterns of behavior to expect from parents (17).

These forces have made it difficult for the family to protect children from undesirable social influences. Modern family life no longer provides children with the secure, protected environment of pretechnological society. Although parents are still as concerned as ever over the welfare of their children, they frequently express uncertainty over how to impose standards of behavior in the home while cultural and social forces outside the home surreptitiously or overtly undermine these standards.

The Youth Culture

The culture reaches directly into the home through the values which American society places on the individual. The typical American family supports these values by stimulating the individual development of children and encouraging their emancipation from the family. If this were not done, a young person would never be free to leave his family, his home town, or his job, to develop his own potentialities. There would be no expectation of a bigger and better future for the new generation; no accommodation to change, but instead an acceptance of the situation into which one was born. Such a philosophy, obviously, would not be compatible with a growing, changing, heterogeneous society. Therefore, the American family, like families in any culture, is actually an instrument for the perpetuation of our type of society.

The benefits derived from a home which has no fixed molds for its members is freedom from regimentation, individual diversity, and opportunity for self-realization. But there are penalties to be paid for these advantages. In order to emancipate himself from the family, a youngster must tear himself away from the ones he loves, break the emotional bonds which were years in forming, and establish new values and goals. While undergoing this emancipation, both parents and children become involved in a sequence of resistance, rebellion, and conflict which generates considerable worry and anxiety in the family.

In other cultures where the family or the kinship group, rather than the individual, is the primary focus of society, this basic conflict between young and old does not exist. The elders retain their influence and position in the family circle and community. This relieves the stress on the individual, for his place in the family is predetermined and secure. Yet, all is not perfect even in communal societies. As Margaret Mead has shown, the Samoan child raised within a large kinship group turns out to lack self-reliance. The Arapesh Indian child grows up emotionally secure with a loving trust for adults, but ill-equipped to live in a society where he must manage his own affairs (46, 47). Each society has its strengths and weaknesses, and the individuals in the society inherit its advantages and disadvantages.

In American society, and in certain other countries of the world, a youth culture has evolved as a means through which the transition of the youngster from home to society is eased. Instead of violently rupturing family ties, a youth's attachments are transferred gradually to the peer group which stands as a buffer between the home and the adult world. The youth culture aids the youngster to achieve a sense of self-identity and provides him with the feelings of personal significance which are vital to him (3, 53, 64).

This youth culture has actually become a subculture, formally recognized by society. It is an important market for special kinds of entertainment, popular music, movies, clothes, and other commercial enterprises. Like its parent culture, adolescent society is not a single entity but varies considerably in terms of its class structure, the size and location of the community, and the social organization of the schools the youth attend. However, it is bound together by common values and special symbols which emphasize freedom from adult control. In liberating themselves from the home, adolescents promote their own activities, develop their own style of life, and enforce the segregation of adolescent society from adult society (8). While this sounds like rebellion, it is the normal process of emancipation encouraged by our society. If the early years of life in the home have been constructive and supportive, the youth culture can be counted on to provide the social experiences which youngsters need to achieve maturity, particularly if parents continue to exercise discreet guidance (53).

Impact of Cultural Influences on the Family

Since the turn of this century there have been vast sociological and technological changes which have changed the pattern of family living. Until a few decades ago, cultural changes proceeded slowly enough to permit a gradual transition from one generation to the next. Parents could control the family environment and regulate the influence of society on children. In recent years the sheer pace of technical progress has provided the younger generation with values, standards, and ideas which parents do not adequately comprehend or accept.

These developments have brought to families feelings of confusion and uncertainty. As old cultural patterns proved inadequate for modern needs in the world of change, home ties became loosened and the possibility for intrafamily friction increased. The appropriate roles of father, mother, and children have become blurred by industrialization and urbanization. The father is no longer the sole breadwinner and protector of the family while the mother stays home to sew, cook, and care for the children. Children no longer accept the authority of parents without dispute. They spend less time in their fraternal home and are more subject to cultural influences which bypass the parents and reach them directly. The current trend toward replacing family-life courses in high school with more academic courses may contribute further to the stresses of family living. Young people are entering marriage without the foggiest notion of what is involved in establishing and maintaining a family. They are getting their preparation for marriage and parenthood from movies, television, magazines, and from each other—sources which hold little promise for improving family life.

All of these factors make it more difficult for people to find security within the family and for the home to fulfill its responsibilities in society. Some authorities feel that a considerable increase in community services to families, including a great deal more parent education, is needed to strengthen the home so that it may fit into modern society while exerting a positive influence on the adjustment of family members (17).

SOCIAL-CLASS INFLUENCES ON ADJUSTMENT

The various cultural factors affecting family life and individual adjustment have been discussed in terms of a typical family and its members. It is necessary now to qualify this general description and point out some of the important differences which exist among people as a consequence of the positions they occupy in society.

Although the United States does not have a caste system as some other countries do, our people still occupy different vantage points in the social structure. Sociologists assign them to various socioeconomic groups based partly on income and wealth and partly on other status factors such as whether a person works with his head or hands; whether he went to college, for how long, and whether it was a public or Ivy League school; how long his family has lived in the community, the clubs and organizations he belongs to, what he reads, his recreational interests, and other prestige symbols. By these characteristics people may be sorted into groups having different life styles and placed at different status levels in society. These status levels, called social classes, have no formal sanction, but they are nonetheless real and have a pervasive influence over the members of the group.

Social-Class Stratification

While it is generally known that social classes exist in our society, the average person has only a vague notion of how he fits into this class structure. A national poll conducted some years ago found that 88 percent of the people considered themselves to be members of the middle class, and the remaining 12 percent thought they were equally divided between the upper and lower classes (20).

Sociologists have found quite a different stratification in society. From studies of rural and urban areas, small towns and large cities, they find evidence of a social class organization consisting of five or six groups arranged in a pyramid as follows (25):

Class	Percent of the Population
Upper	1– 3
Upper-middle	7–12
Lower-middle	20–35
Upper-lower	25–40
Lower-lower	15–25

These figures are not precise because variations are found in different types of communities. However, they indicate that instead of having a bulging middle-class society which overshadows a small upper and lower class, the population has a pyramidal structure with a large lower class at its foundation. While these classes are not divisions of society as rigid as in other countries, there are certain factors which make it difficult for a person to rise above the class into which he was born (45, 59).

Characteristics of Social Classes

Each social class has characteristics which are sufficiently distinctive and powerful to impress on its members values, forms of behavior, habits, customs, and attitudes which distinguish them from other classes (58). Some of the more significant characteristics of the middle and lower classes are summarized below. We shall not consider the upper social classes, since they represent so small a proportion of the total population.

The Middle Classes. In the middle classes are found the white-collar workers, foremen, highly skilled craftsmen, small businessmen, professional and managerial people, and others whose income is derived from fees, salaries, or profits. These people tend to be striving, competitive persons who value progress and education, and conform to the law and to group standards. They are concerned with appearances and what other people think of them. They participate in community affairs through churches, Parent-Teacher Associations, discussion groups, book clubs, civic organizations and other organized groups (28). They emphasize cleanliness, tidiness, restraint, moral conformity, and control of aggressive tendencies.

This middle class, while not the largest class numerically, is said to be the official culture of this country. It is the culture taught in the schools and practiced by recreational and social agencies. It is the "great American public" toward which most advertising, sales campaigns, movies, magazines, newspapers and other media of mass communication are directed (22).

The Lower Classes. The life styles of the lower classes differ in many respects from those of the middle classes. Actually, we need to speak of two lower classes: the upper-lower, the class of the "common man," that includes skilled and semiskilled blue-collar workers with steady jobs, and the lower-lower class which is composed of unskilled wage earners, the foreign-born, tenant farmers, migrant workers, and persons with little education and uncertain employment (25:24). The latter has also been described as the culturally deprived group, the underprivileged, and the disadvantaged.

The upper-lower class is more like the middle class in its aspirations, its anxiety over insecurity, and in some of its customs and values. It resembles the lower-lower class in its struggle for economic existence. However, lower-class people are sufficiently similar in their basic living patterns to be considered as a group (14:264).

Lower-class people are conscious of their group identity to the extent of differentiating between those in the group and those outside it. They feel little responsibility toward people outside the circle of their family, neighborhood, or friends. Within this sphere it is important to be honest and loyal; outside of it, disloyalty and deception are more likely to be overlooked or condoned (31:319).

The lower classes do not emphasize cleanliness and tidiness to the extent that the middle class does, nor do they place so high a value on accomplishment. Their aggressive impulses are less restrained, and sexual restrictions are much looser. The incidence of premarital sexual intercourse in the lower class is said to be seven times higher than among the upper or middle class. From one fourth to one third of all lower-class births are illegitimate (14:264). Relations between husband and wife are also different in lower-class families. Wife beating is almost entirely a lower-lower-class characteristic. Women work harder in these families, while men enjoy more leisure than their wives and usually share this leisure with male companions (41:194).

Members of the lower-lower class marry early and enter the semiskilled and unskilled occupations at an early age. They experience the greatest distress in times of unemployment and usually comprise the bulk of relief cases. They tend to live in the least desirable sections of the community, almost never join social or community organizations other than labor unions, make little use of the public library, subscribe to few magazines, and usually limit their reading to newspapers. The lower-lower class furnishes more than its proportionate share of criminals and delinquents.

Social-Class Differences in Child Rearing

Nowhere do social-class differences express themselves more definitely than in the patterns of family living. Children in the middle-class family are sheltered and closely supervised. They are required to be in the house earlier at night and to work harder on their school lessons than lower-class children. Greater stress is placed on their individual achievement, habits of cleanliness, emotional restraint, and the development of responsibility and self-control. Children are punished not only for what they do but for their intentions and for the long range meaning of their behavior (13, 38).

There is reason to believe that children in middle-class families are subject to considerable stress. Masturbation has been found to be two or three times more common among them than among lower-class children, and thumb sucking occurs three times more often among middle-class than among lower-class youngsters (12, 18). Despite the curtailment of physical freedom, middle-class children enjoy considerable psychological freedom in the home. This is one explanation offered for the low incidence of submissiveness, bullying, and "pecking-order" behavior observed in middle-class play groups (42).

Lower-class families live close together in small, thin-walled, crowded houses or apartments. Their families are large and often include relatives and boarders in the household. Children get in each other's way and must share life more intimately with their siblings and with adults than is true in other classes (4:325). They are taught not to be a nuisance to adults and to stay out of the way. Physical punishment is used liberally to induce obedience and prompt response to commands (38, 66).

Lower-class parents appear to be very permissive in their relationships with young children. They probably nurse their children longer than middle-class mothers do, and are not quite so anxious over matters such as toilet training, weaning, or masturbation (18, 37, 43). Their children are permitted to go to movies alone at an early age and may stay out later in the evening than their middle-class peers. There is less family pride and less concern for appearances or for upholding family status. Children are free to roam the streets with relatively little parental supervision.

This apparent permissiveness in the lower-class home appears to be more a matter of not wanting children around to interfere with parental activities than any concern for developing the child's capacities. The physical freedom of lower-class children does not result in psychological freedom nor in a lower level of anxiety. Children tend to fear their parents and to feel rejected and unworthy because of the lack of close parental ties (42, 43). Parent-child relationships are influenced also by the rate of family disorganization in lower-class homes. There are frequent changes of residence among these people, and a high rate of divorce, desertion, and transitory illegal unions.

In this setting of freedom, lack of privacy, and sexual promiscuity, lower-class children begin their sexual experimentation very early (4:331). Aggression and fighting are also learned early in the life of a lower-class child. He learns to fight children of either sex, and adults if need be, with no regard for sportsmanship or fair play. Fighting is so integral a part of lower-class life that, unless the child becomes a ready and proficient fighter, he loses prestige among his peers and in his family as well (13, 14).

Behavioral Responses to Social-Class Status

As a child grows up in his social-class environment, he is conditioned to behave as the culture dictates. The effects of this cultural imprinting are most evident in the social life of the school. Middle-class children adjust readily to school because it is essentially a middle-class institution, employing mostly middle-class teachers and textbooks, and teaching a middle-class way of life. Lower-class children often find school to be an unreal environment which has little to do with life as they know it in their homes and neighborhoods, and soon develop an antischool attitude (57).

There is much evidence that the cleavage of classes among school children leaves the lower-class child isolated and rejected. One study of elementary-school children in a Midwestern community asked children to name classmates who fitted certain behavioral descriptions and to select their friends among them. The lower-class children were mentioned often as persons not liked and not desired as friends. They had the reputation of being poorly dressed, not good-looking, unpopular, aggressive, dirty, and bad-mannered. This rejection and isolation of lower-class children began in the fifth grade (51).

A study of friendship preferences among high-school students revealed an even more pronounced awareness of social-class symbols. Upper-status children were credited with positive personality traits, such as best-dressed, best-liked, most fun, or real leader. Lower-class children were seldom mentioned as possessing these traits, except by other lower-class children. Both upper- and middle-class students referred to the lower group as "drips" and "jerks," and described them as dirty, smelly, aggressive, and dumb (9).

Other studies (23, 26, 28, 63) support the conclusion that lower-class boys and girls are rejected by their upper-status peers. They are not welcome in school clubs, and are unwanted in the classroom or on the playground. Only when they excel in athletics or can make some other important contribution to the school do they receive recognition from their classmates. Most lower-class children never attain this status. They experience only futility and bitterness in their out-of-class social contacts. Teachers, too, maintain a greater social distance between themselves and lower-class children than they do with middle- and upper-class children. In many instances, the teacher represents a hostile, foreign authority to the lower-class youngster, a person who inflicts punishment and imposes unwanted and meaningless tasks (44).

These conditions force lower-class children into association with their class equals. They seek to achieve a feeling of belonging, by developing a group spirit among themselves, sometimes expressing this spirit through aggression toward those groups who rejected them. Lower-class children's groups set their own standards of behavior, and often disdain the overtures of institutions, clubs, and agencies established to provide recreational opportunities and guidance for them, preferring their own unsupervised freedom. Despite these efforts to find acceptance among themselves, lower-class children show more problem tendencies and greater evidence of emotional instability than do children of higher social status (36). This is significant in light of the fact that among preschool children it is the middle class that shows more symptoms of tension as evidenced by thumb sucking and masturbation. Evidently, emotional pressures on the lower-class child increase as he grows older. Rejection and frustration lead to negative attitudes which carry over into adult behavior and impose serious barriers to adjustment among lower-class people (6, 35:308).

Social-class status affects not only the interpersonal relationships of school children but their educational opportunities as well. Lower-class children profit less from the academic program and have more scholastic problems than their upper-status peers (33, 54). By the time they reach the eighth grade, they are, on the average, 2 years retarded, and academic difficulties increase with the passage of time (5, 13, 16, 39). Many of these youngsters start dropping out of school before they finish the eighth grade, and continue to do so in increasing numbers in high school. Only about 5 to 10 percent of the lower-class children go on to college, while 70 to 80 percent of their upper-class schoolmates get there (24). Even when capable lower-class students receive scholarship aid to go to college, many of them drop out because they lack interest in further education (60). Those who do stay in college credit their high school counselors and teachers rather than their parents for the motivation to do so. In contrast, students from the upper and middle classes who are in college most often mention their parents rather than counselors or teachers as having influenced their decision to continue in school (21).

There are many factors that contribute to the educational

difficulties of the lower-class child, and the end result is that lower-class children receive a poorer education, and less of it, than upper-class children. As a consequence, they can look forward to those postschool jobs commonly filled by members of their class—the ones requiring little education and having low social status (39). Their opportunity for social mobility is curtailed when the schools feed them back into the occupational pursuits characteristic of the social-class level from which they come (11). This process results in frustration, thwarted ambition, and the loss of much human potential, for many of the lower-class children have the intellectual ability to profit from more education than they receive.

Social Class and Maladjustment. As we have shown, the social class structure can be gratifying and supportive for some people and frustrating for others. This is reflected in the nature and extent of maladjustment occurring within the social classes. Numerous studies show that the lower classes are most vulnerable to psychological and social maladjustment, testifying to the steady strain to which they are subjected (19).

In a New England study of patients under psychiatric treatment in hospitals, clinics, and by private physicians, the lower classes were found to comprise three fourths of the patients involved (30). Other studies have shown that the highest incidence of psychosis in a city will be found in the areas characterized by high population mobility, low socioeconomic status, a high proportion of foreign-born, and a high incidence of social and health problems (6, 32, 40).

There are social class differences not only in the incidence or rate of emotional disturbance but also the type which occurs among the various classes. Schizophrenia, for example, one of the psychoses most resistant to treatment, tends to occur ten times more frequently in lower than in upper social classes, and six times more often than in the middle classes (29). The lower classes in general tend to suffer more from the crippling forms of mental illness, while people in higher socioeconomic brackets tend more toward neuroses, psychosomatic ailments, and manic-depressive psychoses (6, 48). Moreover, mental disorders among lower-class patients are difficult to cure, because the lower class person tends to drop out of therapy early, is unresponsive to treatment, and difficult for a middle-class therapist to understand (7).

In searching for explanations for these social-class differences in maladjustment, investigators have found no real evidence of causation, but they have a number of hypotheses. It is possible that upper-class people seek treatment for their emotional ailments earlier than do lower-class people, so that the problem is caught in its early stages when it is treatable. Also, there is good reason to believe that the poorly integrated family life of the lower classes may be a critical factor in their emotional adjustment. The lower classes may be exposed to more psychological stress because of their marginal economic existence, their superficial intergroup relationships, the competitive character of their lives, or the value conflicts which confront them in a middle-class society. A "drift" hypothesis has been advanced recently which holds that mentally disordered individuals tend to drift into the lower socioeconomic classes, or fail to rise out of them, so that environmental stresses and deprivations accumulate here and are passed on from generation to generation (52). No doubt these are all contributing factors which, in varying combinations, make people in the lower classes more susceptible to emotional disorders and maladjustment (6).

SUMMARY

The family is not autonomous in its influence over personality development. To understand how the family performs its functions, it is necessary to look beyond the home into the culture from which it derives its values, customs, and practices. So tightly bound together are culture and family that each is understandable only in the context of the other. Cultural change affects family life, and the family, in turn, supports the culture.

Modern cultural influences have introduced a number of changes in family living which bear directly on the adjustment of individuals within the home. Industrialization, urbanization, and mass communication have leveled the barriers between home and society, so that the culture is no longer mediated entirely by parents but enters directly into the lives of children. The narrowing of the American family to a nuclear unit, family disruptions, working mothers, and early marriages have been described as some of the forces which tend to weaken the hold of the home and encourage youngsters to move out into the wider community. Here they join together for support, creating a youth culture which competes with the family in establishing standards of behavior. All of these factors, and others, have had an influence on the dynamics of family living. But the most significant cultural influence on personality development is the social-class structure of society. Membership in a given social class often determines the pattern of family life and the style of living which its members will adopt. The lower socio-economic classes in our society experience educational, social, and economic deprivations which have far-reaching influences on their behavior and adjustment.

REFERENCES

1. Ackerman, N. W., *The Psychodynamics of Family Life: Diagnosis and Treatment of Family Relationships*, Basic Books, 1958.
2. Bernert, E. H., "Demographic Trends and Implications," in Eli Ginzberg (Ed.), *The Nation's Children, 1: The Family and Social Change*, Columbia, 1960, pp. 24–49.
3. Bloch, H. A., and Niederhoffer, A., *The Gang: A Study in Adolescent Behavior*, Philosophical Library, 1958.
4. Bossard, J. H. S., *The Sociology of Child Development*, Harper & Row, 1954.
5. California Elementary School Administrators Association, *The Neighborhood and the School*, Burlingame, Calif., 1962.
6. Clausen, J. A., and Kohn, M. L., "The Ecological Approach in Social Psychiatry," *Amer. J. Sociol.*, September, 1954, **40**: 140–149.
7. Cole, N. J., et al., "Some Relationships Between Social Class and the Practice of Dynamic Psychotherapy," *Amer. J. Psychiat.*, May, 1962, **118**:1004–1012.

8. Colemans, J. S., *Social Climate in High Schools,* U.S. Office of Education, Publication No. OE 33016, Cooperative Research Monograph No. 4, 1961.

9. Cook, L. A., "An Experimental Sociographic Study of a Stratified Tenth Grade Class," *Amer. Sociol. Rev.,* 1945, **10**:250–261.

10. Cumming, J. H., "The Family and Mental Disorder: An Incomplete Essay," *Milbank Mem. Fund quart.,* April, 1961, **39**:185–228.

11. Davie, J. S., "Social Class Factors and School Attendance," *Harvard educ. Rev.,* Summer, 1953, **23**:175–185.

12. Davis, A., *Social Class Influences on Learning,* Harvard, 1949.

13. Davis, A., "Socio-Economic Influences on Learning," *Phi Delta Kappan,* January, 1951, **32**:253–256.

14. Davis, A., and Dollard, J., *Children of Bondage,* American Council on Education, 1940.

15. Davis, K., "The Early Marriage Trend," *What's New,* Fall, 1958, No. 207.

16. Driggs, D. F., "Relationship Between Intelligence Test Items and Occupation of Parents of School Children," *Research Relating to Children,* U.S. Children's Bureau, Bulletin II, Supplement 2, 1954, p. 23.

17. Dybwad, G., "Family Life in a Changing World," *Child.,* January–February, 1959, **6**:3–9.

18. Ericson, M. C., "Child-Rearing and Social Status," *Amer. J. Sociol.,* November, 1946, **52**:190–192.

19. Freedman, L. Z., and Hollingshead, A. B., "Neurosis and Social Class," *Amer. J. Psychiat.,* March, 1957, **113**:769–775.

20. Gallup, G. H., and Rae, S. F., *The Pulse of Democracy: The Public Opinion Poll and How it Works,* Simon and Schuster, 1940.

21. Gottlieb, D., "Social Class, Achievement, and the College-Going Experience," *School Rev.,* Autumn, 1962, **70**:273–286.

22. Group for the Advancement of Psychiatry, Committee on the Family, *Integration and Conflict in Family Behavior,* Report No. 27, Topeka, Kan., August, 1954.

23. Hand, H. C., *Principal Findings of the 1947–48 Basic Studies of the Illinois Secondary School Curriculum Program,* Superintendent of Instruction, Springfield, 1949.

24. Havighurst, R. J., *American Higher Education in the 1960's,* Ohio State University Press, 1960.

25. Havighurst, R. J., and Neugarten, B. L., *Society and Education,* Allyn & Bacon, 1962.

26. Heintz, E., "Adjustment Problems of Class Status," *Phi Delta Kappan*, April, 1949, **30**:290–293.
27. Hoffman, L. W., "Effects of Maternal Employment on the Child," *Child Develpm.*, March, 1961, **32**:187–197.
28. Hollingshead, A. B., *Elmtown's Youth*, Wiley, 1949.
29. Hollingshead, A. B., and Redlich, F. C., "Schizophrenia and Social Structure," *Amer. J. Psychiat.*, March, 1954, **110**:695–701.
30. Hollingshead, A. B., and Redlich, F. C., *Social Class and Mental Health*, Wiley, 1958.
31. Honigmann, J. J., *Culture and Personality*, Harper & Row, 1954.
32. Hughes, C. C., *et al.*, *People of Cove and Woodlot*, Basic Books, 1960.
33. Institute of Child Development and Welfare, University of Minnesota, *A Survey of Children's Adjustment over Time*, Minneapolis, 1959.
34. Interdepartmental Committee on Children and Youth, *Children in a Changing World*, Golden Anniversary White House Conference on Children and Youth, 1960.
35. Kardiner, A., and Ovesey, L., *The Mark of Oppression*, Norton, 1951.
36. Keller, S., "The Social World of the Urban Slum Child: Some Early Findings," *Amer. J. Orthopsychiat.*, October, 1963, **33**:823–831.
37. Klatskin, E. H., "Shifts in Child Care Practices in Three Social Classes Under an Infant Care Program of Flexible Methodology," *Amer. J. Orthopsychiat.*, April, 1952, **22**:52–61.
38. Kohn, M. L., "Social Class and Parental Values," *Amer. J. Sociol.*, January, 1959, **64**:337–351.
39. Krugman, M., "The Culturally Deprived Child in School," *J. National Educ. Ass.*, April, 1961, **50**:23–24.
40. Leighton, A. H., *My Name is Legion*, Basic Books, 1960.
41. Lindgren, H. C., *The Psychology of Personal and Social Adjustment*, American Book Co., 1953.
42. Maccoby, E. E., *et al.*, "Methods of Child-Rearing in Two Social Classes," in W. E. Martin and C. B. Stendler, (Eds.), *Readings in Child Development*, Harcourt, Brace & World, 1954.
43. Margolin, J., "Reading Failure and Mental Health—Some Research Into the Learning Disabilities," in *The School Administrator and School Mental Health Programs*, Michigan Society for Mental Health, Detroit, July, 1962, pp. 32–34.

44. Mass, H. S., "Some Social Class Differences in the Family System and Group Relations of Pre- and Early Adolescents," *Child Develpm.*, 1951, **22**:145–152.
45. Mayer, K., "The Theory of Social Classes," *Harvard educ. Rev.*, Summer, 1953, **23**:149–167.
46. Mead, M., *Coming of Age in Samoa*, Mentor Books, 1950.
47. Mead, M., *Sex and Temperament*, Mentor Books, 1950.
48. Michael, S. T., and Langner, T. S., "Social Mobility and Psychiatric Symptoms," *Dis. nerv. System*, April, 1963, **24**(Monograph Supplement):S128–133.
49. Murphy, G., *Human Potentialities*, Basic Books, 1958.
50. National Institute of Mental Health, *Highlights of Progress in Mental Health Research, 1961*, Public Health Service Publication No. 919, Bethesda, Md., 1962.
51. Neugarten, B. L., "Social Class Friendship Among School Children," *Amer. J. Sociol.*, 1946, **51**:305–313.
52. Pasamanick, B., "Some Misconceptions Concerning Differences in the Racial Prevalence of Mental Disease," *Amer. J. Orthopsychiat.*, January, 1963, **33**:72–86.
53. Peck, R. F., *et al.*, *The Psychology of Character Development*, Wiley, 1960.
54. Phelps, H. R., and Horrocks, J. E., "Factors Influencing Informal Groups of Adolescents," *Child Develpm.*, March, 1958, **29**:69–86.
55. Population Reference Bureau, Inc., "Spotlight on Marriage," *Population Bull.*, June, 1961, **17**:61–79.
56. Population Reference Bureau, Inc., "The Teen-Age Mother," *Population Profile*, June 3, 1962.
57. Reissman, F., "The Culturally Deprived Child: A New View," *Sch. Life*, April, 1963, **45**:5–7.
58. Reissman, L., *Class in American Society*, Free Press, 1959.
59. Rennie, T. A. C., *et al.*, "Urban Life and Mental Health," *Amer. J. Psychiat.*, March, 1957, **113**:831–837.
60. Smith, S. E., *et al.*, *Are Scholarships the Answer*, University of New Mexico Press, 1960.
61. Springer, N. N., "Influence of General Social Status on Emotional Stability of Children," *J. genet. Psychol.*, December, 1938, **53**:321–328.
62. Stein, M., *et al.*, *Identity and Anxiety: Survival of the Person in Mass Society*, Free Press, 1960.
63. Stendler, C. B., *Children of Brasstown*, University of Illinois, Bulletin No. 59, April, 1949.

64. U.S. Children's Bureau, *Child.,* September–October, 1960, **7:** 200.
65. Vaughan, W. T., Jr., "Children in Crisis," *Ment. Hyg.,* July, 1961, 45:354–359.
66. Woolworth, W. G., "A Basis for Character Education—A Study of the Problem by Teachers and Parents in a School District," *Calif. J. elem. Educ.,* February, 1954, **22:**148–164.

PART II ATTAINING
MATURITY

Chapter 6   The
Self Concept

Having examined the biological and environmental factors which may modify our inherited potentialities for adjustment, we now focus on the subjective world of the individual—the world of personal meaning and internal psychological forces.

As we grow toward maturity, each of us develops a private world comprised of attitudes, feelings, values, perceptions, and expectations which forms a frame of reference through which we view ourselves and interpret the physical and social environment. Psychologists have different names for this private world. Some refer to it as the individual's "self-concept"; others as the "self," or the "ego," or the "sense of self-identity." Although there are academic distinctions among these terms, we shall use them interchangeably and define the self concept or ego as C. R. Rogers does in the following statement (34): "The Self, that organized, consistent, conceptual gestalt composed of perceptions of the characteristics of the 'I' or 'me,' and the perceptions of the relationships of the 'I' or 'me' to others and to various aspects of life, together with the values attached to these perceptions." This self is the mediator of experiences between the individual and the outside world of people and events. While it is only one aspect of the total personality, it must be allotted an important place in the development of adjustment.

EMERGENCE OF THE SELF CONCEPT

There are two important interpretations of the origins of the self which we shall consider: The psychoanalytic concept which emphasizes the unconscious aspects of our inner world, and the genetic interpretations of self which stress maturation, growth, and experience. Both are more or less agreed that the sense of self emerges during the course of growth and that it is of critical importance in personality development (24).

Psychoanalytic Interpretations of the Self

Psychoanalysts place considerable emphasis on the emergence of an inner self as a consequence of the interaction of certain psychic forces or mental energies. These psychic forces, named the id, ego, and superego, operate at various levels of consciousness, and together make up the inner personality.

The id is an inherited mass of energy which is thought to be the repository of our sex drives, mastery drives, pleasure drives, aggressive drives, and other instinctual drives which strive for expression. These are the primitive, uncivilized, and uninhibited aspects of man's nature which seek gratification without concern for the welfare of the individual or society.

The ego is a controlling force which emerges through socialization and represents the conscious aspects of mental life. It has the function of interpreting reality to the id, so that the latter in its blind struggle for expression will not lead the individual into pain or destruction.

In the young child the ego is weak and can exercise only a very slight control over the id. As the child grows, his ego develops and becomes more capable of sensing external dangers and of using thought and reason to create conditions whereby the id may express itself safely. As this process goes on, the ego becomes that aspect of mental functioning which organizes and controls perceptions, protects a person against unreasonable pleasure-seeking tendencies, and makes him aware of the realities of life (3).

The superego consists of the conscience and the ego ideal. The conscience is the prohibitive and punitive aspects of mental ife which distinguishes right behavior from wrong. The ego deal establishes goals or standards toward which the ego strives. Together, the conscience and ego ideal provide a set of inner moral principles which guide behavior.

The conscience is formed initially from internalized symbols of parental control. At first, the young child conforms to the rules of parents because he is rewarded for good behavior and punished for bad behavior. By the time he reaches the third or fourth year of life he has internalized so many parental prohibitions and moral concepts that part of the ego becomes differentiated as the conscience. A few years later this conscience is fully formed and firmly established. As the child grows older, there will be changes in his overt behavior, but the basic moral character laid down in the early years remains with him for the rest of his life (17, 32).

The ego ideal consists of goals or standards by which the ego measures itself and toward which it seeks to grow. The ego ideal emerges gradually out of a series of identifications, first with parents, then with teachers, relatives, peers, and other people. Fantasy figures and fictional characters, such as those derived from movies, radio, television, and books, often enter into this identification process. These images become merged into an ideal self—the person we would like to be. There is a difference between the real self and the ideal self, and people who cannot make this distinction may subject themselves to much frustration and anxiety.

Personality and Development of the Self. Each of us is a different person because of the distinctive pattern of relationship which develops between the id, ego, and superego. Normal development requires the emergence of an adequate ego which is capable of regulating the release of id energies while heeding the superego and adapting to the demands of the external world. If the ego can maintain control over these inner forces, the individual develops as a rational, competent human being.

A home atmosphere where security, affection, and approval are wisely tempered with control and encouragement is the matrix out of which adequate egos emerge. When the child enters school, he has an immature ego which reflects the quality of his early home experiences. In school his ego may be expanded, changed, or undermined, depending upon the success and acceptance he encounters in his academic and social relationships. All children strive to enhance their egos; they want to be appreciated and made to feel important. If they are provided with opportunities to experience such feelings of personal worth in school, ego development can be expected to proceed in a constructive way. Denied these opportunities or subjected to too much failure, isolation, or rejection, they may seek asocial forms of ego-enhancing satisfactions. Many problems of misconduct among school children can be traced back to their efforts to find compensating ego-satisfying experiences when the normal school situation was too threatening or unrewarding.

During the prepuberty years, the child manages to establish a rather stable concept of himself based on childhood values and relationships. With the onset of puberty, these values and relationships change. The youngster's body undergoes a major transformation, leaving him with new sensitivities about himself. These feelings, together with altered social relationships, new glandular functions, and other factors make this a critical period in ego development. The ego is cast loose from its childhood moorings and must be re-established in terms of a new body image, and new personal and social relationships.

During the adolescent years, the ego tends to be unstable and insecure as the individual searches for new attachments, new competencies, and new channels through which to restore his sense of self-identity. As new perceptions and relationships develop, the ego emerges in its mature form. The individual will continue to seek experiences which provide support for his ego and make him feel adequate and approved. But barring a serious mental illness, he will never again go through a major ego transformation such as that involved in the re-establishment of the ego during adolescence (12).

Superego and Id in Personality Formation.   The self concept is not derived from the ego alone. According to psychoanalytic theory, the superego and id also play important roles in the emergence of a sense of identity.

The type of superego a child develops has an important influence on his inner life and the way he views himself and the world. If parents do not do their job well, the superego may be underdeveloped, and the child will lack the inner controls needed to regulate his behavior in a moral and socially approved manner. On the other hand, children who develop too rigid a superego tend to become severely conscientious, perfectionistic individuals who have little fun in life and cannot tolerate others whose standards of conduct are less severe than their own. The kind of superego structure found in well-adjusted people is one which interacts freely with the ego and id, being neither too weak to provide a moral direction to behavior nor so strong that it exerts a tyrannical force over the individual (32).

The id energies must find acceptable modes of expression if the child is to develop an adequate personality. Children need ample opportunity to satisfy their pleasure drives and release energy through play. Too much suppression of their impulses, particularly during the early years, may lead to a restricted personality development, or to the accumulation of energies until they are vented in destructive behavior. If the child is permitted to express his impulses regularly in situations which will not injure himself or others, the id will follow a normal pattern of domestication and be brought under the control of the ego.

Thus, the emergence of the self, according to this theory, is a matter of bringing the three phases of mental life—ego, id, and superego—into a state of suitable equilibrium. If the ego is adequate and capable of harnessing the id energies, and the superego is not overly harsh, the individual may be expected to develop a positive sense of self-identity and a capacity for self-direction (16).

Genetic Development of the Self Concept

Many students of human behavior consider the psychoanalytic interpretations of self-development too mystical and animistic. They view the emergence of self as a developmental process of growth, maturation, and learning which begins in infancy and is controlled, not by internal psychological forces, but by the totality of the individual's growth experiences.

Growth and Individuality. Genetic theories of self-development begin with the newborn infant, "floating in an undifferentiated absolute," incapable of distinguishing between himself and his environment (41:167). In a few years, maturation and the integration of countless learning experiences bring the infant out of this amorphous state of undifferentiation into the distinct awareness of individuality found in early childhood. Gesell and Ilg outline these sweeping changes in the following sequence of behavior descriptions:

At 32 weeks, the infant does not recognize himself in the image which stares at him from a mirror, but he senses a stranger as something different from familiar (13:428). . . .

At 44 weeks, he extends objects to a person without release. Placed before a mirror he sits back and regards the total image (13:318).

Gradually, the child discovers himself, and at two years of age he is a person in his own right:

Johnny is his name, and in his inarticulate psychology, the spoken word Johnny which he hears is nothing more or less than he himself! His name is Johnny as a person.—He will soon use the pronouns *you, me,* and *I,*—a further indication of a fundamental change in the psychology of his self. But he still refers to himself by name (Johnny) rather than pronoun, and if one wishes to secure his *personal* attention it is advisable to address him by *Johnny* rather than *You* (13:337) . . .

The 2½ year old child has a more vigorous sense of self. He says "I want." "I need." He is negative as well as positive. He says, "I don't like." He can state his own sex by negation: "No, I'm not a girl." (13:338) . . .

The three year old has attained a well balanced sense of self. He combines self with another in use of "We." (13:338) . . .

The four year old has an expanding sense of self indicated by bragging, boasting, and out-of-bounds behavior (13:319). . . .

Five years is a rather impersonal age. Self and others are taken for granted (13:319).

Levels of Maturity in Self-Development. Once the child has clarified the distinction between self and nonself, he tends to assert his individuality. He goes through a stage of egocentric behavior where he is almost exclusively preoccupied with gratifying his own wishes and exploring, or exploiting, his immediate environment. Gradually, he becomes aware of the reactions of other people and of the rules governing human relationships. He tests and reacts to these rules and, ultimately, in normal development, integrates most of them into his own behavior. Through a series of such integrations of experience he gradually develops a stable perception of who he is, what he is, what he can and cannot do, and how other people are affected by him (14). Many of the self-perceptions and personality patterns developed in childhood will be revised in later life. Some, however, tend to persist as a basic part of the ego structure laid down in childhood. Many authorities believe that by the age of ten the child has established a personality framework that will remain stable throughout life and that the later structure of personality grows around this framework (21).

Re-Establishment of Self-Identity in Adolescence.   In adolescence the process of becoming an autonomous and self-governing individual takes on new dimensions. The genetic theory of self-development parallels psychoanalytic interpretations at this point. Both agree that the changes brought about by sexual maturity, the eagerness for adult status, and the pressures of society create a totally different psychological environment for the youngster. The adolescent goes through a process of re-identity to free himself from the alignments of childhood and to make sense out of what has gone before in relation to what he now perceives the world to be. He experiments with new behavior, looking for affirmation from his friends and from the adults who mean the most to him. Unconsciously, he revamps his repertory of childhood identifications, revising some and repudiating others, until he emerges with a set of values and identifications which he can accept as his own (10).

Adolescents go through this stage of reidentity with varying degrees of intensity and at different rates. There is a distinct difference between boys and girls in this process. Boys, as a rule, are much more aggressive about attaining autonomy. For example, one hurdle the adolescent must overcome in establishing his own identity is to achieve independence from his parents. Boys commonly go through a series of rough and often painful steps to replace parental standards with standards of their own. They are outspoken and demanding in achieving the right to assert themselves and to cast off the ties of childhood dependency. Girls usually are far less intense about this issue of autonomy. Once they have achieved certain limited goals, such as spending money and choosing clothes, they generally accept the standards of their parents and do not struggle so hard for personal control. The identity issue for the girl is postponed until marriage, when she must make her own decisions and take decisive steps toward establishing independent standards that the boy takes earlier in adolescence (8).

The Self Concept of Adults. When the individual emerges from the adolescent period, he is not a completely transformed person, but his self-identity is at a higher level of integration. He has achieved a composite of perceptions, values, insights, and attitudes which form a relatively stable image of who he thinks himself to be. Normally, he has accepted himself for what he is, and continues to maintain or improve his self-esteem until the middle years of life when many people reflect a downward trend in self-confidence for reasons which have been discussed previously (4).

The most mature stage of ego development is the emergence of the "Self-Other" concept described by G. H. Mead (27). When a person is able to view himself as others view him, he can understand how others behave and how his own behavior may affect them. He becomes capable of transposing himself into the psychological frame of reference of another so that the other person's thinking, feeling, and acting are predictable. This process, termed empathy, greatly enhances his capacity for social behavior. By becoming sensitive to the ego-building processes of other people, he can relate to others in an outgoing manner instead of using them to build his own ego. As a result, he becomes a warm, friendly, understanding person to whom people are attracted (15).

Aspects of the Self Concept. As the psychoanalytic theory of the self embraced the id, ego, and superego, so the genetic theory includes three aspects of the self, called the self-image, the self-ideal, and the self-role. These aspects of the self operate at both conscious and unconscious levels and have different influences on the behavior of the individual.

THE SELF-IMAGE. This is the core of the self concept, the conscious appraisal of oneself. It includes the individual's basic perceptions of what the world is like, and of his own abilities and deficiencies. The self-image is a person's picture of himself, his feelings of adequacy or inadequacy, and how he thinks others look upon him. Some authorities distinguish between the real self and the self-image by describing the self as what you are, and the self-image as what you think you are (18, 39).

An essential factor in the creation of the self-image is one's body image or the perception of the physical self. The child who has physical handicaps, such as impaired vision or hearing, malformation or loss of limbs, speech impediments, and the like is prone to undervalue himself and develop feelings of inferiority and unworthiness. At the supersensitive stage of adolescence, a physical defect which mars the youngster's appearance can become a source of acute sensitivity. In a youth society which places so much stress on physical attractiveness, almost any physical blemish can lead to negative feelings which are incorporated into the self-image (28). So, too, can the color of one's skin, or other physical features which make people different and subject them to rejection or discrimination. The body of a person is a primary channel of contact with the world, and any disturbance of the body image influences what the individual conceives himself to be (31, 48).

Another important factor in the creation of the self-image is the personal interactions which take place in the family. The self-concept is largely learned by emulation of the attitudes and behavior of those few people who are emotionally essential to the growing child. Attitudes toward the self begin to take form in terms of what the child sees reflected about himself by the people who are closest and most important to him. If their words and behavior teach him that he is competent and worthy, these feelings will become a central reference point in his self-image. If he grows up amidst criticism and rejection, or if he cannot live up to the expectations of his parents, he has little opportunity to develop a positive conception of himself. Each rebuff from the people upon whom he is emotionally dependent may add to the proof of his inadequacy and build his perceptions as an unworthy individual (32, 36).

Interpersonal experience outside the home is a third significant influence on the creation of the self-image. The child who can achieve academic success in school, or who has qualities which make him acceptable to his peers, grows up in an environment which is ego-strengthening. Conversely, the child who encounters failure and frustration in school carries a burden of unhappiness which cannot fail to affect his self-image. These experiences with the human and material environment in and out of school reflect back to the individual a picture of himself as a person.

THE SELF-IDEAL.   Each person has an image of himself as he perceives himself to be and another of what he would like to be. The latter is called the self-ideal. It is a composite of desires, aspirations, fantasies, and dreams, derived from a series of interactions with real and imaginary figures.

During his growing years, a child encounters various people whom he admires and after whom he wishes to pattern himself. First, there are his mother and father, then siblings, then a variety of nonfamily figures including other children, teachers, athletes, heroes, movie and television personalities, and fictional figures. Some aspects of the values, accomplishments, and behavior of these people are absorbed into the self-system of the individual and form a pattern of what he would like to be.

Up to this point the formation of the self-ideal parallels the psychoanalytic concept of the ego ideal. Genetic views of the self vary, however, in considering the development of the self-ideal as a continuing process which is not limited to childhood. Adults alter their self-ideals by adopting some of the behavior patterns of significant people with whom they associate. Husbands and wives take on characteristics of one another; friends adopt each other's mannerisms, modes of speaking, and attitudes, and workers emulate their supervisors or employers. A little bit of each person important to us rubs off and is incorporated into our personality structure. Since the self-ideal develops chiefly as a result of interaction with other people, the individual who encounters a large number of people who have a favorable influence upon him has an opportunity to develop a varied and flexible personality.

There are, however, some hazards involved in this process of self-development through identification. The person who identifies with others too easily may not establish his autonomy as a stable, self-directing individual. As Erich Fromm has said (11), when an individual feels too inadequate to set his own course in life, he may seek support from others. He finds his reward in the comfortable feeling of relatedness and dependence which is offered to him by conforming to a group. A person who gives up his individual self and becomes an automaton, identical with millions of other automatons around him, need not feel alone and anxious any more. However, when this happens, he is no longer a self-actualizing person but a conformist who does not dare rise above the crowd.

Another hazard in seeking personal enhancement through identification with others results from acquiring goals which are beyond one's capacity to achieve. If a person internalizes a self-ideal which his own limitations prevent him from realizing, his life may become a tension-filled round of striving for goals which are beyond his reach. The result of this pursuit is often failure, disappointment, and feelings of unworthiness. The self-ideal can serve a constructive purpose in personality development only when it is fashioned in relations to one's abilities, aptitudes, and temperament.

THE SELF-ROLE.   A person's sense of self-identity is influenced by the way other pople react to him as he performs the various roles into which he is cast. We all play many roles in life, and each role involves a different aspect of the self. One of the major tasks of self-development is to keep conflicting roles separate and yet integrate them into a stable pattern of self-identity.

A certain amount of role experimentation is necessary for the development of self-identity. We try on different personalities until we find a few that fit. This process begins with the young child who pretends to be mother or father, or various other imaginary figures, and who can shift from one role to another with ease. Later, as play roles give way to real-life roles, he begins to differentiate which roles provide him with the greatest satisfaction. There emerges a primary role in which he feels most comfortable or into which he is cast by circumstances, around which secondary, tertiary, and other roles are organized. This central-core role, together with the satellite roles which complement and support the central role, is a significant part of the self-identity of the individual (36).

The roles which we assume in life are an outcome of the reciprocal relationship of one's self-image, self-ideal, and personal experience. We identify with the roles we play, sometimes so closely that we may go to pieces when the role is lost. This partially accounts for the personality changes which occur when a person loses his job or his prestige, or when his fortunes change so that he no longer has the status which is important to him. To attain a well-integrated self-concept, we must have an acceptable self-image, a reasonable self-ideal, and a role which enables us to function with satisfaction in the social world (35:16).

SELF CONCEPT AND BEHAVIOR

One of the significant motivating forces in human behavior is the need to preserve the integrity of the self concept. Good or bad, weak or strong, it is this inner sense of self which imposes meaning and order in our lives, and each of us struggles to maintain it.

This struggle becomes more and more acute as an experience approaches the sensitive inner core of the self. We might conceive of our sense of self as having several layers: an outer, relatively impersonal layer, a sensitive stratum below this, and a very sensitive nucleus. Experiences which affect only the outer layer of the self can be handled quite objectively. Those which approach the inner core of personality evoke more emotionalism and anxiety in behavior. As an illustration, a spectator at a football game can discuss the contest impersonally and has no need to become emotional or defensive about it. A player in the game, particularly if he is in a key role, has more difficulty being objective. His ego is involved on a more sensitive level than the spectator's, and he reacts more defensively. As experience strikes closer to the inner core of the self, an individual is more likely to react emotionally because his first concern is to protect his basic ego structure.

Self-Acceptance and Anxiety

Our capacity for developing self-insight and for reacting realistically to experiences seems to be affected by the level of self-acceptance we attain. The person who has a positive self-concept and a strong sense of self-acceptance is not afraid to admit his weaknesses or to incur the disapproval of others. He does not waste his energies protecting himself, hence has more energy available for creative purposes and for social interaction. In contrast, the person with a less confident ego tends to be more inhibited and defensive. He has difficulty facing facts about himself and hesitates to become involved in experiences where failure is possible.

This relationship between self-acceptance, self-insight, and behavior has been studied rather extensively. The reports by Perry (33), Taylor and Combs (44), Mitchell (29), and Klausmeier (23:306) illustrate the general findings of such studies. Perry compared the ability of two groups of fourth-grade children to accept derogatory statements about themselves. One group consisted of well-adjusted youngsters with adequate self-concepts; the other was a group of maladjusted children with a variety of emotional problems. Each group was given a list of statements describing undesirable feelings and actions and asked to check those which they thought described themselves. The adjusted children applied 205 of these derogatory statements to themselves; the maladjusted group accepted only 149. In other words, children who had a high degree of self-acceptance were more critical of themselves, or perhaps, could admit that they had undesirable characteristics without feeling that their self-identity was being undermined.

Taylor and Combs secured substantially the same results with sixth-grade children. They found that children who had adequate self-identity feelings were more able to face facts about themselves and admit to having common faults and weaknesses than children who had a low self-concept.

Studies of college students by Mitchell and Klausmeier showed that self-acceptance had much to do with feelings of competency and with the goals which students set for themselves in college courses. Students with a high degree of self-acceptance tended to set realistic goals for themselves and accepted their success, or lack of it, objectively. Insecure students who had a low concept started similar courses with unrealistically high expectations. Those who did not achieve the success they desired set up progressively lower goals and showed high levels of anxiety, as was to be expected. However, the students with low self-concepts who did achieve or surpass their goals did not enhance their sense of self-esteem. On the contrary, they remained anxious and continued to reflect feelings of incompetence.

These studies support the observation that a person in whom ego strength is at a high level is able to deal with the world objectively. He is open to new experiences and does not develop unmanageable anxiety when exposed to ego-threatening experiences. The individual with a low level of self-acceptance is so involved in protecting his self-identity that he avoids experiences which would help him to develop his full potentialities because they represent too much of a hazard to him. Even when he succeeds, there is always the next experience and the possibility of failure, so anxiety and feelings of threat remain with him (19).

Self-Acceptance and Interpersonal Relations

Turning to another aspect of self-acceptance and behavior, let us examine how self-reference attitudes and feelings affect interpersonal relationships. We are inclined to respond to others in a manner which reflects how we regard ourselves. The self-assured person can be "other-directed" in his dealings with people, because he does not have to use them to satisfy his own needs or to build his own ego. He can give of himself, put others at ease, and contribute to their security by his own lack of anxiety and defensive reactions.

The person who has a low sense of self-acceptance faces quite a different set of forces in his interactions with other people. He has less of himself to give and tends to be egocentric and self-gratifying in his interpersonal relations. He uses people to support his own ego drives and is unable to tolerate situations which do not help him maintain his self-importance. Often he may be an intolerant or prejudiced individual because he projects onto others aspects of himself with which he cannot live comfortably. By finding scapegoats who can be picked on, he builds his own sense of self-importance in an unrealistic and nonadaptive way (30).

An interesting comparison of the differences in attitudes and interpersonal interests of people who have a high sense of self-regard and those with a low sense of self-regard is described by Argyris (2), who studied the personality patterns of workers in a small manufacturing plant. He found distinct differences in life styles which were associated with the self-concepts of these workers. The highly skilled workers expressed a high sense of self-worth, they sought close friendships at work, wanted to work with others, sought variety and challenge in their work world, had personal pride in the quality of work produced, and participated in creative activities outside of work. In general, they presented a picture of expansive interpersonal relations based on a strong sense of self-confidence and a positive self-image.

Low-skilled workers had a correspondingly low sense of self-worth. They preferred to work alone on routine, nonchallenging jobs; they did not form close friendships with others, had no pride in the quality of their work, were not interested in learning other tasks, and participated in noncreative activities outside of work. In brief, a restricted self-concept resulted in a restricted field of personal and interpersonal behavior.

Other studies support the view that one's self-concept has much to do with setting up a psychological chain reaction which tends to accent the individual's social success or failure. The self-assured individual integrates well with other people and thus enhances his sense of security and self-identity. The person who has a low concept of himself avoids people, or displays such competitive, defensive, or dependent characteristics that people are repelled, thus depriving him of sustaining human relationships. Self-fulfillment is a product of human interaction. The ego grows not by always looking into itself but by the extension of self to others.

Self-Esteem and Adjustment

Most psychologists would agree that self-esteem is important to good adjustment. The person who thinks well of himself, and has reason to do so, possesses internal resources which are lacking among people who have feelings of inferiority or who undervalue themselves. The latter, it has been found, show a high incidence of psychosomatic disorders and anxiety symptoms (37).

The effects of low-esteem on adjustment is particularly apparent in some minority groups whom society has cast in inferior roles. Even young children in these groups internalize the role assigned by the culture and reflect attitudes of self-rejection which often lead to violation of social norms through aggressive behavior (43). The fact that such attitudes are more prevalent in some minority groups than in others has led investigators to study the dynamics of this process. One interesting study is reported by McCollum (26), who contrasted the ego development of Negro and Japanese children. He found that Japanese children, on the whole, had a strong identification with their race, culture, and family. As a result, they were able to withstand social prejudice and develop a high level of self-esteem which was reflected in good school achievement and social behavior. Negro children who came from home environments where there was family pride and cultural solidarity also achieved a high level of self-esteem and did well in school. However, Negro children who did not have a strong sense of identity with their race, culture, or family, displayed negative self-concepts. Their achievement in school was below their measured ability, suggesting that lack of success in school was due to a low level of confidence and motivation, rather than lack of intellectual capacity.

School achievement seems to be closely linked to self-esteem, regardless of whether a child is from a minority group. Studies of underachievement among capable children in the general population show a pattern of negative self-attitudes and feelings of rejection and isolation. With such children, remedial measures must include experiences which build the self-concept of the individual. More academic pressure, on the premise that the child is merely lazy, usually aggravates the negative feelings of self-identity which are present and results in more frustration (45).

These studies illustrate how the self-esteem of an individual pre-disposes him to react to his environment in a selective way. This is why manipulation of the external environment is seldom, in itself, an effective way to change a person's behavior.

CHANGES IN THE SELF

The self is never a finished product. As Gordon Allport (1) has said, it is always in a process of "becoming" and never completely stops changing. However, changes in the self-concept are never made easily, particularly after the early stages of childhood when the ego begins to take on a stable pattern. The individual unconsciously develops a set of habits and defense mechanisms which function to protect the ego and prevent any sweeping changes in personality. This is not to say that the self-concept is immutable, but it does mean that changes in the self are seldom made simply by deciding to make them (18).

Lasting changes in the ego structure can be accomplished through a series of experiences which lead to the developmental revision of habits, attitudes, and self-perceptions. Sometimes these experiences are undertaken deliberately by the individual with the intention of self-improvement; sometimes they are planned by teachers and parents, and others who wish to help. In some instances, experiences are thrust upon a person and lead to ego changes which he may not particularly want.

Some Processes of Change

A commonly used technique of self-improvement is that of trying to improve one's self-esteem by enhancing one's self-worth in the eyes of other people. This may be done through beauty aids, through one's manner of dress, through status symbols, or by joining the right groups. These efforts can result in real self-improvement if the individual really increases his capabilities, overcomes objectionable features in his behavior, or otherwise effects basic changes in his personality structure. Often, however, such efforts at self-improvement are limited to the superficial, external aspects of behavior and no real changes occur in the inner personality.

The difficulty with changing the self-concept on a "do-it-yourself" basis is that it is too deeply rooted in emotionally bound attitudes and defense mechanisms to yield easily to superficial measures. These attitudes and defense mechanisms are resistent to persuasion or to good intentions. The individual's defense system is so conceived that any stimulus which is contrary to its structure is treated as a foreign body and either sidetracked or modified to fit into its perceptual organization (22, 40).

Changes in the self-concept are more likely to occur when a skilled therapist or counselor assists the individual. This may be done by working on the attitudes, feelings, and behavior of people who have an influence on him. For example, many child guidance clinics concentrate their efforts on altering the behavior and attitudes of parents so that the home environment exerts a more positive force on the child's ego development. Modifying the school environment by placing a child in a group which will accept him is another illustration of this process. Group forces may make a child a bully or a scapegoat, a leader or an isolate. The group may reward rebellious or unruly behavior, or deny status to those who violate accepted standards.

Matching an individual to a group, or a group to an individual, is as important to adults as it is to children. The small groups with which a person is associated are instrumental in shaping his ego structure by either conferring or withholding the status and recognition that is important to him (38).

Planned group interaction is a technique often used by therapists and counselors to effect changes in the self-concept.

A small group of people having similar problems can find in each other a source of mutual support and derive the impetus needed to make alterations in their self-perceptions. Each member of the group uses the others as a sounding board to express and clarify his feelings, and they reflect back similar feelings so that he discovers that he is not the only one who has problems. By releasing his anxiety in a supportive environment, and in the presence of a person who can help him develop self-insight, the way is cleared for an individual to effect changes in his self-structure. Group psychotherapy is based on this principle of providing stimulation which will cause people to alter their behavior. The action of the group has been likened to that of a cyclotron where particles bounce against each other with cumulative force until all are involved in continuous change.

An illustration of this process is provided by Caplan (5), who followed the progress of some boys having adjustment problems in school. The boys met in small groups with a counselor to discuss their school problems. Once they were satisfied that the counselor could be trusted, they let go the violent and aggressive feelings they had been harboring, stimulating each other as they criticized the school, their teachers, parents, and member of the group. Then they settled down to looking at their personal problems. Over a period of time, definite improvement was noted in the boys' concepts of themselves as worthwhile individuals. Through group interaction they had expressed the emotions which were preventing them from utilizing their full capacities and were motivated to modify their attitudes toward themselves and toward others.

Self-Improvement

We have mentioned previously the difficulties which might be encountered when an individual tries to improve his self-concept on his own. Yet, this can be done if he is capable of facing himself and has the determination to pursue a planned course of self-improvement.

He must first assess his strengths and weaknesses to get a clear view of what he is and what he would like to become. This is the hardest part of the process for few people have the insight and capacity to view themselves in an objective, detached fashion. Too much of the self-structure is shrouded in defensive perceptions to be easily penetrated by introspection. It usually takes the assistance of people who can help him see himself as others see him. Often a wife, husband, relative, or minister can perform this service.

Once the individual has made an assessment of his problems and needs, he is faced with the necessity of planning a series of experiences which could conceivably contribute to the revision of his attitudes and behavior. This may involve joining groups and becoming active in social or intellectual affairs; changing his appearance, voice, or mannerisms; developing new skills and abilities, or a variety of other activities. In any event, action is called for because the ego cannot be changed simply by wishing it to happen.

At this point, a word of caution must be interjected. A person must be wary of forcing himself into experiences for which he is unsuited and which can only lead to further frustration or discouragement. Also, he must have the patience to accept a series of small changes which are undramatic but which may ultimately lead to the desired goals. Obviously, the processes of self-improvement will take time, just as it took time to build the ego structure in the first place. Self-improvement is a difficult process, but it is not beyond the capacity of the individual who seeks to know himself and who has patience, determination, foresight, and some helpful assistance from others.

Involuntary Changes in the Self

Some extensive changes may occur in the self-structure of an individual as a result of stresses, strains, and upheavals beyond his voluntary control. The most obvious illustration of such changes are those that result from the action of alcohol, narcotics, stimulants, and depressants which desensitize the ego and cause it to lose its control over the rational aspects of behavior.

Psychological forces may produce analogous changes in the

ego. Dissociation is one such phenomenon wherein alterations in one's sense of identity occur as a result of environmental circumstances. The person undergoing such an experience may feel like a spectator in the midst of something which seems to be happening to him as an object rather than a person. His ego. appears to split into one part which is having the experience and another watching it, so that he becomes a detached observer of himself. This has been interpreted as a psychological defense system used by people who are trying to avoid intense inner conflict. Sometimes such a person even rejects himself and prefers to live with his idealized self rather than his real self. Such alienation or estrangement from the self is characteristic of many neurotic patients (46).

Dissociation reactions have also been reported by prostitutes who mentally separate their real selves from their bodies and have an apparent lack of anxiety and emotion over their acts. Aviators sometimes experience a feeling of dissociation when flying at high altitudes, describing a floating sensation where they seem to be looking at themselves and the world below in a detached, impersonal way. Prisoners of war have experienced similar sensations when subjected to torture or when watching others being tortured. They report an absence of feeling of self, an inner emptiness, strong sensations of discouragement and no incentive to work, play, cry, or relate to others (41:386).

More familiar illustrations of the phenomenon of dissociation may be seen in the "it-can't-happen-to-me" attitude commonly found among people involved in accidents. This is a protective psychological device which enables a person to exclude from consideration the possibility that a disaster may affect him. Many automobile drivers who violate safety rules display such an attitude, as do aircraft pilots, divers, and others engaged in dangerous work. Without it, no one would dare venture into activities which involve any sort of hazard.

The ego may not only dissociate but, under certain conditions, may seem to merge with other things or people so that a person ceases to function as an independent individual. This may be seen among lovers who lose themselves in one another. Or a person may become so absorbed in his work that he forgets himself completely. Individuals may merge themselves with groups, movements, or missions which leave them with no thoughts or life of their own. Usually the absorption of the ego into another person or activity is a temporary affair, and the individual's self-identity is restored with the passage of time. However, under some conditions of extreme stress, the ego may relinquish its control over behavior to the extent that irreversible breakdown of the self-structure occurs (20). This is a characteristic of some of the psychoses which we shall discuss in a later chapter.

Thus, the ego is both a stable aspect of the personality which is resistant to change, and a fragile structure which can break down, dissociate, or lose its control over conscious behavior. The ability of the individual to develop a self-structure which brings the inner and outer worlds into a harmonious functioning relationship, and to maintain the integrity of this relationship, is a significant index of adjustment.

SUMMARY

The self concept consists of the perceptions, attitudes, feelings and values which characterize the "I" or "me" aspects of personality. It is through this self concept that the individual views himself and his relationships with the external world.

Two theories of the emergence of the self concept have been described. The psychoanalytic theory emphasizes the unconscious interplay of three psychic forces—the id, ego, and superego—the final balance of which produces the inner personality. The genetic theory of self-development stresses growth, maturation, and experience, through which the self-image, self-ideal, and self-role evolve. Both theories seem to merge into a practical agreement that the ego or self-concept begins to form in infancy, expands during childhood, is reformed in adolescence, and assumes a relatively stable form during postadolescence.

The individual is motivated to defend his self-concept, since it is the very essence of his personal identification. People who have succeeded in building a healthy ego have less need to be defensive. They can view themselves with considerable objectivity and have sufficient self-esteem to face failure or frustration without developing unmanageable anxiety. Those who have a low self-concept tend to be highly protective of their sense of self-identity and seek ego-building experiences and security rather than venture into situations where failure is possible.

The self is never a finished product; neither is it readily amenable to change. Efforts at self-improvement are difficult because attitudes, emotions, and habits beyond voluntary control form a protective structure which resists change in the ego. The aid of therapists or counselors, and involvement in group activities, are more likely to effect significant changes in the ego structure.

Sometimes ego changes occur despite the will of the individual. Dissociation, merging of the ego with another person or with a group or activity, and breakdown of the ego are some aspects of this process which will be described more fully in a later chapter.

REFERENCES

1. Allport, G. W., *Becoming: Basic Considerations for a Psychology of Personality,* Yale, 1955.
2. Argyris, C., "Individual Actualization in Complex Organizations," *Ment. Hyg.,* April, 1960, 44:226–237.
3. Bellak, L., "Toward a Unified Concept of Schizophrenia," *J. nerv. & ment. Dis.,* January, 1955, **121**:60–66.
4. Bloom, K. L., *Some Relationships Between Age and Self-Perception,* Unpublished Doctoral Dissertation, Columbia University, 1960.
5. Caplan, S. W., "The Effect of Group Counseling on Junior High School Boys' Concepts of Themselves in School," *J. consult. Psychol.,* 1957, 4:124–128.
6. Combs, A. E., "New Horizons in the Field of Research: The Self-Concept," *Educ. Leadership,* February, 1958, **15**:315–317.
7. Combs, A. W., and Snygg, D., *Individual Behavior,* Harper & Row, 1959.
8. Douvan, E., "Independence and Identity in Adolescence," *Child.,* September–October, 1957, 4:186–190.

9. Erikson, E. H., "Identity and the Life Cycle," *Selected Papers: Psychological Issues,* Vol. 1, International Universities Press, 1959, p. 171.

10. Erikson, E. H., "Youth and the Life Cycle," *Child.,* March–April, 1960, 7:43–49.

11. Fromm, E., "Values, Psychology, and Human Existence," in A. H. Maslow, (Ed.), *New Knowledge in Human Values,* Harper & Row, 1959, pp. 151–164.

12. Geleerd, E. R., "Some Aspects of Ego Vicissitudes in Adolescence," *J. Amer. Psychoanal. Ass.,* July, 1961, 9:344–405.

13. Gesell, A., and Ilg, F. L., *Child Development,* Harper & Row, 1949.

14. Grant, J. D., "Assessment and Evaluation of Delinquent Behavior," in E. M. Bower, (Ed.), *The Psychologist in the School, Bull. Calif. State Dep. Educ.,* Sacramento, August, 1958, 27:7–12.

15. Halpern, H. M., and Lesser, L. N., "Empathy in Infants, Adults and Psychotherapists," *Psychoanal. & psychoanal. Rev.,* Fall, 1960, 47:32–42.

16. Hartmann, H., *Ego Psychology and the Problem of Adaptation,* International Universities Press, 1958.

17. Havighurst, R. J., "Today's Children and Tomorrow's World," *Childh. Educ.,* April, 1961, 37:356–360.

18. Hayakawa, S. J., "Conditions of Success in Communication," *Bull. Menninger Clin.,* September, 1962, 26:225–236.

19. Holmes, C. C., *An Examination of Goal-Directed Behavior in Terms of Level of Aspiration,* Unpublished Masters Thesis, University of Wisconsin, 1959.

20. Horney, K., *Neurosis and Human Growth,* Norton, 1950.

21. Kagan, J., and Moss, H. A., "The Stability of Passive and Dependent Behavior from Childhood Through Adulthood," *Child Develpm.,* September, 1960, 31:577–591.

22. Katz, D., et al., "The Measurement of Ego Defense as Related to Attitude Change," *J. Pers.,* June, 1957, 25:465–474.

23. Klausmeier, H. J., *Learning and Human Abilities,* Harper & Row, 1961.

24. McCollum, J. A., "Improvement of Achievement and Attitudes of Minority Group Children," *Calif. Elem. Administrator,* May, 1961, 24:4, 8.

25. Mahler, M. S., and Furer, M., "Observations on Research Regarding the 'Symbiotic Syndrome' of Infantile Psychosis," *Psychoanal. Quart.,* July, 1960, 29:317–327.

26. Maslow, A. H., "Creativity in Self-Actualizing People," in Anderson, H. H., (Ed.), *Creativity and Its Cultivation*, Harper & Row, 1959, pp. 83–95.

27. Mead, G. H., *Mind, Self, and Society*, University of Chicago Press, 1934.

28. Mendelson, M., *et al.*, "Obesity in Men: A Clinical Study of Twenty-five Cases," *Ann. int. Med.*, April, 1961, 54:660–671.

29. Mitchell, J. V., Jr., "Goal Setting Behavior as a Function of Self-Acceptance, Over- and Under-Achievement, and Related Personality Variables," *J. educ. Psychol.*, 1959, **50**:93–104.

30. Money-Kyrle, R. E., "On Prejudice—A Psychoanalytical Approach," *Brit. J. med. Psychol.*, 1960, **33**:205–209.

31. Moore, M. E., *et al.*, "Obesity, Social Class, and Mental Illness," *J. Amer. Med. Ass.*, September 15, 1962, **181**:962–966.

32. Peck, R. F., *et al.*, *The Psychology of Character Development*, John Wiley & Sons, 1960.

33. Perry, D. C., *Self-Acceptance in Relation to Adjustment*, Unpublished Doctoral Dissertation, University of Florida, 1961.

34. Rogers, C. R., "A Theory of Therapy, Personality, and Interpersonal Relationships, as Developed in the Client-Centered Framework," in Koch, S., (Ed.), *Psychology: A Study of a Science, 3: Formulations of the Person and the Social Context*, McGraw-Hill, 1959, pp. 184–256.

35. Rogers, C. R., *Becoming a Person*, The Hogg Foundation for Mental Hygiene, University of Texas, 1958.

36. Rohrer, J. H., and Edmonson, M. S. (Eds.), *The Eighth Generation*, Harper & Row, 1960.

37. Rosenberg, M., "The Association Between Self-Esteem and Anxiety," *J. psychiat. Res.*, September, 1962, **1**:135–152.

38. Rossberg, R., and Jaques, M., "The Role of the Group in Patient Evaluation, Counseling, and Management," *Personnel & Guidance J.*, October, 1961, **40**:135–142.

39. Rubins, J. L., "The Self-Concept, Identity, and Alienation From Self," *Amer. J. Psychoanal.*, 1961, **21**:132–143.

40. Schlesinger, L., "Why Do We Feel As We Do?", *Adult Leadership*, February, 1957, **5**:242–243.

41. Sherif, M., and Cantril, H., *The Psychology of Ego-Involvements*, Wiley, 1947.

42. Spiegel, L. A., "The Self, the Sense of Self, and Perception," in Eissler, R. S., *et al.* (Eds.), *Psychoanalytic Study of the Child*, International Universities Press, 1959, 81–109.

43. Stevenson, H. W., and Steward, E. C., "Developmental Study

of Racial Awareness in Young Children," *Child Develpm.*, September, 1958, **29**:399–409.

44. Taylor, C., and Combs, A. W., "Self-Acceptance and Adjustments," *J. abnor. soc. Psychol.*, 1952, **16**:89–91.

45. Walsh, A. M., *Self-Concepts of Bright Boys With Learning Difficulties,* Teachers College, 1956.

46. Weiss, F. A., "Self-Alienation: Dynamics and Therapy," *American J. Psychoanal.*, 1961, **21**:207–218.

47. Wittenberg, R. M., *Adolescence and Discipline,* Association Press, 1959.

48. Wright, B. A., *Physical Disability—A Psychological Approach,* Harper & Row, 1960.

49. Zander, A., "Resistance to Change—Its Analysis and Prevention," *Advanced Mgmt.*, January, 1950, **15**:9–12.

Chapter 7　Emotional
Development

Physical growth and development fellow a basic genetic plan, set up at conception, which determines the broad outlines of what the body will be like at maturity. Emotional development is less subject to this genetic plan. Like the growth of the self-concept, emotional maturity is influenced not only by physical factors but by a variety of other conditions and events. A person must acquire emotional maturity; it is not a simple consequence of growth. He must strive for it, and through this striving gradually develop the understanding, experience, and techniques for utilizing his emotions in normal, wholesome ways.

NATURE OF EMOTIONS

Emotions are manifested through both external and internal changes in behavior. Externally, a person undergoing an excited emotional state, such as rage or fear, exhibits a general body posture which prepares him for emergency action. His head may be thrust forward, fists clenched, abdomen contracted, and knees slightly bent, all preparing him for a fight or flight reaction. Or, at the other extreme, a person undergoing emotions of grief, sorrow, or depression will present an appearance of reduced body tension. Muscle tonus is lowered, a vacant, slack look is seen in his face, there is lack of timbre and inflection in the voice, and perhaps a pallor or clamminess to the skin.

Between these extremes of emotionality are various lesser

emotions which are not reflected so dramatically in outward behavior. The processes of self-control or inhibition moderate external behavior, so that a person may experience considerable internal upset and still manage to maintain an outward appearance of normalcy, The effects of such inhibition on the total functioning of an individual can best be understood by examining the extent of physiological changes which occur during an emotional state.

Physiological Aspects of Emotion

Emotions involve widespread changes in physiological functioning. When a person is in an excited emotional state, the adrenal glands are stimulated to release an oversupply of adrenalin into the blood stream; this acts as a stimulant, increasing heart rate and respiration, causing the liver to release more sugar into the blood, and increasing metabolism so that more energy is made available for use. Blood pressure increases, more blood is supplied to the muscles and brain, and, in general, the entire body is mobilized for violent and prolonged activity. As a consequence, the angry or frightened person can hit harder, run farther, lift heavier weights, or climb a tree faster than one who is emotionally calm. However, skilled movements are likely to be impaired by strong emotion. Fear or panic may produce incoordination or muscular clumsiness since the body is geared to gross muscular action rather than to discriminating or delicate movement (11).

In depressed emotional states, organic activity is reduced, metabolism decreases, and the individual finds it difficult to act with his usual speed or strength. This reduced physiological activity leaves him with less than his normal degree of muscular tone, physical energy, alertness, and responsiveness. He must literally force himself to act, and then is likely to find that he cannot perform as adequately as usual. Depressive emotional states are among the least desirable of the emotions from an adjustment viewpoint, because they consume a great deal of the individual's energy, leaving him with little to direct toward solving his problems (30).

Emotions and Mental Activity

The over-all effects of an aroused emotional state is to prepare the body for physical rather than mental activity. When upset emotionally, a person may not "see straight" or "think straight." His perceptions are narrowed and his attention concentrated on the danger facing him, to the extent that other factors in the environment are ignored. He may not even notice that he has been hurt until after the crisis is over and his emotions have subsided somewhat. Many deaths which occur when fires break out in crowded places are due to vain attempts to escape through blocked exits while other clear escape routes are unnoticed.

This narrowing and concentrating of attention mobilizes energy in a specific direction, making it difficult for others to control the behavior of one who is in a state of rage or panic. The child who is "fighting mad" and bent on aggression toward another child is not easily dissuaded from his target by words or entreaties. Something dramatic, such as physical force, may be needed to shift his attention and modify his behavior.

As might be expected, the restricted field of perception and attention which accompanies strong emotion has an effect on learning. The cerebral cortex of the brain may function ineffectively during a state of heightened emotion so that it is difficult for a person to learn, think, or reason. Any learning that does take place may occur within the lower brain centers. This learning is highly specific and results in rigid, stereotyped, and nonadjustive behavior. Learning acquired under emotional stress may cause the individual to react ineffectively because he is not adaptable to changed conditions. He may respond with a habitual action which may not be suited to the occasion and thus intensify the stress experience. Frequently, he is confused and afterwards may not be able to recall the details of his experience (29:94).

While intense emotion may interfere with perception and mental activity, moderate emotion has quite a different effect. A moderate level of emotion makes us alert; we think more clearly, react more efficiently, and are motivated to higher levels of accomplishment. This has been illustrated in studies of the effects of competition on learning. Kagan (15), for instance, has shown that, when competition induces a mild level of emotional energy, boys and girls are stimulated to higher levels of academic achievement, while passive children display less motivation to achieve, less curiosity, and less mastery of academic materials. When emotional energy is controlled, it increases our efficiency and performance, but uncontrolled it mobilizes a person for a particular type of activity and makes him less efficient in other areas of behavior.

Emotions and Awareness

Emotions involve more than physiological change. They are accompanied by a variety of feelings—hope, fear, anger, joy, or some other conscious experience. The emotional experience may originate either in an organic change which can give rise to these feelings, or in feelings which can give rise to an organic change. In everyday experience it seems highly probable that both rather than just one of these mechanisms operate. In some situations we are immediately aware of a danger and react emotionally in terms of this awareness. In other cases the first realization we have of being emotionally involved in a situation may come as a result of realizing we are under physical tension—observing, for example, that our fists are clenched, or the hands are cold and clammy, or that we are smoking excessively, or fidgeting with something.

Unconscious processes also have a great deal to do with the arousal of emotional behavior. Very often we cannot explain why we are feeling frightened or depressed, or in unusually good humor. This is because many of our anxieties, worries, fears, forebodings, or sensations of pleasure are induced by stimuli which are so faint that we are completely unaware of them. Often these stimuli are thoughts, associations, suggestions, or distressing experiences which have been deeply buried within us but which have an emotional force that resists being submerged. In unguarded moments they push into consciousness, create emotional reactions, and have to be suppressed again. All of this takes effort and energy which is a drain on a person's vital capacity. Many accidents are said to be caused by bottled-up emotions which arise unconsciously and distract a person to a point where his coordination and reaction time are reduced and he is unable to evaluate a hazardous situation in time to avoid getting hurt (29:46).

Involuntary Nature of Emotional Reactions

A further complication in the development of emotional control is the involuntary nature of the physiological changes underlying the emotions. The sympathetic division of the autonomic nervous system directs those internal processes which are associated with emotion. This is the automatic segment of our nervous system which consists of a group of nerve cells strung along the spinal cord, with nerve fibers running to both the brain and to essential body organs. They control the heartbeat, blood pressure, digestive processes, gastrointestinal movements, respiration, body temperature, and other physiological processes. Once activated, these processes cannot be regulated by conscious efforts, because the autonomic nervous system is essentially under the direction of the deeper areas of the brain, particularly the thalamus and hypothalamus, which cannot be willed into action. We can no more control the physiological components of emotion than we can control the beat of our hearts (23, 29:91).

This fact is of tremendous significance from the point of view of adjustment. The sympathetic division of the nervous system is slow to act but, once aroused, is persistent, and physiological processes continue long after the external stimulus has been removed. Hence, a person can be persuaded to control his behavior in response to emotion, but once an emotional reaction is started, its physiological aspects must run their course before body equilibrium can be re-established. We shall return to this subject when we consider the process of developing emotional control and emotional maturity.

Feelings and Moods

So far we have been discussing the strong emotions, those which produce rather dramatic effects on behavior. Equally important are the less disruptive but more persistent affective states, such as feelings and moods, attitudes and prejudices. These vary only in degree from the more intense emotions. They, too, are accompanied by disturbances of physiological functioning which, while less widespread or striking in their effects, have many of the characteristics of emotions. Annoyance or irritation, for example, are feelings which induce some muscular tension and some alteration of glandular function. Similarly, a feeling of discouragement differs only in degree from the state of depression described earlier, both being emotions which involve a reduction in the energy level of the individual.

When feelings persist in active form over a long period of time, we refer to them as moods. The quality, frequency, intensity, and duration of moods have a significant influence upon personal effectiveness. Positive moods, such as happiness or hopefulness, tend to increase work efficiency and productiveness, while negative moods, such as worry or apprehension, have an opposite effect. Often, moods are the residue of a more intense emotional experience. A highly pleasurable experience which results in excitement and intense satisfaction usually lasts a very short time. However, it may be followed by a sense of buoyancy which persists for several days and influences one's outlook long after the emotional experience has subsided. A great deal of behavior is influenced by how we feel about things, or the mood we are in. While these mild affective states do not produce marked physical reactions, they have much to do with our attitudes, values, goals, and personal and interpersonal behavior.

Attitudes and Prejudice

Attitudes are tendencies or dispositions to act in characteristic ways in certain situations. Attitudes may be acquired through careful study, analysis of facts, and thoughtful decisions. But more often, they are emotional predispositions to react toward a person, idea, or object with little regard for the realities of the situation. For example, a person who holds a positive attitude toward a certain political party is not open to logical argument. He is likely to accept the facts and beliefs which support his attitude and reject those which do not. He may even distort the facts to fit his preconceptions or actively resist the intrusion of knowledge upon his fixed ideas.

Prejudice of emotional origin merits special consideration because of its extensive influence on personal and social behavior. It predisposes an individual to pass judgment on others in terms of his personal preconceptions, rather than on the basis of fact or reason, and has far-reaching effects on both the persons who practice it and those who are its victims. Prejudice interferes with ego development by distorting the perceptions of an individual and providing him with a means of projecting his own inadequacies on others. It is also detrimental to the development of emotional maturity, because it leads to immature judgments and actions, aggressive and compulsive behavior, hostility, egocentricism, and negative reactions toward people and things which do not fit into the prejudiced person's frame of reference (2, 21).

A number of experiments have demonstrated how a person's biases may impose his own meanings on a situation. For example, Cantril (5) has summarized experiments with a stereoscope which held two different pictures, one seen with the right eye and one with the left. When Zulus in South Africa were presented with pictures of white or colored persons paired with Indians, they saw an overwhelming preponderance of Indians, who represent a threat to them. Mexicans presented with pictures of a bullfighter and a baseball player usually saw the bullfighter, while Americans presented with the same pictures usually saw the ball player. Each person gave meaning to these pictures in terms of his own emotional orientation.

In another study, children in the sixth, seventh, and eighth grades were divided into two groups, one of which was characterized by prejudiced and authoritarian attitudes, the other by unprejudiced and democratic attitudes. The same story was read to both groups. It dealt with how pupils in a certain school reacted to newcomers to their neighborhood, one of whom was a Negro. There was also mention of a fight, although it was only an incidental event in the story. After a short interval the children were asked to reproduce the story. The prejudiced children tended to recall a higher ratio of undesirable qualities of the newcomers, with particular reference to the Negro child and with the fight as the central part of the story. Only a small proportion of the unprejudiced children did this. They managed to keep fairly well to the facts in remembering the story, in contrast with the prejudiced children who distorted the story to conform to their own attitudes (10).

Prejudice makes its appearance at an early age and is widespread in our society. Schools, it seems, are not particularly influential in substituting rational thinking for emotional thinking. According to a study by McNeil (19), prejudiced students become more negative in their attitudes as they go through school. Twelfth-graders were found to have more than twice as many prejudices against racial and religious groups than they held when they were tenth-graders.

Children learn their prejudices from adults and older children with whom they come in contact. This learning is conveyed through inadvertent example as well as through deliberate teaching. As Klein (17:489) points out, prejudice is so widespread in our social structure that it is difficult for a child to elude its influence. So imperceptible is this cultural patterning that the person who harbors prejudices fails to accept them as such and acts as if they were really true, particularly when his own perceptions are reinforced by the groups to which he belongs. Thus, many people never question widespread beliefs which have no foundation in fact. Klein offers as an illustration the following statements:

Frenchmen are sexually more immoral than Americans.
A Catholic cannot be a good American because, when it comes to a showdown, he will obey the Pope rather than the President.
All Negroes are promiscuous.
Jews are notorious international bankers.
Most Jews are capitalists.
Most Jews are Communists.
Scotchmen are stingier than Americans.
Relatively more crimes are committed by foreigners than by native-born Americans.
Atheists are not governed by allegiance to any code of ethics.
All Orientals are deceitful, cunning, and unscrupulous.

Men can reason better than women.

Blondes are more fickle than brunettes.

Americans have a better sense of humor than Englishmen.

Members of the white race are born with better brains than members of any other race, particularly the black race (17:491).

Although not one of these statements is true, thousands of people believe them and react emotionally toward the groups involved. We can conclude that prejudice warps the mental and emotional reactions of people, predisposes them to act with hostility toward others, and interferes with their growth toward emotional maturity.

Emotions and Physical Disorder

A variety of bodily disturbances can be produced by emotional energy which is not discharged through expressive behavior. Many people who cannot find acceptable means of expressing or draining off emotional energy figuratively "swallow their emotions." This internalized emotionality can originate, perpetuate, or intensify physical ailments. So extensive are the organic disturbances associated with emotions that, according to estimates, at least half of the people who consult a private physican for physical illness have no organic pathology. They have physical symptoms but no detectable physical causes for these symptoms (20). The terms "psychosomatic" or "psychophysiological" are used to designate ailments of this type.

Among the long list of psychophysiological ailments which are associated with emotional disturbance are disorders of the gastrointestinal system, such as spastic or mucuous colitis, heartburn, indigestion, and peptic ulcer; disturbances of the circulatory system, including heart palpitations and high blood pressure; genitourinary ailments, such as enuresis; disorders of the reproductive system, such as menstrual difficulties and impotence, and skin ailments, such as eczema, itching, or scaling (12).

Another category of emotionally-induced ailments are the psychogenic disorders. These are disorders of psychological origin which involve no physical alteration or change in body organs. The symptoms may be similar to those of psychophysiological nature, but there is no bodily damage. Nervous fatigue, insomnia, combat hysteria, and pain in various muscles or organs are examples of this type of ailment.

Psychophysiological and psychogenic ailments may have great psychological utility for a person. They give him something tangible to focus upon. It has been found that many people actually resist recovering from physical symptoms and continue to complain of physical discomfort long after their organic ailments have been corrected. By fixing their subjective discomfort on these symptoms they avoid the necessity of having to face their emotional problems, which usually are much more difficult to correct than the physical problems which accompany them (13). This phenomenon is referred to as secondary gain. Although we often regard with suspicion people who seem to be counterfeiting physical symptoms to deceive themselves and others, they are usually doing it without conscious intent in an effort to cope with stress which they can handle in no other way at that particular time.

DIFFERENTIATION OF EMOTIONAL BEHAVIOR

Having described some of the characteristics of emotions, we turn now to the process of emotional growth. As we look at the behavior of an infant, we do not see the variety of emotional reactions which are present in an older child or adult. The immature organism is governed by the principle of mass activity. Due to the incomplete organization of his nervous and muscular systems, when he reacts, he reacts all over; his whole body responds to stimulation, and his reactions are not directed toward a particular goal but are merely expressive of a state of comfort or discomfort (3).

As he grows into childhood and adulthood, differentiation takes place in the emotional behavior of the infant. In place of the all-or-none reaction he will develop a variety of emotions and many shades of feeling, attitudes and moods. He will need to become selective in his emotional response and learn not to react to every stimulus which impinges upon him. He will have to inhibit his emotional expression, develop adequate ways of dealing with his emotions, and bring his emotional behavior into some sort of reasonable consonance with the needs and demands of society.

Selectivity and Delay in Emotional Response

As he matures, the child normally becomes more selective in his reactions to emotional stimuli. Things which once caused him to react emotionally no longer arouse him, either because he has learned adequate ways of dealing with them or because of a change of interest. Commonly, familiarity with a situation removes its emotion-inducing qualities. Hence, a dog which once caused the child to cry and cling to his mother becomes an accepted part of his environment with which he can feel comfortable.

As this process of differentiation goes on, the milder emotional states with their graded, specific, and direct responses become more prominent in the life of the child. More specific and selective interests begin to replace the early generalized interest which the young child indiscriminately displayed in almost every phase of his environment. He becomes increasingly capable of discriminating among the persons, objects, and situations within the range of his perceptions. He is able to evaluate situations and fit his response to them, and to revise his expectations in terms of the situation rather than demand that everything be suited to his requirements. One of the most difficult lessons he must learn is to develop an increasing capacity to withstand delay in the satisfaction of his needs and desires. He must learn to accept the inevitable frustrations of living without being completely upset by them. These things he will normally learn if guided by patient, understanding adults, and if given the opportunity to interact with other children who are learning the same lessons and need to try them on each other.

Control and Expression of Emotion

The expression of emotion is more and more subject to social expectation as the child grows toward maturity. With each stage of development he is expected to gain increasing control over his emotional behavior. It is not enough to find ways of expressing or draining off excess emotional energy; the ways found must be socially acceptable or at least not harmful to others. Failure to abide by these expectations can result in social rejection or social isolation.

To avoid social pressures, an individual learns to adjust his emotional responses to suit the requirements of the situation in which he finds himself. This demands considerable flexibility and social sensitivity, since there is much variation in the social expectations of different groups. For one thing, the closeness of the group has much to do with the forms of expression permitted. More latitude is allowed to emotional expression when we are at home with our families or when we are with a few intimate friends than when we are among strangers or in a more formal social atmosphere. The customs and mores of the social group also have a strong influence on the behavior of the individual. In the lower socio-economic groups, physical and verbal aggression are common and accepted ways of expressing emotion. Similar behavior in the middle and upper classes is likely to be met with severe disapproval. This is one of the troublesome areas of conflict between lower-class children and teachers who try to maintain middle-class standards of behavior in school.

Another factor which influences social expectations is the level of education a person has attained or the professional status he holds. It may be just as illegal for a truck driver to express his anger against another motorist by hitting him on the nose as it is for a professor to do so. But society is less lenient with the professor. As people move up the social scale, they are expected to restrain or inhibit the direct physical expression of emotion. Social sanctions are imposed upon them to temper and revise their emotional responses and to resort more often to verbal and symbolic forms of expression.

It is quite impossible to avoid entirely circumstances which induce emotional reactions. Therefore, it is important to develop channels of acceptable emotional expression which provide relief and make us less susceptible to emotional outbreaks. Some people do this through golf, gardening, swimming, or other forms of physical activity. Some escape from stressful situations by relaxing with a book or viewing television or movies. Others find relief in talking things out with someone, so that their emotions are brought out into the open where their energy can be discharged. While these are substitute forms of emotional expression which do not eliminate the stimuli that evoked them, they are nonetheless adjustive, because they enable a person to regain his physiological equilibrium so that he can later concentrate on finding a constructive solution to his problems. We simply cannot vent our anger on the boss who is causing us to be emotionally upset, because there is the risk of being fired. Nor is it wise to let out this emotion on our family or on other innocent victims. Therefore, hitting a tennis or golf ball, taking a brisk walk, or yelling at a boxing match is often the best way to convert emotions into healthy outlets. When and how to inhibit or discharge emotions is a decision which each of us must make as we assume responsibility for our own behavior.

Emotional control is a necessary part of behavior, but it can be carried so far that it leads to consequences which are as undesirable as uninhibited emotional expression. Too much restraint on the emotions can produce a narrowing of interests, and a lack of spontaneity and initiative as well as the psychosomatic problems described earlier (9). People who overly restrict their expression of emotion are said to lack affect; that is, they are impassive, nothing seems to arouse them, and they lack the emotional vigor needed for healthful living. In extreme cases of emotional disturbance, the psychoses characterized by lack of affect are often more serious and more difficult to treat than those in which emotions are expressed outwardly in the form of hyperactive or manic behavior.

Fixation and Regression

Emotional development may be arrested by several factors which block growth toward emotional maturity, with the result that some aspects of behavior remain on a childish level.

One of these factors is the phenomenon of fixation. In emotional fixation a person does not outgrow some forms of childish behavior and continues to act in ways that are no longer appropriate to his level of development. We see this illustrated in the young bride who throws a temper tantrum when she does not get her own way, because this is how she influenced her parents as a child. The man or woman who never marries and remains devoted to an aging mother may likewise be displaying an immature level of emotional development. Such people fail to mature and remain bound to their childish impulses or dependency needs. This may come about as a result of parental over-protection or other influences which prevent a person from facing the responsibilities of growing up (14).

Another process which indicates immaturity in emotional development is that of regression. This involves the retreat to earlier forms of behavior in the face of frustration. The child who fails to adjust satisfactorily to the demands made upon him in school may revert to thumbsucking, a mode of consolation which perhaps suited an earlier phase of development but which at later ages is no longer acceptable. The adult whose composure breaks down under excessive stress may revert to infantile emotional outbursts; he may run away from life by becoming a chronic alcoholic, using narcotics, ducking from one job to another, or by overeating to the point that he becomes obese (22). Thousands of college freshmen drop out of school after the first few months of the fall term and return home to seek the emotional security of a protected environment. The common occurrence of regression indicates that in many people the mature patterns of behavior they display are often no more than a thin veneer spread over childish forms of adaptation which have not been out-grown (25).

EMOTIONAL MATURITY

How do we judge whether a person has successfully mastered the emotional problems of growing up and arrived at a state of emotional maturity? There is no general agreement on what constitutes emotional maturity. However, English and Pearson offer some reasonable criteria which illustrate the type of behavior that might be expected of a mature person:

1. Be able to work a reasonable amount each day at his job without undue fatigue or strain, and feel that his work is serving a useful purpose.

2. Be able to like, and accept many lasting friendships; and be able to love and be tender and affectionate with a few close friends.

3. Have such confidence in himself that he is not harassed by guilt, doubt, or indecision. He should have enough confidence in himself to be able to oppose impositions upon himself and his family.

4. Be as free of prejudice as possible and treat all men and women with appropriate respect.

5. Be able to give and receive love with joy in a conventional heterosexual way free of guilt or inhibition.

6. Extend his interest in an ever widening circle from self to family, friends, community, state, and nation, and seek to take a part in contributing to the general welfare of mankind.

7. Be interested in advancing his own welfare without exploitation of his fellow man.

8. Be able to alternate work with play, recreation, reading, and the enjoyment of nature, poetry, art, and music.

9. Be free of undue body strains, stresses and tensions when performing his everyday duties, as when confronted with adversity.

10. Be dependable, truthful, open-minded, and imbued with a philosophy that includes a willingness to suffer a little in order to grow, improve, and achieve wisdom.

11. Be interested in passing on his hard-won knowledge to the young (7:420).

Probably no one achieves this ideal of complete emotional maturity. Even well-adjusted adults are not equally mature in all aspects of their emotional behavior. They may be quite advanced and competent in dealing with some aspects of life but immature in others. We all have weak spots in which we are especially vulnerable and, when prodded in these sensitive areas, may do things which are not consistent with our usual pattern of behavior (1). Moreover, the mature person is not perfect; he is simply a person who has achieved emotional balance and stability. He can compromise when necessary, accept or disregard many minor irritations, and tolerate considerable anxiety or frustration. He is capable of facing his problems without incapacitating extremes of emotion, yet can express love, fear, anger, and other emotions when the situation calls for it. In short, emotional maturity implies emotional flexibility—the capacity to react emotionally when it is appropriate to do so, balanced with an ability to moderate behavior in response to the realities of a situation (16:291).

The Process of Emotional Expansion

Growth toward emotional maturity is a process which takes the individual from the narrow self-centeredness of infancy to the other-centeredness of maturity. This process follows a general developmental sequence which is dependent upon both maturation and learning. The typical infant is emotionally receptive; he can accept affection but has no way to bestow it. The young child can give affection to his parents as well as receive it and, normally, is emotionally dependent upon them. In later childhood the process of emotional emancipation begins, and children loosen their ties to parents. Their emotional attachments include others of their own age, and they become less self-centered in their behavior.

The adolescent's resistance to parental authority and his intense identification with his age group marks the crucial period of emotional emancipation. His peer group supports him in his exploration of the wider social world and shares his experiences. But he is not yet emotionally independent. His very fear of being considered different and his compulsive adherence to group customs and fads attest to his emotional dependence upon his age mates (14).

The mature person, having passed through these stages, achieves a level of emotional independence which leaves him free to assert his individuality. He understands and accepts his emotions and has learned to express them in ways that are both socially acceptable and personally satisfying. He no longer has the dependent need for absolute conformity to group codes and customs but is free to maintain a wide range of affectional attachments to others and to shift his attachments with some degree of facility. Thus, the course of emotional expansion takes the individual from the self-centeredness of infancy, to the emotional dependency of childhood, to the adolescent's emancipation from the family, and finally to the broader emotional interaction of the adult, where emotional independence is maintained while interaction with others is expanded.

Emotional Security

At each stage of development the individual needs assurance that his needs will be met either through his own efforts or through the ministrations of others. He needs to feel assured of love, approval, and emotional support when he needs it. With this emotional support he can develop a sense of self-reliance and a confidence in his own ability to manage the emotional problems of living. As his personal competencies develop, he can let go of his supports and form the expanded attachments to others which the process of emotional maturity requires.

This combination of emotional support and freedom is the foundation of emotional security. The emotionally secure person does not feel alone in the world, nor does he feel completely dependent upon others. He can look beyond himself and his own needs and establish rich human relationships which will be satisfying to himself and to others. He will be free to try new experiences, form new friendships, and move out into the expanding social world with zest and confidence.

The person who lacks emotional security is likely to see the world as a hostile environment to which he is exposed. He is in the position of a starving individual whose first concern in the presence of food is his own desperate need. He must satisfy his own emotional needs before he can be concerned with the requirements of other people. This type of behavior perpetuates his emotional insecurity. In centering upon himself, the emotionally deprived person alienates others. He becomes so preoccupied with building his emotional defenses that he loses sight of other rewarding and pleasurable aspects of life.

Our complex, urbanized, competitive society is said to be an important factor in producing emotional insecurity in modern man. It can hardly be denied that economic change, poverty, and threats of war or destruction are conditions which may contribute to feelings of helplessness and insecurity. With the disappearance of our rural forms of life, people have become less certain of themselves and their future, because so many choices and decisions confront them, and so many conditions of living are beyond their understanding or control. They are less stable, because there are more alternatives to choose from and more things to be stabilized before a feeling of emotional security can be achieved (26).

While these conditions may contribute to a general atmosphere which makes it more difficult to achieve emotional security, they do not call for pessimism. A person's emotional life is fashioned within the small intimate groups of which he is a part—his family, companions, school, neighborhood, or work world. Within these small groups it is possible to build emotional supports which contribute to personal security. This places an obligation upon those who have gone through this process to exercise patience, guidance, and understanding with young people, and to provide them with emotional supports when they are needed.

Fostering Emotional Growth

The greatest responsibilty for fostering emotional growth rests with parents and other adults who supervise the early development of children. By the time a child reaches a point in life where he is capable of assuming responsibility for his own actions, he will have built up a complex of attitudes, feelings, and reaction tendencies which in a large measure predetermine his behavior. Therefore, it is important that children be provided with the kind of environment that will encourage the development of a good foundation for emotional growth.

Love is an essential part of an environment which fosters growth toward emotional maturity, but more than love is needed (4). Emotional growth takes place when a child has experiences which help him develop insight into his own behavior and encourage him to take increasing responsibility for his actions. There has to be an atmosphere in the home and in the school permitting children to risk being themselves without fear and providing the emotional support they need to develop a sense of personal competency. The education of emotions is as much a responsibility of home and school as is the education of the mind. To appreciate the feelings of others, one must understand his own feelings. He must learn to recognize his fears, anxieties, sensitivities, and the defensive behavior he uses to express or disguise them. The more insight he has into his own behavior, the more he can realize the common problems he shares with others and develop a good working relationship with people (24).

That many people do not develop such understandings is revealed in the statistics on mental illness, crime, alcoholism, job failure, divorce, and other evidence of inadequate adjustment (20). Many of these problems begin in the home. Overindulgence, overprotection, rejection, neglect, too rigid standards, or responsibilities too great for a child to handle are some of the home conditions which discourage growth toward emotional maturity. Often, parents and teachers limit their training of emotional behavior to the inhibition of disruptive emotions, and give children little help in working off their feelings or learning constructive modes of expression. With the right kind of guidance a child can learn that there are ways to express anger, fear, or hostility without hurting himself or other people. More important, wise adults can see to it that the stresses of life confronting a child at each stage of growth are within his ability to handle. There needs to be an emotional toughening process for each child so that he gradually increases his self-control and his ability to accept frustration and delay. This process should involve a series of graded experiences, extending over a long period of time and operating within a supportive atmosphere. Children who are thrown into the stream of the outside world too early and without adequate support may become toughened emotionally, but often this is a hardening process which does not lead to emotional maturity but to personal and social conflict.

SUMMARY

Emotions, feelings, moods, attitudes, and related affective states have physiological and psychological influences on behavior. They can either stimulate a person's total action system and enhance the quality of living, or restrict his behavior to a point where he is unable to function with full effectiveness. How emotions will affect adjustment depends upon how well the individual progresses through the course of emotional development.

Emotional development has been described as both an educational process and a growth process. Emotional growth begins with the mass action of the infant and progresses through a series of graded experiences toward the goal of emotional maturity. Unlike physical maturity, emotional maturity is not attained by growth alone. Considerable learning is involved in finding suitable means of expressing emotions, developing the ability to delay or inhibit emotional behavior, and adjusting to social expectations. Sometimes fixation or regression will arrest emotional development, so that the individual grows physically but is immature in some aspects of his emotional development. Psychosomatic disorders and other anxiety reactions can occur when emotional growth does not proceed normally toward maturity.

A child who receives adequate emotional support, constructive guidance, and an opportunity to learn how to handle his emotions can be expected to attain sufficient emotional stability and control to assume increasing responsibility for his own behavior. When he achieves maturity, he will be neither overly inhibited nor unduly subject to uncontrollable emotions. He will be able to react emotionally when it is appropriate to do so, and moderate his behavior in response to the realities of a situation. While no one achieves the ideal of complete emotional maturity, most people can attain sufficient understanding of themselves to use their emotions effectively and to establish satisfying relations with other people.

REFERENCES

1. Anderson, J. E., "The Development of Behavior and Personality," in Eli Ginzberg (Ed.), *The Nation's Children, 2: Development and Education*, Columbia, 1960, pp. 43–69.
2. Arter, R. M., "The Effects of Prejudice on Children," *Child.*, September–October, 1959, **6**:185–189.

3. Bayley, N., "The Emotions of Children: Their Development and Modification," in Hountras, P. T. (Ed.), *Mental Hygiene: A Text of Readings,* Merrill, 1961, pp. 145–151.

4. Bettelheim, B., *Love Is Not Enough,* Free Press, 1950.

5. Cantril, H., "Perceptions and Interpersonal Relations," *Amer. J. Psychiat.,* August, 1957, 114:119–126.

6. Coleman, J. C., *Personality Dynamics and Effective Behavior,* Scott, Foresman, 1960.

7. English, O. S., and Pearson, G. H. J., *Emotional Problems of Living,* Norton, 1955.

8. Erikson, E. H., "Youth and the Life Cycle," *Child.,* March–April, 1960, 7:43–49.

9. Frank, L. K., *Feelings and Emotions,* Random House, 1954.

10. Frenkel-Brunswick, E., "Intolerance of Ambiguity as an Emotional and Perceptual Personality Variable," *J. Pers.,* 1949, 18:108–143.

11. Funkenstein, D. H., "The Physiology of Fear and Anger," *Sci. Amer.,* 1955, 192:74–80.

12. Hamilton, M., *Psychosomatics,* Wiley, 1955.

13. Imboden, J. B., *et al.,* "Symptomatic Recovery from Medical Disorders," *J. Amer. Med. Ass.,* December, 1961, 178:1182–1184.

14. Josselyn, I. M., "Psychological Changes in Adolescence," *Child.,* March–April, 1959, 6:43–47.

15. Kagan, J., *et al.,* "Personality and IQ Change," *J. abnorm. soc. Psychol.,* March, 1958, 56:261–266.

16. Klausmeier, H. J., *Learning and Human Abilities,* Harper & Row, 1961.

17. Klein, D. B., *Mental Hygiene,* Holt, Rinehart & Winston, 1956.

18. Kubie, L. S., "Are We Educating for Maturity?", *J. Nat. Educ. Ass.,* January, 1959, 48:58–63.

19. McNeil, J. D., "Changes in Ethnic Reaction Tendencies During High School," *J. educ. Res.,* January, 1960, 53:199–200.

20. Menninger, W. C., *Mental Health, Everybody's Business,* Conference on the Mental Health Needs of Los Angeles, Los Angeles, February, 1961.

21. Money-Kyrle, R. E., "On Prejudice—A Psychoanalytical Approach," *Brit. J. med. Psychol.,* 1960, 33:205–209.

22. Moore, M. E., *et al.,* "Obesity, Social Class, and Mental Illness," *J. Amer. Med. Ass.,* September 15, 1962, 181:962–966.

23. O'Brien, R., "We're Learning More About the Brain," *Today's Hlth.,* August, 1962, 40:32–33.

24. Parent, N., "An Echo in Education," *Ment. Hyg.,* April, 1961, 45:229–234.

25. Powell, J. W., "The Maturity Vector," *Adult Leadership,* February, 1957, 5:252–254.

26. Sanford, N. (Ed.), "Personality Development During the College Years," *J. soc. Issues,* 1956, 12:3–72.

27. Schmideberg, M., "Tolerance in Upbringing and Its Abuses," *Int. J. Soc. Psychiat.,* Autumn, 1959, 5:123–130.

28. Seyle, H., *The Stress of Life,* McGraw-Hill, 1963.

29. Steckle, L. C., *Problems of Human Adjustment,* Harper & Row, 1957.

30. Wilson, D. C., "Dynamics and Psychotherapy of Depression," *J. Amer. Med. Ass.,* May, 1955, **158**:151–153.

Chapter 8   Development and
Decline of Human Abilities

The span of years which an average person can expect to live has increased dramatically during the course of history. Average life expectancy at birth during the time of the Roman Empire is believed to have been about 25 years. In 1800 A.D. it had risen to 35 years, and in 1900 to a little over 47 years. Today, average life expectancy is about 70 years and promises to increase even more. At the present rate of scientific progress, life expectancy is expected to reach 100 years within the next decade or two (36, 37, 38).

This increased life span means that, today, when a person attains mature physical growth, he has completed less than one third of his life cycle. Usually, he will have devoted less than 20 percent of his total alloted years to formal schooling in preparation for the 80 percent of his life yet to come. The young adult will thus emerge from school with the greatest part of life before him. To plan ahead intelligently, he should know something about how human abilities mature and decline, when it is best to prepare for the future, and when he can expect to be most efficient and productive in the use of his abilities.

PHYSICAL AND MOTOR DEVELOPMENT

The period of growth, the period of maturity, and the period of aging are different for various organs and tissues of the body.

The graying of hair, for example, starts in childhood and continues through all ages, although it is most rapid and observable during the thirties. Other tissues have their own timetable of growth, but individual variation makes it difficult to predict the changes that time will bring about in a particular person (16, 51). Meeting one's childhood friends or classmates after a lapse of many years is quite likely to have the startling effects described by Anderson in this incident:

Some years ago I attended the thirtieth reunion of my college class. Because my work had taken me far away I had seen few classmates in the intervening period. Some I recognized without difficulty, despite their gray hair and physical changes, but only with difficulty could others of the group be recognized as the young men they had been many years before. Some were still slender and young in appearance, had active interests, and were getting much out of life; they had made good adjustments and appeared to be very successful. Others had become old and had deteriorated physically, were fat and sloppy both in appearance and action, or had suffered much trouble and worry and were in poor circumstances. Still others had disappeared completely, through death, mental disease, or other difficulties. Some men who had been very prominent as undergraduates were completely out of the picture in their fifties. The great halfback who had been the idol of his class was now in poor health and a minor employee of a classmate who as a quiet youth had attracted little attention, despite high intellectual ability. Several men who were reputed as boys to be both bright and hard workers had achieved distinction and were now centers of attention for their classmates, while others who had promise as young men had failed to come through (3:511).

These changes over a period of 30 years are the outcome of a series of changes which had been occurring gradually and progressively in the intervening period. As we trace the development of these changes, we shall gain some perspective on when and how they occur, and what an individual may expect of his capacities at various stages of life.

Physical and Motor Changes

Among the more obvious changes that occur as life proceeds are alterations in one's physical appearance and capacities. The rise and decline of physical vigor, in particular, is one of the most common indices used to mark the progress of maturity.

The peak of physical efficiency is reached soon after the age of 20 and is followed by a few years of high performance. Then some physical deterioration sets in, beginning as early as the late twenties and continuing to the end of the life span (16). Some of the changes in physical capacity are quite apparent. Physical strength, for instance, is easily measured and shows an increase in both sexes until puberty. After puberty the strength of girls increases little further, while the strength of boys continues to grow into early maturity. Muscle mass increases through the twenties, with the highest point reached at about 24 years. From age 30 to 70, man's physical capacity declines 30 percent as measured by weight-lifting tests (46).

Paralleling these visible physical changes are changes in internal organ structures and functions. Reserve capacity, for example, is reduced. As a person passes maturity, he finds it more difficult to recover his normal powers after physical exertion. The capability of the body to repair itself also deteriorates with time. As a rough index of this deterioration, Steiglitz (48: 49) suggests that for each 5 years we have lived we should add an extra day to the time required to repair an injury. Thus a man of 60 might require 12 days to heal a wound that a 5-year-old would recover from in 1 day. Accompanying this decrease in recuperative powers is a diminishing of reserves for situations that involve physical stress. As we grow older, there is less tolerance of heat and cold, of overeating or starvation, of dehydration or salt depletion, and of other upsets in physiological equilibrium.

Much of this change in physiological function is due to the aging of internal tissues. Arteries harden as people grow old and the walls become thickened, causing circulatory difficulties and often degeneration of brain tissue. Tissue changes make the bones brittle so that fractures occur more easily and are harder to heal. In a fair number of persons there is an increase in blood pressure, requiring reduced activity in order to avoid strain on the heart. Inefficiency in the body's mechanism for excreting some of the by-products of metabolism is thought to underlie many of these physiological concomitants of aging. The accumulation of calcium and calcifiable organic compounds plays an important part in this process. Premature aging has been produced in rats by injecting these products in young animals. A 2-month-old rat so treated develops many of the symptoms found in senile humans, including a wrinkled inelastic skin, bad teeth, cataracts, a hunched back, and calcification of the vocal cords (1).

Progressive changes in physiological functions are rather slight from 21 to 45 years of age. The rate of change increases after 45 and becomes more pronounced after the age of 60 or 70. This emphasizes the need for proper regulation of physical activity and for not subjecting the body to strains which in previous years would have been met easily. Because mental capacities and interests stay ahead of the body's physical capacities, many people die suddenly each year, having forced their bodies to keep up with activities they were capable of mentally but not physically.

Motor performance parallels the growth and decline of physical powers in many respects. Motor coordination increases in quality and at a marked rate up to the age of 13 or 14 years, and more gradually thereafter until it reaches a high point in early maturity. The maximum speed of reaction is attained between 16 and 25 years of age. After that it declines slowly and progressively up to 50 years, and markedly in the fifties and sixties. The oldster, for example, is no match for the 20-year-old in terms of speed of applying the brake in a car, or swerving to avoid an obstacle, or cutting in and out of traffic. If a person's occupation depends on how fast he performs a certain motor task, then it behooves him to look ahead, for he is likely to become less efficient as he ages. But if the quality of a product, rather than the speed of producing it, is the most important criterion of his efficiency, then advancing years are of less significance in determining his success on a job.

Sensory Changes

Sensitivity to pain, vibration, taste, visual accommodation and perception, touch and hearing—all decline as age increases. These changes are due to reduction in the number of elements available for the perception of sensation and probably also to a reduction in efficiency of those which remain.

The progressive changes in vision which take place with age are familiar to most of us. Only 5 out of 100 preschool-age children have a major eye defect, whereas 30 out of 100 elementary and high school students are afflicted with poor vision. By the age of 40, the proportion has increased to 48 out of 100, and by the age of 70, 95 out of 100 people have defective vision (10).

Changes with age affect not only the ability of the eyes to focus on an object but also our perception of light stimuli. Older people are likely to have difficulty in adapting to darkness and in distinguishing between different intensities of light. They usually need much better light to read by than do younger people. The decline of ability to see in the dark may necessitate a night light in the home and avoidance of night driving by older people. A number of other physiological changes in the eye have been noted in older people, including wrinkling of the skin around the eyes, drooping eyelids, little hemorrhages and tearing of eye tissue, increased lacrimation, changes in the cornea and retina, and other structural changes which affect vision (18).

Some degree of hearing loss is normal in aging but usually is less marked than the vision changes described above. Often, sensitivity to high pitches is lost first, followed by progressive losses down the pitch scale. It is quite common to find some decline in the hearing range beginning around the age of 20. The hearing of older people often becomes quite selective. Usually, there must be a certain level of background noise for an older person to hear normal conversation. In a quiet room the older person may be hard of hearing, but in noisier surroundings people automatically raise their voices so that the hearing threshold of the older person is reached and he can hear what is said. Older people also have difficulty with voice discrimination and with the recognition of minimal voice cues. This is thought to result not from organic changes but from the tendency for older people to withdraw from group situations (32).

Similar losses occur in other sensory functions. These do not come on suddenly at a certain age, and there is much individual variation, but they tend to be rather common within a given age group.

INTELLIGENCE AND MENTAL ACTIVITY

As a person ages, there are certain changes in his brain and nervous system which have an effect on his mental activity. Older brain tissues contain fewer nucleotides, the protein compounds which serve as electron carriers and which are essential to cellular respiration (31:37). There is also a shrinkage of brain weight as age progresses. An average 30-year-old person will have a brain weight of 1375 grams, but at 90, brain weight declines to an average of 1232 grams (46). Another factor which is thought to slow up mental processes in older people is the fact that the speed at which nerve impulses are transmitted along single fibers is reduced 10 to 15 percent in older people as compared with younger ones (46). Often, too, small strokes and ailments which interfere with the circulation of blood to the brain occur in the older years.

Such physical and physiological deterioration in the function of the brain and nervous system have an important effect on intellectual processes. However, the influences of these changes on intelligence and the ability to learn are not as great as was once presumed. It was long thought that the ability to learn increases rapidly during childhood and reaches a peak at about 16 years of age, with gradual deterioration thereafter. This has led to describing childhood as the "golden age of learning." Recent studies have shown that this conclusion is largely an artifact of the tests used to measure intelligence. Intelligence tests which were standardized on groups whose maximum age was 16 showed growth in learning ability to stop at this point, because no measurements beyond this age were provided. When the maximum age for test standardization was extended to 18, growth in intelligence was shown to continue to this point. Even now, mental-age scores beyond 22 years and 11 months are not provided on one of the most commonly used individual tests of intelligence (9, 35).

If growth in intelligence is judged solely by quickness of learning, then it is probably true that we reach a peak in our speed of learning at around age 20 and that there is continuous decline thereafter, until at about the age of 80 our learning speed has dropped nearly to that of a 12-year-old (3, 7, 47). However, when time limits are taken off intelligence tests and greater stress is placed on accuracy, it is found that learning ability increases with maturity and that once a peak is reached we continue at this high level until old age sets in. Moreover, life experience contributes to increased understanding and judgment. If these factors are measured by intelligence tests, the ability to think clearly is found to continue well into the advanced years (47:348).

Results will differ depending on whether intelligence and learning ability reach a peak in early adulthood and decline thereafter, and on what types of intelligence tests are used and the conditions under which they are administered. Since intelligence is a complex factor having many aspects, where loss of intelligence with age does appear there are differences in the aspects of intelligence which are affected. Studies have shown that vocabulary and abstract reasoning continue to develop well past adulthood, but ability for practical reasoning reaches an earlier peak of growth (9, 25). Verbal understanding and those abilities which call for information, comprehension, and experience hold up particularly well through the later years of life (2, 13). Memory, however, undergoes a decline, particularly in the last decades of life, due to sclerotic changes in some of the brain's blood vessels. This is a selective memory loss, where memory of general concepts and skills remains intact while recent experiences and names slip away. Many older people can overcome this type of memory loss by concentrating a little harder on remembering names and other data (34).

There is some question whether studies which show a loss of speed in learning and a reduced efficiency in memory and practical reasoning at advanced ages are measuring intrinsic ability or whether other factors are obscuring the picture. The effects of habit, motivation, initial level of intelligence, environmental stimulation, and level of education are factors which are known to influence the way an adult performs on tests of intelligence and the way he utilizes his learning abilities.

Effects of Habit.   In the older person a mass of habits, skills, and attitudes may set up an inertia toward new situations and toward new modes of action which interferes with his performance on intelligence tests or learning tasks. Older people are more prone to select answers which fit into their experience than to make their choice on the basis of the logical merits of a question. They have more difficulty than youngsters in shifting from the performance of one mental task to another as required on intelligence tests. Also, it is probable that they just do not see any sense in many of the questions asked and do not respond to the challenge of a test with the same enthusiasm displayed by younger persons who are accustomed to taking tests and to pitting their abilities against time (54:36).

A person's experience with learning may also influence his performance in later years. What one has learned at a preceding stage of life may impede the acquisition of new learning. This is especially true if his previous knowledge is disorganized or superficial because it was merely memorized or acquired without meaning. Negative emotional reactions toward learning, stemming from too much pressure or from negative interpersonal relations with a teacher or parent, may set up emotional blocks in certain areas of learning. This is a fairly common occurrence with school children and probably carries over into adult life. Its later effects are that a person resists learning not because he is incapable, but because it is associated with the unpleasant pressures experienced in earlier years (4).

Motivation.   Many investigators believe that if older people could be motivated to think seriously about problems presented on intelligence tests they would make a much better showing. The older person does not have the intellectual enthusiasm possessed by a child who is moving up the academic ladder. He is less responsive to rewards or punishments, and usually must see the value of acquiring information and is not inclined to learn just because someone tells him to. A youngster can be coerced to learn, but adults are on their own and must have the desire to learn. It has been found that men and women can, if they wish, master new languages, new ideas, and new types of problem solving, even at the age of 60 or 70, if they are convinced that the learning is useful and are willing to put out the needed effort (55). The lack of motivation on test performance, which several studies reveal (15, 24), stands in sharp contrast to the intellectual performance of older persons who become interested in a hobby or a creative activity, give great amounts of time to it, and show marked improvement in performance.

Level of Intelligence and Education.   There is considerable evidence that the brighter you are the less you decline mentally as you grow older. Terman in his follow-up studies of superior children found that the mental development of this gifted group increased through at least age 50 (53). A four-year study of mental ability in a group of persons 60 and older showed that if a person of 60 has an IQ of 116 or more, his mental ability drops off very slightly as he gets older. Persons in the upper 5 to 10 percent of mental ability tend to remain above the average of young adults until very late in life, as late as age 75 (7, 22).

Education seems to have much to do with maintaining a high level of mental efficiency in the older years. In a study which involved the retesting of 127 men who had been tested with the Army Alpha Test 30 years before as a requirement for entrance to college, Owens (33) found higher average scores in 1950 than were made by the same group in 1919. Men who had over five years of college showed greater increases in their scores on the two tests than those who had four years or less of college. Swanson (52), who studied four groups of superior high school students, using a college aptitude test and readministering the test to the same group 24 years later, found they all showed significant gains in aptitude, especially those who had received bachelors' degrees or higher. Such studies suggest that the higher one's potential mental ability or capacity, and the more this capacity is sharpened through education, the longer mental ability remains at a high level of efficiency.

The Effects of the Social Environment.   In many instances the decline of mental ability may be offset or delayed to the advanced years by stimulating social interaction. Studies of geriatric patients in hospitals for the aged indicate that people deteriorate more rapidly in a nonstimulating environment. Many of the older people who found leisure time oppressive were shown to have lower cerebral blood flow and lower cerebral metabolism (46). If these people are left alone to develop a passive relation to their environment, both mental and physical capacities can be expected to run a downward course. Where old people are encouraged to become involved in social and individual activities and to develop new interests, striking changes in their learning powers and intellectual activities have been observed (41).

Older people have a natural tendency to disengage themselves from interpersonal contacts and to become more cautious and restrained in their behavior. Once set in a pattern of isolation, the psychological structure which accompanies it is so firmly entrenched that only a radical upheaval in a person's environment or outlook will bring about a major change in his life style. Inertia and boredom lead to disillusionment, bitterness, and lack of purpose. This is a tendency now recognized and countered by providing recreation facilities in the numerous housing developments being constructed for "senior citizens" (5, 11, 54).

There is, of course, much individual variation in this decline in socialization and personal effectiveness. Whether a person has a family which accepts him has much to do with his outlook on life. So, too, does his occupation, his level of education, and whether he has achieved distinction or success in his work.

Change in Interests

The narrowing of interest and response as we grow older is not restricted to the advanced years but begins to show up in early adolescence. The child of nine has a broad variety of interests, a great curiosity, and an openness to new ideas. At the age of 13, these interests have decreased materially, and by 17, the individual is at the opposite end of the scale from the

9-year-old, having narrowed his attention to a few interests in which he becomes deeply involved (21).

This reduction of interests points out the necessity for children to have a wide range of exploratory experiences in their early school life in order to locate areas of activity that will become permanent sources of interest. If such interests are not experienced in early life, there is relatively little likelihood that they will be acquired in later life. If a person is not interested in stamp collecting during his school years, it is doubtful that he will become a collector when he retires. If he has no exposure to music or mathematics early in life, he is unlikely to have interest in these subjects later, and there is even less likelihood that he will derive much basic satisfaction from them.

Interests and attitudes toward a subject will have much to do with how one uses his intelligence. A person with positive attitudes toward learning tasks will learn; a person with the same intelligence, but with negative attitudes toward learning, will not learn. The implications of these findings is that childhood and youth are the time to open many doors, to dig into a variety of fields, to explore all kinds of things, and to learn a little about many areas. A bare diet of basic skill subjects or academic studies is too restrictive. Various hobbies and social activities, including aesthetic and athletic experiences, will give the growing person a rich background out of which to select the things he will wish to pursue later. There is no guarantee that the child who studies music will retain an interest in music as an adult. But it is even more possible that if he never had any contact with music as a child he will not seek these experiences as an adult.

Some Conclusions About Intellectual Growth

The evidence cited above points to the conclusion that the quality of learning performance increases from childhood to maturity and can be retained at a high level thereafter in the absence of pathology. So long as a person is in reasonably good health, continues his intellectual interests, and has a well-organized positive set of attitudes toward life, he need not fear the inability to think as he grows older. Individual motivation, the richness of experience, the range of interests, and the social stimulation which one has appear to be important factors in determining whether the growing person retains his learning capacity throughout adult life and well into old age (19).

AGE AND PRODUCTIVITY

Philosophers have long speculated on when man reaches the prime of life, when he is most productive, and when his powers may be expected to decline. Aristotle put man's physical prime at 30 to 35, and his mental prime at age 49, when "his passions have subsided and his experience and judgment has ripened." Plato set age 50 as the proper age to begin philosophical studies and political rule. As we shall see, these ancient philosophers were not far wrong in their calculations.

Lehman (26) has made an extensive study of age and achievement, compiling information on thousands of people in many different fields of endeavor. He found that superior ability and performance in all but a few areas occur much earlier in life than many of us have suspected. The age levels at which superior contributions were made at the greatest average rate in the fields of athletics, science, music, and writing are indicated in the table below.

Field	Age of Greatest Productivity or Success
Athletics:	
Professional football players	22–26
Prize fighters	25–26
Ice hockey	26
Baseball players	27–28
Tennis	25–29
Auto racers	26–30
Golfers	31–36
Science:	
Chemists	26–30
Mathematicians	30–34

Physicists	30–34
Geologists	35–39
Astronomers	35–39
Bacteriologists, physiologists	35–39
Botanists	30–34
Psychologists	30–39

Musicians: (Production of superior music)

Instrumental selections	25–29
Symphonies	30–34
Orchestral music	35–39
Light opera and musical comedy	40–44

Writers:

Poetry	24–31
Short stories	30–34
Comedies	32–36
Tragedies	34–38
Novels, best books, best sellers	40–44
Philosophy	35–39
Economics and political science	30–39

SOURCE: H. C. Lehman, *Age and Achievement*, Princeton, 1959, p. 324.

Thus, it can be seen that man's golden years, as measured by the quality of his accomplishments, are the late 20s, the 30s, and the early 40s. The one exception to this pattern Lehman found was in the field of leadership, where the attainment of success occurred after the age of 50. College presidents, for example, have served most often at 50 to 54, while popes held their positions at the ages of 82 to 92.

Just why achievement should flourish in the early adult years and reach fruition in the early 30s is not easily explained. Lehman suggests that the decline in physical vigor which occurs after the age of 40, and the various bodily infirmities and illnesses which appear with increasing frequency as people grow older, might interfere with productivity. Success itself may impede further creativity, for with success comes promotion, added responsibilities, and a tendency to rest on one's laurels. Personality problems, too, may interfere with productivity, for as people grow older, marital unhappiness, frustrations of many kinds, and emotional disorders occur more often than they do in youth. To these explanations might be added the possibility that scientists usually write their doctoral theses during their 20s and 30s, and thereafter may be too busy earning a living to do much research. Or, as Dennis (12) points out, as scientific output increases, it becomes more difficult for a person to secure adequate outlets for citation of his work.

Whatever the cause may be, it appears that the person who hopes to achieve success must prepare himself early so that he has the necessary background for his productive years. Some authorities feel that the thirties, when many Ph.D.'s are granted, are too late to complete one's education. Too many of the creative years have elapsed before the individual is trained for his life work, and he is left with too few years to make productive use of this training (23, 43). It is especially important that the youth of high achievement potential be identified early and encouraged to complete his basic education with a minimum of wasted time (27).

Individual Variations in Productivity

While there may be certain ages at which productivity seems to reach a peak, there is considerable individual variation in records of successful performance. A glance at some of the significant contributions which were made at advanced ages will show that we cannot be dogmatic about ascribing productivity to certain age groups. For example, Sarah Bernhardt was still on the stage at 77; Goethe completed "Faust" at 82; Verdi wrote "Falstaff" at 80, and "Requiem" at 84; Titian painted both the "Transfiguration" and the "Annunciation" when he was 88; Stradivarius was still giving the world fine violins at 80. These exceptions to the general findings about age and productivity warn against any pessimism about a person's being destined to mediocrity if he does not achieve success in his early thirties or forties. People who are past their middle-years, even those in the sixties and beyond, may have the potentiality for making significant contributions to society. After studying graphs of man's potential and his accomplishments, J. W. Still pointed out considerable discrepancy between what man could do and what he does do. He noted, for instance, that the senile decline theoretically need not occur until some time past the age of 80, but that it actually occurs shortly after the age of 60. Where man could reach the peak of successful mental performance at age 60, he actually reaches the peak at about 35, and declines rapidly after 40 (49). Evidently, as Hans Selye has remarked, too many of us use up our vitality at too early an age and have little left to draw upon in the later years of life (44).

Since about 10 percent of our population is in the 65-and-over group, these facts are important. They suggest the need for planning one's life so that personal and social usefulness continues after what are now considered to be the years "over the hill." For some people it suggests the possibility of two careers, the second of which could come at a time when many of us consider themselves too old to start over. Man's potential seems to be limited largely by his own horizons and his willingness to strive toward success. The physical and physiological obstacles imposed by growing older are being overcome by science and soon may be relatively minor obstructions to a level of productivity which could extend far beyond the point where for most people it now ends. Many of the common conceptions about older workers are even now known to be inaccurate. Studies made by the U.S. Department of Labor have demonstrated that a large proportion of older workers, particularly those between 55 and 64, out-perform the younger ones, are more consistent in the excellence of their performance, and have better attendance and safety records (8). The assumption that after the age of 40 men and women are poor employment risks is inconsistent with what is known about the abilities and potentialities of the later years of life.

FACTORS WHICH AFFECT THE USE OF ABILITIES

Whether a person makes the most of his abilities is often dependent upon the stress to which he is exposed. By stress we mean any kind of assault on the organism. It may be physical stress, such as fatigue, intoxication, trauma, or disease, or it may be psychological stress, which often produces equally extensive disturbances in the organism. Although physical and psychological reactions to stress are not separable, since they often occur simultaneously, we shall separate them for purposes of discussion. Some of the physical stresses which commonly affect adjustment and the use of abilities are described in the following pages. The effects of psychological stress will be treated more extensively in subsequent chapters.

Physical Fatigue

Physical fatigue is known to be a factor which affects an individual's performance. Under certain conditions, chemicals, such as lactic acid, other metabolic waste products, or toxins, may accumulate in a tissue and be transported by the blood stream to other organs. Nerve action, motor performance, and sensory processes may then function at reduced efficiency. Nerves can be fatigued to a point where they are less responsive to stimuli and less able to activate other tissues. Sensory apparatus continuously exposed to a constant stimulus may fatigue an individual so that he is unable to make full use of his senses. Constant, intense visual color, for example, may appear black after protracted exposure because of this effect. Similarly, constant, high noise levels may fatigue the receptors in the ear and cause various forms of partial deafness. In very severe cases of fatigue, such as extreme physical exhaustion, scientists have found cardiovascular damage, epileptic fits, and sometimes congestion and edema of the brain (43).

Physical fatigue may originate in the muscles and spread to other parts of the body, resulting in "jangled nerves," hypersensitivity, irritability, and other symptoms of overtiredness. This is why it is important to take refreshing pauses when working under physical stress. Rest makes oxygen from the air available and permits chemical changes necessary for recovery from fatigue. It has been found that many short breaks during the day are more restful than one or two long ones. Six rest periods of five minutes each, spread out through the day, provide more effective relaxation than one period of thirty minutes. The reason for this is that most of the recovery takes place at the start of the rest period, while less and less benefit is derived from the succeeding minutes (29).

Motivation and Mental Fatigue

Motivation has been found to be an important element in both physical and mental fatigue. When motivation is low, physical fatigue may be experienced very early; when it is high, the evidence of fatigue may not be apparent until the individual becomes exhausted. A highly motivated person may think he is working at a peak level of efficiency while his performance is actually declining (29).

Motivation seemingly creates new sources of energy as a person shifts from one activity to another. After a hard day at classes, a student may feel too tired to study at night. However, he may have plenty of energy to go dancing, attend a play, or even go to a lecture with his favorite companion. We seem to allocate a certain quota of energy to a particular activity and experience tiredness when this energy is consumed. Shifting to another activity makes available another supply of energy.

Studies of mental fatigue generally show that people are capable of mental activity far beyond what they think their limits to be. There is no record of a brain having been damaged by overuse. Usually, disinterest and lack of motivation, together with eyestrain and muscle tension, produce the feelings we call mental fatigue. True fatigue has a selective effect on mental processes, impairing first the higher centers involving for the most part creative thinking, then those which are used in formal reasoning, and finally memory. In other words, it is easier to recall something from memory when we are tired than it is to create new ideas. This has important implications for scheduling one's work to take advantage of periods of high mental efficiency. For most people there is an hourly variation in working capacity, with the most productive hours occurring generally during the first half of the morning, and the least productive hours likely to occur in the late afternoon (42).

Boredom may have a great deal to do with mental efficiency, quite independently of fatigue. Tests have shown that a person who is bored by the work he is doing experiences a slowing down in mental processes and an increase in the errors he makes. Many of us have experienced the type of "mental block" that occurs while adding a column of figures. At times we reach a point where a sum is repeated several times before we can move on to the next sum. Then, for a while we move along adding numbers easily until another block occurs. These blocks may be only a few seconds in duration under normal conditions but occur more frequently under conditions of boredom. The same thing happens in reading passages in a text. Often we finish a page or paragraph and find we really have not read the material at all and must go back and deliberately focus on what we are doing. Boredom is a serious problem with people who have more ability than their jobs call for. Many high-ability students who leave school before their education is completed and take jobs which do not utilize their talents become frustrated people and inefficient workers.

Effects of Other Physical Factors

In addition to fatigue there are a number of other physical factors which may place a person under stress. We shall discuss the influence of alcohol, lack of sleep, nutritional and vitamin deficiencies, and injury and disease to illustrate how physical stress may interfere with an individual's productivity.

Alcohol. Alcohol is one of several drugs commonly used as a stimulant. Many people believe that under its influence they think more clearly, become more alert, and have quicker, more efficient responses. Extensive studies of the effects of alcohol on human beings show none of these things to be true. Alcohol is not a stimulant, but a depressant which acts on the central nervous system. With gradually increasing doses it tends to interfere first with cortical functions which control judgment and restraint. As the concentration in the blood becomes higher, its effects reach deeper areas of the brain and affects both mental and physical performance. It slows down reflexes, increases reaction time, impairs the ability to learn, and produces loss of memory.

Except for the abolition of superficial anxiety, alcohol is a depressant of all neurophysiological and psychological activity. Because judgment and restraint are depressed, the individual *thinks* he is more alert and capable, and that his senses are clearer and sharper than usual. However, when tested on responses, such as time required to sense a red light and react to it by applying the brakes, an individual affected by alcohol can readily be shown to operate well below his normal efficiency (30, 56).

Sleep. The person who cannot sleep at night and has a constant feeling of tiredness during the day may develop what has been called a depressive fatigue state. This is a condition where there is a general feeling of exhaustion which is not relieved by rest. Often these people grow irritable and short-tempered, withdraw from social activity, become annoyed by a variety of small noises, and tend to snap at everybody.

If continued very long, such behavior may lead to a depressed mood and to feelings of helplessness and self-disparagement. When this occurs, the person becomes overwhelmed by his tiredness and cannot fulfill his obligations to family, friends, or job without great difficulty and exertion. Often he withdraws from all pleasurable activities, including television, sports, and social affairs. Many of these people go to physicians for some bodily complaint which prevents them from sleeping, although there may be no organic basis for their difficulty (50).

A normal, healthy person can go without sleep for long periods of time, provided he gets some rest. Laboratory studies have shown that marked deteriorations in behavior will occur after four days without sleep. Irritability, paranoid thinking, visual hallucinations, episodic rage, and deterioration in thinking and motor performance have been induced in normal subjects kept awake for four days or longer. While requirements for sleep will vary for individuals, sleep is important in the energy transfer system of the body. The person who deliberately keeps himself awake for long periods of time, often with drugs, is placing himself in a severe stress situation (28).

Nutritional and Vitamin Deficiencies. Serious undernourishment may lead to increasingly inefficient motor performance. Studies in Nazi concentration camps of severely undernourished persons show the onset of apathy, depression, irritability, and disinclination to think, talk, or move. Even well-nourished persons who are lacking essential elements in their diet can experience distressing psychological and physiological effects. An upset in the normal salt balance of the body may give rise to irritability, depression, and hypochondriacal complaints. An acute lack of the Vitamin B complex, or some of its components, can precipitate psychological symptoms ranging in severity from mild hypochondria to profound psychosis, depending on the degree and duration of the deprivation (43).

While dietary deficiencies affect a person's performance, it is not true that an excess of any of the vital components of nutrition will enhance performance. Most of our normal dietary requirements are met in a balanced food intake. Few people in this country who eat balanced meals have any need for vitamin supplements or special foods. While many people still believe that fish is brain food, or red wine builds blood, these ideas are largely folklore. There is no real evidence to show that special foods or food supplements have any significant effect on increasing personal efficiency or developing specific behavioral characteristics.

Injuries and Disease.   Any agent which damages or upsets the functional integrity of the body can cause temporary or permanent effects on behavior and performance. Accidents, such as burns of the body, can cause edema of the brain and rise of intracranial pressure. Heatstroke can cause swelling, shrinkage, or other changes in brain cells. Excessive exposure to X rays may produce inflammatory lesions in the central nervous system and an increase in cerebrospinal fluid pressure. Any injury which produces anoxia, the cutting-off of oxygen to the brain, may result in hemorrhages, nerve-cell degeneration, or death of some brain tissue.

Many diseases of both an acute and chronic nature can have long-lasting effects on behavior. Focal infections and systemic infectious diseases, such as chickenpox, scarlet fever, measles, mumps, pertussis, Rocky Mountain Spotted fever, typhus, typhoid fever, or encephalitis, can produce lesions in the brain, changes in cerebrospinal fluid pressure, deposit of toxins in the brain, or even destruction of nerve cells. Many children who recover from diseases where a high fever was sustained for several days are left hyperactive, impulsive, and seriously lacking in emotional control. They may become disobedient, destructive, and badly disturbed both at home and at school. Similar effects are produced by a variety of endocrine disturbances, and by certain drugs and poisons, such as lead, carbon monoxide, and arsenicals.

As we shall discuss in the next chapter, many of the effects on the nervous system produced by injury, disease, drugs, or toxins can also be produced by psychological stress. The human organism is capable of great adaptation, but it is also vulnerable to many physical and psychological stresses which may impede or destroy its functions.

SUMMARY

Each individual has a pattern of maturity and decline which is different from that of any other individual. However, there are certain general characteristics of growth which are common among people at various stages of life.

Physical development reaches a peak in the early twenties and declines gradually thereafter. Along with this decline in physical function are internal changes in body structures and functions, including greater susceptibility to disease, some deterioration in recuperative powers, and a reduction in sensory functions. None of these changes occurs suddenly, and few are very pronounced between the ages of 21 and 45. Thereafter, and particularly after the age of 60, the effects of physical decline become more noticeable. Young people need to be aware of these changes as they plan their careers.

Mental activity follows a somewhat different pattern of development and decline than does physical ability. The quality of learning performance increases during childhood and up to maturity. Thereafter it can be maintained at a high level if a person is in reasonably good health, continues his intellectual interest, has stimulating social experiences, and is motivated to use his intellectual capacities.

The age at which man reaches the prime of life and makes the greatest contribution in his particular field of endeavor coincides with the years at which he is at the peak of physical and mental development. Most important contributions are made in the late twenties, the thirties, and the early forties, in all fields except leadership and statesmanship where success is achieved more often after 50. The young person who hopes to make a contribution to society should be mindful of these facts and complete his formal education early enough so that he may take full advantage of his productive years.

Various stresses which impede adequate physical and psychological functioning also interfere with productivity and accomplishment. Included among these are the stresses induced by fatigue, alcohol, nutritional and vitamin deficiency, and the effects of injuries and disease. Psychological trauma may be equally effective in impeding man's adaptive ability and interfering with his productivity.

REFERENCES

1. American Medical Association, "Aging and Calcium Metabolism Linked in Research," *J. Amer. Med. Ass.,* December 29, 1962, **182**:32.
2. Anderson, J. E., "The Development of Behavior and Personality," in Eli Ginzberg, (Ed.), *The Nation's Children, 2: Development and Education,* Columbia, 1960, pp. 43–69.
3. Anderson, J. E., *The Psychology of Development and Personal Adjustment,* Holt, Rinehart and Winston, 1949.
4. Ausubel, D. P., "Can Children Learn Anything that Adults Can . . . and More Efficiently?" *Elem. Sch. J.,* February, 1962, **62**:270–272.
5. Bendig, A. W., "Age Differences on the Interscale Factor Structure of the Guilford–Zimmerman Temperament Survey," *J. consult. Psychol.,* April, 1960, **24**:134–138.
6. Birren, J. E., (Ed.), *A Handbook of Aging and the Individual: Psychological and Biological Aspects,* University of Chicago Press, 1960.
7. Birren, J. E., "Age Changes in Mental Ability," in H. E. Remmers, *et al.* (Eds.), *Growth, Teaching and Learning,* Harper & Row, 1957, pp. 54–62.
8. Bortz, E. L., "The Adult's Potential for Growth," *Sch. Life,* April, 1961, **43**:9–11.

9. Bradway, K. P., and Thompson, C. W., "Intelligence at Adulthood: A Twenty-Five Year Follow-up," *J. educ. Psychol.*, February, 1962, 53:1–14.

10. Covey, J. K., and Bakal, C., "Myths and Facts About Eye Care," *Today's Hlth.*, June, 1962, 40:8–9.

11. Cumming, E., *et al.*, "Disengagement—A Tentative Theory of Aging," *Sociometry*, March, 1960, 23:23–35.

12. Dennis, W., "The Age Decrement in Outstanding Scientific Contributions: Age or Artifact?", *Amer. Psychol.* August, 1958, 13:457–460.

13. Dibner, A. S., and Cummins, J. F., "Intellectual Functioning in a Group of Normal Octogenarians," *J. consult. Psychol.*, April, 1961, 25:137–141.

14. Eichorn, D. H., and Bayley, N., "Growth in Head Circumference from Birth Through Young Adulthood," *Child Develpm.*, June, 1962, 33:257–271.

15. Friend, C. M., and Zubek, J. P., "The Effects of Age on Critical Thinking Ability," *J. Geront.*, October, 1958, 13:407–413.

16. Garn, S. M., "Growth and Development," in Eli Ginzberg, (Ed.), *The Nation's Children, 2: Development and Education*, Columbia, 1960, pp. 24–42.

17. Ghiselli, E. E., "Relationship Between Intelligence and Age Among Superior Adults," *J. genet. Psychol.*, June, 1947, 90: 131–142.

18. Gordon, D. M., "The Aging Eye," *Seminar Rep.*, Merck, Sharp & Dohme, Fall, 1961, 6:8–14.

19. Halfter, I. T., "Aging and Learning: An Achievement Study," *School Rev.*, Autumn, 1962, 70:287–302.

20. Inhelder, B., and Piaget, J., *The Growth of Logical Thinking From Childhood to Adolescence*, Basic Books, 1958.

21. Institute of Child Development and Welfare, *A Survey of Children's Adjustment Over Time*, University of Minnesota Press, Minneapolis, 1959.

22. "Intelligence and Geriatrics," *Clearing House*, November, 1960, 35:169.

23. Jensen, A. R., "The Improvement of Educational Research," *Teachers Coll. Rec.*, October, 1962, 64:20–27.

24. Jerome, E. A., "Thinking Ability in the Aged," *Proceedings of the International Research Seminar on Social and Psychological Aspects of Aging*, University of California, Berkeley, 1960.

25. Jones, H. E., "Intelligence and Problem-Solving," in J. E. Bir-

ren, (Ed.), *Handbook of Aging and the Individual,* University of Chicago Press, 1959, pp. 700–738.

26. Lehman, H. C., *Age and Achievement,* Princeton, 1953.

27. Lehman, H. C., "The Age Decrement in Outstanding Scientific Creativity," *Amer. Psychol.,* February, 1960, 15:128–134.

28. Luby, E. D., *et al.,* "Sleep Deprivation: Effects on Behavior, Thinking, Motor Performance and Biological Energy Transfer Systems," *Psychosom. Med.,* May–June, 1960, 22:182–192.

29. Maier, N. R. F., *Psychology in Industry,* Houghton Mifflin, 1955.

30. National Institute of Mental Health, *Alcoholism,* Public Health Service Publication No. 730, Bethesda, Md., 1961.

31. National Institute of Mental Health, *Highlights of Progress in Mental Health Research,* Bethesda, Md., Publications and Reports Section, January, 1959.

32. Olsen, I. A., *Discrimination of Auditory Information as Related to Aging,* Unpublished Doctoral Dissertation, Washington State University, 1962.

33. Owens, W. A., Jr., "Age and Mental Abilities: A Longitudinal Study," *Genet. Psychol. Monogr.,* 1953, 48:3–54.

34. Penfield, W., "The Thread of Experience," *What's New,* Abbott Laboratories, Summer, 1962, 228:6–8.

35. Pinneau, S. R., "Conventional and Deviation IQs for the Stanford-Binet," in *Testing Today,* Houghton Mifflin, December, 1959, pp. 4–6.

36. Population Reference Bureau, Inc., "How Many People Have Ever Lived on Earth?", *Population Bull.,* February, 1962, 18: 1–19.

37. Population Reference Bureau, Inc., "New Emphasis on the Elderly," *Population Profile,* February 26, 1962.

38. Population Reference Bureau, Inc., "U.S.A. Population Growth: Projections to 1980," *Population Bull.,* May, 1959, 15:38–59.

39. President's Council on Aging, *The Older American,* GPO, 1963.

40. Pressey, S. L., "Toward Earlier Creativity in Psychology," *Amer. Psychol.,* February, 1960, 15:124–127.

41. Rae, J. W., *et al.,* "Geriatric Rehabilitation in County Hospitals," *J. Amer. Med. Ass.,* May 12, 1962, 180:463–468.

42. Rapaport, A., *et al.,* "Group Stress," in Mental Health Research Institute, *Third Annual Report, 1958–59,* University of Michigan, Ann Arbor, 1959, pp. 11–12.

43. Selye, H., "The General-Adaptation Syndrome in its Relationship to Neurology, Psychology and Psychopathology," in A. Weider, (Ed.), *Contributions Toward Medical Psychology: Theory and Psychodiagnostic Methods,* Vol. I, Ronald, 1953, pp. 234–274.

44. Selye, H., *The Stress of Life,* McGraw-Hill, 1963.

45. Selznick, G. J., and Larkins, J., *What Is Known About Young Adults,* Survey Research Center, University of California, Berkeley, 28 pp., mimeographed, 1961.

46. Shock, N. W., "The Physiology of Aging," *Sci. Amer.,* January, 1962, **206**:100–110.

47. Steckle, L. C., *Problems of Human Adjustment,* Harper & Row, 1957.

48. Steiglitz, E. J., "The Personal Challenge of Aging," in C. Tibbitts, (Ed.), *Living Through the Older Years,* University of Michigan Press, 1951.

49. Still, J. W., "Man's Potential—And His Performance," *New York Times Magazine,* November 24, 1957, p. 37.

50. Stoeckle, J. D., and Davidson, G. E., "Bodily Complaints and Other Symptoms of Depressive Reaction," *J. Amer. Med. Ass.,* April 14, 1962, **180**:134–139.

51. Stoughton, R. B., "Physiological Changes from Maturity Through Senescence," *J. Amer. Med. Ass.,* February 24, 1962, **179**:636–638.

52. Swanson, E. O., *A Follow-up Study of College Trained vs. Non-College Trained High School Graduates of High Ability,* Unpublished Doctoral Dissertation, University of Minnesota, 1953.

53. Terman, L. M., and Oden, M. H., *The Gifted Group at Mid-Life: A Thirty-Five Years' Follow-Up of the Superior Child,* Stanford, 1959.

54. Wallach, M. A., and Kogan, N., "Aspects of Judgment and Decision Making: Interrelations and Changes With Age," *Behav. Sci.,* January, 1961, **6**:23–36.

55. Watson, G., *What Psychology Can We Trust?* Teachers College, 1961.

56. Zappella, D., "Psychological Effects of Alcohol," *Calif. Hlth.,* August 15, 1960, **18**:25–28.

PART III PSYCHOLOGICAL STRESS AND ADJUSTMENT TO STRESS

Chapter 9   Psychological Stress

We have described some of the physical stresses which may impede the full use of a person's abilities. These are readily understood, since they involve direct interference with the functions of the body. Psychological stress operates in a much less tangible manner. Without introducing any foreign agents or physically attacking the body in any way, psychological stress can produce reactions which are fully as incapacitating as those resulting from disease, injury, or physical trauma. Indeed, as we explore the nature of psychological stress, it will be seen that such stress may be even more harmful to adjustment than physical insult, because its origins often are obscure and thus less amenable to prevention or treatment.

SOME SOURCES OF PSYCHOLOGICAL STRESS

Psychological stress may arise from any aspect of the environment or from within the individual himself. We shall describe some sources of stress in the social and cultural environment, in the home, and within the individual. However, the student should be cautioned not to view these sources as operating independently of one another. Usually, the forces from which psychological stress are produced are interwoven like tangled threads, so that it is seldom possible to separate them.

Social and Cultural Stress

Poverty, unemployment, competition, social status, social isolation, and social change are but a few of the social and cultural forces which may place people under stress. We shall delve briefly into some aspects of social isolation and social change to show how such forces may give rise to psychological stress.

Modern urban living forces many people to live in isolation from one another. Despite the fact that they spend a large proportion of their time working among other people, this relationship is often impersonal and mechanical. Many people are merely cogs in a working world where no one really cares for them as persons. Frequently, they are separated from their families and intimate friends, and live as lonely, out-of-touch human beings in quiet isolation. In the large cities are many such lonely souls who eat alone, go to movies alone, and spend much of their time reading, or at spectator activities where they are isolated from human warmth and companionship. For many of these people, leisure is a source of boredom and frustration, and week ends and holidays a vacuum which they are unable to fill. The high rate of personal and social maladjustment found among social isolates in our large cities testifies to the intensity of the strain under which these people live (15, 19, 28).

Certain groups in our society are exposed to considerably more social stress than others because of the onlooker roles into which they are cast. Some authorities ascribe many of the problems of youth to the spectator status into which adult society forces them. The late adolescent in particular is socially isolated in that he can no longer function as a child, yet is too young to marry, largely excluded from employment, and not permitted to take part in the political aspects of community life. It is little wonder that many of them turn against the adult culture and form their own society (39). Even greater social isolation is experienced by millions of migrant workers, members of minority groups, and others who are denied full participation in the social, political, and economic life of society. Whatever isolates an individual from the support of the social structure and denies him the warmth of human interaction can be expected to burn deeply into the psychological structure of his personality (33, 38).

Rapid social change is another modern source of psychological stress. Although we have survived the influences of the telephone, radio, television, automobile, jet aircraft, and space probes in the current century, the social changes brought about by modern technology have displaced many people from their customary modes of living. Studies show that this uprooting process, whether physical or psychological, is often a traumatic experience. For example, studies of the emotional breakdowns among soldiers in World War II found that the change of moving from civilian to military life was one of the greatest stresses experienced by soldiers. More emotional breakdowns occurred before the men were in combat, and often before they went overseas, than under actual fighting conditions (28). Corresponding reactions have been observed among Africans who were removed from a semiprimitive form of existence in their tribal villages and placed in new industrial settlements. This rapid social change was too much for the natives. Many developed a crippling form of anxiety characterized by fear of bewitchment, apprehension, and homicidal or self-destructive tendencies (21). The displacements caused by automation, urban renewal, or the disappearance of an industry and way of life may similarly expose people to special stresses which have a major influence on their behavior.

Stress in the Home

The home is our primary source of security and emotional support. This has been demonstrated in many ways and in many places. One of the most dramatic illustrations of this point was the observation made in England during World War II that children who were separated from their families and housed in the country to escape the bombing of cities showed greater signs of stress than those who stayed with their parents and had to seek protection in bomb shelters each night (28).

However, the home may become a primary source of stress to its members. The very efforts of parents to make children into socialized human beings involve the deliberate application of a whole series of stresses. The blocking of desires and wishes, the modification of actions, the threats of disapproval or rejection, and the effects of discipline are forms of stress which almost every child experiences in the process of growing up. Parents who fail to impose controls on children and who do not provide them with opportunities to experience the realities of life create a home environment in which actual and potential stress may be as great as in homes where children are rejected or abused (36).

The closeness of family ties makes the home an effective incubator for the spread of stress among its members. Children are particularly susceptible to parental concern over illness, money, food, possessions, social status, or other factors relating to family life. The anxiety of parents over such matters communicates itself to children as surely as measles or chickenpox infections are passed from one person to another. Children cannot be shielded from all the worries of a family, nor should they be. Since a major developmental task is to learn to face reality and to tolerate a normal amount of stress, the family is the best place in which to learn to do this. However, in some families, the atmosphere of stress is so intense that, rather than serving as a supportive environment, the home is actually injurious to its members. Various studies of the readjustment of patients discharged from mental hospitals show that these people often do better if they are not returned to their own homes but are sent to a boarding house or to some other neutral environment (8).

Stress Within the Individual

Many people carry within themselves conflicts, sensitivities, unfilled aspirations, and a variety of other stress stimuli which have become a part of their personality structure. This internal source of stress is deep-seated and not easily modified by such things as changing jobs, marriage partners, or neighborhoods, because the individual is actually reacting to himself.

Frequently, sources of stress within an individual operate on an unconscious level. Just as a virus may invade the body and stimulate physiological reactions while the individual is unaware of what is going on, so psychological stress can exert its influence below the level of awareness. A person may be unable to understand why he feels and acts as he does, yet he persists in his established patterns of behavior even if it gets him into difficulty. Only through a process of therapy can these unconscious origins of stress be disclosed and irrational behavior made intelligible (2).

The internalization of stress stimuli on an unconscious level is a complex process which is not entirely understood. It is probable that repression and conditioning are important factors in this process. Repression is the involuntary forcing into the unconscious of painful or threatening stimuli. This results in a complex of submerged wishes, thoughts, desires, and feelings, the origins of which are not usually known to a person. More will be said about the process of repression in the following chapter.

Conditioning helps explain why to some people feelings, thoughts, and symbols of danger are as real as an actual physical hazard. Many years ago, the Russian physiologist, Ivan P. Pavlov, demonstrated that the clicking of a metronome, or certain other sounds, lights, or odors, could be substituted for food and produce in an animal all the emotional and physiological reactions that normally occur when he is fed. Similar reactions occur in humans, so that they react to internalized symbols of threat even before an active threat is presented or long after it has passed. Feelings of helplessness, disturbing inner doubts, and apprehension are just as difficult to live with when they are produced by internalized symbols of threat as when they come from some actual threatening situation (2).

ACUTE AND CHRONIC STRESS

Ordinarily, the longer a stress continues to act on an individual, the more strain or tension he will experience. A person can hold his breath for a few seconds without discomfort, but continued holding of the breath puts him under a severe strain. Similarly, he can tolerate psychological stress for a short time, but continued stress will make heavy demands on his energies and adaptive capacities.

In the physical realm, continued stress may cause the body to become capable of sustaining the strain. For example, if a person does not use his arm muscles very much during the year, a few hours of hard labor will make him very stiff and sore. But if the activity is continued, the muscles adapt and the individual becomes capable of physical activity over a long period of time. Moreover, he can stop and rest, or discontinue physical exercise and gain quick relief from the physical stress.

The body does not accommodate so readily to psychological stress. If the stress is not overpowering, a person may develop new competencies to meet the demands or learn to live under some tension. But continued psychological stress which keeps a person under constant pressure requires some continued kind of reaction. If the stress is mild, just enough to keep a person mobilized, the emotional stimulation is just enough to keep him on his toes. However, under chronic emotional stress, the strain on the body interferes with one's ability to react in a normal, intelligent way. Behavior then is directed toward relieving discomfort rather than solving the problems which are the source of tension.

The accumulation of tension resulting from a succession of stresses is often the cause of a blow-up after a seemingly inconsequential experience. The frequency of the expression, "that's the last straw," indicates that such reactions are a rather common occurrence. The cumulative effect of such stresses is materially enhanced if there has been no opportunity to drain off at least some of the tension into activity. Where such draining off occurs, the immediate stress is relieved and the intensity of the reaction to subsequent situations is reduced. This is why it is well for a person to be actively involved in some form of recreation or hobby which will provide an outlet for the excess energy that stressful living produces.

SOMATIC REACTIONS TO PSYCHOLOGICAL STRESS

In Chapter 7 we described the function of the autonomic nervous system in activating the internal organs of a person when he was experiencing a strong emotion. As we look a little deeper into how the body reacts to stress, we shall see why it is that real physical disorders can be produced by psychological stimuli. These disorders are no less real or less painful because they are brought about by psychological stress rather than through disease or injury.

Glandular Reactions

A variety of glandular activity occurs when an individual is subjected to psychological stress. In some chronic stress conditions the adrenal glands produce a corticoid named desoxycorticosterone, or DCA, which diminishes excitability of the nervous system. A few crystals of DCA are sufficient to anesthetize fish. This product is thought to be associated with depression, apathy, and general feelings of weakness and fatigue.

In acute stress experience the excretion of pituitary hormones is activated. An increase in production of the adrenocorticotropic hormone, ACTH, of the pituitary gland occurs under emotional stress. This substance regulates the discharge of adrenal hormones into the blood stream (37). One of these adrenal hormones, hydrocortisone, has been studied extensively. Hydrocortisone levels of the blood rise during states of excitement and diminish during periods of calm. Experiments with normal subjects have shown that even an exciting film can cause a rise in blood hydrocortisone concentrations while a bland nature film will lower it. The experience of real emotional stress produces much more dramatic fluctuations in the hydrocortisone levels of the blood (30).

Thyroid activity has also been associated with emotional stress. Underactivity of the thyroid may lead to emotional blunting. When sheep are deprived of their thyroid gland, they no longer react to stimuli like normal animals but plod along complacently, hardly responding to changed conditions, or even to sharp stimuli like a pistol shot. Many phlegmatic, depressed, or chronically tired people have been shown to have low levels of thyroid functioning. High-strung, sensitive, touchy people often have an excess of thyroid activity (23).

Ovarian activity is another glandular change frequently associated with stress. Almost half of all women in the reproductive period of life display cyclic emotional instability around the menstrual period. This has been called premenstrual tension and usually is accompanied by symptoms of irritability, fault-finding, flares of temper, emotional depression, crying spells, or heightened sensitivity. The ovarian hormone, progesterone, is implicated in this upset of physiological equilibrium (32).

These and many other glandular responses to psychological stress have been reported. Glandular activity usually represents a widespread mobilization of the body resources, involving enzymes, hormones, metabolic functions, and other disturbances which affect the total behavior of a person (18).

Gastrointestinal Reactions

In contrast with the general upheaval associated with glandular response to stress, reactions involving the gastrointestinal system commonly are localized and defensive in nature. Often they are focused around the portals of entry and exit of the body and involve the mouth, throat, opening of the esophagus to the stomach, of the stomach to the bowels, the anus, and related structures. When stress is encountered, a person may symbolically eject the stimulus by vomiting, by diarrhea, and, in some cases, by loss of bowel control. In lesser stress there are feelings of nausea, belching, dryness of the mouth or excess salivation, and other ejection-riddance reactions (43).

Along with these active observable reactions are physical changes in internal organs. The reactions of the stomach have been studied extensively, using people whose stomach linings have been exposed as a result of surgery. The stomach has been found to react with characteristic symptoms to certain emotional experiences. Fear or a horrifying experience can cause a sinking feeling in the stomach which is accompanied by a blanching of the mucous membrane similar to the manner in which the face turns pale. Following the blanching, motor activity ceases and the stomach increases in size until nausea occurs. Similar reactions can be produced by worry and may be sustained over long periods of time.

In anger or hostility, when a person's face turns red, the stomach lining also turns red. Acid production is more than doubled, and vigorous contractions begin. In sustained resentment the same reactions occur and persist, often accompanied by heartburn and gnawing pain. It isn't difficult to see why people who have such stomach reactions are prone to peptic ulcers. When the stomach lining is engorged and red, and acid secretions high, the stomach is more subject to hemorrhage and pain. Even talking about unpleasant problems which arouse anger can cause gastric contractions and acid secretion. An angry person many appear outwardly calm and serene, but his stomach reveals his true state of distress (42).

The large bowel responds to stress much like the stomach. By administering barium salts and using X-ray photography, the bowel has been studied under various conditions of emotional stress. Persons who have feelings of dejection and futility commonly have an elongated, slack bowel which is practically motionless. Under the stress of fear or panic, the bowel narrows and conspicuous contraction waves appear, often resulting in diarrhea. People who develop ulcerative colitis have been found to have a hyperactive, tense colon with small hemorrhagic lesions and with an increased secretion of the enzyme lysozyme which can damage the protective lining of the intestine and expose it to ulceration (43). In all of these conditions a person may maintain a calm exterior while he is churning inside. The bowel and stomach, it seems, are better indicators of how we really feel than is our external appearance. The persons most likely to develop ulcers are those who experience chronic internal agitation, regardless of their outward behavior. Schizophrenics, it has been found, have an extremely low rate of ulcers. Withdrawn from reality, they are not subject to the agitation and anxiety which makes the normal person produce this response to stress (14, 26).

Other Physical Reactions to Stress

The body reacts in many other ways to psychogenic stress. There is hardly a part of the human body that cannot be damaged by tension. We shall mention but a few of the more common reactions affecting the cardiovascular system, the respiratory system, the teeth, and the skin.

Cardiovascular Reactions. A standard test of heart function is to check the heart action during rest, provide a short period of exercise, then recheck the heart. In normal, healthy people, the heart rate should return to the resting state within about two minutes after exercise. When an individual is under stress, the heart continues to behave as it did during exercise or only slowly returns to the resting level of performance (43). These same reactions can be produced when the patient does not exercise at all but is exposed to stressful interviews, or to threats such as drawing a blood sample. The more anxious the person is, the longer his heart functions in an exaggerated manner (13).

Associated with response of the heart to stress are certain muscular reactions which give rise to the pain and shortness of breath that a tense person may experience. During stress the diaphragm is flattened and shortened, causing a tightness or cramp in the chest and inability to take a deep breath. The muscles around the ribs and shoulders may undergo sustained and sometimes forceful contractions, adding to the feeling of discomfort. It is these muscular reactions which sometimes cause a tense person to feel he is having a heart attack (43).

Constant tension can have even more serious effects on the circulatory system. The steady discharge into the blood stream of powerful glandular products, which occurs when a person is under stress, may be more than the body can handle. One effect is the migraine headaches which occur when arteries in the head dilate and become filled with blood. Another is the rise in blood cholesterol levels which can contribute to the development of atherosclerosis, a thickening of the artery walls which impedes circulation. The formation of blood clots which may lodge in the vessels of the heart or brain—a most serious consequence of continued tension—is caused by the narrowing of the small arteries and the increase in blood viscosity. Thus, constant emotional tension may do more than merely make a person nervous or miserable; it can jeopardize his life.

Dental Caries. There is some indication that tooth decay may be affected by stress. Dentists have observed that people have a greater incidence of tooth decay during periods of anxiety and frustration than when their lives are proceeding smoothly. One dentist who kept records on three children in a family over a period of years found that the middle child, a girl of twelve who was neither as bright nor as attractive as her siblings and was always being picked on, had the greatest incidence of dental caries, and this incidence was higher during periods of stress. A similar reaction was noted in another young girl who had hoped to get married upon graduation from high school but had to go to work instead. Caries occurred at a high level during the intervening year until she did get married, and subsided thereafter.

These reactions are thought to result from metabolic disturbances occurring during periods of emotional stress which cause chemical changes in the saliva. Some confirmation of this possibility comes from the medical life histories assembled at Cornell University. One of the main conclusions reached through the study of many people over a period of years was that "the great majority of the cluster of illness episodes that occurred in the lives of every group occurred at times when they perceived their life situations to be unsatisfying, threatening, over-demanding, and productive of conflict, and they could make no satisfactory adaptation to these situations" (16). Further confirmation of the possible relationship between dental caries and emotional stress comes from a study made on Navajo Indian children who were removed from a reservation and placed in a boarding school. The children had received good dental care on the reservation through the U.S. Public Health Service. At school they brushed their teeth, ate a balanced diet, and lived in clean warm dormitories under optimum health conditions. Despite such care, a large number of children developed a gum infection similar to trench mouth. The cause of the infection could not be traced to any physical factors. The investigators concluded that the emotional stress induced by moving these children from the permissive, seminomadic life of the reservation, where they practically ran wild, to the regimented, authoritative environment of the boarding school produced physiological reactions which enabled the otherwise benign organisms living in the mouth to become active and set up an infection (25).

Asthma and Allergies of the Respiratory Tract. The mucous membranes of the nose, mouth, throat, and the upper respiratory system are sensitive to psychological stress. Common responses are swelling, hemorrhaging, ulceration, dilation, turgescence, hypersecretion, pain or obstruction. These reactions may give rise to asthma, rhinitis, and other allergic symptoms (43).

The histories of patients with asthma often contain instances of attacks following emotional events. Asthmatic attacks have been produced experimentally simply by presenting people with symbols of stimuli associated with their allergies. In one patient a severe attack was induced by the sight of a goldfish in a bowl; in another, by a picture of a horse (9). It has been observed that some children who have allergic reactions to eggs develop symptoms only when their parents argue at the breakfast table. Some ragweed-sensitive children get hay fever only on the first day of school. Others develop asthmatic symptoms every Christmas, although they are around evergreens all year. Perhaps this is why it is sometimes necessary to remove asthmatic individuals from the emotional effects of the environment before their attacks can be brought under control (41).

The Skin. Just as mucous membranes may show increased sensitivity to food, pollen, drugs, and other things, during periods of emotional stress, so the skin reacts to psychological symbols of danger. Ring-finger dermatitis, for example, has been observed among women who had conflicts over marriage. The dermatitis is limited to the area under the ring and does not shift to another finger when the ring is shifted. Eczema of the thumb, of the external ear, and of the eyelids has been associated with emotional stress. This dermatitis is thought to have a symbolic significance related to problems which affect the particular locale of the irritation. In some rare cases a weeping eczema covering the entire body has occurred in response to severe psychological stress (34).

Observations of patients with acne have shown that, during periods of stress, changes occur in the output of the small glands in the skin which secrete the sebaceous or oily fluid. While experiencing anger, a person may secrete 25 times more sebum than is normal for him. In remorse or depression, there is a relative decrease of sebum output. One study found that patients with the worst cases of acne were those who experienced intense anger followed by depression or remorse (43). Inflammatory skin reactions have also been traced to the release from the nerve endings of a hormone-like substance called Neurokinen, which stimulates blood vessel dilation and causes skin flare-ups (31).

Many other physiological reactions to stress are known. Civilian populations subjected to the emotional stresses of World War II were observed to show reactions of excessive sweating, diffuse aches and pains, dizziness and fainting, impotence in males and menstrual anomalies in females, disturbances of urination, insomnia, and extreme fatigue. Obviously, the physiological reactions to stress can be very extensive and incapacitating (37).

Diffuse Motor Reactions. Stress can induce in an individual a surge of energy which seeks release through motor activity. When no useful motor activity is available, the individual is likely to engage in a variety of useless movements, including restless pacing, gnawing of the knuckles, repeated rubbing of the chin, biting of the lip or nail, inability to sit still, ceaseless smoking, and other forms of physical nervousness.

Temporary nervousness in response to an acute stress situation is an entirely normal occurrence. A worried person has an excess of nervous energy that he does not know what to do with. If expectant fathers could be put to working chopping wood or boiling water, their energy could be drained off into some useful activity rather than into distressing motor and visceral responses. Unless a person engages in some type of physical activity, constant exposure to stress can lead to a condition of motor nervousness which keeps him jumpy and hyperactive even when there are no immediate pressures upon him. When all this evidence is put together, it would seem to indicate that excessive tension comes out somewhere in the body, sending a message to take it easy or suffer the consequences.

ANXIETY AS A RESPONSE TO STRESS

Anxiety is a state of dread or apprehension, characterized by an uncomfortable, vague, diffuse feeling of uneasiness. It is quite a common reaction to pyschological stress and often accompanies the physiological responses discussed above.

Anxiety may range in intensity from mild states of apprehension, such as being nervous about an interview, to acute terror or anguish. It can even occur during sleep and give rise to nightmares or night terrors. One of the most distressing aspects of anxiety is the feeling of helplessness it creates. Often, the individual cannot identify the stress which has given rise to anxious feelings, or, if he can, there is nothing he can do about it. This state of emotional upset, if continued very long, can produce depressive reactions, generalized nervousness, psychosomatic ailments, and other distressing or handicapping conditions (4).

Some Effects of Anxiety

As we have mentioned previously, anxiety is not all bad. Some kinds of anxiety would be considered completely natural, normal, and even healthy. It is natural for a soldier to be anxious before a battle, for an athlete to be tense before a game, or for an inexperienced orator to be nervous before a speech. In these instances the anxiety is in response to some pending event and usually is dissipated when the crisis has passed.

Anxiety is also an important part of the child-rearing process. Without it, it is doubtful whether a person would develop a superego or conscience. In his earliest experiences in the home, a child begins to learn which activities will be approved or disapproved. Disapproved activities will arouse anxiety, and an effort normally will be made to exclude them from behavior and to incorporate approved activities. If the child experiences no anxiety at all about his behavior, then the foundations for an antisocial personality are laid for later delinquency or other forms of irresponsible action.

The role of anxiety in learning has been studied rather

extensively and shows both positive and negative effects. Anxiety is the basis for much creative effort and often becomes a stimulus to progress. People who are free of anxiety are unlikely to be motivated to learn or to take any action regarding the problems they encounter. They may become drifters or floaters in school. On the other hand, students who have a manageable level of anxiety have an extra supply of energy to devote to their learning tasks (17).

When the level of anxiety reaches a point where it becomes distressing, learning is definitely impeded. The individual becomes so concerned with relieving his anxiety that he cannot attend to the learning task at hand. His perceptions are narrowed, and he tends to focus upon himself and his own feelings rather than on what is going on around him. Therefore, it is not surprising to learn that studies of school children show strongly anxious pupils tending to be nearly two years retarded in mental and educational development, despite a normal level of intelligence (35:74).

The effects of anxiety on creativity and imagination have been investigated among children at different ages. These studies show that as youngsters encounter anxiety-producing pressures, their creativity becomes more restricted. At 4½ years of age, children are usually highly imaginative, but 6 months later, when they enter school, there is a definite decrease in originality. A period of recovery follows, until the age of 9, when peer approval becomes a significant stress. Other decreases in creativity are found at age 13, the onset of early adolescence, and at age 17, when the transition to college, work, or military service is confronted. Although similar studies of adults have not been made, anxiety can be expected to have the same depressing effects on creative thinking among adults as it does among children (40).

Guilt

Guilt is a form of anxiety arising primarily from inner conflicts. The demands and prohibitions of parents, coupled with the moral and social sanctions of the culture, conflict with an individual's desires or actions and create feelings of guilt.

Guilt feelings may lead to several types of behavior, the most common being remorse, compunction, and self-punishment. Remorse and compunction often are reflected in efforts to bring about reconciliation through gifts, kind deeds, or helpfulness. The youngster who has received a deserved spanking is often quite contrite after his emotions have subsided and tries hard to please the punisher. The husband who has forgotten a wedding anniversary similarly relieves his guilt feelings through gifts which may be more extravagant than they would have been had they been presented at the appropriate time.

The guilty person may feel sorry for his thoughts, wishes, or misdeeds and seek to punish himself in various ways. Usually, the source of the guilt is below the level of consciousness, and the behavior of the individual in response to this unconscious guilt is not entirely explainable even to himself. Various masochistic, or self-punishing, acts may occur, including denying oneself any pleasurable activities, hard work, and forms of atonement ranging from excessive preoccupation with religion to acts of philanthropy or devotion to public welfare. Accident proneness is also considered to be an unconscious attempt at self-punishment.

In children the anxiety resulting from guilt feelings is often reflected in behavior which unconsciously is designed to provoke punishment. They seem deliberately to persist in doing things calculated to annoy or irritate their parents or teachers. When punishment is forthcoming, the feelings of guilt are relieved, the slate cleared, and the cycle started anew. This is a fairly normal occurrence, and the person who administers the punishment should not develop anxiety himself over the part he is forced to play in it.

Conflict and Frustration

When an individual is confronted with the necessity of choosing between several incompatible action systems, he is in a conflict situation. Sometimes none of the avenues open to him are desirable. Or they may all be desirable, but if he takes one he must give up others that are important. If he is completely blocked and can find no solution to his conflict, he experiences frustration. These are situations which engender feelings of anxiety. They fill a person with ambivalent desires that make him want to fight and to run away, to love and to hate, to speak up and be silent, to take a chance and to play it safe. He remains under tension because he can make no decision.

Conflict and frustration may, and often does, result from environmental restraints, restrictions, or hazards. However, environmental factors are only potential sources of conflict or frustration. Whether a person actually develops anxiety over such situations depends on his personal values and motivation. The golf enthusiast who has planned to play on a certain day is frustrated when rain interferes with his plans. The person who cares little about golf will experience no frustration in connection with the same situation. The environmental factors are the same in both instances, but differences in personal motivation and values influence the reactions to the situation. Therefore, we must think of frustrating situations existing in terms of the needs, goals, or wishes of the individual, as well as the external situation. This is sometimes disconcerting to people who think others should behave in a certain way in response to certain situations and are dismayed when they do not. For example, psychotherapists are often frustrated by the lack of response of lower-class patients who neither value nor understand their disorders or the efforts made to alleviate them. Teachers, too, are often upset by the standards and values of lower-class children who are not motivated to learn. We must understand the wishes, needs, values, and goals of individuals if we are to interpret their reactions to external circumstances with any degree of accuracy.

PATTERNS OF REACTION TO STRESS

People vary considerably in the manner in which they react to psychological stress. Some are so marginally balanced that even a minor threat can precipitate a serious upheaval. Others are more mature, capable, and stable, and can withstand tremendous stress before they go to pieces (6).

Variability occurs also in the types of reactions which stress calls forth in different individuals. Laboratory studies have shown that each person has a characteristic mode of reaction to stress and that this behavior is brought into play automatically when he responds to stress stimuli.

It would take many pages to describe adequately the varieties of human reaction to stress which have been identified. Fortunately, it is possible to group these reactions into two major categories for analysis. These are the aggressive or fight reactions, and the withdrawal or flight reactions. While this is a rough grouping which obscures the true complexities of individual behavior, it will help us gain a general understanding of some common patterns of reaction to stress.

The Aggressive Response

The aggressive reaction is a primitive response which appears early in life. It is seen in the crying, thrashing around, and other expressions of displeasure displayed by the infant. Young children normally go after what they want and try to overcome any obstacle that stands in their way. The spectacle of a three-year-old kicking at a closed door is a familiar illustration of this. A child normally does not learn to withdraw or run away from a hazard or obstacle until he has had some unpleasant experience with it.

As adults, some people continue to fight for what they want and are aggressive, competitive, and striving. To fight against obstacles is a healthy form of adjustment if it gets problems solved and meets the needs of the individual without coming into conflict with society. However, if this is the only way a person knows to cope with stress, he will have difficulty as his social environment increases in complexity and he needs to become more sensitive to the reactions of other people. Thus, an active approach to threat can be good or bad, realistic or unrealistic, depending upon the person and the circumstances.

Individuals who are unable to tolerate more than a minimal level of tension are likely to discharge their energy into premature aggressive action. Unstable and immature people are particularly prone to nonpurposeful aggression which does not solve their problems or relieve their anxiety. A young child, for example, who is frustrated because his parents ignore him or favor a sibling, is quite likely to show his aggression by refusing to obey, by destroying something, or by wetting his bed. The adult who uses his car as an instrument of aggression is displaying a similar form of nonadjustive behavior. Such actions may temporarily reduce the feelings of anxiety and discomfort, but they have little effect on the stress itself (6).

The Withdrawal Response

People who seek safety by withdrawing from a stress situation usually direct their anger or irritation inwardly toward themselves rather than against the stress-producing stimulus. Often they feel ill-treated, depressed, and even angry with themselves for acting as they do. Yet, their tendency to withdraw, either physically or psychologically, is an automatic response which is difficult to control (12).

It is sometimes wise and reasonable to withdraw from a threatening situation. A strategic retreat may be more sensible than a futile assault against an insurmountable obstacle. But when this withdrawal becomes an automatic reaction rather than a realistic response to circumstances, then the individual perpetuates his frustration by leaving his problems unsolved. The visceral and emotional tensions which accompany this anger reaction are not eliminated by avoiding the stress which creates them. These continuing tensions often lead to psychosomatic ills or to a state of chronic anxiety (24). Patients suffering from ulcerative colitis frequently use such phrases as "helpless," "despair," "hopelessness," "overwhelmed," "too much to cope with," and "too much expected of me" to describe their feelings. They feel an underlying anger and hostility, but there is little overt expression of this anger either verbally or through actions (11).

The course of good adjustment requires a person to learn to deal with his stresses. Sometimes he has to delay his responses long enough to formulate plans and mobilize his resources. At other times he may have to attack the problems which can be attacked, or compromise, or accept substitute gratifications. Flexibility, rather than a stereotyped pattern of reaction to stress, provides the best chance for achieving a reasonable state of adjustment (29).

STRESS TOLERANCE

We have pointed out that stress can be damaging to personality development or it can add zest to life, depending on whether the stress is within the limits of one's capacity to adjust. People do, in fact, seek situations which place them under stress. They enjoy games of skill and chance, and like to match wits, or skill, or strength with others because of the challenge they experience. By encountering and overcoming obstacles a person can bolster his sense of adequacy and develop a feeling of accomplishment. Without some challenge, some difficulty to surmount, or crisis to resolve, we would be deprived of experiences which are essential for ego development.

The type of stress which produces tensions that we can do nothing about, which does not let us relax, and is beyond our ability to handle, poses some severe adjustment problems. There is no easy formula for avoiding such stress or for coping with it. The best defense is to develop a tolerance to stress, so that we do not react to everything that happens to us but limit our reactions to things that are important enough to get disturbed about.

The development of stress tolerance is a learning process that begins in early childhood and is largely dependent upon wise guidance by parents. A child has to experience stress if he is to become progressively more capable of dealing with it. He has to learn to accept substitute goals when necessary, and become accustomed to certain delays in the satisfaction of his wishes. These are difficult lessons to learn, and a child needs protection from problems which are beyond the scope of his developing powers as well as leeway to attack those problems which are within his capacity to handle. Too much protection or too little emotional support may be equally detrimental to the development of adequate methods for handling stress.

The inability of many adults to tolerate more than a minimum amount of stress indicates that this developmental process does not always operate smoothly. Many of us reach adulthood clinging to inadequate ways of responding to stress. We use such terms as "temperamental," "unpredictable," "volatile," or "overly inhibited" to describe the immature reactions of adults. The adult cannot expect the sympathy and support given to a child; he is expected to handle his own problems. Yet, adults, too, need human support when exposed to stress. People feel more comfortable when other people are around to share their problems. We tolerate stress much more easily in the presence of a friend, relative, or sympathetic person than we do when we are alone or in the presence of a stranger (20).

Despite our best efforts to develop a mature level of stress tolerance, we cannot expect to insulate ourselves entirely from stress stimuli. A person needs to be alert to the early warning signals of tension, so that he can do something before it overwhelms him. Such symptoms as chronic fatigue, depression, stomach upsets, heartburn, nervousness, anxiety, and others which we have described, should be considered as a warning that something is wrong and that it is time to either stop and take stock of what is going on or seek professional help. Such alertness may not prevent all his problems, but it may often enable a person to do something about them before they become too severe.

SUMMARY

Psychological stress can produce tensions which are fully as incapacitating as injury done to the body by physical stress. Many physiological reactions occur in response to psychological stress. These include reactions of various glands and organs: gastrointestinal, cardiovascular, cutaneous, respiratory, and muscular responses, among others.

Anxiety often accompanies these physiological reactions as an emotional response which may either promote or hinder adjustment. Moderate anxiety is useful in the child-rearing process and contributes to creativity and motivation for learning. When anxiety becomes intense, its positive values are eliminated, and it becomes an obstacle to reasoned behavior by narrowing one's perceptions, obscuring intellectual function, and focusing attention on internal problems.

People vary considerably in their reactions to psychological stress. A large number develop aggressive patterns of reaction and expend their energy in attacking the stress-producing stimulus. Many others seek safety in withdrawal from stress and direct their energies inwardly. Either reaction, if unsuited to the circumstances, and if it becomes a stereotyped pattern of behavior, may interfere with the individual's adjustive capacity.

Psychological stress can contribute to adjustment by providing a challenge to the individual and enabling him to develop a sense of accomplishment through pitting his abilities against obstacles. The less desirable effects of stress are those which keep people under continuing tension. The development of stress tolerance will enable a person to disregard many annoyances and limit his reactions to situations which are really important. This process is never perfected, and even the best adjusted person needs to be alert to the physiological and emotional symptoms of tension so that he can do something about them before they become overwhelming.

REFERENCES

1. Azima, H., and Azima, F. J. C., "Studies on Perceptual Isolation," *Dis. nerv. System, Monogr. Suppl.*, July, 1957, pp. 80–86.
2. Bertalanffy, L. V., "Some Biological Considerations on the Problem of Mental Illness," *Bull. Menninger Clin.*, March, 1959, 23:41–51.
3. Braceland, F. J., "Feelings of Loneliness," *The Third Annual Forum on Human Relations*, Hartford, Conn., Connecticut Mutual Life Insurance Co., 1961.
4. Braceland, F. J., "The Individual—Challenge of the Future," in *Society Challenges the Individual*, Report of the Mental Health Lectures in Hartford, Conn., Connecticut Mutual Life Insurance Co., March, 1962, pp. 21–29.
5. Brady, J. V., "Ulcers in 'Executive' Monkeys," *Sci. Amer.*, October, 1958, Reprint No. 425, pp. 3–6.
6. Brody, E. B., "Borderline State, Character Disorder, and Psychotic Manifestations—Some Conceptual Formulations," *Psychiat.*, February, 1960, 23:75–80.

7. Brosin, H. W., "The Primary Processes and Psychoses," *Behav. Sci.*, January, 1957, **2**:62–67.

8. Cumming, J. H., "The Family and Mental Disorder: An Incomplete Essay," *Milbank Mem. Fund Quart.*, April, 1961, **39**:185–228.

9. Dekker, E., and Groen, J., "Reproducible Psychogenic Attacks of Asthma," *J. psychosom. Res.*, February, 1956, **1**:58–67.

10. Dunham, W. W., "Social Structures and Mental Disorders: Competing Hypotheses of Explanation," *Milbank Mem. Fund Quart.*, April, 1961, **39**:259–311.

11. Fullerton, D. T., *et al.*, "A Clinical Study of Ulcerative Colitis," *J. Amer. Med. Ass.*, August 11, 1962, **181**:463–471.

12. Funkenstein, D. H., *Mastery of Stress,* Harvard, 1957.

13. Glickstein, M., *et al.*, "Temporal Heart-Rate Patterns in Anxious Patients," *Arch. Neurol. Psychiat.*, July, 1957, **78**:101–106.

14. Gosling, R. H., "Peptic Ulcer and Mental Disorder—II," *J. psychosom. Res.*, 1958, **2**:285–301.

15. Harrington, J. A. and Cross, K. W., "A Preliminary Investigation of Leisure in Psychiatric Patients," *Ment. Hyg.*, October, 1962, **46**:580–597.

16. Hinkle, L. E., Jr., and Wolff, H. G., "Ecologic Investigations of the Relationship Between Illness, Life Experiences, and the Social Environment," *Ann. intern. Med.*, December, 1958, **49**:1373–1388.

17. Hochbaum, G. M., "Modern Theories of Communication," *Child.*, January–February, 1960, **7**:13–18.

18. Houssay, B. A., "The Status of Endocrinology in 1985," *What's New,* Abbott Laboratories, 25th Anniversary Issue, Number 220, 1960.

19. Jackson, C. W., *et al.*, "The Application of Findings from Experimental Sensory Deprivation to Cases of Clinical Sensory Deprivation," *Amer. J. Med. Sci.*, May, 1962, **243**:558–563.

20. Kissel, S., *Social Stimuli and Reduction of Stress,* Unpublished Doctoral Dissertation, University of Buffalo, 1961.

21. Lambo, T. A., "Malignant Anxiety," *J. ment. Sci.*, May, 1962, **108**:256–264.

22. Langner, T. S., "Environmental Stress and Mental Health," *Address Delivered to the American Psychopathological Society,* February 20, 1959, New York, 12 pp., mimeographed.

23. Liddell, H. S., "Conditioning and Emotions," *Sci. Amer.*, January, 1954, Reprint No. 418, pp. 2–10.

24. Marshall, S., "Personality Correlates of Peptic Ulcer Patients," *J. consult. Psychol.,* June, 1960, 24:218–223.

25. Mills, L. F., "Epidemic in a Navajo School," *Bull. Menninger Clin.,* July, 1962, 26:189–194.

26. Mirsky, I. A., "Physiologic, Psychologic and Social Determinants of Psychosomatic Disorders," *Dis. nerv. System,* February, 1960, Supplement, 21:550–556.

27. Murphy, G., "New Vistas in Personality Research," *Personnel & Guidance J.,* October, 1961, 40:114–122.

28. Murphy, H. B. M., "Social Change and Mental Health," *Milbank Mem. Fund Quart.,* July, 1961, 39:385–445.

29. Murphy, L. B., "Preventive Implications of Development in the Preschool Years," in G. Caplan (Ed.), *Prevention of Mental Disorders in Children,* Basic Books, 1961, pp. 218–248.

30. National Institute of Mental Health, *Highlights of Progress in Mental Health Research, 1960,* Public Health Service Publication No. 824, Bethesda, Md., 1961.

31. National Institute of Neurological Diseases and Blindness, *Highlights of Progress in Research on Neurological and Sensory Disorders, 1961,* Public Health Service Publication No. 893, Washington, 1962.

32. Page, R. W., "Frequently Encountered Menstrual Problems," *Seminar Rep.,* Merck, Sharp & Dohme, Fall, 1961, 6:16–22.

33. Pflanz, M., "Socio-Psychological Aspects of Peptic Ulcer," *J. psychosom. Res.,* February, 1956, 1:68–74.

34. Sanger, M. D., "The Psyche and Dermatitis," *State of Mind,* Ciba, March–April, 1959, 3:No. 2.

35. Sarason, S., *et al., Anxiety in Elementary School Children,* Wiley, 1960 .

36. Schmideberg, M., "Tolerance in Upbringing and Its Abuses," *Int. J. soc. Psychiat.,* Autumn, 1959, 5:123–130.

37. Selye, H., "The General-Adaptation-Syndrome in Its Relationships to Neurology, Psychology and Psychopathology," in A. Weider (Ed.), *Contributions Toward Medical Psychology: Theory and Psychodiagnostic Methods,* Vol. I, Ronald, 1953, pp. 234–274.

38. Sifneos, P. E., "A Concept of Emotional Crisis," *Ment. Hyg.,* April, 1960, 44:169–179.

39. Sorenson, R., "Youth's Need for Challenge and Place in Society," *Child.,* July–August, 1962, 9:131–138.

40. Torrance, E. P., "Cultural Discontinuities and the Develop-

ment of Originality of Thinking," *Except. Child.,* September, 1962, **29**:2–13.

41. Tuft, H. S., "Significance of the Psyche in the Asthma-Eczema-Urticaria-Rhinitis Syndrome," *State of Mind,* Ciba, December, 1958, 2:No. 10.

42. Wolf, S., and Wolff, H. G., "Life Situations, Emotions, and Gastric Function: A Summary," in A. Weider (Ed.), *Contributions Toward Medical Psychology: Theory and Psychodiagnostic Methods,* Vol. I, Ronald, 1953, pp. 290–314.

43. Wolff, H. G., "Life Stress and Bodily Disease," in A. Weider (Ed.), *Contributions Toward Medical Psychology: Theory and Psychodiagnostic Methods,* Vol. I, Ronald, 1953, pp. 315–367.

Chapter 10   Coping

with Anxiety

People who face their problems and do something constructive about them are most likely to make an adequate response to psychological stress. However, the origins of our problems are not always known, and, if known, not always correctable. Therefore, we must expect to experience anxiety at times, and be prepared to cope with it when it arises. Since anxiety is a reaction which no one can tolerate very long or very often, nature has provided some psychological and behavioral devices which help us to reduce the intensity of anxiety or avoid it altogether. These devices are called defense mechanisms or mechanisms of adjustment. They provide a means whereby a person may regulate his feelings, thoughts, perceptions, and actions so that the anxiety he does experience is at a level he can handle.

CLASSIFICATION OF DEFENSE MECHANISMS

We owe to psychoanalytic theory the concept of defense mechanisms as ways of coping with anxiety. Psychoanalysts originally described these devices as mental mechanisms, limited to the manipulation of conscious and unconscious mental processes (8). Psychologists have expanded the meaning of this term to include behavior and emotions, as well as mental processes, so that these devices are now commonly referred to as mechanisms of adjustment rather than mental mechanisms.

Mechanisms of adjustment include a wide range of behavior for which there is no completely satisfactory classification (2:78). Therefore, we have grouped the most common mechanisms into the following three categories which represent different ways of coping with anxiety:

MECHANISMS OF DECEPTION. These mechanisms tend to alter or mask the individual's perception of a threat by reconstructing his attitudes and feelings so that he senses no threat. Included here are the mechanisms of rationalization, projection, displacement, repression, and suppression.

MECHANISMS OF SUBSTITUTION. These mechanisms attempt to change the tension-laden situation by substituting safe, attainable goals for hard-to-get or threat-inducing goals. The mechanisms of compensation, substitution, reaction formation, sublimation, and egocentricism are classified in this category.

MECHANISMS OF AVOIDANCE. These mechanisms enable the individual to remove himself, psychologically, from a threatening situation. The mechanisms of fantasy, regression, negativism, identification, and some types of somatic reactions are included here.

The mechanisms to be discussed do not always fit into these discrete categories and may often overlap several categories. However, this functional classification will help to clarify the general nature and utility of these devices.

MECHANISMS OF DECEPTION

A person may insulate himself from psychological stress by so altering his interpretations of a situation that he does not feel threatened. He may exclude disagreeable perceptions from awareness, reinterpret them so that they appear different from what they really are, or convince himself that they do not apply to him. Of course, this technique does not alter the forces which are troubling the individual any more than raising an umbrella stops the rain. But they do enable him to manipulate his feelings and mental processes so that tensions do not have too formidable an impact upon him.

Rationalization

One of the most commonly used mechanisms of deception is rationalization. This is a device whereby a person provides himself and others with plausible reasons for behavior rather than admit the actual reasons which are too painful for him to acknowledge. He justifies, excuses, or explains away his behavior, so that what has been done or is being planned appears right and acceptable. In this way he avoids discomfort and makes peace with himself.

Children learn very early to explain their behavior in a way that will earn social approval and avoid punishment. In time they come to believe these explanations, because rationalization helps them to avoid the guilt and anxiety that might result if they had to face the consequences of their thoughts and actions. Later, rationalization becomes built into behavior as a protective mechanism.

The person who rationalizes does not deliberately distort the truth. He usually is quite unconscious of his motives and not aware that he is twisting the facts to protect his self-esteem. The executive, for instance, who discharges a subordinate whose competency is a threat to his own security, does not acknowledge this insecurity as the reason for his actions. In fact, he would deny it if it were brought up. Instead, he finds some acceptable reason for his decision and thus protects his self-esteem (10).

Rationalization is often a very helpful device. It makes us feel better about playing golf when we should be mowing the lawn, or going to a dance when we should be studying. For common, relatively unimportant incidents, rationalization has value in enabling people to do what they want to do without having to pay for their pleasures with feelings of guilt. But, like other deceptions, this form of behavior must be used in moderation. The overuse of rationalization may remove a person so far from his real problems that he may end up with a crisis which cannot be dodged.

Projection

The tendency to shift the responsibility for an act or thought from oneself to an outside agency or to another person is a common psychological defense. This process is called projection. It enables a person to alter his perception of a painful or threatening situation so that he does not carry the blame for it. The baseball player who strikes out but claims that the umpire or the bat was at fault, the golfer who breaks his clubs after a poor showing on the link, the little boy who is constantly tattling on other children, and the clerk who defends his own inadequacies by claiming the boss is out to get him are some familiar illustrations of the mechanisms of projection.

A special form of projection is known as displacement. This is the technique of shifting a response or reaction from its original object to another which is less dangerous. For instance, the child who is reprimanded by his mother may feel hatred toward her. Because of a fear of punishment or feelings of guilt, he does not dare express hatred toward his mother, so he displaces his reactions to his dog. Or he may become a problem in school. Many an unsuspecting teacher or classmate becomes an object of displacement because of hostile feelings created in the home. Some of our likes and dislikes of people, things, or ideas may be traced to this process of displacement. Since this mechanism operates on an unconscious level, we frequently cannot account for the reason why we like or dislike certain things, or why we are hostile to some people and friendly to others (3:44–68).

Repression

Repression is an unconscious process wherein shameful thoughts, guilt-producing memories, painful experiences, or distasteful tasks are removed from awareness or forced below the level of consciousness. This process has been discussed previously in connection with the manner in which the ego and superego deal with the impulses of the id.

Since repression operates through nonconscious processes, the individual is not aware of what is going on. The ego protects itself from anxiety by forcing into the unconscious those experiences which have been distasteful and by resisting the emergence of thoughts and memories which might threaten the complacency or emotional well-being of the person.

The process of repression has been verified by experiments on recall in learning. Things learned under pleasant circumstances are much more readily recalled than things learned under unpleasant circumstances (23, 27). Further evidence is provided by case studies compiled by psychiatrists, which reveal that the hates, anguish, and suffering that parents induce in children are excluded from recall in later life as if these experiences had never occurred. Children frequently vow to get even with a parent "when I grow up," but usually the process of repression intervenes to remove the painful memories of past experiences so that the shameful inclinations, thoughts, and wishes of childhood are forgotten. The individual may be left with feelings of guilt, resentment, or hostility, but the experiences which induced these feelings cannot be remembered at will (12).

Suppression

Suppression is the deliberate, conscious control of one's hazardous and undesirable thoughts or impulses. This mechanism serves the same purpose as repression but involves the conscious intent to put things out of mind. When a person decides that it is best not to think about certain inclinations or commit certain acts, or when he deliberately forces out of his conscious mind certain desires, then he is using the mechanism of suppression.

We frequently are required to grit our teeth and restrain ourselves from hasty action, or to force out of mind aggressive inclinations which might lead to unpleasant consequences. Everyday life is filled with instances where a person must suppress his reactions toward a wife, husband, friend, parent, or traffic officer. If he did not do so, he might precipitate a real emotional crisis. Not only are actions suppressed, but other stimuli which induce worry, tension, or anxiety are likewise forced out of mind. Over a period of time, these suppressed reactions take their place in the unconscious mind along with the products of repression. Thus, while the conscious mind is cleared of thoughts and experiences which are uncomfortable for the individual to acknowledge, these thoughts and experiences are not lost, but stored in the unconscious reservoir of the mind.

For many years, the notion that past experiences were stored away in the unconscious mind was considered to be an unproved assumption of psychoanalysis. Recently, some experimental evidence has been provided to support this concept. Penfield's (20) experiments with the electrical stimulation of the brain has revealed the existence of something akin to the "stream of consciousness" described by William James and other early philosophers and psychologists. By touching an electrode to various portions of the temporal cortex, a conscious person was made aware of random periods of past experience. Things heard and seen in the past were heard and seen again, and the thoughts and emotions which occurred at that period of time passed through the patient's mind again. When the electrical stimulation was removed, the experience ceased; when the current was reapplied, the experience reappeared.

Just where and how these past experiences and emotions are stored in the brain is not clear. It would seem that relatively permanent neuron paths are established in the brain by an experience and that electrical stimulation of this path reactivates the thread of experience as it was on the day it originally occurred. This interpretation coincides very closely with the psychoanalytic theory that an experience of any kind is never completely erased from the mind but remains forever at unconscious levels where the right combination of stimuli may cause it to be reactivated.

Adjustive Value of Mechanisms of Deception

The mechanisms of deception which we have described have some utility in that they help to ease the tensions of living. They enable the individual to exclude distracting or disconcerting perceptions so that he is not constantly harassed by psychological stress. A person is thus enabled to get on with the business of living without having to dissipate his energies combating a succession of minor emotional crises.

While mechanisms of deception do not in themselves solve any problems, they gain time for the person, and time may accomplish what the mechanisms themselves cannot do. The passage of time may work a reorientation in the attitudes or feelings of an individual so that what was a crisis earlier in life is looked back upon as merely "growing pains." Circumstances may become altered, or a person's capacities may develop as he matures, so that earlier threats no longer affect him at a later date. Many of us who have endured sorrows, such as the death of a parent, know how time can soften hurts, change one's perspective on life, and erase its pains.

However, mechanisms of deception cannot be given full approval as adjustive techniques because considerable disorganization of behavior may result from their continued use. The thoughts, memories, and action patterns forced out of the conscious mind by repression or suppression are frequently laden with emotional forces which continue to exert pressure on the unconscious level. The energy that it takes to keep these events submerged may drain emotional capacities to a point where the individual becomes overly inhibited and has little zest for life.

Similarly, rationalization, in its exaggerated form, is seen as an element of the delusions which characterize severe personality disorders, while projection, carried to extremes, becomes the organized persecution complexes of the psychotic person. Any of the mechanisms of deception may lead to behavior and adjustment problems because they enable a person to dodge reality. If he is removed too far and too often from reality, he may have increasing difficulty facing up to the many problems of living which cannot be avoided.

MECHANISMS OF SUBSTITUTION

In many instances where people are cut off from the goals they desire or are faced with obstacles or threats which can neither be denied nor resolved, they resort to mechanisms of substitution to extricate themselves from such situations. These mechanisms enable a person to relieve his anxiety by altering his goals. Instead of exposing himself to repeated frustration by pursuing something he cannot have, he attains substitute satisfactions through psychological devices which permit him to change direction without loss of self-esteem. This is not a deliberate process where, for example, a college student who is not accepted by a fraternity decides to become active in student government in order to gain recognition. It is, rather, an automatic adjustment process which defends the ego from feelings of failure or unworthiness. Mechanisms of substitution provide satisfaction and relieve tension without exposing a person to the conscious realization that he is settling for something less than what he really wants. There appears to be a sex difference in the use of substitution as a defensive device. Men tend to turn to substitute goals more often than women. The latter are more likely to seek help from others in pursuing their desired goals than to alter their goals or activities (1).

Compensation

We know that when an arm is lost, the other arm makes up for the loss by becoming stronger. If a lung is lost, the other lung compensates for it. As a mechanism of adjustment, compensation performs a similar function in enhancing self-esteem by overcoming a person's failure or deficiency in one area of behavior through satisfaction achieved in another area. Through this mechanism, a person may be able to cover up for a weakness, counterbalance failure, achieve prestige, or relieve himself of emotional pressure.

Compensation is frequently used by children to relieve the frustrations and anxieties developed in an adult-dominated world. This mechanism is seen at work in gangs where the smallest boy may become the most daring in order to achieve status among the older boys. The seemingly irrational behavior of children is more usefully thought of as attempts to compensate for frustration than inherent deviltry or wickedness. Bullying, vandalism, and even stealing may be compensations for the denial of certain satisfactions rather than deliberate incorrigibility.

The compensations of adults are not so frequently of the asocial nature that childhood compensations assume. The adult, having an awareness of the social consequences of his actions, learns to select compensations which will be acceptable to society. Many of these compensations may materially improve his mode of living. For example, people who engage in hobbies or in community projects to compensate for their unhappiness at work or boredom at home may become involved in enterprises that make a fundamental difference in their lives. In such cases, compensation may have a wholesome influence on adjustment.

On the other hand, compensation may have some distinctly negative influences on adjustment. Overuse of this mechanism may develop habits of seeking the easiest way out. If a person is frequently satisfied with attaining lesser goals than he originally desired, he may develop attitudes of resignation or defeat, or inferiority feelings which prevent the full realization of his abilities. The person who overcompensates may do equal injury to himself by becoming a nuisance or a menace to others. People who become aggressive and domineering to compensate for physical inferiority, or who have a fanatical urge for power, or who harbor strong prejudices, reflect some of the less desirable aspects of compensation.

Thus, compensation may be a very useful mechanism when directed into wholesome channels. However, a person cannot always control his adjustive reactions. Compensating behavior is often selected on a chance basis and tends to persist as habit patterns. Unless an individual develops some insight into this process, the compensations which make him feel better may not contribute to his long-range adjustment.

Substitution

Substitution is a device which makes it possible to discharge tensions by diverting one's energies from a desired goal to some substitute. This process is sometimes called transferred compensation, since there is a change of goal as well as of activity. In compensation, a person may alter his activity but pursue the same goal. If he seeks recognition, he may seek it through aggressive behavior rather than personal accomplishment, but he continues to strive for recognition. When substitution is used as a mechanism of adjustment, he may give up trying to attain recognition and turn to eating, for instance, as a means of relieving anxiety. Eating then becomes a substitute activity, replacing a form of satisfaction which the individual cannot attain (4).

Substitution is a useful mechanism of adjustment only when

the substituted goal is sufficiently akin to the desired goal to have some adjustive value. Unless this condition prevails, attaining the substitute goal will provide only transitory relief from emotional tension. Hence, it is not surprising to learn that compulsive eaters have been found to be immature, lacking in impulse control, and often suspicious, hostile people. Their eating does not relieve anxiety but merely allays it. Therefore, it is not an adequate substitute goal (6, 18).

Reaction Formation.   This is a special type of substitution which takes place when the original desire or impulse is heavily laden with guilt feelings. The substitute activity adopted to relieve these feelings is a complete reversal of one's attitudes or behavior. Under such conditions the alcoholic becomes rigorously nonalcoholic and denounces all drinkers; the atheist joins a church and becomes an ardent reformer; the child who has hostile thoughts toward his parents showers them with love and kindness. Similar behavior is demonstrated when people are confronted with anxiety-provoking situations which they must overcome or endure. Medical students when first confronted with a cadaver turn to joking and laughing to overcome their fear or revulsion. Soldiers about to engage in battle have been noted to behave in the same manner. Like reactions are observed among people confronted with a common threat, such as loss of employment. The mechanism of reaction formation serves as a safety valve, relieving tensions and anxiety by causing the person to behave in a manner opposite to what the situation might appear to call for.

Sublimation

Sublimation is the redirection of emotional drives from prohibited goals or desires into socially acceptable modes of behavior. When a person is forced to inhibit his impulses or inclinations, or finds desired goals unattainable, sublimation provides him with approved channels for release of emotional energy.

This mechanism was originally applied by psychoanalysts to the diversion of sexual energies into other forms of behavior. Great works of art, music, and literature have been described as the sublimated outpourings of sexual energy. This interpretation of sublimation has been expanded to include the redirection of energies other than the purely sexual urges. Thus, interest in teaching, nursing, and social work has been described as sublimation of maternal urges; aggressive tendencies may be sublimated into athletics; throwing oneself into one's work may be a redirection of emotions arising in the home; religion may be a sublimation of deeper impulses which a person is unable to express in any other way. In each instance, the individual channels his activity into emotionally satisfying enterprises. However, the substitute activities may not always take the place of the satisfactions which would have been derived from attaining the original and desired goals, and an underlying current of anxiety may remain within the individual.

Egocentricism

Egocentricism is an effort to establish oneself as the center of attention. The egocentric person appears to need constant reinforcement of his ego. In a child, the quest for self-reassurance is a normal aspect of development. Attention-getting devices, such as asking questions, getting in the way of adults, minor infractions of rules, and mischievous pranks which arouse parents, are forms of self-centered behavior common to many children.

As he grows, the child should become less self-centered, and his demands for attention should give way to a large measure of self-sufficiency and independence. Egocentricism in an adult represents a fixation of behavior at the childish, narcissistic, or self-love, level. The adult who must be the life of the party, who is unhappy being alone, whose extroversion is so extreme that he must always be at the center of the stage, may be reacting to an underlying insecurity. As long as he receives a full quota of attention, his ego is bolstered and his anxiety kept under control. But when attention is not forthcoming, his anxiety returns and he may resort to eccentric behavior, antisocial acts, or attention-getting devices. Egocentric people are often single-purpose individuals, with an intense drive for success, who find it difficult to get along with others despite their desire for acceptance (17).

The Adjustive Value of Mechanisms of Substitution

The mechanisms of substitution are potentially more adjustive than the mechanisms which distort one's perceptions of threat. The person who uses mechanisms of substitution is at least making an active attack on his problems rather than evading them. He senses the threatening situation and tries to do something about it by changing his goals or activities so that he does not remain under emotional tension. Compensation and sublimation are probably the most effective of the adjustive mechanisms in that they may lead to real emotional satisfaction and continuing adjustment.

However, as has been pointed out, these mechanisms are only potentially adjustive. If they are misused or overused, then the person may overcome one conflict only to create another within himself or with society. Temporary relief of tension through any of these mechanisms carries with it the possibility that, if the substituted activity does not continue to work, the underlying source of anxiety will become reactivated and the person will again be under stress. Mechanisms of substitution, like all adjustive mechanisms, serve primarily to make a person feel more secure and comfortable. They do not alter the factors which create insecurity or discomfort.

MECHANISMS OF AVOIDANCE

Laboratory experiments have shown that when a situation becomes too stressful it is common for an organism to "leave the field." This may be either a physical or a psychological escape from the emotional stress of a frustrating situation. For example, it has been observed that goats who become frustrated when run through mazes to reach food will rear up on their hind legs and peer over the fence instead of continuing toward their goals. Similarly, sheep "stall for time" and try to avoid a frustrating task by nibbling at stray tufts of vegetation, even grazing on the bare cement floor of the laboratory during difficult conditioning experiments.

Children have been noted to behave in a like manner. When faced with an unsolvable problem, consisting of locating the door to food when the food is concealed behind a different door each time, one child stuck to the task for a little while, then told the examiner, "I must go home now." Falling asleep is another device used to escape from such stressful situations (15).

The mechanisms of avoidance are techniques which enable a person to leave the scene of conflict psychologically. They provide an escape from emotional stress and afford protection from external and internal threats when life becomes too oppressive.

Fantasy

Fantasy is a mental mechanism which enables a person to substitute imaginary for real satisfactions. The stress of everyday life sometimes becomes difficult to endure, and it is quite common for people to seek some relief from continuing tension. We all utilize some form of fantasy to tide us over long periods of waiting or to escape from our problems long enough to relax and gain a new perspective on things. Modern society has capitalized on this need for mental escape by providing a number of ready-made fantasies for us. Movies, television, radio, novels, plays, spectator sports, and other forms of entertainment are fantasy-like activities which offer needed relaxation for many people.

A danger involved in the use of this mechanism is that fantasy life might become more desirable than real life. People who constantly escape into books, attend an endless stream of movies, or remain glued to the television or radio may cut themselves off from reality. Instead of facing their problems, they escape into a fantasy world. If carried too far, this world of fancy may become more satisfying than the real world. This occurs in some of the more serious adjustment disorders where the daydream is confused with reality. There are cases on record where adolescents have become so addicted to television that they neglected their school and home duties and developed a general apathy toward everything except the television. They surrendered so completely to fantasy that psychotherapy was required to wean them from the screen and bring them back to reality (16). Thus, fantasy, like a habit-forming drug, may provide great comfort and relaxation if used in small doses, but we must be wary lest we become habituated to its use.

Regression

Regression is a process of relieving anxiety or escaping stress by falling back upon the thoughts, feelings, or behavior which worked successfully during an earlier period of life. In using this mechanism, the individual appears to be defining himself as someone younger and retreats from a higher to a lower level of functioning (22). Behavior of this type is common among children who find it difficult to meet the developmental tasks of their age and revert to the dependency and irresponsibility of their younger years. Adults use this same mode of behavior when they cast off their restraints at conventions or carnivals and act with the carefree abandon of their younger days.

Regression, like many of the mechanisms described previously, may have temporary value as a release from tension or unpleasantness. Occasional regression, in the form of kicking over the traces at a college reunion, or returning to the old home site to relive childhood memories, has no harmful effect on personality. But constant retreat from one's problems by living in the past or resorting to childish patterns of thought and behavior may seriously impair personality development. In extreme cases of regression, a person returns so completely to an infantile stage that he is unable to wash or feed himself, or even control his excretions. Few people regress to this extreme, but it is not uncommon for regression to make a person dependent, indecisive, and afraid of change or new ventures.

Negativism

This is an avoidance mechanism which protects the ego by resisting involvement in threatening activities. Negativism is a psychological refusal to enter into a tension-producing situation. It is a kind of stubborness—a resistance against the suggestions or wishes of other people. Somehow, this resistance becomes so satisfying to the individual that he may actually be willing to endure some suffering in order to maintain his stand. We see this in lovers' quarrels where neither party will admit error, and each seems to derive more pleasure from being unyielding than from making up. The person who persists in opposing a group enterprise, knowing full well that his resistance will result in exclusion from the group, is using the same device.

Often the negativistic person knows how he is behaving and realizes that his actions are not entirely proper, yet he cannot change, because negativistic behavior makes him feel strong, righteous, immovable, a master of the situation. This internal satisfaction is direct and immediate and displaces the more distant benefits which might result from a more rational and co-operative type of behavior. Actually, this mechanism is an ineffective way of adjusting to tension. No problems are solved by negativistic behavior, regardless of the amount of temporary satisfaction derived from the process.

Adjustment Through Somatic Reactions

We have discussed psychogenic and psychophysiological ailments as reactions to emotional stress. These physical ailments or symptoms of physical ailments are often used as adjustment devices. They enable a person to withdraw gracefully from a difficult situation without experiencing feelings of guilt or failure. A sore throat, a convenient headache, a strained back, and other physical ailments have at one time or another been used by most of us to get out of unpleasant or difficult situations. In such cases, the ailment is real in that it has some organic basis. However, where psychogenic mechanisms are involved, the person does not actually have an ailment but feels that he does. Yet, he is not malingering or pretending. If he feels his throat is too sore to talk, he actually cannot talk. But within a short time after the passing of the crisis situation, the vocal paralysis is suddenly relieved and he is well again. People who use this device to get out of difficulties are usually tense, insecure people, who would rather dodge a problem than face it (11).

School phobia is an interesting application of this mechanism of adjustment in children. There are some children who have a morbid dread of going to school. When faced with the prospect of doing so, they may develop a fever, vomit, or experience cramps, diarrhea, headaches, and other distressing symptoms (21:56). Such reactions are seldom seen on school holidays and usually disappear at the end of the school day.

Analysis of many cases of school phobia has indicated that underlying the fear of school is a fear of being separated from the mother. In most instances, the mother, usually unconsciously, has maintained the child in a state of dependency to satisfy her own needs or to allay her own anxieties (7). As long as life is more or less tranquil, these children can get along fairly well in school and quite often succeed academically. But any crisis in the home, such as illness of the mother, a family fight, or the threat of moving, may stir up the undercurrent of insecurity and dependency in the child and bring on defensive physical symptoms (14). The school phobia is merely a displacement of anxiety from the home to the school and takes the form of physical resistance to separation from the mother. Obviously, the person, young or old, who solves his problems in this manner does nothing to improve his lot and may be even more vulnerable to subsequent frustrations.

Identification

Identification is a process of deriving personal satisfaction through the activities of an agent external to oneself. This external agent may be another person, a group, an object, or even an idea.

Identification with a person is the most common use of this adjustment mechanism. Indeed, this is a vital part of the ego-development process. As a boy grows, he normally identifies with his father. Through a process of introjection he actually takes on some of the characteristics of his father. Later, he identifies with other males and gradually develops a typically masculine set of interests and ways of behaving.

A similar process of identification and introjection goes on with girls as they grow into their feminine roles. There is considerable cross-identification between the sexes, and identification with teachers, other children, and many fictional or fantasy figures. Through this process the child establishes his ego ideals and reaches beyond his own capacities to derive satisfaction from what others do.

Social groups may also become objects of identification. Students bask in the glory of their football team, or fondly refer to the *alma mater* after graduation. Lodges, clubs, fraternities and sororities serve a similar function in providing vicarious satisfactions to their members and often establish symbols and rituals to foster this identification. Even one's possessions may become an object of identification. Some people make great sacrifices to acquire a new car, an impressive house, a good mailing address, or an extensive wardrobe of clothes which gives them a feeling of importance. In instances where a person has identified with these symbols to a point where his self-esteem is wrapped up in them, he may undergo considerable emotional trauma if he loses them or is forced to give them up.

The frequency with which identification is used and the normalcy of its use in the growth process should not obscure some of the hazards which accompany this mechanism of adjustment. Television, comics, and movies have been accused of providing aggressive models and themes for children to identify with and of stimulating them to emulate the behavior and actions of these models. While the evidence on this point is not entirely conclusive, parents generally must be on the alert to provide children with socially desirable objects of identification and to guide this process along channels of wholesome growth (5, 9, 24).

Sometimes identification is carried too far, and an individual derives so much satisfaction from the accomplishments of others that he neglects his own life. This occurs when a parent becomes so wrapped up with the achievements of his children that he hardly has a life of his own. In extreme cases, the process of identification may proceed to a point where a person not only achieves satisfaction through the accomplishments of another person but loses his own identity and actually becomes that person. The end product of this process is seen in psychotics who believe themselves to be someone else and live as this person in a world of irreality.

Adjustive Value of Mechanisms of Avoidance

The tendency to take flight from a distressing or dangerous situation is a normal defensive maneuver of living things. The snail escapes danger by withdrawing into its shell, the pill bug rolls itself up into a hard little ball, the clam snaps itself shut.

When it is no longer threatened, each organism resumes its normal mode of living.

Man uses this same technique when he shuts himself off psychologically from situations which are too threatening to him. By refusing to function under painful conditions, he insulates himself from disruptive reactions and protects his nervous system from unbearable irritations. Such behavior has a self-protective value just as long as the person can keep his escape mechanisms under control and can get back to reality at the appropriate time. Often, however, this process of avoidance gets out of control and tends to insulate a person from all of his problems rather than merely protecting him from minor irritations. He may begin to feel like a quitter, or a helpless puppet who can not direct his own destiny. Feelings of guilt, shame, and hurt pride are common among people who withdraw from life too often. These feelings may lead to depressive reactions, to the "fed-up" attitudes which make a person want to chuck it all and get away somewhere, or even to the progressive loss of contact with reality (26). Thus, mechanisms of avoidance can provide some temporary relief from tension, or they can lead a person along a path of withdrawal from life which may result in serious adjustment problems.

THE FUNCTION OF ADJUSTMENT MECHANISMS

While we have separated adjustment mechanisms into discrete behavior patterns for discussion purposes, an individual seldom employs a single mechanism in reacting to stress. More often, the combined effects of several mechanisms enter into the process of adjustment. Thus, a person may compensate for a feeling of inadequacy by regressing to an earlier stage of life where he identifies with a parent figure who was alive at that time.

The selection of mechanisms of adjustment is not a matter of deliberate choice. The boy who could not make the football team does not decide to compensate for his failure by becoming an outstanding scholar. He tries the sources of satisfaction which worked for him previously, until he finds something that will relieve his anxiety and support his sense of self-esteem. This is a learning process involving trial and error rather than reason, and is based on feelings rather than logical analysis. Successful stress-relieving devices become reinforced and continue to function even after they have lost their initial utility. This process begins early in life. By the age of three or four, even the most normal and happy children already have a repertoire of defense mechanisms. Once established, these defenses become an integral part of the personality, and the individual will hold on to them until he discovers better ways of adjusting to psychological stress (25).

The use of adjustment mechanisms is not limited to people who are having difficulty with the problems of life. Everyone uses ego-defense techniques at one time or another to protect himself from the minor irritations of life and to conserve his energies so that major problems can be met more effectively. Every normal person rationalizes to some extent, projects some of his inadequacies upon others, or enjoys the pleasures of fantasy for a while. One's adjustment is influenced not so much by the defense mechanisms used as by the use to which they are put. Defenses only become pathological when they become rigid, fixated, and used to the extent that they interfere with the resourceful and realistic handling of problems (19).

The merits of adjustment mechanisms hinge upon the extent to which they enable the individual to become a fully functioning, competent person. In evaluating the adjustment techniques, the following criteria may be applied:

1. Does the mechanism reduce the tensions felt by the individual and minimize his anxieties?
2. Is the mechanism socially approved?
3. Does the mechanism facilitate further adjustment?

If the mechanism does not relieve tension, then it is obviously of no value to the individual. However, internal tensions must not be relieved at the expense of incurring the disfavor of society. To do this would create new tensions as rapidly as the old ones are relieved. The social factor is an essential criterion for evaluating the merits of the mechanisms. Finally, unless the adjustment technique enhances the ability of the individual to analyze his problems and attack the fundamental origins of his anxieties, he is making no progress toward an adequate adjustment to life (13:366–388).

SUMMARY

When people experience threat, tension, irritation, failure, or other forms of psychological stress, it is natural for them to take defensive action. The most constructive approach to such problems is to face them and solve them to the best of one's ability. However, there are times when even the most capable person finds himself in a situation where he can do nothing about the origins of his psychological stress and is forced to protect himself from rising anxiety and from threats to his self-concept. This is when the mechanisms of adjustment come into play. Mechanisms of deception may be used to remove the perception of threat; mechanisms of substitution enable a person to find satisfaction in non-threatening areas, and mechanisms of avoidance enable him psychologically to leave the field of tension.

These adjustive techniques evolve through a process of learning. If they succeed in making the individual feel better, they are reinforced and become established as involuntary habit patterns. They then come into play automatically when psychological stress is encountered, much in the manner we use reflexes when a blow is aimed at us. Some of these defense mechanisms are useful in that they make life more tolerable by insulating us from constant emotional irritation. Others may lead to serious problems of personality disorganization if used excessively or inappropriately. Defense mechanisms, in themselves, do not solve problems or make them go away, but if self-insight is applied to their use, they may help a person develop techniques for coping with the everyday stresses of living.

REFERENCES

1. Anderson, J. E., *Experience and Behavior in Early Childhood and the Adjustment of the Same Persons as Adults,* Institute of Child Development, University of Minnesota, Minneapolis, 1963.

2. Argyris, C., *Personality and Organization,* Harper & Row, 1957.
3. Bonney, M. E., *Mental Health in Education,* Allyn & Bacon, 1960.
4. Bruch, H., "Disturbed Communication in Eating Disorders," *Amer. J. Orthopsychiat.,* January, 1963, **33**:99–104.
5. Carskadon, T. R., *et al., Television for Children,* Foundation For Character Education, Boston, 1957.
6. Conrad, S. W., "The Psychologic Implications of Overeating," *Psychiat. Quart.,* April, 1954, **28**:211–224.
7. Eisenberg, L., "School Phobia: A Study in the Communication of Anxiety," *Amer. J. Psychiat.,* February, 1958, **114**:712–718.
8. Fenichel, O., "The Study of Defense Mechanisms and Its Importance For Psychoanalytic Techniques," in H. Fenichel and D. Rapaport (Eds.), *The Collected Papers of Otto Fenichel,* Norton, 1954.
9. Gitlin, I., "Television and Children—A Look At the Research," *Child Stud.,* Summer, 1960, **37**:33–36.
10. Hayakawa, S. I., "Conditions of Success in Communication," *Bull. Menninger Clin.,* September, 1962, **26**:225–236.
11. Holmes, T. H., "Low Back Pain, Tension and the Psyche," *State of Mind,* March, 1958, **2**:No. 3.
12. Holzman, P. S., "Repression and Cognitive Style," *Bull. Menninger Clin.,* November, 1962, **26**:273–282.
13. Hountras, P. T., *Mental Hygiene: A Text of Readings,* Merrill, Columbus, Ohio, 1961.
14. Kahn, J. H., and Nursten, J. P., "School Refusal: A Comprehensive View of School Phobia and Other Failures of School Attendance," *Amer. J. Orthopsychiat.,* July, 1962, **32**:707–718.
15. Liddell, H. S., "Conditioning and Emotions," *Sci. Amer.,* January, 1954, Reprint No. 418, pp. 2–10.
16. Meerloo, J. A. M., "Reading Block and Television Apathy: An Alarm for Parents," *Ment. Hyg.,* October, 1962, **46**:610–616.
17. Merton, R. K., and Kitt, A. S., "Reference Group Theory and Social Mobility," in R. Bendix and S. M. Lipsit (Eds.), *Class, Status and Power: A Reader in Social Stratification,* Free Press, 1953, 409–410.
18. Moore, M. E., *et al.,* "Obesity, Social Class, and Mental Illness," *J. Amer. Med. Ass.,* September 15, 1962, **181**:962–966.
19. Murphy, L. B., "Preventive Implications of Development in the Preschool Years," in G. Caplan (Ed.), *Prevention of Mental Disorders in Children,* Basic Books, 1961, p. 218–248.

20. Penfield, W., "The Thread of Experience," *What's New*, Abbott Laboratories, Summer, 1962, **228**:6–8.

21. Sarason, S., *et al.*, *Anxiety in Elementary School Children*, Wiley, 1960.

22. Szalita, A. B., "Regression and Perception in Psychotic States," *Psychiat.*, February, 1958, **21**:53–63.

23. Taylor, J. W., *An Experimental Study of Repression with Special Reference to Success-Failure and Completion-Incompletion*, Unpublished Doctoral Dissertation, Washington University, St. Louis, 1952.

24. Wertham, F., *Seduction of the Innocent*, Holt, Rinehart & Winston, 1954.

25. Witkin, H. A., *et al.*, *Psychological Differentiation*, Wiley, 1962.

26. Youmans, E. G., "Human Relations in School Administration," in A. D. Albright *et al.*, "School Administration and the Human Sciences," *Bull. Bureau School Serv.*, University of Kentucky, College of Education, September, 1961, **34**:39–80.

27. Zeller, A. F., "An Experimental Analogue of Repression: III. The Effect of Induced Failure and Success on Memory Measured by Recall," *J. exp. Psychol.*, 1951, **42**:32–38.

Chapter 11   The

Deterioration of Adjustment

When defense mechanisms cease to be effective, behavior may deteriorate into a persistent state of maladjustment. In Chapter 1 we cited some data which, in general, suggested that maladjustment is not at all rare in our society. These figures were based largely upon cases known to hospitals, physicians, clinics, and other agencies. There is reason to believe that maladjustment in the general population exceeds the estimates derived from these sources. Recent studies sponsored by the Joint Commission on Mental Illness and Health, which was appointed by Congress to assess the problem of mental illness in the United States, found that one person out of every five in our population has felt on the verge of a nervous breakdown at some time during his life (10). Another investigation, in which a carefully selected sample of the people in one of our major cities was interviewed, showed that 20 percent had severe or incapacitating mental and emotional symptoms, and that another 60 percent had tensions which impaired their effectiveness (20). Such data indicate that symptoms of the deterioration of adjustment are likely to be encountered rather frequently among the people we meet in everyday life.

The severity of maladjustment is gauged by the extent to which the individual's feelings, perceptions, and behavior deviate from the normal, and how far removed he is from reality. In the milder forms of maladjustment the individual maintains contact with reality, but certain aspects of his behavior are exaggerated or distorted. These maladaptive types of reaction are classified as behavior or personality disorders. As maladjustment becomes more accentuated, behavior becomes more rigid; there is more extensive disorientation toward reality and a greater predominance of irrational reactions and distressing emotional symptoms. Maladjustment of this type is referred to as neurosis. In the most severe forms of maladjustment, the psychoses, the individual undergoes considerable personality disorganization, and his detachment from reality becomes more frequent and extreme.

There is no clear distinction between these various forms of maladaptive behavior. Normal behavior usually is distinguishable from extreme psychosis, but between these extremes are many gradations of behavior which are not easily differentiated. The normal merges imperceptibly into the borderline, the borderline into the neurotic, and the neurotic into the psychotic, with much overlapping of characteristics. Most normal people, at one time or another, experience emotional crises which resemble maladjustive behavior. Most maladjusted people, in certain aspects and at certain times, are remarkably rational in their behavior. In this chapter we shall describe some of the symptoms of maladjustment and discuss the personality disorders. The next chapter will deal with the more severe forms of maladjustment, the neuroses and psychoses.

SYMPTOMS OF MALADJUSTMENT

There are a number of behavioral symptoms which reflect a deviation from normal patterns of response and adjustment. Some are so widespread that few of us go through life without encountering people in whom they are reflected. Included here are such patterns of behavior as the following:

Belligerence. Walking around continuously with a chip on the shoulder, ready to argue or quarrel at the slightest excuse, or even without an excuse.

Excessive moodiness. Spells of the blues, or feeling down in the dumps; feeling a great deal of the time that nothing is worthwhile or really matters.

Exaggerated worry.   Continuous anxiety about nothing at all, or entirely out of proportion to the cause.

Suspiciousness and mistrust.   A persistent feeling that the world is full of dishonest, conniving people; that everyone is trying to take advantage of me.

Selfishness and greediness.   Lack of consideration of the needs of others; a "what's in it for me" attitude about almost everything.

Helplessness and dependency.   A tendency to let others carry the burden; difficulty in making decisions.

Poor emotional control.   Exaggerated emotional outbursts out of proportion to the cause, and at inappropriate times.

Daydreaming and fantasy.   Spending a good part of the time imagining how things could be, rather than dealing with them the way they are.

Hypochondria.   Worrying a great deal of the time about minor physical ailments; experiencing imaginary symptoms of illness (16:3).

These, it will be recognized, are reactions which occur occasionally for most of us, last a while, and then disappear. Even when such behavior occurs more frequently, we would not classify these people as seriously sick. They may not be too stable or dependable, too agreeable, or too happy, but neither are they so disorganized that their behavior could be called pathological.

The symptoms of maladjusted behavior are more extreme, pervasive, and persistent than the reactions described above. We shall discuss these symptoms under the categories of reality distortions, mental aberrations, affect distortions, motor reactions, and personality disorganization.

Reality Distortions

Man's contact with reality is established through his perceptions. If these perceptions are faulty, then his behavior will be unrealistic and distorted. Maladjusted people may have a variety of distorted perceptions, because they unconsciously attempt to restructure their environment so that they can make some kind of purposeful response to it. The observer may not understand these responses because he cannot understand the perceptions to which these people are reacting.

Illusions and hallucinations are two forms of perceptual distortion which seriously affect an individual's interpretations of reality. Illusions are sensations which are misinterpreted by the individual, or which he forms into inaccurate perceptions. The physical phenomenon of illusion occurs when we think we see a lake in the desert, or a body of water lying ahead of us on a paved road. Or we may experience the illusion of heat when suddenly touched by a cold object. The illusions of a disturbed person are more exaggerated and persistent than these transitory experiences. For example, he may interpret air currents or the touch of his clothes as insects crawling over his body, causing him to tear off his clothes to get rid of the insects. Or when he sees people talking or laughing together, he is certain they are talking about him or laughing at him. He may refuse certain foods because they taste as if they have been poisoned, or put out all lights because he feels they are aiming death rays at him. These are the types of reality distortions created by illusions. In each instance the person senses something but distorts its meaning and reacts to this distorted perception.

Hallucinations are disorders of perception which are not founded on sensory experiences but are created within the individual. He sees, hears, and feels things which no one else can sense, because no external stimuli are present. He may see snakes crawling around the room, or feel sound beams tearing into him, or suffer from an incessant buzzing in the head. These hallucinations are not just imagined; they are experienced with great intensity, and produce behavioral reactions which may appear bizarre because the observer cannot perceive the stimuli to which the individual is reacting.

Mental Aberrations

A disturbed person is likely to display a variety of defective patterns of thinking, and disorders of consciousness and memory. Defective thinking may take the form of a flight of ideas where ideas pour out in great profusion but without logical order. Often such a person will start a sentence, hit a key word, and, without finishing his original thought, proceed off on another idea which was triggered by the new stimulus.

Another characteristic of disordered thinking is irrelevance. Here what a person says may be in logical form, but it has no relation to what is going on. A peculiar fragmentation of thought prevents him from relating thoughts to one another in the way most people do. He may be asked, "Where do you live?" and respond, "Today is my birthday" (1). Verbal dissociation is usually present also, and there is a splitting of words from one group of ideas into another, so that the result is a queer jumble of disconnected words which make no sense. In such disrupted thinking processes, the person cannot order what he wants to say. Fragments of sentences come to his mind which he feels compelled to utter, and the outcome is confused and unintelligible communication (23).

Delusions, paranoid ideas, and obsessions are additional forms of disordered thinking. Delusions are false or improbable beliefs which have no relation to experience or reason. There are several kinds of delusions, such as delusions of having committed a crime, delusions of having an incurable disease, delusions of grandeur in which the person thinks he is wealthy or a great historical figure, delusions of worthlessness where he feels totally incompetent, and delusions of persecution where the individual feels something or someone is out to "get" him. The following statement, which the author received through the mail, reflects the confused thinking and irrational beliefs contained in some delusions of persecution:

The invisible insects and animals forced the invisible human beings to convey these thoughts to me. The reason animals force human beings to print props, remodel, redecorate, move buildings, and get rejuvenated and have telephones, go on the radio and enslave human beings is because they think they add richness of thought to America.

Insects can become human beings by getting rejuvenated into larger animals. The larger animals will get killed at 30 years of age. They will be used as electricity from 5 to 25 years. Then they will be taken into the female human being and become babies.

Delusions of persecution may become organized into paranoid ideas. The paranoid person is extremely sensitive, humorless, and rigid. He thinks no one likes him and that everyone is out to do him harm. He may not wait until this harm actually occurs but try to prevent it through physical, verbal, or legal action. He goes around with a chip on his shoulder, fighting against every little imagined slight or infringement on his individual rights. Such attitudes make these people obnoxious, or at least difficult to deal with (19). In extreme cases, they may become so aggressive that society must take steps to protect itself from them (6:495). Delusions of persecution affect not only individuals but even groups. The mass delusions related to religious symbolism or to political causes have at times given rise to retaliatory practices which do not reflect to the credit of civilized man (13).

Obsessions are another common characteristic of disordered thinking. Almost everyone has had some mild obsessional experience where he could not get a tune out of his mind or kept worrying about whether he turned off the electricity before leaving on a vacation. These thoughts can be very disconcerting. When they crowd out all other thoughts and so overwhelm the person that he can think of nothing else, they become obsessions. A person may be fully aware of how illogical his ideas are, but he cannot force them out of mind. Not only must he live with them all day, they even appear in his dreams, giving him no relief from his anxieties. Sometimes to reduce the effects of obsessions, an individual resorts to certain compulsive forms of behavior which will be described later (2).

Associated with disorders of thinking are disorders of consciousness which affect a person's orientation in time and place. He may not be able to tell what day or month it is, what place he is in, or the time of the day. People, places, time, and events whirl about in disordered confusion. In some cases, aphasia is present, and the individual cannot connect thoughts and speech, or he may lose the ability to use some of his senses.

Inability to focus attention on anything is another symptom of this disorder. Establishing contact with such a person is difficult because his attention tends to drift off to other things when someone is talking to him. In extreme cases, a condition of stupor may occur, where consciousness is withdrawn to the point that no response at all can be elicited from the person. All of these symptoms may occur without any identifiable organic damage to the brain.

Memory disorders occur when a person unconsciously resolves his conflicts by blotting out certain parts of his experience. He dissociates himself from unpleasant circumstances by taking mental flight into a state of amnesia. Amnesia may take several forms. There is simple or circumscribed amnesia, where the person loses all memory of a certain period of time, while events before and after this period are remembered. Retrograde amnesia is a condition where the amnesia extends backward from a certain time and the person cannot recall what happened up to that point. In antegrade amnesia the person can recall past events but cannot remember what he just heard or read. Paramnesia is a memory of something which never happened—a sort of persistent hallucination. Hyperamnesia is an unnatural acuteness of memory wherein the person vividly recalls a past event to the extent that he relives it. He may, for example, believe that he is still drowning or still being beaten, if these were the things he had experienced.

These amnesias may last for a few days or weeks, or continue for years, or until adequate therapeutic measures are applied. Except for the specific memory loss he experienced, the person usually shows unimpaired intellectual and perceptual abilities. Usually, he remains in his environment and can function adequately except in the blacked-out areas of consciousness. If he actually flees from his predicament, becoming amnesic and wandering away, suddenly waking up somewhere unable to recall how or why he got there, the condition is called a fugue. He may take on a new identity and even begin a new career or start another family. Actually, however, this condition is rarely encountered in real life and is confined to a few extreme cases which appear in the literature (6:468–469).

Affect Distortions

We speak of feelings and emotions as the affective aspects of behavior. Among the many affective disorders which may occur among maladjusted people are exultation, transient rage, depression, and phobias. Each is an uncontrollable form of reaction which produces significant alteration of behavior.

Exultation is an exhilarated, effusive response to stimuli which are either not observable to other people or which would have little effect on a normal person. The exulted individual is overstimulated, hyperactive, and often talks endlessly and loudly. Transient rage is an exaggeration of the temper tantrums seen among children. These uncontrollable temper reactions in adults result in strong emotional upheaval which can lead to destructive action. Usually, such people will have a particular stimulus to which they respond with rage reactions, while remaining calm in all other areas of behavior. Since this stimulus may be within themselves, their temper outbursts occur without external provocation, making their behavior unpredictable and sometimes dangerous (1).

Depression is a disorder of emotion which we have discussed previously. It may serve the needs of the maladjusted individual by enabling him to manipulate others through forcing them to be concerned over him. The depressed person would deny that his reactions have any utility, since he feels so miserable, yet he clings to his feelings and symptoms and resists efforts to alleviate them (3, 22).

Phobias are affective disorders with persistent irrational fears. We all have unreasonable fears which cause us some trouble. For example, we may get sinking feelings in our stomach or nervous flashes in our legs when peering over the side of a skyscraper. However, we do not refuse to enter the building because of these feelings; we are not overwhelmed by these fears, but simply try to avoid those things which bother us.

The person who develops a true phobia may get along quite

well as long as he can avoid the phobia situation. However, when this phobia is attached to ordinary objects or situations which he cannot avoid, then he is in real trouble. For example, if he cannot ride a bus or in an auto without developing heart palpitations, breathing difficulties, and profuse sweating, then he will have problems holding a job or going anywhere away from home. Actually, this is the objective of some phobic symptoms. They represent a fear which has been displaced from something that is the real source of anxiety to something else which acts as a sort of camouflage. Finding the true sources of a phobia is a difficult therapeutic task. Some 135 phobias have been named, ranging from acrophobia, fear of high places, to zoophobia, fear of animals. Each such fear has its own origins and utility, and develops in response to some need of the individual (5).

Motor Reactions

Many of the perceptual, mental, and emotional symptoms which we have discussed are accompanied by deviations in motor behavior or overt actions. We have mentioned the hyperkinesis or over-activity which is seen in states of exultation, and the psychomotor retardation or slowing down of muscular activity and coordination, which occurs in depression.

Compulsive acts are a form of motor behavior which indicate that a person is having difficulty maintaining control over his volition and action. Compulsions are irresistible impulses to perform certain acts which in some way relieve anxiety. Often they are associated with obsessions, hence the term obsessive-compulsive reactions. In these cases, the individual resorts to acts or rituals which relieve his obsessions and repeats these in unvaried form over and over. Some people wash their hands so often that the skin becomes raw and cracked; others will not turn a doorknob unless a tissue or clean cloth is used, or they may feel compelled to disinfect dishes and even furniture after each use. Bedtime rituals are frequently followed in precise and prescribed ways of laying out clothes, arranging blankets and pillows, and other careful, meticulous preparations.

Compulsive people pay minute attention to the details of

their acts and avoid any variation in the way they are per-formed. They behave as if the only way they can ward off danger or secure relief from fears, anxieties or obsessions is to routinize their lives so thoroughly that everything happens on schedule and there is little chance for the unexpected to occur. Many times these people will say, "I know it is silly, but I just don't feel right until I do it." They realize that their behavior is illogical, but they cannot avoid doing it without experiencing strong anxiety (21:156).

Usually, compulsive acts do no harm to anyone except the person who engages in them. There is a type of compulsion which has more serious consequences both for the individual and for society. These are the manias, deliberate, purposeful, and uncontrollable acts of aggression toward people, property, or toward the individual himself. The compulsion to set fires is called pyromania; to steal, kleptomania; to kill, homicidal mania; to drink excessively, dipsomania; and there are many others which have not been given names. Usually, these people live relatively rational lives until their anxieties accumulate to a point where they must be relieved through a particular com-pulsive act. After committing this act, they feel relaxed and often go home and sleep soundly. If apprehended during a manic act, the only explanation they can offer is that they just could not help themselves (21:158).

Personality Disorganization

Some disturbed people undergo a depersonalization process in which their sense of self is undermined. During treatment these people may make comments to the therapist such as "I'm a fine example of nothingness," "I feel empty," "I just exist," "I feel like a blob of protoplasm," and similar expressions of worthlessness which indicate that they feel hopelessly inade-quate. They may neglect their personal appearance and present a picture of abject apathy and gross self-neglect (17).

Another form of personality disorganization is a separation of roles to the point where the individual is a different person at different times. This is known as multiple personality—the Dr. Jekyll-Mr. Hyde reaction which has been depicted in fiction.

Few people undergo the complete personality reversals described in such stories. More often, the disturbed person will go through periods when he feels he just is not himself and where one aspect of his personality becomes dominant for a while. Except for some types of psychoses, most disturbed people maintain enough grasp on reality so that they do not lose their identity completely when undergoing one of these role shifts (6:470).

Origins of Symptoms of Maladjustment

Now that we have described some of the symptoms of maladjustment, we turn to the question: How do these symptoms arise?

In Chapter 2 we discussed the biological foundations of behavior, pointing out how genetics, biochemistry, endocrinology, and other biological sciences have contributed to the interpretation of human behavior. These sciences provide some insights into the maladjustment process by duplicating, in the laboratory with normal people, many of the symptoms exhibited by people who are having adjustment problems. Auditory and visual illusions, and feelings of revulsion or disgust, can be produced in normal people through electrical stimulation of various areas in the temporal cortex of the brain (18). Acute states of excitement, depression with suicidal thoughts, impairment of judgment, perceptual distortions, flight of ideas, and disturbances in thinking have been created by lysergic acid, Psilocybin, or by sensory deprivation (12). Euphoria, restlessness, feelings of unreality, depressive reactions, agitated depression, delusions, hallucinations, feelings of depersonalization, and bizarre behavior —all have followed the administration of cortisone products to patients suffering from medical ailments (4). Certain glandular products are capable of inhibiting neuron excitability by setting up blocks at the synapses. This prevents the organism from bringing into play the areas of the brain in which the record of our experiences and previous judgments resides, thus short-circuiting the communication channels so that disordered thoughts and ideas arise (14).

Just how these electrical, chemical, metabolic, and glandular activities occur, and whether they actually operate outside the laboratory, are questions which have not been answered satisfactorily. Obsessive thoughts may be produced by drugs or by electrical stimulation, but they are also produced by life situations, such as a long siege of trouble, sickness, tragedy, or hard luck (7). Whether these life experiences cause biological, chemical, or electrical changes in the brain and nervous system, which in turn produce symptoms of maladjustment, is not yet clear. There is some support for this theory, since symptoms of maladjustment may not appear until a person has undergone considerable tension. He may go along for years suffering from anxiety and stress reactions and give no indication of what he is undergoing. These stresses have a cumulative effect; they pile up until some single incident, a precipitating cause, breaks down the last line of resistance and brings forth the symptoms of disturbance. Whether these life experiences are stored in the form of electrical charges, as in a condenser, or wear down resistance through persistent biological or chemical action, are problems now under study. Each person has a different threshold of tolerance to accumulated stress, but much remains to be learned about how this threshold is developed.

PERSONALITY DEVIATIONS

We have described some of the symptoms of maladjustment without trying to attach them to specific disorders. It is not possible to fit people into definite categories of disorder on the basis of the symptoms they exhibit. Indeed, symptoms can often be deceiving, for two people with the same ailment can display very different symptoms, while two other people with different ailments can exhibit similar symptoms. At best, we can group a collection of symptoms into a pattern, called a *syndrome*, give this syndrome a name, and proceed to discuss it as if it were a definite entity. We shall follow this procedure in discussing the personality deviations, but the reader is cautioned to keep in mind that there is much overlapping between categories, and many differences among individuals within each of the groups thus arbitrarily established.

The term personality deviations is used here to refer to a

group of people in our society who are not maladjusted in a clinical or legal sense but who have developed behavior patterns which are socially unacceptable and personally inadequate. No one knows how many people there are in this category, but the number is estimated to run into millions. They are the ones most likely to be involved in suicides, automobile accidents, and credit difficulties; they make up a large proportion of the chronically unemployed, the public charges, and the "skid-row" population, and often have a history of juvenile or adult court offenses (15).

There is no precise way to classify these varied personality disorders. The only standard nomenclature available, that recommended by the American Psychiatric Association in its *Diagnostic and Statistical Manual*, is not very helpful, because it was devised primarily to gather statistics from mental hospitals. Therefore, for ease of discussion, we shall group the less serious personality disorders into a few arbitrary categories on the basis of their predominant behavior patterns. People in these groups are found in the general population, where they get along reasonably well, but with considerable emotional incapacitation (24).

The Eccentric Group

Most of us have encountered people whose mannerisms, appearance, or habits set them apart from the ordinary or usual. These eccentrics cannot or will not see themselves as others see them, and often have a complete disregard for what others think. Included here are the wastrel; the incorrigible liar; the person seen on city streets or walking along railroad tracks, wearing heavy clothes in the summertime, dirty, disheveled, talking to himself or to an inanimate object; people who fill their rooms with collections of string or bottles or other strange objects. These people are not just rugged individualists; they are so divorced from reality that they live outside the mainstream of society.

There are more serious forms of eccentricity which denote some basic personality changes. Some women dress and act like men; some men adopt feminine mannerisms, and wear feminine clothes and perfume; some people are parasitic, living off their families and refusing to contribute to their welfare in any way. These people, and many like them, may know that they are different from others, but have ceased to care. While they are not sufficiently detached from reality to be classified as neurotic or psychotic, any increase in the intensity of such patterns of thought or behavior could lead to serious maladjustment (8).

The Inferior Group

There are some people who have developed so low a self-concept that they make life needlessly trying for themselves and for others. The person who feels so fundamentally inferior that this feeling radiates into areas where he need not feel inferior is said to have an inferiority complex. Thus, a man may be a poor golfer, a fair accountant, and an average conversationalist, but his basic inferiority makes him feel small, weak, and insignificant in all these areas. Such a person may call attention to his inadequacies and in this way unconsciously appeal for sympathy, or he may withdraw from social contacts. The withdrawn, inferior person is often seen walking along the street with his eyes glued to the sidewalk, so that he does not have to meet the eyes of others or exchange greetings. He may even cross the street to avoid meeting people.

In the social area, the inferior person may become a source of annoyance, because his whining, self-deprecating habits make people feel uncomfortable. His inability to converse with others and his evident nervousness and discomfort may chill a social gathering and isolate him even more. Or, if he puts on an air of aggressiveness and becomes overbearing, autocratic, and commanding, in an effort to obscure his underlying feelings of inadequacy, he may become equally objectionable to other people. Inferior people may be aware of their reactions and of their effects but are unable to overcome the basic fearfulness and sensitivity that they feel.

The Antisocial and Dissocial Groups

This category includes a group of individuals within our society who are self-centered, calloused toward the rights and privileges of others, and concerned primarily with the satisfaction of their own desires. The antisocial group includes people who will lie, steal, cheat, fight, or use any other means to gain their own ends. They form extremely weak relationships with other people and have no loyalty to anyone except themselves. Most of them have a history of affectional deprivation in childhood, with no opportunity to establish sincere relationships with anyone meaningful to them. In this category we find unethical businessmen, confidence men, unprincipled politicians, prostitutes, and assorted delinquents and criminals who operate as "loners." Considerable depersonalization may be involved in antisocial behavior, since the individual does not apply to himself the codes of conduct which others live by. His values and perceptions of society are so distorted that he invites social ostracism and thereby intensifies his own anxieties and hostilities. Even when he tries to solicit friendship, his lack of sensitivity to the feelings and reactions of others may cause him to be rebuffed or ignored so that his antisocial tendencies are reinforced.

Some dissocial individuals are able to establish close personal relations with others to form a group whose values are opposed to those of society. There are, for example, families of criminals or delinquents, members of which are bound together by very close ties. The group designated as the culturally deprived, and the members of gangs and of certain minority groups, develop considerable in-group cohesiveness and loyalty. These people may be quite competent and adequate within their own circles, but because their values and behavior are rejected by the larger society, they are subject to social, emotional, legal, and economic pressures which prevent them from leading full and useful lives (6:497).

The Dependent Group

Classified as the emotionally dependent group are those people who are passive and indecisive, who lack initiative, and lean upon others for support and protection. They are rather pathetic individuals, whose lives are submerged in the lives of others. The dependent person finds it difficult to make decisions or to stand up for his own rights. He is so insecure and fearful that situations which seem quite ordinary to normal people become formidable obstacles for him. This may involve facing an examination, seeking a job, or any other situation where his ego is exposed to possible rebuff or failure.

Failure to achieve emancipation from the home is a common occurrence among dependent people. Because of emotional ties to the security and protection of the home, dependent people undergo a real crisis when it comes time for them to establish their own adult status. Many of them never achieve true adult maturity and independence. They may cling to their aging parents and never marry. If they do marry, they tend to select a mate who will care for them, rather than one with whom a mature marital relationship could be established.

Dependent people may get along reasonably well as long as their source of protection remains secure. If favored with a comfortably safe, routine job, where decisions and initiative are not demanded, they can earn a living and contribute to society. But with the undercurrent of fear and insecurity which dominates their lives, dependent people are always in danger of losing their protective supports and slipping into a state of personal inadequacy.

The Sexual Deviate Group

Some people find release from their anxieties through sexual practices which are contrary to the ethical and moral standards of society. Among the more common sexual deviations are exhibitionism, where the individual achieves gratification by exposing his genitals in a public place; pedophilia, where the sex object is a child; rape, excessive masturbation, and homosexuality. There are other forms of sexual perversion which are encountered more among severely disturbed persons than among those who are classified as having personality deviations.

The sexual deviate is often quite normal in appearance and in his general behavior. His sexual deviation is the avenue he uses to release his tensions so that he can function adequately in other areas of living. When apprehended, the deviate can seldom give a rational explanation for his behavior. He only knows that his anxiety builds up until he is forced to engage in deviate practices to relieve it, and no other activity will do this for him. Many of these people are married and have normal sexual experience in the home. Just why they seek deviate sexual experience is difficult to ascertain, since such behavior rarely takes place where it can be observed, and social taboos make people reluctant to discuss these practices. Despite all the efforts which have been made to understand deviate sexual behavior, the causes for these practices remain pretty much a mystery.

Transient Personality Disorders

Most people who have personality aberrations learn to live with their problems and peculiarities, and never suffer a more serious type of behavioral disorder. However, their lives are in precarious balance, and exposure to sudden or acute stress can accentuate their anxiety and make them vulnerable to more serious forms of maladjustment. This process occurs often enough so that the term transient personality disorder has been ascribed to it. When a transient personality disorder occurs, the individual's symptoms are intensified and, for a time, he becomes neurotic or even psychotic.

Transient personality disorder is not limited to people with personality deviations. Seemingly normal people may develop such reactions at certain critical periods of life. At these times the ego becomes overwhelmed, and the individual is without defensive resources to combat anxiety. He may verbalize his feelings in expressions, such as "I just couldn't take any more," or, as one young man said, "I felt tired of living, tired of everybody, just tired." During these states, suicide may be considered or other irrational acts committed by such a person.

These crises are most likely to occur at adolescence, after childbirth, during the climacteric or change of life, during senility, or at other times when the stresses of life become particularly accentuated. Transient personality disorders occur during adolescence with sufficient frequency that the term adjustment reaction of adolescence is used to describe this type of behavior. This is more than just the ups and downs of emotional instability which many adolescents undergo. It involves an extensive disorganization of behavior. To illustrate, a fifteen-year-old-school girl suddenly began to scream and wave her arms around in class, saying that she had a buzzing in her head that was getting louder and louder. The principal had to remove the girl from school and take her home. The teacher had noticed progressive changes in behavior over a three-month period during which the girl had become withdrawn, seclusive, and noncommunicative. The mother found a diary which contained thoughts of suicide and of murdering people, and described many physical symptoms the girl was experiencing. Medical examination revealed no physical abnormalities, and psychiatric care was required to restore this girl to normalcy.

Another illustration of this type of disorder is the psychological disorientation which occurs among some mothers after the birth of a baby. The mother may reject the baby and become severely depressed, often sobbing uncontrollably. This is called a puerperal reaction when it is of short duration, or a post-partum psychosis when it is more extensive and overwhelming (11). These conditions have all the aspects of serious emotional disorder but differ primarily in that they are either self-limiting or readily amenable to therapy.

SUMMARY

Maladjusted behavior is reflected in a variety of symptoms indicating deviations in a person's mental and emotional orientation, in his actions and relations with other people, and in his personality structure.

A disturbed person may experience reality distortions in which the world is interpreted through unreal perceptions, such as illusions and hallucinations. He may exhibit mental aberrations in which the flight of ideas, irrelevance, verbal dissociation, and delusions make it difficult for him to communicate with other people. Paranoid delusions, obsessions, disorders of consciousness, and memory disorders may create for him a world which is quite different from that experienced by normal people.

Affective disorders usually accompany these mental aberrations. Exultation, transient rage, depression, and phobias are some of the more extreme forms in which affective disorders are expressed. Motor reactions, in the form of hyperkinesis, psychomotor retardation, compulsions, and manias, are some ways in which inner disturbances are expressed in behavior. Maladjustment may also affect the personality, and particularly the ego structure of the individual, resulting in feelings of depersonalization or in extreme role shifts described as multiple personality.

All these symptoms do not occur at the same time nor with the same intensity in maladjusted people. They occur in various combinations, sometimes dramatically and openly, sometimes subtly and insidiously. As maladjustment becomes more accentuated, these symptoms are more prominent, behavior is more erratic, and there is greater disorientation toward reality. The end point of this process is the extreme form of maladjusted behavior called psychosis. Between normality and psychosis are several gradations of maladjustment which cannot be categorized accurately in terms of their symptoms but which lend themselves to a rough classification into the personality disorders and the neuroses. In this chapter we have described some personality disorders which we have arbitrarily named the eccentric group, the inferior group, the anti-social and dissocial group, the dependent group, and the sexual deviate group. The behavior of these people is not pathological in a clinical sense, but differs sufficiently from normal behavior that many of these individuals are living unhappy, inadequate, or socially unacceptable lives. Relatively few of the millions of people in this category are institutionalized, except for those who violate the laws of society, but most could profit from therapeutic assistance.

REFERENCES

1. American Medical Association, "GPs Should Be Alert to Possible Psychosis in Patients," *J. Amer. Med. Ass.*, April 13, 1963, **184**:51.
2. Blau, A., "Benign Schizophrenia," *Arch. Neurol. Psychiat.*, December, 1957, **78**:605–611.

3. Bonime, W., "Depression as a Practice: Dynamic and Psycho-therapeutic Considerations," *Compreh. Psychiat.,* June, 1960, 1:194–198.

4. Cobb, S., "Some Clinical Changes in Behavior Accompanying Endocrine Disorders," *J. Nervous and Mental Disease,* February, 1960, 130:97–106.

5. English, O. S., "The Phobic Patient as Encountered in General Practice," *State of Mind,* Ciba, January–February, 1959, 3:No. 1.

6. English, O. S., and Pearson, G. H. J., *Emotional Problems of Living,* Norton, 1955.

7. Evans, H. S., "Man Divided Against Himself," *Listen,* May–June, 1960, 13:8–11.

8. Ginsburg, S. W., "The Neuroses," in P. T. Hountras (Ed.), *Mental Hygiene,* Merrill, 1961, pp. 403–418.

9. Groen, J., "Psychosomatic Disturbances as a Form of Substituted Behavior," *J. psychosom. Res.,* 1957, 2:85–96.

10. Gurin, G., *et al., Americans View Their Mental Health,* Joint Commission on Mental Illness and Health, Monograph Series No. 4, Basic Books, 1960.

11. Hayman, A., "Some Aspects of Regression in Non-Psychotic Puerperal Breakdown," *Brit. J. med. Psychol.,* 1962, 35:135–145.

12. Malitz, S., *et al.,* "Some Observations of Psilocybin, a New Hallucinogen, in Volunteer Subjects," *Compreh. Psychiat.,* February, 1960, 1:8–17.

13. Malzberg, B., "The Distribution of Mental Disease According to Religious Affiliation in New York State, 1949–1951," *Ment. Hyg.,* October, 1962, 46:510–522.

14. Marrazzi, A. S., "The Action of Psychotogens and a Neuro-Physiological Theory of Hallucination," *Amer. J. Psychiat.,* April, 1960, 116:911–914.

15. Metropolitan Life Insurance Company, "Human Factors in Motor Vehicle Accidents, *Statist. Bull.,* May, 1962, 43:8–10.

16. Milt, H., *How to Deal with Mental Problems,* National Association for Mental Health, 1960.

17. Nikelly, A., "Goal-Directedness: A Practical Goal for Psychotherapy," *Ment. Hyg.,* October, 1962, 46:523–526.

18. Penfield, W., "The Interpretive Cortex," *Sci.,* June 26, 1959, 129:1719–1725.

19. Schwartz, D. A., "A Re-View of the 'Paranoid' Concept," *Arch. gen. Psychiat.,* April 1963, 8:349–361.

20. Srole, L., *et al., Mental Health in the Metropolis: The Midtown Manhattan Study,* Vol. I, McGraw-Hill, 1962.
21. Steckle, L. C., *Problems of Human Adjustment,* Harper & Row, 1957.
22. Stoeckle, J. D., and Davidson, G. E., "Bodily Complaints and Other Symptoms of Depressive Reaction," *J. Amer. Med. Ass.,* April 14, 1962, **180**:134–139.
23. Szalita, A. B., "Regression and Perception in Psychotic States," *Psychiat.,* February, 1958, **21**:53–63.
24. Thorpe, L. P., Katz, B., and Lewis, R. T., *The Psychology of Abnormal Behavior,* Ronald, 1961.

Chapter 12   Severe
Disorders of Behavior

Neuroses and psychoses are severe disorders of behavior, which reflect considerable personality deterioration. These disorders have many symptoms in common but differ essentially in the extent to which the person is incapacitated. The neurotic may have many troubles but, usually, can function within the bounds of reality and interact with people fairly well. The psychotic is more detached from reality, more disoriented, and more severely impaired in his interpersonal relationships. Either disorder may be sufficiently serious to require hospitalization; however, the majority of neurotics, and a large proportion of the psychotics, can be treated on an outpatient basis in clinics or hospitals, or by private physicians. Unfortunately, many neurotics and psychotics are receiving no treatment of any kind.

THE NEUROSES

The term neuroses means literally "full of nerves"; hence, it is not surprising that neurotic disorders frequently are confused with true nerve diseases, such as neuritis or neuralgia, and with other loosely defined conditions, described as "nervousness," "nerve weakness," and "nervous breakdown." Before proceeding with a discussion of the neuroses, we should clarify some of these popularly held notions regarding nervous conditions.

The term nervousness generally is used to describe a tense,

hyperactive person who cannot sit still, displays various forms of motor restlessness sometimes described as the "jitters," and has a number of tension-reducing mannerisms such as nose picking, nail biting, and the like. However, the fact that such a person is tense, high-strung, or keyed-up does not necessarily make him neurotic.

Nerve weakness is alleged to be a tired, worn-out feeling, due to a run-down condition of the nervous system. The term is used frequently in promoting the sale of "nerve tonics." There are very few nervous conditions brought on by an impairment of the nervous system, and nerve tonics have little effect on a person unless he happens to be suffering from a vitamin deficiency, or the tonic is liberally fortified with alcohol or sedatives.

Nervous breakdown may mean anything from a polite name for a psychosis to plain physical exhaustion. As in the case of nerve weakness, there is no actual breakdown in the function or organic integrity of nerve tissue. The impairment which exists is in the individual's adjustive capacities.

These and other popular terms used to describe various nervous reactions should not be confused with the true neuroses.

The Nature of Neurosis

The nature of human neurosis can perhaps be better understood by examining neurotic behavior in animals. Experimental neurosis has been induced in sheep and goats by subjecting the animals to a rigid and unvarying pattern of light signals, followed by electrical shock. The most striking and persistent symptoms displayed by these neurotic animals was an acute sensitivity to possible danger, and an inability to deal with danger when it occurred. The neurotic animal was in a constant state of readiness for something to happen, and the slightest sound caused an immediate acceleration of its heart rate and an increase in muscular tension. Yet, despite this alertness, the neurotic animal was incapable of dealing with actual danger. On several occasions, dogs invaded the pasture where the experimental animals were kept, and their victim invariably was one of the neurotic sheep. While normal animals protected themselves by staying together and escaping as a flock, the neurotic animal fled in panic by itself and was picked off (37).

Underlying neurotic disorder in humans is a core of anxiety similar to the accentuated sensitivity of neurotic animals. This anxiety is experienced as diffused dread, plus various physiological reactions which are disproportionate in intensity to any real threat confronting the individual. Defensive reactions to this basic anxiety are often irrational, because the individual is responding to forces which he cannot identify. He maintains a vigilance or a state of psychological and physiological arousal against symbols and unconscious forces which he interprets as threats. Consequently, his behavior may be compulsive, immature, inappropriate, and unproductive, as far as adjustment is concerned (33).

Neurotic people often are quite aware of their condition. Many of them read books and study their problems so thoroughly that they can carry on intelligent discussions with the therapist, using all the correct terminology. However, mere awareness does not help them overcome their difficulties or relieve their symptoms. There is a wide gulf between intellectual awareness of a neurotic disorder and the elimination of neurotic behavior.

Origins of Neurotic Behavior

There are many theories regarding the origins of neuroses. We shall touch upon three which appear to have the most support at the present time.

One point of view is that a neurosis results from the arousal of intense and painful anxiety, followed by the development of exaggerated ego defenses to cope with this anxiety. As further stress is encountered, secondary defenses arise to protect the original ego defenses. The result is a complicated structure of neurotic habit patterns, designed to help the individual maintain some semblance of self-integrity in the midst of a hostile psychological environment (18).

A number of circumstances can activate this chain of events, but most often it stems from childhood experiences within the family. Case histories of adult neurotics frequently reveal restrictive patterns of parent-child relationships. The typical family patterns encountered are those in which protective, anxious parents prevent the child from growing up; perfectionistic parents make the child feel he can do nothing right; overly strict parents make him feel mistrusted or ashamed of his natural impulses; and rejecting parents make the child feel worthless and unloved. In each case, threats to the sense of selfhood, and conflicts over submitting to the parents or following a course of self-realization, lead to the use of defense mechanisms. When these mechanisms fail to relieve his anxiety, the child engages in a complicated series of neurotic maneuvers to avoid further damage to his self-integrity.

In such a course of events, the actual neurotic breakdown may come on rather suddenly. Sometimes it follows a physical illness or accident; or it may be triggered by emotional events, such as domestic turmoil, economic crisis, disappointment in love or work, or by a major catastrophe such as death of a loved one. In each case, however, the final event is merely the precipitating cause, not the actual cause, of neurosis. Past events had made the individual vulnerable to this final upset.

A neurosis may emerge at any stage of development but occurs most frequently in the late teens or in early adult life. The incidence of neurosis varies only slightly among the age groups beyond fifteen. Neurosis as a disorder is relatively rare among younger children. This may be due to the reluctance of examiners to classify children as neurotic, and a tendency to use the classifications of personality disturbance or emotional maladjustment instead. However, neurotic symptoms are common among children below the age of fifteen. Withdrawal, temper tantrums, enuresis, aggressiveness, destructive behavior, and other neurotic traits may have their beginnings as early as the preschool age (47).

Another view of the neuroses emphasizes a conditioning process which occurs when a child grows up under the influence of parental anxiety or when he is deprived of maternal affection and care during the early years of life (12, 43). A considerable body of evidence points to the mother as the parent who is instrumental in determining a child's susceptibility to later neurotic disorders. Extensive investigations have shown that mothers who do not relate well to their infants, particularly during the first year of life, can predispose the child to neurotic responses to stress (17). Research conducted by Roudinesco and others, referred to in Chapter 4, has shown that if the mother is absent from the home during the first year of life and if no substitute mothering is provided, the basic foundation for later personality disorganization is laid.

Animal experiments have further documented this effect of the mother on the development of neurotic behavior. In his experiments at Cornell University, Liddell (37) took a mother goat and her twin kids, aged three weeks, and confined one kid to a room alone, while the other was kept with its mother. Both kids were subjected to electrical shocks which were synchronized with an overhead light that went off before the shock was applied and came on during the shock. As the conditioning proceeded, the little goat who was alone began to move cautiously around the room close to the wall, finally cowering against the wall in one corner of the room. Its twin, in the other room with its mother, continued to move freely around the room and did not develop a neurotic pattern of behavior. A follow-up test was conducted two years later, using eight goats which had been conditioned in this manner. All were re-exposed to the same darkness signals and electric shocks. By the twentieth day, the four goats which had their mothers with them during their earlier experiences showed no evidence of neurotic behavior, while the other four exhibited signs of experimental neurosis.

While the loss of a mother during early childhood does not inevitably lead to neuroses, studies of adult neurotics show a much higher incidence of mother loss than that which occurs in the normal population. This factor must be considered as an important aspect of the conditioning theory of neurosis, in that maternal bereavement in childhood can set up a chain of events which contributes to the reinforcement of anxiety (4).

A third view of the origin of neurosis has been advanced by those who look upon this disorder as an organic disease. Since certain drugs relieve the symptoms of some forms of neurosis, this idea has much popular appeal. In certain types of neurosis, physiological activities different from that of normal people have been discovered. These include slower sedimentation of the blood, increased viscosity of the blood serum, increased red blood count, an excess of phosphorus in the urine, and hyperacidity of the stomach (56). An increased excretion of epinephrine and related substances has been found among neurotics, and improvement in their condition is accompanied by a lowered excretion of these substances. While investigators do not go as far as to say that these physiological factors cause the neuroses, their discoveries have opened a new line of research.

Forms of Neurosis

Neurotic illnesses or psychoneuroses (the terms are used here interchangeably) are classified into several groups according to the person's predominant symptoms. The most generally accepted classifications are the psychasthenic neuroses, the neurasthenic neuroses, and the conversion reactions.

Psychasthenic Neuroses. These are ailments in which a person exhibits a vast range of troublesome mental and emotional symptoms. The psychasthenic may be fear-ridden by unreasonable dreads or phobias; he may have obsessions and compulsions, display unreasonable elation, constant depression, discouragement, apathy, or overinhibition. Some talk incessantly, while others are withdrawn and uncommunicative.

ANXIETY NEUROSIS. This is a form of psychasthenia in which, in addition to generalized feelings of anxiety and apprehensiveness, the individual has acute anxiety attacks which may last from a few minutes to a few hours. During these attacks, he is in a state of near panic and often experiences palpitation, sweating, tremor, dizziness, and a tightness in the chest. These attacks may occur without warning and usually cannot be attributed to any single factor or circumstance. At times, anxiety neurosis may be expressed through hostile actions directed toward oneself, which may lead to suicide attempts (58).

Neurasthenic Neuroses. In these neuroses, sometimes described as nerve weakness or fatigue states, anxiety is expressed through vague physical symptoms as well as through exaggerated emotional reactions. The neurasthenic displays various diffuse physical reactions, which might include hypochondria, insomnia, constant tiredness, indigestion, nausea, vomiting, constipation, diarrhea, headache, or dizziness. The most common physical symptom is a loss of feeling of well-being. The person complains of fatigue, tiredness, or "heavy" feelings, often so overwhelming that daily activities are difficult to perform. These feelings may vary from being tired all the time to inability to get out of bed in the morning. Attempts at rest or relaxation often make the victim more uncomfortable, irritable, and tense. This physical lassitude may cause the person to withdraw from other people, to snap at those he must live with, and to be annoyed by minor noises such as children at play. He knows he is irritable, and tends to feel guilty about it, but resists help even when he realizes that he needs it (59).

Conversion Reactions. Formerly called hysteric neuroses or hysteria, this is a form of disorder in which specific physical symptoms assume the function of insulating the troubled individual from his anxiety (5). In our discussion of adjustment mechanisms, it was shown how a sore throat or headache might serve as a convenient way of getting out of a disagreeable situation. Conversion reaction is an extension of this behavior. The function of some body part is lost, distorted, or impaired to a point where normal functioning is impossible. There may be a paralysis of the limbs, intense aches and pains, deafness, blindness, loss of voice, or tremors of the head or hands. An anesthesia may develop, in which the victim becomes insensitive to pain. Or he may develop fits or seizures, or faint at the least provocation. Physical examinations persistently indicate that the body is sound and able to function, yet the hysteric is not pretending; his ailment is real to him, and he is just as disabled as if he had a physical disease or disorder (66).

Exaggerated emotional reactions usually accompany these physical symptoms. There is a high incidence of attempted suicide in this group, as well as feelings of hypersensitivity, irritability, impulsiveness, and frequent mood swings (50). Some hysterics are highly suggestible; they read all the material they can get on the illness they are supposed to have and then develop many of the symptoms described (16). The cures effected by faith healers or miracle workers are thought to result from the exercise of suggestion on such hysterically ill people.

Neuroses may take many other forms which defy classification. Some neurotic disorders engulf the total life of a person; others are limited to a specific area of activity. Whether or not neurotic reactions cause the individual serious trouble depends on the types of symptoms he develops, how well they are disguised or balanced by other traits, and what events in life occur to accentuate or minimize them. Some neurotics can function successfully in one type of situation and with certain types of people, but go completely to pieces when circumstances become less favorable. Often these people go from doctor to doctor, seeking a cure for their physical complaints, but never completely cooperating with the physician, because their physical symptoms hide the real problem and removal of these symptoms would focus attention on conflicts that are too painful to face (22).

THE PSYCHOSES

Psychoses differ from neuroses primarily in the extent to which the ego has lost control over the personality, and in the more extensive disorganization of thought processes, emotions, and behavior. The neurotic may be a tense, unhappy individual, but his ego strives to maintain control, and he is often capable of living with his family and maintaining himself in society. The psychotic undergoes a gross loss of contact with reality and usually requires close care and supervision. As nearly as we can tell, there are several million psychotics in this country. Since less than half this number can be counted among patients at hospitals, clinics, or private physicians, large numbers of psychotics must be unrecognized and untreated in the general population (36, 47).

Psychoses are generally classified into two broad groups: the organic psychoses and the psychogenic or functional psychoses. Organic psychoses are disorders in which there is damage to the brain or central nervous system due to infection, trauma, drugs, the degenerative changes of old age, or other physical disability. The psychogenic or functional disorders include many of the same symptoms as are found in organic psychoses, but there are no significant physical, structural, or physiological changes in the brain or nervous system to account for them. We shall limit our discussion to the common forms of functional disorder, since most other types of psychoses are primarily a medical concern. The schizophrenic reactions and the affective disorders account for most of the ailments in the functional group. Psychopathic and sociopathic disorders, and paranoia and paranoid conditions, are functional disorders which represent only a small percentage of the psychoses, but because the actions of these people are often dramatic and much publicized, we shall spend a little time describing them.

About half the people who develop psychoses have a functional disorder. Schizophrenic reactions comprise the majority of these functional psychoses. There are many types of schizophrenia, the most common being (1) simple schizophrenia or dementia praecox, (2) paranoid schizophrenia, (3) catatonic schizophrenia, and (4) hebephrenic schizophrenia. In addition, the term *schizoid personality* is used to designate behavior which is not entirely schizophrenic but is tending in that direction. Also, the term *autism* is applied to some forms of schizophrenia which occur in children. Together these disorders are called schizophrenic reactions. They affect the largest and the youngest group of patients admitted to mental hospitals. About one fourth of the new admissions to mental hospitals are so diagnosed, and the median age of patients is in the early thirties. However, because these disorders last for many years, a large proportion of the long-term inmates of mental hospitals are in the schizophrenic category.

General Symptoms of Schizophrenic Behavior

Schizophrenia has so many forms and symptoms that it is impossible to give a complete and adequate description of it. Symptoms differ in terms of the age of the person, the personality development before the onset of symptoms, the culture in which he is reared, and many other factors. There are a few common threads of reaction which, more or less, run through most of the types of schizophrenia. These include a breakdown in the selective inhibiting functions of attention, disturbances of ego concept and body image, regression, and bizarre behavior. These do not occur uniformly in all schizophrenic reactions but are seen often enough to be classified as prominent symptoms of these disorders.

The breakdown in the selective inhibiting functions of attention causes the schizophrenic to be swamped by a tide of incoming impressions, which he is unable to sort out or communicate effectively. Consequently, he can neither attend fully to his surroundings nor react to them realistically. Disturbances of body image are reflected in the difficulty he experiences in associating himself with his body. Usually, he perceives his hands and feet to be smaller than normal, and is confused about where various organs of the body are located and what they are like. Bizarre behavior takes on many forms, including postural oddities, regression to infantile behavior, meaningless repetition of certain words and sounds, odd statements, apathy, and varied reactions to the many delusions, hallucinations, and thought distortions which are experienced (42, 64). In addition to these general symptoms, each type of schizophrenia is differentiated by its own particular set of symptoms.

Simple Schizophrenia. Simple schizophrenics are immature, withdrawn, timid, seclusive, indifferent people who are childlike in their interests and activities, highly suggestible, and easily led into trouble. They are incapable of much effective work, other than simple, repetitive tasks. Often, they appear to be mentally retarded, but this may be due to immaturity and apathy rather than to an impairment of intellectual capacity. As the disease progresses, profound regression of behavior occurs. Older patients may just sit and vegetate, or lie in bed completely apathetic and helpless, unable to care for their most elementary needs, such as feeding, washing, or elimination.

Paranoid Schizophrenia. The paranoid schizophrenic is dominated by an elaborate system of sounds, forces, beliefs, and people, which fills his world with sinister meanings. He is a hapless victim of persecution by various lights, rays, waves, spirits, or people. The most basic threat is that he will cease to exist and either become a part of another person or be absorbed by someone or something. Sometimes he develops exalted hallucinations or delusions and considers himself to be a great ruler, or as possessing much wealth or special powers. These people usually have a grievance about something and want to express it, but their thoughts and words are garbled and disorganized. Because the threats they experience are real and vivid, their behavior may be unpredictable and sometimes violent (55). However, it is said that there is less danger of violence in walking through the wards of a mental hospital than in walking through some of our city streets at night.

Catatonic Schizophrenia. This type of schizophrenia is characterized by a seeming suspension of volition. Catatonics develop a stupor or mutism, during which they are unable to utter a word for long periods of time, then suddenly burst into a voluble streak which again subsides into mutism. Or they may assume a position of muscular rigidity (catalepsy), such as a kneeling position with hands clasped as in prayer. This position is held for hours or days, and any attempt to move the person is resisted. In such immobile states, the catatonic does not swallow, saliva dribbles from his mouth, he does not eat, and may not eliminate until natural peristalsis or urination occurs. He may suddenly emerge from his catalepsy and become violent and destructive, then return to a state of immobility. Sometimes these people appear to be quite normal after a siege of catalepsy, but often they act in unpredictable ways and seem to have little control over their behavior (3).

Hebephrenic Schizophrenia. This is the classical "village looney." The hebephrenic's behavior is incongruous, confused, and silly. He laughs and smiles inappropriately, talks to himself, and seems to enjoy life in a weird, childish way. Sometimes he becomes so childish and undisciplined that he urinates on the floor or smears feces on the walls. His speech and thought processes shift rapidly and have little relation to what is going on around him. He will answer questions directed to him, but his answers usually have nothing to do with the question asked, often consisting of disconnected, meaningless words.

Autism and Childhood Schizophrenia. Schizophrenia may occur during the first few years of life. One form of this ailment found among young children is called autism. The autistic child usually has difficulty in learning to speak. He may parrot meaningless phrases, or grunt to express himself, but cannot communicate effectively. Some autistic children are withdrawn and unresponsive even to their parents. Often they become attached to an object like a doll or blanket and will shriek if it is taken away (19, 53).

The play of autistic children is compulsive, aimless, repetitive, and seems to give them little enjoyment. If left to themselves, they will repeat a movement for hours, such as sifting sand or pebbles through their fingers. They are so far removed from reality and so unamenable to control that they cannot function with other children in a public school setting (28).

There are other forms of childhood schizophrenia in which behavior is not so completely deteriorated as in autism. Some schizophrenic children get along quite well during the early years of school, and their work may be average or above average, particularly in areas which call for rote learning. Many learn to read without apparent effort but with little or no comprehension. Often they are described by teachers as sweet, gentle, easy to get along with, passive, and dependent. Usually by the age of ten or eleven, symptoms of bizarre behavior and incongruous emotional reactions becomes evident. Serious behavior flare-ups and acute schizophrenic episodes involving somatic complaints, phobias, body image distortions, hallucinations, and other symptoms, become more frequent in late adolescence and can be expected to result in a disabling psychosis unless therapeutic intervention takes place (9).

The Affective Psychoses

The predominant symptoms of the affective psychoses are extreme variations in emotional reaction. As many as twenty varieties of affective psychoses have been described. We shall limit our consideration to the two major disorders of this group, the cyclothymic psychoses and the involutional psychoses.

Cyclothymic Psychosis. This ailment, often called manic-depressive psychosis, occurs most commonly in the middle years of life, around the early forties, and affects 5 to 10 percent of the patients admitted to mental hospitals. It is an ailment which involves cyclic changes in mood, varying from a manic or elated phase to depression, with alternating periods of normalcy. At times, the normal period extends over several years, so that it is difficult to distinguish between recovery and the quiescence of symptoms.

In the manic state of this disorder, the person is overactive, excited, and talks rapidly and profusely. His judgment is faulty and he may enter into ventures which he cannot possibly fulfill. He may throw money around, shout, tear off his clothes, and become violent. Fatigue usually ushers in a period of normalcy or depression. As he quiets down, the patient often expresses regret over his lack of self-control. In the depressive state the person is overwhelmed with feelings of impending disaster. He may become morose, cringe in a corner, and lose interest in life, or his depression may be of the agitated type with much crying and wringing of the hands. Many depressives begin to feel better after a while, even without treatment, but relapses are frequent and the danger of suicide is always present (10, 50).

Cyclothymia rarely occurs in children in the form of a psychosis. The early stages of this disorder are more often reflected in the form of cyclothymoid personality. These are anxious youngsters, beset with many fears and bodily disturbances, who have frequent crying spells and mood swings. Periods of hyperactivity and negativism become more frequent as the child grows older, reaching a peak in adolescence, when the individual may become grossly disabled for several years. Following adolescence, the disorder often subsides spontaneously and may not recur until late adulthood (2).

Involutional Psychosis. Previously called involutional melancholia or psychotic depression, this disease affects about the same proportion of patients as cyclothymia but occurs later in life, generally between the ages of 48 and 58. Women develop this disorder almost three times more often than men.

As the name implies, the involutional melancholic is an extremely sad and depressed person. His orientation in time may be so confused that he continues to grieve over a sorrow which occurred years ago as though it had just happened. The mere mention of the sorrow will bring on a flow of tears. Accompanying the depression are various symptoms of bodily distress, such as loss of weight, feelings of weakness or exhaustion, loss of appetite, and disturbed sleep. Some patients are very apathetic and just sit at a window with an expression of extreme dejection, staring at a fixed object for hours at a time. Others are so painfully distressed that they pace the floor, moaning and wailing.

There is much similarity between the symptoms of involutional psychosis and the depressive stages of cyclothymia. The two ailments are difficult to distinguish and often are diagnosed on the basis of age. There is, however, a difference in prognosis. The chances for recovery from cyclothymia are good, particularly if the first attack occurs between the ages of 21 and 30. These patients are responsive to electroshock and psychotherapy, and spontaneous recovery without treatment occurs quite often. Involutional psychosis is of longer duration, and spontaneous recovery is not usual. Therapy must often be continued over a long period of time and is most effective where the duration of the illness has not been over two or three years. Long-standing, chronic cases of involutional melancholia may require more heroic treatment, including psychosurgery.

The Lesser Psychoses

Two other types of psychoses, which together make up only about 2 percent of the patients admitted to mental hospitals, are worthy of mention because of their effect on society. These are the psychopathic and sociopathic personality disorders in one group, and paranoia and paranoid personality in the other.

The psychopath is not necessarily the sadistic monster so often portrayed on television and in novels. He may be quite a harmless person who, because he lacks inner controls, gets himself into one jam after another. Not understanding the consequences of his actions, and being unaware of his effects on other people, he may do many bizarre things. If he believes himself to be a wealthy man, he may go around the country passing worthless checks and living in luxury. He may proclaim himself to have rare healing powers and offer his wondrous services to all who suffer. He may be so uninhibited and child-like in his concepts of proper behavior that he has no com-punctions about knocking on the door of any house and asking to use the bathroom. The psychopath receives many rebuffs and hard knocks from society, but he does not learn from his experiences and keeps right on repeating the same mistakes and getting into the same difficulties. In a mental hospital where he is known, has a definite routine to follow, and someone to provide the controls he lacks, the psychopath can get along quite well and usually is a competent worker.

The sociopath has quite a different influence on society. His out-of-bounds behavior has a strong antisocial quality, which society cannot ignore. Included here are some of the hardened criminals, compulsive homicidals, and various unprincipled people who benefit from the sorrows of others. The typical criminal sociopath has a stormy history which usually includes early delinquency, frequent fights, difficulties in school, ina-bility to hold a job, poor marital adjustment, a police record, and often excessive use of alcohol and drugs (20). He is difficult to reform because he denies, even to himself, the consequences of his behavior and maintains a picture of himself as clever and unreachable (54).

A few studies have been made of the childhood behavior of people who later became psychopaths or sociopaths. In general, they tend to show that, as children, these people were aggres-sive, competitive, and tried to manipulate others through ex-tortion or ingratiation. They readily resorted to cheating and foul play in order to achieve their goals. Their schoolwork usually was poor, although they often displayed good ability to memorize. Their aggressiveness often made them leaders among their peers, but they would repeatedly get themselves and their followers into trouble. When apprehended, they would try to avoid punishment by acting remorseful, but had no anxiety about their acts and would return to their usual pattern of behavior (32).

The paranoid person is distrustful, suspicious, hostile, and has many imagined enemies. His delusions are transitory and his behavior erratic. He does not undergo the extensive personality deterioration seen in paranoid schizophrenia. At times, he may feel and act rationally and have the appearance of a normal person. However, if stimulated to react in the particular area where he has paranoid tendencies, he quickly becomes irrational and hostile.

When the suspiciousness of the paranoid becomes certainty, when his doubts become delusions, and his imagined thoughts hallucinations, he has developed paranoia. The symptoms of paranoia are generally organized around a single theme and are continuous. Paranoid personality and paranoia may cause a person to commit violent acts against all kinds of imagined adversaries, resulting in some instances in serious hazards to the welfare and safety of innocent people.

ORIGINS OF THE PSYCHOSES

There are many myths, fables, and superstitions about the origin of psychoses. In the early days of man's history, bad blood, evil spirits, devils, and demons, received most of the blame for these disorders. Later, injuries, infections, masturbation, excessive use of alcohol and tobacco, and the strain of modern living (even in 1854!) were implicated as the cause of mental disorders. Today, after decades of scientific investigation, there still remains a lack of agreement on how functional psychoses arise.

Two major schools of thought prevail at the present time. One, which is supported by biologists, neurologists, physiologists, and allied scientists, considers these disorders to be strictly biochemical in origin, with various proponents emphasizing heredity, glandular dysfunction, metabolic disturbances, neurological changes, or physiological processes. The other major group, consisting of some psychiatrists, psychologists, sociologists, and professional people who have a social orientation toward human behavior, considers these psychoses to be psychosocial disorders, brought on by maladaptations to the stresses of life. The latter place great emphasis upon the forces which shape personality during the developmental process. There are other points of view, and a number of compromises among the various schools of thought, but the biochemical and the psychosocial views represent the basic patterns of thought regarding the nature and origins of the nonorganic psychoses (28).

Biochemical Viewpoints

Many of those who support the biochemical hypothesis attack psychosocial explanations of behavior as descended from ancient superstition and from mystical concepts of the soul. They emphasize that the scientific approach has already discovered many important physiological facts about psychoses and that, if a cause for these disorders is ever found, it will be found by those who are searching for biological and physiological causes. In recent years, many millions of dollars have been provided by public and private agencies for research into the causes of mental illness, and most of this research has been in the biochemical fields. As a result, many investigations have been conducted, and a number of new and promising leads discovered. Yet, time after time, it has been found that the new facts offered with great enthusiasm by early researchers are not substantiated by later and more rigorous research. Considerable controversy exists over what physiological knowledge can be relied upon to explain the origins of functional psychoses (30, 31).

Genetic Origins. In Chapter 2 we described some of the early studies on the hereditary transmission of personality and adjustment characteristics. These studies showed a high incidence of mental disturbance in some families and even in generations of these families. However, these were primarily statistical studies, and their weakness lies in being unable to rule out the nongenetic factors which can influence the development of mental disorders (29). Research has not provided clear evidence that the functional psychoses are transmitted in accordance with accepted genetic laws.

This is not to say that genetics are unimportant. On the contrary, genes are enormously important, but our knowledge of how they work is still imperfect, and it has not yet been shown that they exercise complete control over man's personality development (7, 60). It is hoped that the extensive studies now being made into the genetic structure of cells will some day lead to a better understanding of the relationship between somatic and psychological functioning (51).

Glandular Factors. There has been a great deal of study on the effects of the endocrine glands on mental illness. It has long been known that the pituitary, adrenal, thyroid, pineal, and sometimes the ovarian glands can produce behavior disturbances, if their secretions are either deficient or excessive. The process by which behavior changes are produced by glandular products was a mystery until modern research devoted itself to tracing certain metabolic processes in the body and finding out what happens to glandular products. For example, studies of the adrenal gland have revealed an adrenochrome stage in the metabolism of adrenalin. If this stage is prolonged, psychotic symptoms are produced (46). The activities of other endocrine glands have also been studied, and there is little doubt that glandular disturbance and mental disease go together. However, it is not yet clear whether endocrine disturbances produce the symptoms of psychoses or are concomitants of the over-all disturbance. Many psychotics who have abnormal amounts of endocrine products in the blood stream have been shown to return to normal levels as they recover from their ailments. Yet, the use of hormones to cure psychoses has not met with much success.

Physiochemical Factors. A number of investigations have indicated that the chemical processes going on in psychotic people differ from those found in normal people. The incomplete metabolism of certain proteins in psychotics results in the excretion in the urine of chemicals which, when purified and injected into animals or normal humans, produce many of the symptoms of psychoses (44, 62). The blood plasma of schizophrenics has also been shown to have noxious products which do not exist in normal people. Extracts of schizophrenic blood serum injected into normal humans have produced temporary schizophrenia. A protein named taraxein is one of the products which has been indicted as responsible for this effect (21).

Some of the other changes in bodily metabolism of schizophrenics which have been reported reveal a higher tolerance to histamine than normal people have, and a higher protein level in the ventricular fluid of the brain (57, 63). However, as interesting and promising as these explorations into the biochemical bases of psychosis have been, no metabolic product has been found which will clearly differentiate a psychotic person from a normal person. The best that can be said about these studies is that, with increased precision in methodology, the chemical and physiological bases of psychoses may become increasingly significant in coming years (14, 34).

Organic and Physiological Factors. For more than a century, physicians have been trying to find an organic defect in the brain which would account for the functional psychoses. Medical history reports no success in this effort, and modern research has done little better. A recent report of autopsies performed on the brains of 50 schizophrenics and 200 people who were not psychotic found nothing more significant than a thickening of the smaller cortical blood vessels in the brains of schizophrenics, and this was not held to be the cause of the psychosis (26).

There is some statistical evidence that injury to the brain may be an important element in the later development of psychoses, even though no structural changes are revealed upon autopsy. One study which compared the life histories of schizophrenic children with their normal siblings found that 40 to 53 percent of the schizophrenics had suffered brain injuries, either prenatally or immediately after birth, while only 6 to 9 percent of their normal siblings had sustained such injuries (61). Thus, organic factors cannot be ruled out as a cause for functional psychoses, although the relationship is still unproven.

Some recent investigations have turned from a search for structural changes in the brain to a study of differences in the manner in which the brain operates in psychotics and in normal people. A number of studies on the electrical activity of the brain are under way. Russian scientists have been exploring the electrophysiological activity of the brain through the use of a system of batteries and lights. In healthy individuals they found a bio-electric mosaic that was in constant movement. Brain electricity made lights go off and on constantly, much like an electrical advertising display. In schizophrenics, the electrical activity was less dynamic, becoming more and more inert as the disease progressed. When schizophrenics were given various drugs, electrical activity in their brains increased or decreased as behavior became more normal or more disturbed (48). However, electroencephalographic studies conducted in this country have not been able to relate brain waves to psychoses with sufficient precision to be used as a diagnostic measure (1).

Another type of study, conducted at the Harvard Medical School, had to do with measuring the structural and physiological maturity of the central nervous system in schizophrenics. The chemical composition of the cerebrospinal fluid was found to provide an index of maturity. Adult schizophrenics had a level of neuraminic acid, a component of the brain's gray matter, which was comparable to that found in children under the age of seven years. A tentative theory was advanced that schizophrenia may result from the arrested development of the nervous system (6).

Many other channels of investigation are now being pursued in the search for biochemical causes for the functional psychoses. These studies are provocative, but they have not as yet produced conclusive evidence for distinguishing psychotics from normals in terms of the genetic, glandular, chemical, metabolic or physiological processes that have been measured. This issue remains a basic source of controversy between scientists who seek an organic explanation for the psychoses and those who look to life stresses for the origins of these disorders.

Psychosocial Views

Many behavioral scientists view the neuro-glandular-chemical disturbances of the psychoses as symptoms rather than causes. The real origins of functional psychoses are thought to arise from the family and the culture. There is much support for this point of view in the evidence derived from the home and social backgrounds of people who develop functional psychoses.

Psychotogenic Families. The family genesis of psychoses has been under study for many years. The general findings have been that there is a high correlation between personal psychopathology and family psychopathology. Not all psychotics come from homes where parents are poorly adjusted. However, early family relationships which undermine the child's ability to master his environment and develop his own individuality are known to play a vital role in the causation of psychoses (40).

Most studies of the family life of psychotics have focused on the mother. The predominant pattern of relationship between mothers and children who later became schizophrenic is one where the mother is restrictive toward the child, denies him his individuality, and makes him dependent upon her. She constantly exposes him to pathological thinking and anxiety-producing situations by vacillating in her requirements and demands so that the child does not know what responses to make (41). In families where one sibling becomes schizophrenic and another does not, it has been found that the emotional entanglement of the mother with the psychotic child was more intense, while the nonpsychotic child was more often left alone, particularly during adolescence. Often the psychotic sibling was a sick or unusual infant who required more attention than the others, so that the dependent mother-child relationship developed early in life (65).

A type of family pattern encountered among people who later developed paranoid personality, psychotic depression, or sociopathic personality is one where the father was the dominant parent and the mother weak and submissive. The father was inconsistent, harsh, erratic, and sometimes brutal in the treatment of the child. The mother made no demands and gave the child no support. The child protected himself in this hostile, unpredictable environment by introjecting his anger and projecting blame upon others. When these devices failed, paranoidal tendencies, aggression, and self-destructive impulses emerged (23).

There are other types of disturbed family relationships which may influence the development of psychoses. Most are characterized by an unresponsiveness of the parents to the emotional needs of the children, a tendency to compete for the child's loyalty, and an undermining or derogation of one parent by another. In a confused, intensely anxious family environment, the child is handicapped in achieving his own identity. If he develops a psychotic disorder, the nature of this disorder will be closely related to the manner in which his personality was permitted to function during his early experiences in the family (15).

Sociocultural Factors. There are two types of social forces which may have an effect on the occurrence of mental disorders. The first is traumatic and widespread social upheavals, such as war and depression. The second is the enduring, pervasive forces which affect everyday living from childhood to old age. Of these, the latter seem to be most potent in shaping adjustment. War and depression cause great suffering and disruption in the way of life of entire nations, but they do not appear to result in a significant increase in the incidence of mental disorder. Studies in Britain and in the United States have shown that neither in World War II nor in the Great Depression of the 1930s did the incidence of admission to mental hospitals increase (49).

On the other hand, social forces which isolate people from human companionship, which render them unstable and mobile so that they have no roots in society, or which gnaw away at them through poverty and low social status, seem to tax the adjustive capacities of people most severely (11). The life pressures exerted by social-class membership have been studied most extensively, and a direct relationship has been shown between social-class status and the type and incidence of psychosis. As mentioned earlier, schizophrenia is six times greater among the lower classes than in the middle class. Middle-class people have a higher incidence of psychosomatic disorder, and upper-class people are more prone to manic depression. Thus, one's social-class membership predetermines what ailment he will develop. Even when they get the same mental disorder, the social classes differ in the symptoms they display. Among a group of schizophrenics who were having delusions, it was found that delusions of upper-class patients centered around religious and grandiose themes, while lower-class patients had delusions of inferiority. Social-class membership produces different stresses on people, and the lower classes are most vulnerable to the severe mental disorders (35, 39, 45).

Synthesis of Fact and Theory

After reviewing the studies on the genetic, biochemical, physiological, and sociocultural origins of psychoses, we see that there is no preponderance of evidence to support any one hypothesis to the exclusion of all others. Most serious students today are inclined to accept a theory of multiple causation for the psychoses. A reasonable synthesis of current knowledge suggests the view that the psychotic is born with an inherited constitutional vulnerability to this disorder. Whether he actually acquires a psychosis depends upon his psychological, social, and physical development. If his life experiences overtax his adjustive capacities, he undergoes internal physiological changes and behavioral modifications which interfere with the function of the brain and upset his emotional equilibrium. These changes render him less capable of meeting the stresses of life, distort his mental, emotional, and behavioral processes, and force him to take refuge in a world of irreality. This is a simplified interpretation of the etiology of functional psychosis, but it takes into account most of what is now known about these conditions and helps to explain why mental illness is so complex and varied a disorder (8, 24).

Recovery from Psychosis

More hospital beds are occupied by psychotics than by patients suffering from any other single illness. Yet, psychiatrists tend to be optimistic about recovery from the psychoses. They point out that more and more of these people are being returned to their homes and jobs as a result of modern therapeutic procedures (13). It has been estimated that from 60 to 85 percent of the new cases of psychoses and about two thirds of the chronic cases could be cured and the patients returned to gainful employment in the community, if proper care were provided (25).

While there appears to be justification for this optimism,

follow-up studies of patients discharged from mental hospitals do not always support claims for high recovery rates. One extensive study made in England reported that 86 percent of the patients treated in a general hospital psychiatric unit over a ten-year period were discharged as cured. But they also found that during the same period, 41 percent of the patients had relapses which required further treatment, and another 18 percent had milder relapses which did not require treatment (52). With such a high rate of relapse, there is a question as to whether a person is cured when his symptoms subside. Some authorities think that the changes which a psychotic undergoes can never be reversed completely and that all we can hope for is to get his behavior within the range of normality so that he can function in a supportive environment outside the hospital. We shall pursue this subject further in the next chapter.

SUMMARY

Neuroses and psychoses are mental and emotional disorders which disable millions of people in the United States. The neuroses are thought to arise out of the accumulated stress experiences of an individual and to emerge when normal defense patterns become rigid and nonadaptive. There are several forms of neurosis, some of which incapacitate a person almost completely, others affecting only a certain aspect of his personality. Despite the handicaps under which they function, neurotics attempt to maintain control over their behavior and to remain in contact with reality. Many of them continue to perform their roles in home and community while laboring under severe emotional burdens.

Psychosis is characterized by more extreme loss of control over behavior and by a gross severance with reality. In many cases, the behavior of psychotics disintegrates so completely that the individual requires close care and supervision lest he harm himself or others. The origin of psychoses has been studied extensively, but much remains to be learned. The organic psychoses have been traced to physical and physiological changes in the body which interfere with the normal function-ing of the brain, nervous system, or other bodily processes. The functional psychoses, which affect many millions of people, have not been linked to any clearly identifiable cause. Most serious students today believe that the person who develops a functional psychosis is born with an inherited constitutional vulnerability to this disorder. Whether he actually develops a psychosis depends upon his physical, social, and psychological development. If the stresses encountered in life overtax his adjustive capacities, he may undergo internal physiological changes and behavioral modifications which upset his emotional equilibrium. The symptoms he develops as he undergoes these changes depend upon the nature of his previous personality development and the forces which have affected it.

The prognosis for recovery from the neuroses and functional psychoses is good. There is considerable optimism that, given early and effective treatment, these people can be restored to a useful life. Although the relapse rate is high at the present time, modern therapeutic procedures are becoming more effec-tive, and if the proper supportive environment can be pro-vided by the community, a majority of the people now confined to mental hospitals could be rehabilitated and restored to useful and productive citizenship.

REFERENCES

1. American Medical Association, "Psychotic, Epileptic Wave Patterns Studied," *J. Amer. Med. Ass.,* December 29, 1962, **182**:33.
2. Anthony, J., "Manic-Depressive Psychosis in Childhood," *J. Child Psychol. Psychiat.,* January, 1960, **1**:53–72.
3. Arieti, S., "Volition and Value: A Study Based on Catatonic Schizophrenia," *Brit. J. med. Psychol.,* 1961, **34**:129–141.
4. Barry, H., Jr., and Lindemann, R., "Critical Ages for Maternal Bereavement in Psychoneuroses," *Psychosom. Med.,* May–June, 1960, **22**:166–181.
5. Berblinger, K. W., "The Quiet Hysteric and His Captive Re-spondent," *Dis. nerv. System,* July, 1960, **21**:386–389.

6. Bogoch, S., "Cerebrospinal Fluid Neuraminic Acid Deficiency in Schizophrenia," *Arch. Neurol.*, August, 1958, **80**:221–227.

7. Böök, J. A., "Genetical Etiology in Mental Illness," in *Causes of Mental Disorders: A Review of Epidemiological Knowledge, 1959*, Milbank Memorial Fund, New York, 1961, pp. 14–33.

8. California Department of Mental Hygiene, "Research—The Ultimate Hope," *Calif. ment. Hlth. Progr.*, August–September, 1962, **3**:6–7.

9. Cobrinik, L. H., "The Manifestations of Plasticity as Seen by the Clinical Psychologist," *Amer. J. Orthopsychiat.*, March, 1963, **33**:305–306.

10. Donnelly, J., "Human Personalities and Their Ills," in *Society Challenges the Individual*, Report of the Mental Health Lectures in Hartford, Conn. Connecticut Mutual Life Insurance Co., 1962, pp. 3–10.

11. Dunham, W. W., "Social Structure and Mental Disorders: Competing Hypotheses of Explanation," *Milbank Mem. Fund Quart.*, April, 1961, **39**:259–311.

12. Eysenck, H. J., *Behavior Therapy and the Neurosis*, Pergamon Press, 1960.

13. Felix, R. H., "Psychopharmacology and Psychiatry," *J. Ark. Med. Soc.*, November, 1961, **58**:223–229.

14. Fessell, W. J., *The Blood Proteins in Functional Psychoses: A Review of the Literature and Unifying Hypothesis*, California Department of Mental Hygiene, Research Division, DMH Project 59–1–14, No. 38, January 23, 1962, 33 pp., mimeographed.

15. Fleck, S., "Family Dynamics and Origin of Schizophrenia," *Psychosom. Med.*, September–October, 1960, **22**:333–344.

16. Flynn, W. R., "On the Psychology of the Shaking Palsy," *Psychiat. Quart.*, April, 1962, **36**:203–221.

17. Garner, A. M., and Wenar, C., *The Mother-Child Interaction in Psychosomatic Disorders*, University of Illinois Press, 1959.

18. Ginsburg, S. W., "The Neuroses," in P. T. Hountras (Ed.), *Mental Hygiene*, Merrill, 1961, pp. 403–418.

19. Goldfarb, W., "Self-Awareness in Schizophrenic Children," *Arch. gen. Psychiat.*, January, 1963, **8**:47–60.

20. Guze, S. B., "Psychiatric Illness and Crime with Particular Reference to Alcoholism: A Study of 223 Criminals," *J. nerv. ment. Dis.*, June, 1962, **135**:52–59.

21. Heath, R. G., *et al.*, "Behavioral Changes in Nonpsychotic Volunteers Following the Administration of Taraxein, the

Substance Obtained from Serum of Schizophrenic Patients," *Amer. J. Psychiat.*, April, 1958, 114:917–920.

22. Hirschfeld, A. H., and Behan, R. C., "The Accident Process. I. Etiological Consideration of Industrial Injuries," *J. Amer. Med. Ass.*, October 19, 1963, 186:193–199.

23. Hitson, H. M., and Funkenstein, D. H., "Family Patterns and Paranoidal Structure in Boston and Burma," *Int. J. soc. Psychiat.*, Winter, 1959, 5:182–190.

24. Hoff, H., "The Multifactorial Approach in Psychiatry," *J. Neuropsychiat.*, April, 1960, 1:173–181.

25. Howard, B. F., "An Optimistic Report on Total Rehabilitative Potential of Chronic Schizophrenias," *Arch. gen. Psychiat.*, October, 1960, 3:345–356.

26. Howie, D. L., "Some Pathological Findings in Schizophrenics," *Amer. J. Psychiat.*, July, 1960, 117:59–62.

27. Jackson, D. D., "Schizophrenia," *Sci. Amer.*, August, 1962, 27:65–74.

28. Jackson, D. D., *The Etiology of Schizophrenia*, Basic Books, 1960.

29. Kallman, F. J., *Heredity in Health and Mental Disorder*, Norton, 1953.

30. Kety, S. S., "Biochemical Theories of Schizophrenia," Part I, *Sci.*, June 5, 1959, 129:1528–32.

31. Kety, S. S., "Biochemical Theories of Schizophrenia," Part II, *Sci.*, June 12, 1959, 129:1590–96.

32. Krippner, S., "Sociopathic Tendencies and Reading Retardation in Children," *Except. Child.*, February, 1963, 29:258–266.

33. Kubie, L. S., "The Fundamental Nature of the Distinction Between Normality and Neurosis," *Psychoanal. Quart.*, 1954, 23: 167.

34. Landsman, T., "Factors Influencing Individual Mental Health," *Rev. educ. Res.*, December, 1962, 32:464–475.

35. Langner, T. S., "Environmental Stress and Mental Health," in P. H. Hoch and J. Zubin (Eds.), *Comparative Epidemiology of the Mental Disorders*, Grune & Stratton, 1961, pp. 32–44.

36. Leighton, D. C., "The Distribution of Psychiatric Symptoms in a Small Town," *Amer. J. Psychiat.*, March, 1956, 112:716–723.

37. Liddell, H. S., "Conditioning and Emotions," *Sci. Amer.*, January, 1954, Reprint No. 418.

38. Lovatt, M., "Autistic Children in a Day Nursery," *Child.*, May–June, 1962, 9:103–108.

39. Lucas, C. J., et al., "A Social and Clinical Study of Delusions in Schizophrenia," J. ment. Sci., November, 1962, 108:747–758.
40. McCord, W., "The Familial Genesis of Psychoses," Psychiat., February, 1962, 25:60–71.
41. McGhie, A., "A Comparative Study of the Mother-Child Relationship in Schizophrenia," Brit. J. med. Psychol., 1961, 34: 209–221.
42. McGhie, A., and Chapman, J., "Disorders of Attention and Perception in Early Schizophrenia," Brit. J. med. Psychol., 1961, 34:103–116.
43. Mackay, R. P., "A Neurologic Theory of the Neurosis," Neurol., October, 1962, 12:657.
44. Masuda, M., "Urinary Aromatic Metabolites in Schizophrenia," J. nerv. ment. Dis., February, 1960, 130:125–133.
45. Myers, J. K., and Roberts, B. H., Family and Class Dynamics in Mental Illness, Wiley, 1959.
46. National Institute of Mental Health, Highlights of Progress in Mental Health Research, 1961, Public Health Service Publication No. 919, Publications and Report Section, Bethesda, Md., 1962, pp. 6–20.
47. Pasamanick, B., "A Survey of Mental Disease in an Urban Population, VI. An Approach to Total Prevalence by Age," Ment. Hyg., October, 1962, 46:567–572.
48. "Pavlovians Stress Electrical Study," Med. News, November 9, 1960, 6:2.
49. Reid, D. D., "Precipitating Proximal Factors in the Occurrence of Mental Disorders: Epidemiological Evidence," Milbank Mem. Fund Quart., April, 1961, 39:229–258.
50. Robins, E., and O'Neal, P., "Culture and Mental Disorder: A Study of Attempted Suicide," Human Org., Winter, 1958, 16:7–11.
51. Roessler, R., and Greenfield, N. S., Physiological Correlates of Psychological Disorder, University of Wisconsin Press, 1962.
52. Rohde, P., and Sargant, W., "Treatment of Schizophrenia in General Hospitals," Brit. Med. J., July 8, 1961, 2:67–70.
53. Schachter, F. F., et al., "Childhood Schizophrenia and Mental Retardation: Differential Diagnosis Before and After One Year of Psychotherapy," Amer. J. Orthopsychiat., July, 1962, 32: 584–594.
54. Schmideberg, M., "Psychotherapy of the Criminal Psychopath," Arch. crim. Psychodynamics, Fall, 1961, 4:724–735.

55. Searles, H. F., "The Sources of the Anxiety in Paranoid Schizophrenia," *Brit. J. med. Psychol.,* 1961, 34:129–141.
56. Selye, H., "The General-Adaptation-Syndrome in Its Relationships to Neurology, Psychology and Psychopathology," in A. Weider (Ed.), *Contributions Toward Medical Psychology: Theory and Psychodiagnostic Methods,* Vol. 1, Ronald Press, 1953, pp. 234–274.
57. Sherwood, S. L., "Relation of Behavior to Cerebral Ventricular Fluid Protein Levels," *Arch. Neurol.,* August, 1962, 7:146–159.
58. Sifneos, P. E., and McCourt, W. F., "Wishes for Life and Death of Some Patients Who Attempted Suicide," *Ment. Hyg.,* October, 1962, 46:543–552.
59. Stoeckle, J. D., and Davidson, G. E., "Bodily Complaints and Other Symptoms of Depressive Reaction," *J. Amer. Med. Ass.,* April 14, 1962, 180:134–139.
60. Stromgren, E., "Genetics and Mental Health," *Child.,* March–April, 1958, 5:49–54.
61. Vorster, D., "An Investigation Into the Part Played by Organic Factors in Childhood Schizophrenia," *J. ment. Sci.,* April, 1960, 106:494–522.
62. Wada, J., and Gibson, W. C., "Behavioral and EEG Changes Induced by Injection of Schizophrenic Urine Extract," *Arch. Neurol. Psychiat.,* June, 1959, 81:747–764.
63. Weckowicz, T. E., and Rall, R., "Skin Histamine Test in Schizophrenia," *J. nerv. ment. Dis.,* July–September, 1957, 125:452–458.
64. Weckowicz, T. E., and Sommer, R., "Body Image and Self-Concept in Schizophrenia," *J. ment. Sci.,* January, 1960, 106:17–39.
65. Yi-chuang Lu, "Mother-Child Role Relations in Schizophrenia," *Psychiat.,* May, 1961, 24:133–142.
66. Ziegler, F. J., *et al.,* "Contemporary Conversion Reactions," *J. Amer. Med. Ass.,* October 26, 1963, 186:307–311.

PART IV   READJUSTMENT AND THE PREVENTION OF MALADJUSTMENT

Chapter 13   Therapy
and Readjustment

People can and do recover from the severe forms of maladjustment. Sometimes, recovery occurs spontaneously, helped along by the passage of time and by changes in the circumstances of living. More often, the assistance of a professional therapist is needed to restore the individual's functional capacities and set him on the road toward readjustment.

In this chapter we shall describe the forms of treatment which a therapist may employ. These fall into two general categories: the somatic therapies and the psychological therapies. Somatic therapies are techniques used to modify certain physiological processes which are considered to be the source of behavior disturbances. Psychological therapies seek to rehabilitate the individual by restoring or rebuilding his mental and emotional competencies. Usually, a combination of treatment is needed for the rehabilitation of a given person. The selection of therapeutic procedures depends on the nature and duration of the illness, and on the skill and convictions of the therapist.

SOMATIC THERAPIES

In our discussion of the origins of maladjustment, we described some of the physiological and metabolic processes which are thought to influence behavior. Somatic therapies attempt to alter these processes through the use of drugs, shock, surgery, and other techniques that affect physiological functioning.

These are drastic and sometimes dangerous forms of treatment, which require the supervision of a qualified physician.

Drug Therapy

The use of drugs or chemicals for the treatment of emotional disturbances is a relatively new therapeutic technique, although its origins have been traced back 30 centuries to the physicians of India.

Over 90 percent of the drugs now in use for treating psychiatric disabilities have been introduced since 1950. The first of these drugs to receive popular acclaim were the tranquilizers or ataractic drugs. The term ataractic is derived from a Greek word, meaning freedom from disturbance of mind or passion. Tranquilizers have the ability to produce sustained relief from anxiety, reduce hostility and aggression, and lower excitability, without inducing marked sedation.

There are two categories of ataractic drugs: the major tranquilizers and the minor tranquilizers. The major tranquilizers are largely derivatives of the organic chemical phenothiazine. They include the original tranquilizer chlorpromazine, which is marketed under the trade name Thorazine, and more recent derivates such as Sparine, Pacatal, Promazine, Thioridazine, and others. These are powerful chemicals, and their use usually is restricted to the more serious types of emotional disorders. However, it is estimated that chlorpromazine has been prescribed for over 50 million patients since its discovery (5).

The minor tranquilizers were developed to treat milder emotional problems and bring relief from common nervous tension and anxiety. These drugs are largely derivatives of the synthetic organic chemical meprobamate, known to many people as Miltown or Equanil. Over a billion tablets of the minor tranquilizers are consumed in this country each year (40).

Since the introduction of tranquilizers, a great many other drugs have become available for the treatment of emotional disturbances. Collectively they are called psychoactive drugs, meaning drugs which are capable of modifying mental activity. In addition to the tranquilizers, they include chemicals which stimulate mental and emotional activity, and those which free the mind by expanding the range of consciousness and sharpening the perceptions.

The stimulants, antidepressants, or energizers are drugs, such as Benzedrine, Dexedrine, and Ritalin, which increase vigilance, raise the level of intellectual energy, and make the patient more accessible to psychological therapy. These are "mood lifters," useful in cases of melancholia and depression, and in certain types of behavior problems of children.

Drugs which free the mind, such as lysergic acid diethylamide (LSD), are said to shorten the time required for psychotherapy. They revive memories, thus enabling the patient to relive childhood events, and stimulate self-expression so that the therapist can gain insight into the causes of maladjustment more quickly (7).

Many other drugs are used for psychotherapeutic purposes, but these are the major ones. The consumption of psychoactive drugs has reached such tremendous proportions that over 100 million dollars are spent on them each year.

Effects of Psychoactive Drugs.   When first introduced, psychoactive drugs were heralded as miracle cures for psychiatric ailments. They were described as a major breakthrough in the practice of psychiatry which would eliminate the need for restraints and shock treatment, and reduce confinement in mental institutions to just a few months (23).

Today, there is more modesty in the claims made for these drugs. For all their demonstrated usefulness, psychoactive drugs have not proved to be suitable for all people, and there is considerable doubt about the long-range safety and usefulness of the more potent medicines. Some studies suggest that the drugs themselves have no lasting therapeutic value and that it is the warm personal attention of the doctor, rather than the medication, which produces improvement in the behavior of patients. In fact, many investigations have found that, given proper care, a placebo or inert substance such as milk sugar can be substituted for the psychoactive drug which a patient had been taking, and he will continue to improve about as well as he did while under medication (46).

An experiment conducted in an English hospital is typical of the findings of many studies where placebos are substituted for drugs without the knowledge of either patients or attendants. Two wards of disturbed, chronically ill patients were placed on chlorpromazine for several months until definite improvement in behavior was observed. Then, a placebo was substituted for drugs in one ward without the knowledge of patients or attendants. At the same time, musical evenings, physical training, occupational therapy and other activities were started for the patients. For six months, while one ward was receiving nothing but milk sugar, there was continued improvement in the behavior of patients. Then placebos were withdrawn, and, within a short time, patients began to show signs of increased disturbance. The conclusion of this study was that improvement of the hospital environment was at least as effective as tranquilizers in altering the behavior of patients, and that drugs may be an unnecessary expense and hazard in the management of disturbed patients (38).

There are some psychiatrists who believe that much of the success credited to psychoactive drugs might well be the result of increased attention given to patients by doctors and nurses. After being virtually ignored for years, the patients suddenly receive more care than they ever had, and because they respond, it is assumed that the drugs were working wonders. However, this issue is still being debated. Many investigations conducted by careful and competent research workers show a reversal of improvement when placebos replace medication. More experience with the use of psychoactive drugs is needed before this question can be resolved (17).

Another controversy in the evaluation of psychoactive drugs relates to the permanency of the improvements due to them. Some mental hospitals claim that, with the aid of modern drugs, they now discharge over three fourths of the patients admitted with functional psychoses. But several studies show that, unless these patients continue on medication, the relapse rate is high, at least 25 to 35 percent (12). This raises the question of whether the patients were really cured of their illness when discharged from the hospital, or if they merely appeared to be better because their symptoms were masked. Some medical people say that psychoactive drugs are chemical crutches and that patients are dependent upon them to keep their symptoms under control. The counterargument is that, through the use of drugs, a person who would otherwise be totally incapacitated is enabled to live a productive life. An analogy is made to the treatment of diabetics, epileptics, heart patients, asthmatics, and others, who are never cured of their ailments but, with the help of medicines, carry on their life functions quite effectively. Whether this analogy can be applied to the use of psychoactive drugs is far from certain, since they have not been in use long enough to evaluate the effects of their use over a lifetime.

Hazards of Psychoactive Drugs.   Practically all the psychoactive drugs have been observed to produce side-effects, some of which are serious hazards to the physical well-being of the individual. The major tranquilizers are known to produce neurotoxic reactions in some people. One study of almost 4000 patients found that nearly 40 percent developed reactions similar to a neurological disorder called Parkinson's Disease. Symptoms included rigidity of limbs, face, and neck; tremors of the hands; oily or waxy facial skin; gait disturbances, including stooped, rigid posture and shuffling steps; and drooling (4). Other side effects of the major tranquilizers are lowered blood pressure, dryness of the mouth, pronounced increase in appetite and weight, frequency of urination, incontinence, jaundice, blood diseases, dermatitis, and, with high dosages, seizures and permanent liver damage. Many of these side-effects disappear when the drug is discontinued; some, however, have been known to persist for months after the phenothiazines were stopped (11, 43).

Nor are the minor tranquilizers, meprobamates and similar compounds, completely safe. Although they are said to be of low toxicity, they have been known to produce skin rashes, chills, fevers, and gastrointestinal disturbances. Some people develop a physical dependency upon these drugs, and addiction similar to barbiturate addiction has occurred. In others, a feeling of apathy, boredom, futility, and emptiness has resulted from the continued use of meprobamates (43).

Other psychoactive drugs have equally disturbing influences

on some people. LSD has been noted to produce a proneness toward suicide in some instances; Rauwolfia compounds may cause serious mental depression; energizers may stimulate a person for a short time and then lead to a serious letdown feeling; depressants may cause mental impairment, irritability, disorientation, and auditory hallucinations (43). Obviously, the psychoactive drugs are not to be taken as freely as people now consume aspirin.

Despite the hazards involved in the use of these drugs, under proper medical supervision they are a valuable adjunct to the therapist. They do not cure psychiatric disorders, in the sense of restoring normal thought processes and emotions or reestablishing ego controls, but they make it easier for the psychotherapist to accomplish these goals. In more refractory cases, it is largely through the use of drugs that the influences of psychotherapy can be brought to bear upon a patient. There is reason to believe that, as scientists discover the precise mode of action of psychoactive drugs on the human organism, the hazards of their use may be minimized and their therapeutic effects controlled more precisely than is possible at present (52).

Shock Therapies

Before the introduction of psychotropic drugs, shock therapy was used quite extensively in the treatment of severe maladjustment. Shock therapy is a violent, imperfectly understood method of jolting the brain and nervous system so that the patient is rendered amenable to rehabilitative forms of therapy. The shock itself has only a temporary effect, and its greatest value is to interrupt a serious depression, quiet an excited person, and restore the patient to the world of reality so that he can be reached through psychotherapy.

One of the oldest forms of shock therapy involves the use of insulin, which produces a coma by reducing the sugar content of the blood. Immediately after emerging from the insulin coma, the patient is usually in good contact with reality for an hour or so, and this period is used for psychotherapy. Through the combined use of insulin shock and psychotherapy, the patient becomes free of his symptoms for longer and longer periods of time and may eventually recover. This treatment has been particularly effective for some types of schizophrenia.

Metrazol shock consists of injecting the organic drug metrazol into a person. Within several seconds a severe epileptic-like seizure results, followed by unconsciousness. This treatment is seldom used today, because convulsions are so violent that broken bones or other injuries may result. Also, the feeling of impending death or sudden annihilation, experienced by many patients before the convulsions, is too traumatic a sensation to be repeated very often.

Electroshock therapy (EST) or electroconvulsive therapy (ECT) is the most commonly used shock treatment. Electrodes are fastened to the temple or forehead and a strong electrical current is passed through the brain for about half a minute. When the current is applied, there is first a flexion of the body, then a series of tonic and clonic reactions. The tonic phase is a sudden rigidity of muscles; the clonic phase, a series of convulsions with jerking contractions of the extremities. The entire reaction generally lasts about 60 seconds. The patient remains unconscious for 10 to 30 minutes and then usually sleeps for many hours. When he awakes, he has no recollection of what happened to him and may complain of a headache or general aches and pains.

This is a heroic form of treatment, and the patient must be protected from breaking an arm or leg, from biting his tongue, or suffering respiratory arrest during the convulsions. Some patients receive several such treatments a day, sometimes hundreds over a period of years. Others are helped by short treatments, in which the convulsive effects are reduced through the use of anesthesia or muscle relaxants. No one knows exactly what happens when the electrical current pulses through the brain, but, in many cases of psychotic depression and catatonic schizophrenia, electroshock therapy is the only treatment that has an effect on the patient (1, 30).

Psychosurgery

It has been found that, by severing the nerve fibers connecting the prefrontal lobes of the brain with the thalamic center of the brain stem, the behavior of hyperactive psychotic patients can be moderated. Prior to 1935, this operation was called prefrontal lobotomy or leucotomy. The surgeon made two openings in the skull, one on each side of the temple, through which he inserted an instrument and severed nerve fibers. Since 1936, a modification of this technique, called transorbital lobotomy, has been in use. A sharp, slender instrument is introduced through the bony part of the eye socket into the frontal lobe of the brain and swung through an arc of 30 degrees, cutting the nerve fibers in its path.

The theory behind psychosurgeory is that, by severing the pathways between the forebrain, which is important in higher thought processes, and the thalamus, which is an important center of emotions, the emotional tone accompanying an individual's thoughts and memories is diminished. This procedure does not remove the source of a patient's emotional disturbance, but relieves him from the torment of disturbed thoughts and ideas, fears, hallucinations, and other internal stimuli which keep him in a constant state of agitation. This treatment is claimed to be particularly useful in some cases of psychotic depression, schizophrenia, and intractable neuroses. One survey of 10,000 patients who had been treated by leucotomy over a period of 12 years found that 60 percent of the group profited from this operation (42).

However, psychosurgery is by no means a safe form of treatment. Sometimes it results in profound personality changes, including intensified selfishness, indifference to moral obligations, unconcern over the consequences of acts, emotional instability, and even in seizures and death. Psychosurgery is now considered an extreme measure, to be used only on people who have not responded to any other form of treatment and who are likely to remain totally incapacitated by their illness (27, 44).

Other Somatic Therapies

Physical therapy, hydrotherapy, carbon dioxide inhalation, and narcotherapy are additional forms of somatic treatment used in some hospitals.

Physical therapy and hydrotherapy involve the use of massage, heat, stimulating showers, or relaxing baths to either tone up or quiet a patient. Drugs and electroshock treatment have largely supplanted these procedures in many hospitals.

Carbon dioxide inhalation is sometimes used with cases of hysterical conversion reaction, and with certain phobias, psychomotor disorders, and depression. The patient takes 20 or 30 breaths of a mixture of 30 percent carbon dioxide and 70 percent oxygen, and lapses into unconsciousness. On awakening, he is more amenable to psychotherapy than before treatment. This is another form of therapy used on an empirical basis without full knowledge of the physiological or psychological processes involved (22).

Narcotherapy or prolonged narcosis is a form of sleep therapy introduced by Russian psychiatrists prior to World War II. Drugs are used to put a patient to sleep for 12 to 22 hours per day, over a period of several days or weeks. Patients are aroused only for cleaning, feeding, and toileting. The long period of rest is thought to restore the functioning of the nervous system to an optimum level and make the person more responsive to drugs, psychotherapy, or shock treatment. Success has been reported with some types of neuroses and psychoses, but the relapse rate is high, and drugs or psychotherapy must be continued in order to maintain the improvements secured under narcotherapy (16, 32).

PSYCHOLOGICAL THERAPIES

The use of psychological methods for the treatment of mental and emotional ills dates back to the priests and medicine men of earlier civilizations, who used magic, incantations, music, suggestion, and other methods of exorcising the evil spirits which were thought to be the cause of disturbed behavior. Modern psychological therapy, however, is founded on principles of human behavior rather than on the concept that some external force has invaded the body.

Psychological therapy may be performed by any mature individual who is a good listener and can provide some assistance to a troubled person. However, this is a very limited form of therapy which is applicable only to situations where the problems are relatively superficial. Professional therapists are trained to do more than merely listen or offer advice. They help a person vent his feelings, a process called emotional catharsis, and then seek to reinforce his inner resources as well as assist in solving immediate problems. Trained therapists may be counselors, whose efforts are limited to certain prescribed areas of adjustment, or psychotherapists, who probe more deeply into the personality structure.

Counseling

Counseling is a form of therapy confined largely to problems which can be worked out on an operational level. These problems generally fall in the areas of vocational choice, marriage and family life, school problems, job-related problems, and interpersonal relationships. Professional counselors are people who have had special training in counseling as part of the preparation required by their occupations. Many ministers, attorneys, educators, psychologists, police officers, probation workers, social workers, nurses, physicians, and others in the service professions, have such training. The function of a trained counselor is to provide information, offer reassurance and support, and help the troubled person find a way out of the difficulties which confront him.

Since counselors are not usually trained in psychotherapy, they must be careful not to permit a person to reveal too much of himself, or probe too deeply into the dynamics of his problems. When it becomes evident that the person's expressed problems are merely symptoms of a more fundamental personality disorder, the counselor should refer the individual to a psychotherapist (15).

Psychotherapy

Psychiatrists, clinical psychologists, and others who are qualified to practice psychotherapy, attempt to help an individual rebuild his impaired functions as well as solve his immediate problems. Unfortunately, psychotherapy operates under two handicaps which tend to limit its usefulness. One is the length of time it takes to achieve results; the other, its dependency upon verbal communication.

Psychotherapy, like medicine, has emergency applications which produce immediate results, and long-term treatment which is more lasting but where improvement is not immediately observable. Emergency psychotherapy has proved quite successful in helping people over an acute emotional crisis. After a disturbed person has had a chance to pour out his panic reactions, his symptoms often subside, and the help of a psychotherapist at this point may result in a quick recovery or prevent further breakdown.

Treatment psychotherapy must usually continue for months and sometimes years before there is an improvement in the person's condition. This is quite a financial drain on many people, and, discouraged by the lack of observable results, they may discontinue treatment before psychotherapy has had a chance to take effect.

Another important limitation to psychotherapy is that it is largely dependent upon the patient's ability to communicate with the therapist. He must have enough mental capacity, emotional stability, and motivation to describe his thoughts, feelings, and experiences, and to understand the interpretations offered by the therapist. Severely deteriorated people and mental defectives are unable to do this. Nor is psychotherapy very helpful with the lower social-class individual who neither understands the process nor is willing to carry on with it for the length of time required. People such as these cannot be reached by psychotherapy, except at rather superficial levels. They often drop out of therapy after the initial interview. The greatest success of psychotherapy is achieved with upper-status, educated people who are motivated toward self-improvement and who carry through with the treatment to its conclusion (34, 39).

Psychoanalysis

Sometimes called depth psychotherapy, psychoanalysis is a form of psychotherapy which seeks to effect a radical change in the basic personality structure. The essence of psychoanalytic therapy lies in reconstructing those phases of the past which still exist in the individual's unconscious and restrict his capacity for emotional growth and maturity. By re-experiencing repressed emotional conflicts which had not been resolved at an earlier stage of life, the person is helped to give up neurotic modes of gratification and re-form his personality on a higher level of maturity (33).

Psychoanalysis is even more demanding of intellectual understanding and financial resources than psychotherapy. Therefore, its range of usefulness is more restricted. The shortest period of treatment which could justifiably be called psychoanalysis would be 6 months to a year. Even when an individual can afford to spend this amount of time and money, the treatment does not always result in a fundamental and permanent alteration in the personality structure. Psychoanalysis achieves its greatest success with neurotics of above average intelligence, whose illness has not progressed to a point where serious personality deterioration has occurred.

Group Therapy

Psychotherapy with groups of 10 or 12 persons began around 1905 and is now a well-established practice. This technique was developed partly because of a shortage of psychotherapists and partly because some people derive more help from a group situation than from individual psychotherapy.

The purpose of group therapy is to stimulate interaction among patients having similar difficulties. Through this means, conflicts and tensions are brought out dramatically, and many people experience considerable relief from learning that they can vent their anger and reveal shameful thoughts and wishes without losing the respect and acceptance of others. The therapist also profits from these group sessions, because in a short time he can observe a range of behavior that would take many hours to uncover in individual therapy sessions (25).

Some people prefer group therapy, because it provides them with a chance to isolate themselves within the group or to discuss someone else's problems without revealing their own. However, it has been found that even those who appear aloof from the group and do not contribute to the discussion can profit from the group sessions. With these withdrawn patients, the group experience serves as a reinforcement of what they gain in individual contacts with a therapist. By listening to others discuss problems similar to their own, they are helped to acquire a feeling of belonging and to derive security and confidence from the group (48).

Therapy groups may use different techniques, depending on the therapist, the patients, and the situation. Psychoanalytic therapists have used dream interpretations, for example, as a springboard for eliciting associations from the group members and encouraging the expression of anxieties (29). Psychodrama or role playing has been used by others as a technique for patients to act out their problems. Psychodramas have even been recorded, then played back to the patients, who offer solutions to the problems presented and discuss similar problems in their own experience. Closed-circuit television is a new technique which shows considerable promise as an aid to group therapy. Here psychodramas and group discussions are portrayed on the screen and followed by audience discussion under the direction of the therapist. In one situation where this was tried, two thirds of a group of schizophrenics and involutional psychotics showed improvement in behavior. Disturbed patients became quiet and attentive, and destructive patients became absorbed in the program instead of tearing their clothes and raving or ranting (35, 50).

In recent years, the family has become the focus of group therapy efforts. Through a series of conferences with parents, children, and relatives, the therapist attempts to modify the behavior of both the disturbed individual and his family. He helps them to explore their relationships, and express thoughts and feelings not previously verbalized, so that they will develop some insight into how they are affecting one another. This interaction among family members leads to a restructuring of roles, so that the disturbed member of the family group is provided with more understanding and support than he had been receiving (8).

Since a great deal of anxiety can be activated in groups, group therapy is a technique which must be under the direction of a person who is qualified to provide individual therapy when necessary. Group discussions are used frequently in schools for counseling purposes, and among adult groups for the sharing and clarification of common problems. If the leader of these discussions is not a qualified therapist, he must exercise caution in permitting the group participants to expose their personal problems to a point where embarrassment and anxiety result.

Aids to Psychotherapy

There are a number of therapeutic aids which a therapist may use to facilitate the diagnosis and treatment of his patients. We have described how drugs, shock treatment, psychodrama, television, and group interaction may be used in conjunction with psychotherapy. Other therapeutic aids in common use include hypnotism, narcoanalysis, clinical tests, books, films, music and art, and modification of the environment.

Hypnotism and Narcoanalysis.   Hypnotism has gone through cycles of popularity and decline as a therapeutic aid. It was introduced as a diagnostic and treatment technique by European physicians in the latter half of the nineteenth century, then fell into disrepute when magicians, amateur psychologists, and quacks began to use it for entertainment and exploitation of gullible people. Today, hypnotism is used with caution, even by qualified psychotherapists, because experience has shown that anxiety, panic states, hysterical dissociation, suicidal depression, and paranoia may at times follow the inexpert use of this procedure. In the hands of a skilled practitioner, who has a thorough understanding of behavior psychodynamics, hypnotism can shorten the therapy process by enabling the patient to reveal problems which would take a longer time to expose if they had to be uncovered through usual interview techniques (3).

Narcoanalysis is a technique which may accomplish the same ends as hypnotism and is frequently used as a substitute for it. A sedative drug, such as sodium pentothal, is administered to the patient until he becomes groggy but not unconscious. In this condition of "twilight sleep," he is encouraged to talk about his emotional conflicts and describe past events which are submerged below the level of mental awareness. With inhibition reduced by the drug, the patient relates experiences which had been excluded from consciousness and enables the therapist to get at the source of his troubles. This technique was used for therapeutic purposes in World War II to reduce the crippling effects of combat neurosis by permitting the patient to release powerful and intense emotional conflicts which he had repressed.

Clinical Tests. An additional method which assists patients to reveal their emotional difficulties is through the use of projective tests. Among the more commonly used tests are word-association tests, where a person is given a stimulus word and asked to react to it quickly with another word; the Rorschach Test, which requires the interpretation of ink blots; the Thematic Apperception Test, where a picture is presented and the individual asked to tell what it means to him; the Rosenzweig Picture-Frustration Study, which uses comics to which the individual adds words to make a story, and many other similar devices. These projective tests do not in themselves provide a diagnosis for a specific ailment. By encouraging the person to express his feelings, thoughts, attitudes and emotions they contribute to the clinical impressions of the therapist and help him formulate an analysis of the patient's problems.

Books and Films. The use of books as a therapeutic aid to human adjustment is called bibliotherapy. There are times when books serve a useful purpose as means through which people can escape temporarily from their tensions and frustrations. The vicarious experiences secured when a reader identifies with real or fictional characters who have problems similar to his own may broaden his insight and help him modify his behavior. Bibliotherapy has been used successfully with schoolchildren for improving human relations in the classroom, and has had some application in institutions for delinquents and even in mental hospitals. It has also been helpful in group therapy situations where selected books are used to provide an impersonal situation around which to base group discussions (21).

Films may serve the same purpose as books and may be even more dramatic in their effects by portraying characters and situations with which the viewer may identify. The therapist who knows his patients well can select films for the particular impact desired and, in this way, bring to the surface reactions which can be used either in individual or group therapy sessions to develop insight and stimulate discussion. Here, again, it must be noted that certain films developed around emotional problems of living can arouse anxiety in a group and should not be used for entertainment or by persons who are not qualified to handle this anxiety (2).

Art and Music. Some disturbed people have difficulty expressing their feelings in words but can express them through art or through music. This has led to the use of art and music for diagnostic and therapeutic purposes. Art has been used diagnostically by specialists, interpreting a person's drawing and paintings through observing his use of colors, figures, and the themes he expresses in his work. Music has been used in auditory projection tests, in which recordings of familiar tunes and sounds are played and the patient asked to describe the memories, thoughts or feelings aroused.

Art and music may also serve as media through which some individuals can release their tensions and anxieties. By either producing or reacting to art or music, an individual's feelings and emotions are aroused so that he becomes more amenable to psychotherapy. This mode of treatment has been found useful in some cases where the individual has so submerged his affective reactions that he cannot be reached by the therapist (19, 51).

The therapeutic value of art and music will depend largely upon the sensitivity of the individual and upon his past associations. These media are by no means the soothing or healing agents which some people have claimed them to be. Music, for example, may have diverse effects on people. Some familiar melodies may recall pleasant childhood memories; others may bring up painful experiences and arouse anxiety. There are even cases on record where music has created panic reactions and caused intensification of an illness. With some people, music and art may be a helpful adjunct to therapy, with others they have no affect, and in some cases they can make the situation worse (47, 49).

Environmental Therapy. A person's environment is a vital part of his psychological adjustment. Few enduring changes in psychological reactions can be attained if he remains in an environment that plays a major part in creating his problems. This concept has been used extensively in the rehabilitation of disturbed and delinquent children who come from undesirable home situations. By placing them in foster homes or in institutions, the youngsters are removed from negative environmental pressures and given an opportunity to modify their behavior in a healthier atmosphere.

Mental hospitals have carried this form of treatment a step farther by structuring the environment of patients so that their life experiences become a part of the therapeutic treatment. This therapeutic structuring of the environment is called environmental or milieu therapy. It consists of providing patients with experiences through which pressures and responsibilities are built up gradually in a protected situation, until the individual is functioning within the hospital much the same as he would be required to function in his own community. Usually, work experiences are provided, so that patients can learn to accept supervision and authority, and renew their confidence in their own ability to do something worthwhile. Along with this vocational activity, patients are given opportunities for social interaction through various forms of recreation, study, and group activity, so that they learn again to live with other people. When they reach a point where the structured environment of the hospital is no longer necessary, they may be transferred to a "Halfway House," or protected shelter outside the hospital, where they receive a minimum of professional help and supervision. This process shortens the length of time spent in mental institutions and returns patients to the community as soon as they are able to function on their own (10, 24, 31).

Milieu therapy has proved so effective that many states are now working toward the elimination of large mental institutions located far from the homes of patients. They are establishing smaller centers close to communities so as to minimize the trauma a disturbed individual experiences when he is separated from his family and familiar surroundings, and confined to a strange hospital where he has no identity. Some states are carrying this plan to the point of not confining disturbed patients to a hospital at all. Instead, they provide day-treatment centers within the community. The patient lives at home and comes to the center during the day to work, participate in recreational and social activities, and be treated. One such day center, opened a few years ago, was so successful with this mode of treatment that two thirds of its psychotic and severely neurotic patients were spared from spending years in a mental institution (52).

Effects of Psychological Therapy

Now that we have described the major forms of psychological therapy, we must turn to the question: Does psychotherapy cure emotional ailments? We have seen that somatic therapies are not a cure in themselves but are used more often to relieve symptoms or to prepare a patient for psychotherapy. As we look at the results of psychotherapy, we find no clear answer to whether this form of treatment is any better than somatic therapy or no therapy at all. One eminent psychologist, H. J. Eysenck, has stated that the best figures available on the results of psychotherapy show that two out of three patients treated are either improved or cured, but that an equal number who are not treated show spontaneous remission of symptoms. In other words, those in psychotherapy might have achieved the same recovery if left alone (13, 14). Further support of this viewpoint is provided by a follow-up study of one thousand children, treated at a child guidance clinic, who were compared with an untreated group. The findings indicated that there was no difference in the adjustment made by the treated and untreated children (26).

Even physicans who refer their patients to psychiatrists do so with reservations. As one physician wryly remarked: "My alcoholics talk thirty minutes then go home and drink; my fat ones talk thirty minutes then go home and eat; my anxious ones talk thirty minutes then go home and swallow fingernails and tranquilizers. I know patients who have taken psychotherapy for years without results" (20).

Evidence of this sort is disquieting, but psychiatrists and other clinicians point out that all it means is that there is a lack of significant statistical data. They cite the many cases of people who, through psychotherapy, were relieved of handicapping symptoms and enabled to perform functions they could not carry on before therapy. Perhaps this clinical evidence is not entirely valid from a research viewpoint, but there seems to be little doubt that each year therapists somehow manage to help thousands of disturbed people to recover enough of their vital capacities so that they can live useful lives instead of vegetating in a custodial institution. These people may not be cured of their ailments, but if their symptoms are brought under control so that they can work, take care of their families adequately, and carry on a reasonably normal existence, they are no worse off than the millions of people who are living with physical disorders that are never cured (37, 41).

Pseudotherapy

Many people are unwilling to invest the time and money required by psychotherapy, and cast about for an easy solution to their emotional problems. These easy solutions are offered freely by magazines, newspapers, books, public lecturers and others who cater to public demand. A few dollars spent at almost any magazine stand will yield an armful of magazines and paperbacks which provide quick tests of personality, ratings of marital success, stories on how others have overcome handicaps similar to yours, and a great deal of advice on problems ranging from child care to marital disharmony. More of this can be found in syndicated columns of newspapers where personal problems are analyzed and a solution proposed by a writer who knows no more about an individual than what is contained in his letter.

Another type of assistance offered to troubled persons is the public lecture conducted by experts with questionable titles, who offer to teach the secrets of success in business and show how to overcome personality weaknesses, all in 10 or 12 lessons. One lecturer advertised private lessons in "self-psychoanalysis" to accomplish this. Or people are offered records and tapes for self-hypnosis to ". . . relieve pressures and anxieties, and eliminate undesirable habits. . . ." Other gadgets, lessons, books, or machines are advertised and demonstrated, each supported by testimonials from satisfied users.

The possibility that such remedies will actually help an emotionally disturbed person is rather remote. Occasionally, an article or lecture may have some therapeutic effect by relieving an individual's anxiety, raising his hopes, or persuading him to change his habits. However, these instances are rare, and seldom will real changes in personality be brought about through such sources. More often, the individual simply wastes his time and money trying one remedy after another. This can become a serious matter if the process continues to a point where emotional difficulties become aggravated so that professional therapy has less chance to succeed (18).

SUMMARY

The major forms of treatment used in the rehabilitation of maladjusted persons may be classified into two broad categories, somatic therapy and psychological therapy.

Somatic therapy is the treatment of emotional disorders by physical methods, such as drugs, shock, or surgery, which are meant to modify physiological processes. This treatment is based on the theory that behavior deviations are symptoms of disturbed physiological processes and that restoration of physiological homeostasis will result in improved behavior.

Psychological therapy is aimed at strengthening the individual's mental and emotional resources so that he can function more effectively. The simplest form of psychological therapy is counseling, where problems are worked out on an operational level without attempting to alter the psychodynamic functioning of the individual. Psychotherapy goes beyond the solving of practical problems and tries to restore the individual's functional capacities. Psychoanalysis is a form of depth psychotherapy which attempts to rebuild the personality structure.

There are a number of aids or adjuncts to psychological

therapy which may be used to facilitate diagnosis or treatment. These include hypnotism, narcoanalysis, clinical tests, books, films, art, music, psychodrama, and television. The somatic therapies, particularly drugs and shock treatment, are used, usually in conjunction with psychological therapy, in the treatment of seriously disturbed patients. Environmental or milieu therapy is an adjunct to psychotherapy which has grown in importance as a form of treatment. It consists in structuring the environment so that personality changes are brought about in an individual. Milieu therapy is used extensively in psychiatric hospitals and other institutions where it is possible to regulate the lives of patients and provide them with therapeutic experiences.

Despite the variety of treatments available, personality is not easily changed, and the process of readjustment is lengthy and expensive. This has led many people to seek quick cures through the advice offered by various media of public communication. There has also been considerable quackery practiced by untrained people who use suggestion and persuasion to effect temporary relief of symptoms. The hazard of such pseudotherapy is that it may cause a person to delay getting proper treatment for his real problems.

REFERENCES

1. Abse, D. W., "Electroconvulsion Therapy and Electrostimulation," *J. Amer. Med. Ass.,* October 12, 1963, **186**:176–177.
2. Allen, W. H., *Audio-Visual Communication Research,* Systems Development Corporation, Santa Monica, Calif., September 20, 1958, 89 pp., mimeographed.
3. Auerback, A., "Attitudes of Psychiatrists to the Use of Hypnosis," *J. Amer. Med. Ass.,* June 16, 1962, **180**:917–921.
4. Ayd, F. J., Jr., "A Survey of Drug-Induced Extrapyramidal Reactions," *J. Amer. Med. Ass.,* March 25, 1961, **175**:1054–1060.
5. Ayd, F. J., Jr., "Chlorpromazine: Ten Years' Experience," *J. Amer. Med. Ass.,* April 6, 1963, **184**:51–54.
6. Balint, M., and Balint, E., *Psychotherapeutic Techniques in Medicine,* Charles C Thomas, 1962.
7. Belden E., and Hitchen, R., *An Investigation of the Use of LSD–25 in the Treatment of Hospitalized Alcoholics,* Cali-

fornia Department of Mental Hygiene, Research Division, Prepublication copy No. 110, October 30, 1962.

8. Bell, J. E., *Family Group Therapy*, Public Health Monograph Number 64, Public Health Service Publication No. 826, GPO, Washington, 1961.

9. Brill, N. Q., and Storrow, H. A., "Prognostic Factors in Psychotherapy," *J. Amer. Med. Ass.*, March 16, 1963, 183:913–916.

10. Cumming, J., and Cumming, E., *Ego and Milieu*, Atherton Press, 1962.

11. Druckman, R., *et al.*, "Chronic Involuntary Movements Induced by Phenothiazines," *J. nerv. ment. Dis.*, July, 1962, 135: 69–76.

12. Ellsworth, R. B., and Clayton, W. H., "The Effects of Chemotherapy on Length of Stay and Rate of Return of Psychiatrically Hospitalized Patients," *J. consult. Psychol.*, February, 1960, 24:50–53.

13. Eysenck, H. J., "Further Comments on Relations with Psychiatry," *Amer. Psychol.*, 1954, 9:157–158.

14. Eysenck, H. J., "The Effects of Psychotherapy: An Evaluation," *J. consult. Psychol.*, October, 1952, 16:319–324.

15. Farnsworth, D. L., "Concepts of Educational Psychiatry," *J. Amer. Med. Ass.*, September 8, 1962, 181:815–821.

16. Faure, H., "Sleep-Induced Group Psychotherapy," *Int. J. Group Psychother.*, January, 1960, 10:22–38.

17. Felix, R. H., "Psychopharmacology and Psychiatry," *J. Ark. Med. Soc.*, November, 1961, 58:223–229.

18. Frank, J. D., *Persuasion and Healing: A Comparative Study of Psychotherapy*, Johns Hopkins, 1961.

19. Freeman, R. V., and Friedman, I., "Art Therapy in a Total Treatment Plan," *J. nerv. ment. Dis.*, October, 1956, 124:421–425.

20. Garber, R. S., "What Do Other M.D.'s Think of Psychiatrists?" *Psychiat. Rep.*, Smith, Kline & French, January–February, 1963, pp. 16–20.

21. Gilberstadt, H., *et al.*, "Reading Preferences as Related to Diagnosis of Psychiatric Patients," *Ment. Hyg.*, January, 1963, 47:89–95.

22. Hawkings, J. R., and Tibbets, R. W., "Carbon Dioxide Inhalation Therapy in Neurosis," *J. Mental Science*, January, 1956, 102:52–59.

23. Joint Commission on Mental Illness and Health, *Action for Mental Health*, Basic Books, 1961.

24. Jones, M., "Social Rehabilitation with Emphasis on Work Therapy as a Form of Group Therapy," *Brit. J. med. Psychol.*, 1960, 33:67–71.

25. Levin, S., "Some Comparative Observations of Psychoanalytically Oriented Group and Individual Psychotherapy," *Amer. J. Orthopsychiat.*, January, 1963, 33:148–160.

26. Levitt, E. E., *et al.*, "A Follow-up Evaluation of Cases Treated at a Community Child-Guidance Clinic," *Amer. J. Orthopsychiat.*, 1959, 29:337–347.

27. Lewin, W., "Observations on Selective Leucotomy," *J. Neurol., Neurosurgery & Psychiat.*, February, 1961, 24:37–44.

28. Lewis, F. A., Jr., "Community Care of Psychiatric Patients Versus Prolonged Institutionalization," *J. Amer. Med. Ass.*, October 27, 1962, 182:323–326.

29. Locke, N., *Group Psychoanalysis: Theory and Technique*, New York University Press, 1961.

30. Menninger, K., "The Prescription of Treatment," *Bull. Menninger Clin.*, September, 1960, 24:217–249.

31. Mesnikoff, A. M., "Ward Group Projects as a Focus for Dynamic Milieu Therapy," *N.Y. J. Med.*, August 1, 1960, 60:2395–99.

32. Moore, D., "The Use of Sleep Therapy in Psychiatric Treatments," *Med. J. Australia*, January 4, 1958, 1:9–11.

33. Novey, S., "The Principle of 'Working Through' in Psychoanalysis," *J. Amer. Psychoanal. Ass.*, October, 1962, 10:658–676.

34. Overall, B., and Aronson, H., "Expectations of Psychotherapy in Patients of Lower Socioeconomic Class," *Amer. J. Orthopsychiat.*, April, 1963, 33:421–430.

35. "Psychotherapy by Television," *What's New*, Abbott Laboratories, Late Winter, 1958, No. 204, pp. 2–5.

36. Queredo, A., "Mental Health Programs in Public Health Planning," *Ment. Hyg.*, October, 1962, 46:627–654.

37. Rassidakis, N. C., *et al.*, "A Follow-up Study of Schizophrenic Patients: Relapse and Re-Admission," *Bull. Menninger Clin.*, January, 1963, 27:33–40.

38. Rathod, N. H., "Tranquillisers and Patient's Environment," *Lancet*, March 22, 1958, 1:611–613.

39. Riessman, F., "Some Suggestions Concerning Psychotherapy with Blue Collar Individuals," *Amer. J. Orthopsychiat.*, March, 1963, 33:293–294.

40. Rodman, M. J., "Drugs for the Age of Anxiety, *Registered Nurse*, July, 1957, 20:48–53.

41. Ruesch, J., "The Treatment of Acute Psychoses," *J. Neuro-psychiat.*, August, 1962, Supplement, 3:S122–129.
42. Sargant, W., and Cantab, M. B., "The Present Indications for Leucotomy," *Lancet*, June 9, 1962, 1:1197–2000.
43. Schiele, B. C., "Newer Drugs for Mental Illness," *J. Amer. Med. Ass.*, July 14, 1962, 181:126–133.
44. Scoville, W. B., "Late Results of Orbital Undercutting," *Amer. J. Psychiat.*, December, 1960, 117:525–532.
45. Selling, L. S., "A Clinical Study of Miltown, a New Tranquilizer Agent," *J. clin. exp. Psychopath.*, January–March, 1956, 17:7–14.
46. Sheard, M. H., "The Influence of Doctor's Attitude on the Patient's Response to Antidepressant Medication," *J. nerv. ment. Dis.*, June, 1963, 136:555–560.
47. Sommer, D. T., "Music in the Autobiographies of Mental Patients," *Ment. Hyg.*, July, 1961, 45:402–407.
48. Spotnitz, H., *The Couch and the Circle: A Story of Group Therapy*, Knopf, 1961.
49. Stein, J., "Music Therapy Treatment Techniques," *Amer. J. Orthopsychiat.*, April, 1963, 33:521–528.
50. Tucker, H., *et al.*, "Television Therapy," *Arch. Neurol. Psychiat.*, January, 1957, 77:57–69.
51. Zanker, A., and Glatt, M. M., "Individual Reactions of Alcoholic and Neurotic Patients to Music," *J. nerv. ment. Dis.*, April, 1956, 123:395–402.
52. Zemlick, M. J., and McMillan, T. M., *Day Treatment—A Study Of A Year's Operation*, California State Department of Mental Hygiene, Research Division, Pre-publication copy No. 43, January 30, 1962.

Chapter 14   Mental
Hygiene

Scientists have been studying human behavior for many years but have not come up with a formula which would guarantee a wholesome, well-adjusted personality. The best that can be offered at the present time is a body of general principles and practices, derived from many areas of human activity, which are collectively called mental hygiene.

There have been many attempts to define mental hygiene, but this field is a hybrid which eludes precise definition. It consists not only of a body of knowledge, but also of a way of life, a set of values, and a quality of interpersonal relationships. Rather than become embroiled in a discussion of definitions, we shall direct our attention to those aspects of mental hygiene which have been shown to have some practical value in preventing mental and emotional disorders. We shall discuss the concepts of primary prevention and secondary prevention, as they relate to human adjustment, and describe some of the mental hygiene programs that have been developed in recent years.

PRIMARY PREVENTION

Primary prevention focuses on the prevention of maladjustment at its points of origin. It is concerned with prenatal care, fetal development, obstetrics, infant care, and other medical matters, because problems of adjustment begin where life begins. What happens to the growing human organism in the home, school, and community is also an important aspect of primary prevention. Hence, mental hygiene is not limited to the fields of medicine and psychology, but extends into economics, sociology, government, education, and other areas which directly or indirectly affect human welfare.

Prevention in the Prenatal and Infancy Periods

The prevention of maladjustment begins with ensuring the birth of healthy, undamaged infants. Medical science has made great progress in reducing infant mortality and preventing birth defects. With proper prenatal and postnatal care, most mothers can start their babies out in life physically fit. Yet, it is estimated that at least half the mental retardation in this country is caused by physical damage that could have been prevented (41). Thousands of mothers in this affluent nation receive little or no medical care and, as a result, give birth to infants who are handicapped unnecessarily (2, 16). Babies are sustaining neurological impairment because they are born prematurely; metabolic disorders which could be modified through proper diets are producing many cases of mental retardation, and mothers are giving birth to defective children as a result of contracting communicable diseases during the term of pregnancy, when proper medical care could prevent or ameliorate the effects of these diseases (15, 18, 44). There is little doubt that improved medical care programs are needed if we are to prevent much of the physical damage which is now occurring at the very beginnings of life.

There is need, too, for improved psychological services to mothers. An anxious, nonacceptant mother can do great psychological damage to the infant during its prolonged state of helplessness and dependency. Some mothers need psychological reassurance or help with their own emotional problems before they can give an infant the warm, intimate physical comfort so necessary to his healthy emotional development. Many mothers also need help in understanding normal growth patterns and in interpreting the seriousness of the various behavior problems which occur among children. The quality of the environment established by the parents and the quality of the physical and psychological care given the child between the ages of two and six are important determiners of the adult's adjustment (4). With the age of marriage decreasing, the psychological preparation of young people for parenthood is becoming a more urgent requirement for the prevention of maladjustment among children (7).

Mental Hygiene and the Family

Primary prevention is concerned with parent education, but it must also look beyond the family to the factors which are instrumental in determining how a family will function. It is easy to blame parents for what happens to children, but many parents are what they are because of the circumstances under which they live; and before their behavior can be changed, these circumstances must be altered (19).

Families who live under economically depressed conditions have special difficulty in providing children with a wholesome environment for psychological growth. Youngsters growing up in impoverished homes are subject not only to economic hardship but to cultural deprivations, lack of educational opportunities, low social status, low self-concepts, attitudes of defeat and hopelessness, and feelings of resentment and hostility. Many of these children later become inadequate parents themselves and continue the cycle of deprivation and frustration into the next generation.

The importance of this problem is reflected in the fact that one out of every five families in the United States had an annual income below three thousand dollars in 1960 (41). This is about half of what is considered necessary to maintain an average standard of living for a family of four. Economic deprivation is thus a mental hygiene problem of significance. This is not to say that children in more economically favored families do not also suffer some forms of deprivation. Psychological and emotional deprivation occurs at every socioeconomic level. Yet, it cannot be denied that youngsters born into economically depressed families are subject to more severely environmental stresses and deprivations than those in the middle and upper classes. Communities which ignore the needs of these people can expect a high incidence of family disintegration, and a higher rate of mental defects, retardation, delinquency, and emotional disturbance than would prevail if the necessary assistance were provided to make the home a unifying and constructive force in the development of children (38).

Prevention in the School

In the last few years a heated controversy has raged over what the proper role of the school is. A very vocal and influential segment of the population believes that schools should concentrate on teaching academic skills and knowledge to children, and leave to the home, the church, and community matters of emotional health, character development, and adjustment (28).

Another faction contends that the school cannot limit itself to academic training; that this is the logical place for a program of mental hygiene, because the school is the one institution with which almost every citizen has long and continuous contact. They would have schools take an active part in preventing juvenile delinquency, and in dealing with the emotional factors that lead to reading disabilities, school dropouts, venereal disease, and the many other behavior problems exhibited by students. Some would even have the schools provide therapy for children, and, if need be, for their parents.

This controversy is still very much alive today. School board members have been elected or defeated, and administrators appointed or discharged, on the basis of whether they favored or opposed progressive education, basic education, life adjustment education, and other issues related to this contention. Currently, it appears that pressure for academic excellence has taken precedence over mental-hygiene considerations in the schools. Subject matter is being stressed more heavily than it has been for a generation, and pushed lower and lower in the grades, as colleges and universities raise their entrance requirements (9). Educators have also taken sides in this matter, and there is a highly visible reluctance on the part of some school people to initiate or support mental-hygiene activities (8).

Regardless of one's point of view, the academic success

achieved by a child, his relationships with other children and with his teachers, and the total environment of the school are potent forces in affecting emotional growth and adjustment. Whether the schools will it or not, they are influencing the emotional development of children. In the interests of the child's adjustment, mental hygienists maintain that this influence should be planned and organized rather than permitted to occur incidentally with uncertain effects (27). When we discuss some of the mental-hygiene programs undertaken by school districts, it will be seen that many schools are recognizing this responsibility and are concerned with both the intellectual and emotional growth of children as shared aspects of the school curriculum.

Prevention in the Community

The development of wholesome adjustment is inextricably related to the social fabric of the community. The values and goals of a community, its form and quality of government, the freedom and opportunities accorded to its citizens, and the attention devoted to the welfare of individuals—all influence the community climate and its social health. Well-adjusted individuals are not readily produced in a sick community. A community where thoughtlessness, discrimination, greed, selfishness, prejudice, hate, and strife flourish will have a high incidence of delinquency, divorce, crime, strikes, and other evidences of personal and social disorder (23).

The factors which should prevail in a community where human welfare is valued are fairly well-known. There must be a concern for employment opportunities, decent housing, churches, schools, recreational facilities, public health and safety, welfare services, and other community facilities which can contribute to the public welfare and build defenses against personal and social breakdown. Extensive sociological research has shown that neighborhoods, towns, and cities where people are willing to devote their time, money and energy to improving the living environment for all its members have comparatively few problems of maladjustment. Conversely, communities where apathy, selfishness, and disregard for individual needs prevail offer a fertile soil for the nourishment of maladjustment and social disorganization.

Scope of Primary Prevention

The primary prevention of mental and emotional disorders is the by-product of a concern for human welfare. This concern begins with the provision of medical services that will assist children to develop healthy bodies and minds. A happy childhood, spent in a serene household with loving care from competent parents, is the next prerequisite for mental health. Schools which help children develop their capacities to the fullest extent and teach them how to work with other human beings can contribute significantly to the way people develop emotionally. In the community, the choice of good companions, steady work, recreational facilities, decent housing in wholesome surroundings, churches, and social agencies which can assist people who have problems are vital aspects of an environment which facilitates the development of mental health.

The cost to society of providing these preventive services is high, but not as high as the billions of dollars now being spent on mental illness, crime, and other social disorders. Nor can a price be placed on the wasted lives brought on by maladjustment. If this nation is to make full use of its human resources, financial support must be provided for prevention as well as rehabilitation. The greatest dividend to society might be realized by concentrating preventive efforts on children and youth. If preventive activities were focused upon the preschool through late adolescent years—ensuring each child a good start in life, opportunity to mature emotionally, to find a job, acquire a habit of work, and achieve an integrated ego structure—the impact of maladjustment in later years would be less severe, and, if it occurred, more easily treated (42).

SECONDARY PREVENTION

Our knowledge of human behavior is too imperfect and our facilities too inadequate to expect primary prevention in itself to provide a solution to the problems of maladjustment. Therefore, a program of secondary prevention is an essential supplement to primary prevention. This involves the early detection and treatment of mental and emotional disorders.

Secondary prevention depends, first, upon discovering maladjustment before an individual's behavior has deteriorated too seriously. Through the efforts of various official and volunteer agencies, a concerted campaign of public education is being conducted to acquaint people with the nature and symptoms of mental illness, so that they will seek treatment when it is needed. Television, radio, newspapers, popular magazines, and other channels of communication have been used extensively to make the public aware of mental disorder as an illness which can be treated, and to combat the superstition and fatalism with which these ailments have been viewed. This educational program has had the effect of increasing the public's willingness to provide care and treatment for the mentally ill instead of hiding them away in remote state institutions (3).

Another phase of the educational program in secondary prevention is the orientation of professional people toward mental-health goals and concepts. This is being done through training programs, workshops, institutes, lectures, and other devices aimed at the service professions. Nurses, physicians, ministers, attorneys, peace officers, probation and welfare workers, teachers, and others who deal with human problems have become more alert to the symptoms of emotional disturbances and are referring many more people for treatment early in the course of their disorder.

The other aspect of secondary prevention is to provide effective treatment when and where it is needed. As mentioned in the preceding chapter, it has become evident that local clinics and hospitals will have to replace the large, remote state institutions, if people are to receive proper treatment. Each community should have ready access to facilities such as guidance and counseling centers, adult psychiatric services, home care treatment, follow-up clinics, rehabilitation centers, and private therapy services, if long delays are to be avoided in bringing people the help they need. It is just as absurd to require a person suffering from an emotional illness to wait six months to a year for treatment as it is to delay the treatment of a tubercular patient for a similar length of time. Yet, waiting lists are the rule rather than the exception in most community clinics and hospitals. In the following sections, we shall describe some of the efforts that are being made to improve this situation, and to make primary and secondary prevention programs a more effective force in safeguarding the mental health of the community.

MENTAL-HYGIENE PROGRAMS

As we survey what is now being done for the prevention and treatment of mental disorders, the picture is quite different from what it was half a century ago. Then, people refused to recognize these disorders as illnesses and established "insane asylums" to get the mentally ill out of the way. Today, mental-hygiene programs are so widespread and diversified that it would be impossible to describe them all within the limitations of this text. The illustrations which follow are but a small sample of the many activities which have been developed in the last few years to improve the quality of living among a large segment of our people (24, 43).

Programs at the National Level

A wide variety of mental-hygiene services are offered by official agencies of the United States Government, and by volunteer or private agencies. In terms of the money expended, the number of people involved, and the over-all impact on the nation, the activities of the federal government are most significant.

The government entered directly into mental-health activities in a major way when Congress passed the National Mental Health Act in 1946. Although many services which could be called mental hygiene were being offered before that date, this act authorized the federal government to participate officially in a comprehensive program for the prevention of mental illness and for the promotion of more positive mental health among the general population.

The National Institute of Mental Health. The National Institute of Mental Health was established in 1949 to carry out the intent Congress expressed by the National Mental Health Act. Through this agency the states are provided with many financial grants and services. Direct help is offered to communities for establishing clinics, organizing preventive and educational services, training professional staffs, and research. The institute has served as a pump primer by requiring the states to match federal funds, dollar for dollar. However, once the program was under way, the states far exceeded this matching requirement. Before the National Mental Health Act was enacted, state wide mental-health programs were practically nonexistent. Now, they are operating in every state and territory, and instead of merely matching federal funds, states allocate fourteen dollars for every federal dollar (35).

In addition to its support of state activities, this institute conducts extensive research and clinical programs in its own facilities. Its budget has increased over 14 times since it was established. In 1963, over 143 million dollars were being expended by this agency in its campaign against mental illness. Recently enacted legislation made available 329 million dollars for construction of community health centers, research and treatment facilities, and other assistance to the mentally ill and the retarded. Most of this money is disbursed through the National Institute of Mental Health (34).

Other Federal Services. Many other federal agencies which are not primarily responsible for mental health are making important contributions in this field. Among these are the Children's Bureau, the Office of Education, and the National Institute of Child Health and Development.

The Children's Bureau was organized almost half a century ago to improve health services for infants and children. This is done primarily through funds distributed to the states, and through the assistance rendered by the professional staff. With the help of the Children's Bureau, many states have expanded services for mentally retarded children, for children of migrant families, and for orphans, delinquents, and crippled children.

This bureau also has been instrumental in increasing the number of child-welfare workers serving communities, strengthening parent education programs, and expanding maternal and child health services. These activities will be recognized as important in the primary prevention of behavior disorders (37).

The U.S. Office of Education, in addition to its responsibility for gathering and disseminating information about the public schools, is concerned with many programs that affect the adjustment of children and youth. It seeks to develop closer relationships between schools and communities, encourages the early discovery of potential maladjustment, and aids schools in securing better guidance services, visiting teachers, and remedial programs for academically retarded children. It helps initiate work programs to keep youngsters from dropping out of school, and rehabilitation programs for those who leave school before graduation. This office exerts its influence primarily by providing grants and funds to local schools, colleges, and universities to conduct research or to try out various means of coping with existing problems. Expert consultation services and many forms of information are made available to aid the local communities in carrying out these activities.

The National Institute of Child Health and Human Development was created by Congress in 1962 to study human beings through the total life span, from preconception to old age. Its major responsibility is to discover what constitutes normal growth and how the process of development, maturation, and decline can be influenced to favor the growth of healthy infants, children, adults, and older persons in our society (33).

Many other federal agencies are performing valuable mental-hygiene functions incidental to their major responsibilities. To mention only a few: the U.S. Public Health Service is active in reducing the toll of death and disability from disease, accidents, and poisoning; the Bureau of Public Assistance helps maintain and strengthen family life; the Department of Justice provides camps and facilities for rehabilitation of youthful offenders; the Department of Labor keeps watch over the working conditions for youth, and provides counseling and placement services; the Department of Agriculture works with millions of parents each year in developing a healthy home life for children; the Veterans Administration provides long-term care and extensive clinical treatment for psychiatrically disabled military people. So many federal agencies are providing so many services in this field that it has been necessary to establish an Interdepartmental Committee on Children and Youth to help these agencies work together and to avoid overlapping of functions (21).

Private and Volunteer Organizations

The preventive projects undertaken by private groups and volunteer organizations, while not so extensive as federal activities, are an important part of our national mental hygiene program. Private efforts frequently do the pioneer work in a field and pave the way for the better-financed government agencies to step in when the worth of an activity has been demonstrated. Organizations such as the National Association for Mental Health, first established in 1909, have had a significant influence on improving the care of patients in mental hospitals and on organizing preventive mental hygiene programs. This association was instrumental in establishing volunteer mental-health organizations in most of the states. It carries on an active campaign to educate citizens on the facts of mental illness, influences legislation, prints and distributes literature, and in various other ways promotes mental-hygiene programs in the nation.

Other organizations such as the Hogg Foundation of Texas, the Milbank Memorial Fund of New York, and numerous private philanthropic foundations have done a great service to the mental-health movement by stimulating research, issuing publications, financing training programs, and establishing hospitals and clinics. In 1962, the American Medical Association provided a great impetus to mental hygiene efforts by holding the First National Congress on Mental Illness and Health. It is now a policy of the association to combat mental illness through improved training programs for physicians, more research, and better treatment. It is hoped that this policy will encourage all physicians to be more concerned over mental illness, rather than leave these problems largely in the hands of the psychiatric specialists.

State Programs

The organization of mental hygiene services in the states parallels that at the national level. Each state has an official mental hygiene authority and unofficial volunteer or private agencies working in the field of mental health. The mental health authority of the state is usually vested in the department of mental hygiene, the department of public health, or the department of social welfare. Its function is to maintain liaison with the federal mental hygiene agencies, supervise state hospitals, clinics, and treatment facilities, and organize and conduct prevention programs.

Traditionally, the primary effort of state mental hygiene agencies has been focused on the treatment of mental illness. Although many states are introducing modern practices, such as day hospitals, after-care clinics for patients discharged from state institutions, public-health nursing services, foster-family care, work opportunities, and other rehabilitative services for the mentally ill, the major portion of state mental-hygiene budgets generally is allocated to the support of custodial institutions (23). However, state agencies are developing more effective preventive programs. One type of service which has gained wide acceptance provides professional consultation to the staffs of local agencies. In many states, psychiatrists, psychologists, and social workers, employed by the state, meet with the staffs of community agencies for conferences devoted to improving the skills of these people in handling the emotional problems they encounter. This is not an effort to make junior psychiatrists out of welfare workers, nurses, juvenile police, and the like, but an educational program designed to increase the understanding and perception of individuals who have special responsibilities for the welfare of other people.

Another preventive service commonly provided by the state mental-hygiene authority is mental-health education for the public. Films, plays, pamphlets, posters, speakers, and other educational devices are made available to community groups interested in mental health, or are used in seminars, workshops, and meetings organized by the state agency. Some states provide special training for their health department personnel, so that doctors and nurses who visit homes or conduct clinics can offer instruction in mental hygiene to mothers and children. Other states have organized traveling clinics, consisting of teams of psychiatrists, psychologists, social workers, and nurses, that provide services to communities which have no clinics of their own. In addition to diagnosing and prescribing treatment for the cases brought to the clinic, these teams offer training to local doctors, nurses, and other professional people, so that treatment can be continued when the clinic staff moves on to another community.

Supplementing the services furnished by the state mental hygiene authority, other governmental units in the states are engaged in mental health education of one type or another. It is common, for instance, to find the state health department carrying out mental-health education in connection with its public health services; education departments encourage the development of guidance and counseling programs in the schools, and subsidize special programs for mentally retarded and physically handicapped children; agriculture departments through demonstration units and extension services provide basic child-rearing information and youth activities for rural families. These are but a few examples of the many mental-hygiene programs now under way, which indicate that the states are showing an increased interest in the mental health of their people.

Unofficial State Programs. Unofficial groups are active in every state, supporting the work of official state agencies in improving the care and treatment of the mentally ill and in organizing preventive mental hygiene programs. Most states have a volunteer mental-health association which is affiliated with the National Association for Mental Health and performs parallel functions at the state level.

Community Programs

Some communities have a variety of organizations which provide mental-hygiene services. Among these are welfare bureaus, public health departments, family service agencies, medical and guidance clinics, juvenile police, recreation departments, church groups, service clubs, children's aid societies, and youth groups of many types. In the larger cities will be found special homes and schools for children who are in trouble, neighborhood clubs and recreation centers, camp facilities, housing developments, and other special facilities. Mental-health associations and similar organizations function in most of the larger cities to provide information regarding available treatment facilities, and to keep the public informed of educational programs and other mental hygiene services. One city has a welfare information service which advertises: "Your Trouble is Our Business . . . and Help is as Near as Your Telephone." People are invited to phone this agency to talk over their troubles or secure a referral to a clinic or to other community services.

In recent years, the move toward suburbia has created in many large urban centers a depressed slum area from which a high incidence of personal and social disorders arise. Supported by funds from private foundations and government agencies, these cities are making a major effort to reduce the social, economic, cultural, and educational handicaps existing in their slum belts (25, 26). Most of the programs now under way are focused primarily on children, since it has been found that an impoverished home in a run-down neighborhood places children at a serious disadvantage when they encounter the highly verbal requirements of a school. These youngsters have difficulty learning to read, experience failure and frustration, lag behind in their schoolwork, and leave school as soon as they are old enough to join the growing reservoir of untrained and unemployable manpower.

To break this chain of events, some cities are organizing programs to supplement the work of schools. Preschool children are taken to zoos, museums, farms, airports, fire stations, and other community centers to enrich their background of experience. Recreation programs, day camps, summer camps, health and psychological services, and special tutoring centers are provided for older children. Adolescents are offered a modified school program and part-time jobs. The jobs are intended to help these young people recognize the need for education and prevent school dropouts. These programs have succeeded in reducing the dropout rates in many metropolitan high schools and have salvaged many youngsters who might otherwise have drifted into unemployment, despair, or delinquency (17).

Community programs for the culturally deprived have been extended to adults as well as children. In 1960, almost 3 million people in the United States were unable to read or write, and millions more with less than five years of schooling were functionally illiterate. These people lacked the minimum skills necessary to secure and hold a job. Total federal, state, and local expenditures in welfare payments for their support exceed 4½ billions dollars per year (11). Some cities have attacked this problem by trying to upgrade welfare recipients through making attendance at evening schools a condition of staying on relief. Classes were organized to teach them how to read and write, and to develop skills that would qualify them for employment. Such programs have met with considerable success. In many instances it was found that these people were so appreciative of an opportunity to improve their lot in life that the compulsory features of the plan were unnecessary.

Programs of this nature are not reaching all the culturally deprived children and adults, but they are demonstrating that these people can be made into productive citizens, if community programs of the types described are started early enough and sustained long enough (26).

Another significant type of community mental-hygiene activity of recent origin is the provision of facilities for people who need immediate emergency treatment for an emotional crisis. People who are upset, or feel they are going to pieces because of a severe stress, need emotional first aid to help them through this critical period. They cannot wait six months to be seen at a clinic; sometimes six hours may be crucial. For such people, walk-in clinics have been tried in some cities. No appointments are required; people simply present themselves at the clinic and ask to talk with a therapist. These clinics have met with an overwhelming response. One clinic found over a hundred people waiting on the first day it opened its doors. Thereafter, it was necessary to close the doors five minutes after opening time each day, because so many people crowded in that it took the staff the rest of the day to handle them. This experience graphically illustrates the great need that exists for emergency facilities (13).

School-District Programs

In the past half century, school districts have expanded their services to children tremendously. Special personnel, many of whom were unheard-of at the turn of this century, are now employed by schools to help meet the emotional needs of children. These include attendance supervisors, case workers, psychometrists, social workers, visiting teachers, counselors, speech therapists, school psychologists, and other specialists skilled in identifying and alleviating the stress and anxiety of children. In addition, some of the larger school districts have fully staffed guidance clinics which not only treat children but provide assistance to teachers and parents so that therapy may be continued in the classroom and at home (29).

Special schools and classes are provided in many districts to help children who are not doing well in the regular classroom. Some schools maintain ungraded classrooms, where a small group of children having learning or behavior problems are given individual attention by a special teacher. These children participate in some of the regular school activities but are segregated most of the day for a modified program of instruction.

Some large school districts have special schools, where a staff of teachers, psychologists, psychiatrists and other specialists provide a rehabilitation program for children who were unmanageable in the regular school. Instead of the usual academic curriculum, vocational training is emphasized in an effort to prepare these youngsters for employment (6). Other school operate a work-experience program as part of the regular curriculum for students who have academic, social, or personal problems. Students are placed on jobs, for which they are paid, and attend school a few hours a day. Motivation is provided by requiring that they succeed in school and on the job in order to continue in the program (36, 40).

School districts have found that the success of a mental-hygiene program is dependent on the contributions made by informed, competent, sympathetic teachers, who are assisted by mental health specialists. To utilize fully the potential of the school as a primary agency for preventing maladjustment, in-service training programs are organized for teachers. This has been done through university extension classes in the local community, consultation and discussion sessions with psychiatrists and psychologists, child and youth study groups, seminars, human relations classes, and other training devices (25). Teachers who go through such experiences tend to become more considerate and humane in their treatment of children. They are less anxious about behavior which they find difficult to manage, and more capable of providing a therapeutic environment in the classroom (1, 32, 39). Significantly, it has been found that, where emphasis is placed on meeting the emotional needs of children and improving human relations in the school, there are gains in learning, work habits of pupils improve, interest in school work increases, and truancy and vandalism decline. In other words, as teachers introduce mental hygiene practices into the curriculum, there is no loss in academic achievement, but an over-all improvement in all aspects of child development (22).

EFFECTS OF MENTAL-HYGIENE PROGRAMS ON PREVENTION OF MALADJUSTMENT

The ferment of activity in the mental hygiene field has been going on for many years. It is reasonable to ask what these efforts have accomplished, and Congress established the Joint Commission on Mental Illness and Health to prepare an answer to this question. The final report of this commission is a sober reminder of how much remains to be done in the field of mental hygiene (23).

Mental illness, it was shown, is not really declining. True, the statistics show a decrease in the number of patients residing in mental hospitals, but this is merely a paper decrease, representing a shift in the residence of patients. Instead of remaining in the hospital for years, they are treated briefly and released to convalesce at home or in some intermediary residence. This results in an apparent reduction in hospital population, while first admissions continue to climb.

Another current fact is that few places in this nation have enough clinics or professional staffs to care adequately for the emotionally disturbed. To meet current needs, the number of mental-hygiene clinics would have to be doubled, psychiatrist hours increased one third, psychologist hours 80 percent, and psychiatric social worker and other professional time 89 percent. At the rate we are now training professional people, the number of professional workers will never catch up with population increase, unless a massive national effort is made (5, 43).

The demand for mental-health services which can be expected in the future is now reflected in what is being done for certain vulnerable groups of children. For example, only about one out of five of the nation's mentally retarded children are enrolled in special education programs in the public schools. Similar inadequacies exist in the care of physically handicapped children, the culturally deprived, children of broken or parentless homes, predelinquents, and many others. From this group of uncared-for children, we can expect a steady stream of maladjusted, socially inadequate, dependent people in the years to come (41).

Just why our society is not handling its mental health problems more adequately is a matter of conjecture. There are several intriguing hypotheses that might be considered. One is that the public perception of mental illness is still one of fear and superstition. Despite all the information that has been disseminated in the past few years, many people continue to think of mental illness as a shadowy, eerie thing, while mental hygiene is associated with brainwashing, thought control, subliminal stimulation, hypnotism, and other bizarre practices. People feel a great deal of anxiety about allying themselves with a movement that carries a stigma of personal inadequacy, as mental illness does, and with practices that still have not been completely distinguished from those of the medicine man. These attitudes may underly the apathy toward mental illness, which exists in our society, and explain why there has been no all-out support for a public-health program to combat mental illness, as there has been for physical ailments, such a poliomyelitis, tuberculosis, or cancer, which have less emotional connotation (30).

Another aspect of this problem is the financial commitment needed to conduct a mental-hygiene program of the required proportions. There would have to be a heavy investment in clinics, staff, educational and social welfare agencies, and other services, but the dividends from this investment would not be evident for a generation or more. The public is not yet willing to take the gamble of spending money now to save lives and money in the future. It is still easier to secure funds for expanding a mental hospital than it is to employ professional people to carry on preventive mental-hygiene activities in a community. A similar situation exists with respect to mental-health research. Most of this is short-term research, planned to show quick results. There is not nearly enough basic research, such as that carried on in the study of cancer and heart disease, which is designed to discover necessary scientific knowledge. Some critics say we shall never learn much more about controlling mental illness if research continues to emphasize crash-program solutions to immediate problems.

In summary, an objective view of the progress and problems in the field of mental hygiene shows that many important advances have been made in the last few decades, but that the problems have increased faster than the remedies. The Joint Commission on Mental Illness and Health recommends that this nation double and triple its expenditures for the prevention of mental illness, and that facilities, services, and research be given the priority that mental illness as a major public-health problem warrants. Anything short of this determined effort will ensure that the problem is transmitted to the next generation, and the next, growing in proportion each time.

SUMMARY

Mental hygiene is concerned with the primary prevention of maladjustment by improving the physical, psychological, social, and economic conditions under which people live, and with secondary prevention which seeks to minimize the effects of maladjustment once it develops.

Many public and private agencies have developed programs to achieve these goals. The federal government, particularly since passage of the National Mental Health Act in 1946, has developed a comprehensive program for the prevention of mental illness and the promotion of mental health among the general population. The impetus of the federal government is reflected in state mental-hygiene programs, by which clinical services, educational activities, treatment facilities, and social welfare services have been improved tremendously in recent years. Local communities and schools have likewise shown increasing concern with the personal, social, and emotional welfare of adults and children, and are offering a broad range of services designed to meet the needs of people of all ages.

However, despite all that is being done, mental and emotional disorders continue to exist. This does not mean that mental-hygiene programs are ineffective. Rather, it indicates that more of these programs are needed and that they must be better organized, better financed and better supported by the public. Mental illness can be controlled if it is given the priorities it warrants as a major public health problem.

REFERENCES

1. Allinsmith, W., and Goethals, G. W., *The Role of Schools in Mental Health,* Basic Books, 1962.
2. American Medical Association, "Mental Health Conference Stresses Treatment at Local Level," *J. Amer. Med. Ass.,* March 16, 1963, **183**:37.

3. American Medical Association, "Non-Political Attack on Mental Illness," *J. Amer. Med. Ass.,* March 16, 1963, **183**:38.

4. Anderson, J. E., *Experience and Behavior in Early Childhood and the Adjustment of the Same Persons as Adults,* Institute of Child Development, University of Minnesota, Minneapolis, 1963.

5. Bahn, A. K., "Gains in Outpatient Psychiatric Clinic Services, 1961," *Ment. Hyg.,* April, 1963, **47**:177–188.

6. Bower, E. M., "The Emotionally Handicapped Child and the School: Present Research Plans and Directions," *Except. Child.,* January, 1960, **26**:232–242.

7. Braceland, F. J., "The Individual—Challenge of the Future," in *Society Challenges The Individual,* Report of the Mental Health Lectures held in Hartford, Connecticut, Connecticut Mutual Life Insurance Co., March, 1962, pp. 21–29.

8. Call, J. D., "Preventive Mental Health in the Schools," in Krugman, M., (Ed.), *Orthopsychiatry and the School,* American Orthopsychiatric Association, 1958, pp. 159–168.

9. Clausen, J. A., and Williams, J. R., "Sociological Correlates of Child Behavior," in H. W. Stevenson, *et al.* (Eds.), *Child Psychology,* 62nd Yearbook of the National Society for the Study of Education, Part I, 1963, pp. 62–107.

10. Cohen, L. D., *State Activities in Mental Health Education,* Public Health Services Publication Number 863, National Institute of Mental Health, Bethesda, Md., 1961.

11. Cohen, W. J., *Adult Basic Education Act of 1962: Hearings Before the Committee on Education and Labor,* 87th Congress, Second Session, House of Representatives Committee on Education and Labor, GPO, February, 1962.

12. Daniels, E. M., "Psychiatrists in the School," *Nat. Educ. Ass. J.,* March, 1960, **49**:11–12.

13. Delman, A., "Emotional First Aid: New Hope for the Disturbed," *Today's Hlth.,* September, 1962, **40**:30–31.

14. Educational Research Service, National Education Association, *Special Programs for the Disadvantaged,* Circular No. 2, February, 1963.

15. Eichorn, D. H., "Biological Correlates of Behavior," in H. W. Stevenson, *et al.* (Eds.), *Child Psychology,* 62nd Yearbook of the National Society for the Study of Education, Part I, 1963, pp. 4–61.

16. Eisenberg, L., "If Not Now, When?" *Amer. J. Orthopsychiat.,* October, 1962, **32**:781–793.

17. Ford Foundation, *The Society of the Streets,* 477 Madison Ave., New York, June, 1962.
18. Gruenberg, E. M., "The Prevention of Mental Disorders," *J. Chronic Dis.,* March, 1959, **9**:187–198.
19. "Human Rehabilitation in the Sixties," *Amer. J. Orthopsychiat.,* July, 1963, **33**:589–590.
20. Hurewitz, P., "The Use of Group Procedures with Children, Teachers and Parents in the Prevention and Treatment of Normal Adjustment Problems in Elementary Schools," *Amer. J. Orthopsychiat.,* March, 1963, **33**:374–375.
21. Interdepartmental Committee on Children and Youth, *Annual Report, 1961–62,* U.S. Children's Bureau, Washington, 1962.
22. Jackson, E. H., *A Four Year Project in the Elementary School for Emotionally Handicapped Children,* Unpublished Doctoral Dissertation, University of Southern California, Los Angeles, 1962.
23. Joint Commission on Mental Illness and Health, *Action for Mental Health,* Basic Books, 1961.
24. Kaplan, L., *Mental Health and Human Relations in Education,* Harper & Row, 1959.
25. Kipfer, J. F., *Michigan School Mental Health Project, 1955–1959,* Michigan Society for Mental Health, Inc., 153 East Elizabeth St., Detroit, Mich., 1959.
26. Kohler, M. C., and Freedman, M. K., *Youth in the World of Work,* Taconic Foundation, 666 Fifth Ave., New York, October, 1962.
27. Lafferty, J. C., "Special Services—A Tight Little Island," in *The School Administrator and School Mental Health Programs,* Michigan Society for Mental Health, Inc., 1528 Woodward Ave., Detroit, 1962, pp. 21–31.
28. Lerner, M. J., and Heyer, R., "A Study of the Critics of the Public Schools," *J. educ. Res.,* September, 1963, **57**:3–10.
29. Lichter, S. O., *et al., The Drop-Outs,* Free Press, 1962.
30. McNeil, E. B., *et al.,* "The School Mental Health Program," in M. G. Gottsegen, and G. B. Gottsegen (Eds.), *Professional School Psychology,* Vol. II, Grune & Stratton, 1962, pp. 102–122.
31. Michael, S. T., and Langner, T. S., "Social Mobility and Psychiatric Symptoms," *Dis. nerv. System,* April, 1963, **24**(Monograph Supplement):S128–133.
32. Moustakas, C., "Human Relations Seminar at the Merrill-Palmer School," in *Basic Approaches to Mental Health in the*

Schools, a reprint from the *Personnel and Guidance Journal,* 1960, pp. 30–37.

33. National Institutes of Health, "Mental Health Bill Signed; New Era in Treatment Seen," *NIH Rec.,* November 5, 1963, **15**:1–6.

34. National Institutes of Health, *Public Health Service Publication Number 81,* GPO, 1963.

35. National Institute of Mental Health, *The National Mental Health Program and the States,* Public Health Service Publication No. 629, Bethesda, Md., 1962.

36. Newman, R. G., "The Assessment of Progress in the Treatment of Hyperaggressive Children with Learning Disturbances Within a School Setting," *Amer. J. Orthopsychiat.,* July, 1959, **29**:633–643.

37. Oettinger, K. B., "A Half Century of Progress for All Children," *Children,* March–April, 1962, **9**:43–51.

38. Pasamanick, B., "Some Misconceptions Concerning Differences in the Racial Prevalence of Mental Disease," *Amer. J. Orthopsychiat.,* January, 1963, **33**:72–86.

39. Peck, B., and Prescott, D. A., "The Program at the Institute for Child Study, the University of Maryland," in *Basic Approaches to Mental Health in the Schools,* reprint from *Personnel and Guidance Journal,* 1960, pp. 7–14.

40. Phillips, E. L., and Norris, G. H., "Results from Special Techniques of Teaching Emotionally Disturbed Children," *Except. Child.,* October, 1959, **26**:64–67.

41. President's Panel on Mental Retardation, *A Proposed Program for National Action to Combat Mental Retardation,* GPO, October, 1962.

42. Rassidakis, N. C., *et al.,* "A Follow-up Study of Schizophrenic Patients: Relapse and Readmission," *Bull. Menninger Clin.,* January, 1963, **27**:33–40.

43. Robinson, R., *et al., Community Resources in Mental Health,* Basic Books, 1960.

44. Schwartz, A. D., "Preventing Mental Illness and Preventing Mental Health," *Calif. Hlth.,* September 1, 1959, **17**:36–37.

45. Torribio, J. A., "The Development of a Mental Health Education Program for Index Personnel," *Calif. Hlth.,* September, 1961, **19**:33–36.

INDEXES

Index of Names

Abse, D. W., 319
Ackerman, N. W., 115
Albright, A. D., 245
Allee, W. C., 66
Allen, W. H., 319
Allinsmith, W., 342
Allport, G. W., 17, 139, 145
Anderson, H. H., 146
Anderson, J. E., 66, 168, 172, 192, 243, 343
Anthony, J., 291
Argyris, C., 145, 244
Arieti, S., 291
Armstrong, C. M., 67
Aronson, H., 321
Arter, R. M., 168
Asch, S. E., 67
Auerback, A., 319
Ausubel, D. P., 17, 192
Ayd, F. J., Jr., 319
Azima, F. J. C., 220
Azima, H., 220

Bach, G. R., 93
Bahn, A. K., 343
Bakal, C., 193
Balint, E., 319
Balint, M., 319
Baroff, G. S., 41
Barry, H., Jr., 291
Batt, J. C., 39
Bauer, W. W., 68
Bayley, N., 169, 193
Behan, R. C., 293
Belden, E., 319

Bell, J. E., 320
Bellak, L., 145
Bender, L., 40
Bendig, A. W., 192
Bendix, R., 244
Berblinger, K. W., 291
Bercel, N. A., 40
Bernert, E. H., 115
Bertalanffy, L. V., 220
Bettelheim, B., 169
Birren, J. E., 192
Blair, A. W., 67
Blau, A., 264
Bloch, H. A., 115
Blood, R. O., Jr., 94
Bloom, K. L., 145
Bogoch, S., 292
Boll, E. S., 94
Bonime, W., 265
Bonney, M. E., 244
Böök, J. A., 40, 292
Bortz, E. L., 192
Bossard, J. H. S., 78, 94, 115
Bossio, V., 95
Bower, E. M., 67, 146, 343
Bowlby, J., 94
Braceland, F. J., 67, 69, 220, 343
Bradley, C., 42
Bradway, K. P., 193
Brady, J. V., 220
Brill, N. Q., 320
Brockway, I. V., 87, 94
Brody, E. B., 220
Bronfenbrenner, U., 94
Brosin, H. W., 221

Browning, C. J., 94
Bruch, H., 244
Burton, W. H., 67

Caldwell, B. M., 94
Call, J. D., 343
Cantab, M. B., 322
Cantril, H., 147, 155, 169
Caplan, G., 67, 96, 141, 222, 244
Caplan, S. W., 145
Carskadon, T. R., 244
Cattell, J. B., 94
Chapman, J., 294
Chesrow, E. J., 67
Chess, S., 67
Chorost, S. B., 94
Clark, W. W., 67
Clausen, J. A., 40, 115, 343
Clayton, W. H., 320
Cobb, S., 40, 265
Cobrinik, L. H., 292
Cohen, L. D., 343
Cohen, W. J., 343
Cole, L. E., 40
Cole, N. J., 115
Coleman, J. C., 67, 169
Colemans, J. S., 116
Combs, A. E., 145
Combs, A. W., 135, 145, 148
Conrad, S. W., 244
Cook, L. A., 116
Cornell, E. L., 67
Covey, J. K., 193
Cross, K. W., 221
Crutchfield, R. S., 67
Cumming, E., 193, 320
Cumming, J. H., 116, 221, 320
Cummins, J. F., 193

Daniels, E. M., 343
Davidson, G. E., 195, 266, 295
Davie, J. S., 18, 116
Davis, A., 116
Davis, K., 67, 116
Dekker, E., 221
Delman, A., 343
Dennis, W., 184, 193
Dibner, A. S., 193
Dollard, J., 116
Donnelly, J., 292

Douvan, E., 67, 145
Driggs, D. F., 116
Druckman, R., 320
Dunham, W. W., 221, 292
Dybwad, G., 116

Earle, A. M., 94
Earle, B. V., 94
Edmondson, M. S., 147
Ehrenwald, J., 94
Eichorn, D. H., 193, 343
Eisenberg, L., 244, 343
Eissler, R. S., 147
Elder, G. H., Jr., 94
Elias, L. J., 67
Ellsworth, R. B., 320
English, O. S., 162, 169, 265
Erickson, M. C., 116
Erikson, E. H., 67, 146, 169
Evans, H. S., 265
Eysenck, H. J., 292, 320

Faegre, M. L., 94
Farnsworth, D. L., 17, 320
Faure, H., 320
Faust, M. S., 67
Fein, R., 17
Felix, R. H., 40, 292, 320
Fenichel, H., 244
Fenichel, O., 244
Fessell, W. J., 292
Fleck, S., 292
Fleege, U. H., 68
Flynn, W. R., 292
Frank, J. D., 320
Frank, L. K., 169
Freedman, L. Z., 116
Freedman, M. K., 344
Freeman, R. V., 320
Frenkel-Brunswick, E., 169
Friedman, I., 320
Friedman, M., 40
Friend, C. M., 193
Fromm, E., 17, 133, 146
Fullerton, D. T., 221
Funkenstein, D. H., 68, 169, 221, 293
Furer, M., 146

Galdston, I., 18
Gallager, J. R., 68

Gallup, G. H., 116
Garber, R. S., 320
Garn, S. M., 40, 193
Garner, A. M., 95, 292
Geiger, R. S., 40
Geleerd, E. R., 146
Ghiselli, E. E., 193
Gibson, J. E., 40
Gibson, W. C., 295
Gilberstadt, H., 320
Ginsburg, S. W., 17, 265, 292
Ginzberg, E., 40, 115, 168, 192, 193
Gitlin, I., 244
Glatt, M. M., 322
Glickstein, M., 221
Goethals, G. W., 342
Goldfarb, W., 72, 95, 292
Goldstein, K., 40
Golomb, S. W., 40
Goodman, H. O., 40
Gordon, D. M., 193
Gosling, R. H., 221
Gottleib, J. S., 40
Gottlieb, D., 116
Gottsegen, G. B., 344
Gottsegen, M. G., 344
Grant, J. D., 146
Green, J., 17
Greenfield, N. S., 294
Groen, J., 221, 265
Gruenberg, E. M., 344
Gurin, G., 17, 265
Guze, S. B., 292

Halfter, I. T., 193
Halpern, H. M., 146
Hamilton, M., 169
Hand, H. C., 116
Hariss, D. B., 87, 95
Harrington, J. A., 221
Hartmann, H., 146
Havighurst, R. J., 68, 116, 146
Hawkings, J. R., 320
Hayakawa, S. J., 146, 244
Hayman, A., 265
Heath, R. G., 292
Hebb, D. O., 33, 41
Heffernan, H., 68
Heintz, E., 117
Herndon, C. N., 40

Heyer, R., 344
Hinkle, L. E., Jr., 221
Hippocrates, 21, 22
Hirschfeld, A. H., 293
Hirsh, J., 17
Hitchen, R., 319
Hitson, H. M., 293
Hoch, P. H., 41, 293
Hochbaum, G. M., 221
Hoff, H., 293
Hoffman, L. W., 117
Hollingshead, A. B., 116, 117
Holmes, C. C., 146
Holmes, T. H., 244
Holzman, P. S., 244
Honigmann, J. J., 95, 117
Horney, K., 146
Horrocks, J. E., 68, 118
Hountras, P. T., 169, 244, 265, 292
Houssay, B. A., 41, 221
Howard, B. F., 293
Howie, D. L., 293
Hughes, C. C., 17, 117
Hunt, J. McV., 17, 68
Hurder, W. P., 41
Hurewitz, P., 344
Hurlock, E. B., 68
Hyden, H., 41

Ilg, F. L., 68, 128, 146
Imboden, J. B., 169
Inhelder, B., 193

Jackson, C. W., 221
Jackson, D. D., 293
Jackson, E. H., 344
Jacobs, P. E., 17
Jahoda, M., 17
Jaques, M., 147
Jenkins, C. G., 68
Jensen, A. R., 193
Jerome, E. A., 193
Jersild, A. T., 68
Jervis, G. A., 95
Jones, H. E., 193
Jones, M., 321
Josselyn, I. M., 68, 169

Kagan, J., 146, 152, 169
Kahn, J. H., 244

Kallman, F. J., 25, 41, 293
Kanner, L., 95
Kapłan, L., 344
Kardiner, A., 117
Katz, B., 266
Katz, D., 146
Keller, S., 117
Kerenyi, A. B., 42
Kety, S. S., 293
Kimball, B., 76, 95
Kipfer, J. F., 344
Kissel, S., 221
Kitt, A. S., 244
Klatskin, E. H., 117
Klausmeier, H. J., 135, 146, 169
Klein, D. B., 156, 169
Knobloch, H., 41, 42
Knoebler, M., 68
Koch, S., 147
Kogan, N., 195
Kohler, M. C., 344
Kohn, M. L., 40, 115, 117
Krasner, L., 41
Kretschmer, E., 22
Krippner, S., 293
Krugman, M., 117, 343
Kubie, L. S., 18, 68, 169, 293

Lafferty, J. C., 344
Lambo, T. A., 221
Landis, P. H., 95
Landsman, T., 293
Langner, T. S., 118, 221, 293, 344
Larkins, J., 69, 195
Lasko, J. K., 95
Lauterbach, C. G., 96
Leeds, M., 68
Lehman, H. C., 182, 183, 194
Leighton, A. H., 18, 117
Leighton, D. C., 18, 293
Lemkau, P. V., 68
Lerner, M. J., 344
Lesser, L. N., 146
Levin, S., 321
Levitt, E. E., 321
Levy, D. M., 81, 82, 95
Lewin, K., 68
Lewin, W., 321
Lewis, F. A., Jr., 321
Lewis, R. T., 266

Lichter, S. O., 344
Liddell, H. S., 221, 244, 271, 293
Lidz, T., 95
Lindemann, E., 18
Lindemann, R., 291
Lindgren, H. C., 117
Lipsit, S. M., 244
Lipton, E. L., 96
Little, J. K., 18
Locke, N., 321
Lombroso, C., 22
Lovatt, M., 293
Luby, E. D., 194
Lucas, C. J., 294
Lucas, C. M., 68
Lund, F. H., 41

Maccoby, E. E., 68, 117
McCollum, J. A., 138, 147
McCord, W., 95, 294
McCourt, W. F., 295
McGhie, A., 69, 294
Mackay, R. P., 294
McMillan, T. M., 322
McNeil, E. B., 344
McNeil, J. D., 156, 169
Mahler, M. S., 146
Maier, N. R. F., 194
Malitz, S., 41, 265
Malzberg, B., 265
Margolin, J., 117
Marrazzi, A. S., 41, 265
Marshall, S., 222
Martin, W. E., 117
Maslow, A. H., 68, 146
Mass, H. S., 117
Masuda, M., 294
Mayer, K., 118
Mead, G. H., 130, 147
Mead, M., 103, 118
Meerloo, J. A. M., 95, 244
Mendelson, M., 147
Menninger, K., 321
Menninger, W. C., 169
Merton, R. K., 244
Mesnikoff, A. M., 321
Michael, S. T., 118, 344
Mills, L. F., 222
Milt, H., 265
Mirsky, I. A., 222

Mitchell, J. V., Jr., 135, 136, 147
Money-Kyrle, R. E., 147, 169
Moore, D., 321
Moore, M. E., 147, 169, 244
Moss, H. A., 146
Moustakas, C., 344
Murphy, G., 38, 41, 118, 222
Murphy, H. B. M., 222
Murphy, L. B., 222, 244
Murray, J. M., 69
Mussen, P., 95
Myers, J. K., 294

Neiser, E., 95
Neugarten, B. L., 116, 118
Newman, R. G., 345
Niederhoffer, A., 115
Nikelly, A., 265
Norman, V. B., 18
Norris, G. H., 345
Novey, S., 321
Nursten, J. P., 244

O'Brien, R., 169
Oden, M. H., 195
Oettinger, K. B., 345
Oettinger, L., Jr., 41
O'Kelly, E., 195
Olsen, I. A., 194
O'Neal, P., 294
Overall, B., 321
Ovesey, L., 117
Owens, W. A., Jr., 179, 194

Page, R. W., 42, 222
Parent, N., 170
Parnell, R. W., 23, 42
Pasamanick, B., 41, 42, 118, 294, 345
Patterson, F., 69
Pearson, G. H. J., 162, 169, 265
Peck, B., 18, 345
Peck, R. F., 95, 118, 147
Penfield, W., 194, 229, 245, 265
Perlman, I. R., 18
Perry, D. C., 135, 147
Persky, H., 42
Pfeiffer, J., 42
Pflanz, M., 42, 222
Phelps, H. R., 118
Phillips, E. L., 95, 345

Piaget, J., 193
Pinneau, S. R., 194
Powell, J. W., 170
Prescott, D. A., 345
Pressey, S. L., 194
Pringle, M. L. K., 95
Prugh, D. G., 96

Querido, A., 321

Radke, M. J., 96
Radler, D. H., 69
Rae, J. W., 194
Rae, S. F., 116
Rall, R., 295
Rapaport, A., 194
Rapaport, D., 244
Rassidakis, N. C., 321, 345
Rathod, N. H., 321
Redl, F., 69
Redlich, F. C., 117
Reid, D. D., 294
Reiss, M., 42
Reissman, F., 118
Reissman, L., 118
Remmers, H. H., 69
Rennie, T. A. C., 118
Richmond, J. B., 94, 96
Riessman, F., 321
Roberts, B. H., 294
Robins, E., 294
Robinson, R., 345
Rodman, M. J., 321
Roessler, R., 294
Rogers, C. R., 18, 123, 147
Rohde, P., 294
Rohrer, J. H., 147
Rosanoff, A. J., 25, 42
Rosenberg, M., 147
Rosenfeld, G. B., 42
Rosenman, R. H., 40
Rossberg, R., 147
Roudinesco, J., 96, 271
Rouman, J., 87, 96
Rowland, R. L., 18
Rubens, J. L., 147
Ruesch, J., 322
Russell, S. M., 69
Rust, R. M., 18
Rutherford, E., 95

Sanford, N., 170
Sanger, M. D., 222
Sarason, S., 42, 222, 245
Sargant, W., 294, 322
Sawry, J. M., 18
Schachter, F. F., 294
Schacter, H., 68
Schaffner, B., 96
Schiele, B. C., 322
Schlesinger, L., 69, 147
Schmideberg, M., 18, 96, 170, 222, 294
Schwartz, A. D., 345
Schwartz, D. A., 265
Scoville, W. B., 322
Searles, H. F., 295
Sears, R. R., 76, 96
Selling, L. S., 322
Selye, H., 170, 185, 195, 222, 295
Selznick, G. J., 69, 195
Shagass, C., 42
Sheard, M. H., 322
Sheldon, W. H., 22, 23, 42
Sherif, M., 147
Sherwood, S. L., 295
Shock, N. W., 195
Sifneos, P. E., 222, 295
Slater, P. E., 42
Smith, M., 68
Smith, M. B., 18
Smith, S. E., 118
Snygg, D., 145
Solomon, P., 42
Sommer, D. T., 322
Sommer, R., 295
Sontag, L. W., 69
Sorenson, R., 222
Spiegel, L. A., 147
Spock, B. M., 69
Spotnitz, H., 322
Springer, N. N., 118
Srole, L., 19, 266
Steckle, L. C., 170, 195, 266
Steiglitz, E. J., 195
Stein, J., 322
Stein, M., 118
Stendler, C. B., 117, 118
Stevenson, H. W., 148, 343
Steward, E. C., 148
Still, J. W., 195
Stoeckle, J. D., 195, 266, 295

Storrow, H. A., 320
Stoughton, R. B., 195
Straus, B. V., 92, 96
Stromgren, E., 43, 295
Stroup, F., 19
Swanson, E. O., 179, 195
Symonds, P. M., 96
Szalita, A. B., 245, 266

Tasch, R. J., 96
Taylor, C., 135, 148
Taylor, J. W., 245
Telford, C. W., 18
Terman, L. M., 195
Thompson, C. W., 193
Thorpe, L. P., 266
Tibbets, R. W., 320
Tibbitts, C., 195
Toolan, J. M., 96
Torrance, E. P., 222
Torribio, J. A., 345
Tucker, H., 322
Tuft, H. S., 223

Unger, S. M., 43

Vath, W. R., 43
Vaughan, W. T., Jr., 119
Vogel, W., 96
Vorster, D., 43, 295

Wada, J., 295
Wallach, M. A., 195
Walsh, A. M., 148
Watson, G., 195
Watson, J. B., 83, 96
Wattenberg, W. W., 69
Weckowicz, T. E., 295
Weider, A., 195, 222, 223, 295
Weil, A. A., 43
Weiss, F. A., 148
Wenar, C., 95, 292
Wertham, F., 245
Wheelis, A., 19
Williams, J. R., 343
Wilson, D. C., 170
Wistill, J., 184
Witkin, H. A., 245
Wittenberg, R. M., 148
Wolf, S., 223

Wolff, H. G., 221, 223
Woolworth, W. G., 119
Wortis, J., 43
Wright, B. A., 148

Yi-chuang Lu, 295
Youmans, E. G., 245

Zander, A., 148

Zanker, A., 322
Zappella, D., 195
Zeller, A. F., 245
Zeller, W. W., 69
Zemlick, M. J., 322
Ziegler, F. J., 295
Ziskind, E., 43
Zubek, J. P., 193
Zubin, J., 293

Index of Subjects

Academic achievement and emotions, 152
Academic retardation, 112
Accidents and emotions, 152
Achievement, and age, 182–185
  at advanced ages, 184
  of athletes, 182
  of musicians, 183
  of scientists, 182, 183
  of writers, 183
Acne, 210, 211
Acrophobia, 254
Acute stress, 203, 204
Adaptation and adjustment, 13
Adjustive behavior, 11–14
Adjustment, and anxiety, 14
  and ego strength, 144
  and normality, 12
  and perfection, 15
  and personality, 8
  and self-esteem, 138, 139
  and social sensitivity, 10
  and tranquility, 14
  as a process, 8
  criteria of, 9–11
  cultural influences on, 97–114
  defense mechanisms in, 224–243
  deterioration of, 246–263
  development of, 15
  dynamic equilibrium in, 11
  emotional maturity in, 10, 162–167
  in middle age, 53
  in old age, 54, 55
  influence of psychological stress on, 199–219

Adjustment (*Continued*)
  inheritance of, 21–27
  meaning of, 7–8
  mental hygiene concepts of, 8
  prenatal influences on, 324
  self-perception in, 10
  severe disorders of, 267–290
  social aspects of, 8
  social class influences on, 105–114
Adolescence, 49–52, 101, 102, 129, 131, 164, 262, 263
  body image in, 131
  emotional emancipation in, 164
  marriage in, 101, 102
  re-identity in, 129
  self-image in, 131
  transient personality disorders in, 262, 263
Adolescent period, 49–52
Adolescents, and parent conflicts, 51
  and television, 236
  group activities of, 51
  influence of father on, 74–76
  neurotic symptoms in, 50
  personality patterns of, 50
  social isolation of, 200
  worries of, 50
Adrenal glands, 36, 150, 205, 284
Adrenochrome, 284
Adrenocorticotropic hormone (ACTH), 205
Adulthood, 52
Adults, self-concept in, 130
Affect distortions, 253, 254
Affection, need for, 60

Affective psychoses, 278–280
Affective states, 154
Age and productivity, 182–185
Age of marriage, 101, 102
Aggression as a stress response, 216, 217
Aging, 174–182
  intelligence and mental activity in, 176–182
  physical aspects of, 171–176
  sensory changes in, 174–176
Alcohol and human efficiency, 188, 189
Alcoholism, 6
Allergies, 210
Amnesia, 252
Amniotic membrane, 28
Anoxia, 27, 28
Antimetabolites, 36
Antisocial personality, 259, 260
Anxiety, age of, 3
  and adjustment, 14
  and creativity, 213
  and creation of unrest, 64
  and life style, 36
  and self-acceptance, 135, 136
  coping with, 224–243
  definition of, 212
  effects of, 212, 213
  guilt, as a form of, 213–214
  in child rearing, 212
  in learning, 213
  in neuroses, 269
  in the home, 202
Anxiety neurosis, 272
Aphasia, 251
Art in psychotherapy, 314
Asthma, 210
Ataractic drugs, 300
Atherosclerosis, 208
Attitudes, 154
Auditory projection tests, 314
Authoritarian father, 77, 78
Autism, 71, 275, 278
Autonomic nervous system, 153

Behavior, 11–14, 20–39, 57, 62–65, 97–114, 134–144, 145–167, 171–191, 199–219, 267–290
  adaptive, 13
  adjustive, 11–14
  and body build, 21

Behavior (Continued)
  and brain function, 30–35
  and emotions, 149–167
  and maturity, 63
  and normal growth, 57
  chemical influences on, 36
  cultural influences on, 62, 63, 97–114
  deterioration of, 171–191
  effects of birth trauma on, 29
  effects of injury and disease on, 190, 191
  effects of prejudice on, 155–157
  embryonic roots of, 27
  glandular influences on, 35, 36
  group influences on, 61
  influence of heredity on, 21–27
  maladjusted, degrees of, 12
  metabolic influences on, 36
  postnatal influences on, 29–30
  prenatal influences on, 27–29
  psychobiological origins of, 20–39
  psychological stress in, 199–219
  selective, 64–65
  self-concept in, 134–144
  severe disorders of, 267–290
  social class influences on, 105–114
Behavior disturbances, chemical factors in, 33
Behavior patterns, establishment of, 65
Behavior problems in children, 30
Bibliotherapy, 313
Biochemical changes in psychoses, 284–286
Biochemical origins of psychoses, 283
Biochemical research, 26
Biological differences, sources of, 24
Biological functioning, social influences on, 37, 38
Biological needs, 59–60
Birth trauma, 29
Blood-brain barrier, 32
Body build, 21–22
Body image, 131
  in ego development, 126
  schizophrenia, 276
Body types, 21–24
Boredom, 187, 188
Brain, aging of, 176
  and emotions, 151
  and sensory stimulation, 34

Brain *(Continued)*
  effects of injury and disease on, 190,
    191
  electrical activity of, 31, 285, 286
  electrical stimulation of, 256
  of schizophrenics, 285, 286
Brain chemistry and behavior, 33
Brain function and behavior, 30–35
Brain injury, 29, 285
Brainwashing, 33
Brain waves, 32
Broken families, 99, 100
Broken homes, 6

Carbon dioxide therapy, 307
Cardiovascular reactions to stress, 208
Catalepsy, 277
Catatonic schizophrenia, 275, 277
Cerebral damage, 29
Character and adjustment, 8
Character disorders, 12
Chemical balance in body, 36
Chemical influences on brain function,
  32, 33
Childhood, emotions in, 158–162
Childhood schizophrenia, 30, 278
Child rearing, social class differences in,
  109–113
Children, 30, 44–52, 71–78, 82–85, 88–90,
    91–93, 100-103, 109–113, 138, 158–
    162, 166, 167, 180, 181, 270, 271,
    275–278, 281, 327
  autistic, 278
  discipline of, 82–85
  effects of position in family on, 85–93
  emancipation from home, 103
  emotional development of, 158–162,
    166, 167, 327
  first born, 86–88
  friendship preferences of, 111
  growth of interests in, 180, 181
  in democratic homes, 84, 85
  in early and middle childhood, 46, 47
  influence of father on, 73–78
  maternal deprivation in, 71–72
  middle-born, 88–89
  neuroses in, 270, 271
  normal stages of growth, 44–52
  of broken homes, 100
  of minority groups, 138

Children *(Continued)*
  of working mothers, 100, 101
  only, 91–93
  origins of behavior problems in, 30
  prepsychotic, 275, 278, 281
  puberty stage, 47–49
  schizophrenic, 30, 278
  social class differences in, 109–113
  uncared for, 340
  youngest, 89–90
Chlorpromazine, 300
Chronic stress, 203, 204
Clinical tests, 313
Clinics, 338, 340
  adequacy of, 340
  guidance, 338
  walk-in, 338
Colitis, 207, 217
Community influence on adjustment,
  327
Compensation, 231, 232
Compulsions, 254, 255
Compulsive eaters, 233
Conditioning, 64, 203, 270, 271
  and stress, 203
  in neuroses, 270, 271
Conflict, 91, 214, 215
Conscience, 58, 81, 124, 125
Consultation services, 339
Conversion reactions, 273, 274
Cortical activity and sensory depriva·
  tion, 33–35
Cortisone products and brain action,
  256
Counselors, 308
Crime, 7
Criminal types, 22
Cultural imprinting, 110
Cultural stress, 199–201
Culturally deprived, 108, 336–337
Culture, and social class, 105–114
  influence on adjustment, 8
  influence on behavior, 97–114
  influence on family, 98–105
  influence on individual, 62, 63
  of youth, 103, 104
  sources of stress in, 199–201
Cyclothymic psychoses, 279
Cyclothymoid personality, 279

Day centers, 316
Defective thinking, 249, 250, 251
Defense mechanisms, 140, 224–243
    classification of, 224, 225
    description of, 226–243
Delinquents, 60
Delusions, 250, 251
Dementia praecox, 275
Dental caries as stress response, 208, 209
Deoxyribonucleic acid (DNA), 26
Dependency, 260, 261
Depersonalization, 255, 260
Depression, 49, 150, 189, 253, 279, 280
    and sleep, 189
    in puberty, 49
    psychotic, 279, 280
Dermatitis, 210
Deterioration of adjustment, 246–263
Development, 55–58, 171–176
    basic principles of, 55–58
    individual variations in, 56
    motor, 171–176
    physical, 171–176
Developmental tasks, 57, 58
Differentiation of emotions, 158–162
Dipsomania, 255
Discipline, 82–85, 202
    in the home, 82–85
    use of stress in, 202
Disease and behavior, 190, 191
Disorientation, 251
Displacement, 227
Disruption of families, 99–101
Dissocial personality, 259, 260
Dissociation, 143
Distortions of reality, 248, 249
Disturbed families, 286–288
Divorce, 6, 102
Dizygotic twins, 24, 25
Domination, 80, 81
Drop-outs, college, 6
Drug addiction, 6
Drug therapy, 300–304
Dynamics of growth, 58–65

Eccentrics, 258–259
Economic deprivation, 325
Ectomorphs, 22
Eczema, 210

Education, and adjustment, 15
    and mental decline, 179
    in mental hygiene, 329
Ego, and human interaction, 138
    and self-acceptance, 135
    breakdown of, 143, 144
    changes in, 139
    defense of, 139, 224–243
    development of, 125, 126
    dissociation of, 143
    function of, 124
    reformation in adolescence, 50
Ego development and prejudice, 155
Ego enhancement, 126
Ego-ideal, 125
Ego strength, 136
Egocentric behavior, 129
Egocentricism, 137, 234
Electrical energy, in brain, 31
Electroconvulsive therapy, 305
Electrocortical activity, 31–32
Electroencephalograph, 31
Electrograph, 31
Electroshock and endocrine glands, 36
Electroshock therapy, 305
Emancipation from family, 103
Emergency mental health care, 337
Emergency psychotherapy, 309
Emotional behavior, differentiation of, 158–162
Emotional breakdown among soldiers, 201
Emotional control, 153, 161, 190, 191
Emotional development, 47, 149–167
    fixation and regression in, 161, 162
    in early and middle childhood, 47
Emotional disorder, vulnerability to, 38
Emotional disturbance, brain waves in, 32
    during growth spurts, 56
    incidence of, 5
Emotional energy, discharge of, 157, 160, 161
Emotional expansion, 164
Emotional expression, 10, 160–161
Emotional growth, 158–162, 166, 167
Emotional insecurity, 165, 166
Emotional maladjustment, extent of, 4–7

Emotional maturity, and prejudice, 155
    criteria of, 162, 163
    development of, 164
    in adjustment, 10
Emotional reactions, involuntary nature
    of, 153
Emotional restriction, 54, 161
Emotional security, 165, 166
Emotional states, 150
Emotional stress, 3, 151
Emotional upset, 151
Emotions, and awareness, 152
    and mental activity, 151, 152
    and physical disorders, 157–158
    control and expression of, 159–162
    in accidents, 152
    influence on learning, 178
    nature of, 149–167
    physiological effects of, 150
    unconscious processes in, 152
Empathy, 130
Endocrine function and psychological
    37
    and chemical balance, 36
        stress, 36
Endocrine glands, and behavior, 35, 36,
    and psychoses, 284
Energizing drugs, 300, 304
Environmental therapy, 315
Excitement, 149
Exhibitionism, 261
Exultation, 253

Family, cultural influences on, 98–105
    democracy in, 84, 85
    disciplinary practices in, 82–85
    group therapy, 311
    mobility, 98
    ordinal position of children in, 85–93
    parent-child interactions in, 78–82
    psychological forces in, 70–93
    role of father in, 73–78
Family disintegration, 326
Family ties, 98
Family unit, 98–101
Families, disturbed, 78, 286–288
Fantasy, 236
Father, absence of, 76, 77
    authoritarian, 77, 78

Father (Continued)
    influence in home, 73–78
    influence on adolescents, 74, 75
Fathers of psychotic children, 287
Fatigue, 186–188, 272–273
    mental, 187, 188
    nerve, 186
    physical, 186
    psychological, 272–273
    sensory, 186
Feelings, 153, 154
    of guilt, 214
Fetus, activity of, 29
    chemical influences on, 27
Films in psychotherapy, 314
Fixation, 161, 162
Fraternal twins, 24, 25
Frustration, 10, 214, 215
Frustration tolerance, 159
Fugue, 252
Functional psychoses, 275–282, 289

Gastrointestinal reactions in stress, 206,
    207
Genes, 26
Genetic development, of psychoses, 283,
    284
    of self-concept, 127–134
Gerontology, 55
Glands, 35, 36, 150, 151, 284
    adrenal, 36, 150
    and psychoses, 284
    influence on behavior, 35, 36
    thymus, 35
    thyroid, 35
Glandular factors in psychoses, 284
Glandular reactions in stress, 205–206
Glial cells, 32
Gonads, growth of, 48
Group contagion, 61
Group forces and ego change, 140
Group identity and social class, 108
Group influences, on behavior, 61
    on emotional expression, 160–161
Group interaction, 141
Group psychotherapy, 140, 141
Group status, need for, 61, 62
Group therapy, 140, 141, 310–312
    purpose of, 310
    techniques of, 311

Growth, and behavior, 57
  and individuality, 45, 128
  basic principles of, 55–58
  during adolescence, 49–52
  dynamics of, 58–65
  effect of chemicals on, 28
  emotional, 158–162
  fixation and regression in, 161, 162
  in interests, 180, 181
  individual variations in, 56
  irregularity in, 56
  of preschool child, 45, 46
  spurts and plateaus in, 56
  stages of, 44–45
Guidance clinics, 338
Guilt, 213–214

Halfway house, 315
Hallucinations, 34, 249
Harvard Growth Studies, 49
Hearing loss, 175
Hebephrenic schizophrenia, 275, 277, 278
Heredity, and body build, 21
  environmental influences on, 27
  factors modifying influence of, 27
  facts and theories of, 21–27
  in psychoses, 283, 284
  sources of evidence on, 24
Hidden delinquency, 5
Hogg Foundation, 333
Home, democratic atmosphere in, 84, 85
  disciplinary practices in, 82–85
  effects of mass communication on, 102
  effects of urbanization on, 102
  influence of father in, 73–78
  parent-child interactions in, 78–82
  psychological forces in, 70–93
  stress in, 201–202
Homeostasis, 59
Homes, impoverished, 325
Homicidal mania, 255
Homosexuality, 261
Hormones, adrenal, 205
  in stress, 205
  ovarian, 206
Human abilities, 171–191
Human behavior, theories of, 20
Human needs, 58–65

Humors of the body, 21
Hydrocortisone in stress, 205
Hydrotherapy, 306
Hyperamnesia, 252
Hyperkinesis, 254
Hypnotism, 312
Hysteric neuroses, 273, 274

Id, 124, 127
Ideal self, 125
Identical twins, 24, 25
Identification, as an adjustment mechanism, 239, 240
  in adolescence, 129
  in ego development, 239
  in personality development, 132, 133
  in superego formation, 125
  with father, 74, 76
Infancy, adjustment in, 70–72
Infant, emotional development of, 158
Infantile autism, 71
Inferiority, 259
Illusions, 34, 249
Immaturity, 162
Impoverished homes, 325
Inadequate mothering, 30
Independence, struggle for, 130
Individual, sources of stress in, 202, 203
Inherited characteristics, 21–27
Inhibition, 150
Injuries and behavior, 190
Insecurity, emotional, 165, 166
Insulin therapy, 304
Intellectual growth, 181, 182
Intelligence, and interests, 181
  and mental decline, 179
  effects of age on, 176–182
Intelligence tests, 176
Interdepartmental Committee on Children and Youth, 333
Interests and age, 180, 181
Internalization of stress stimuli, 203
Interpersonal relations, 78–82, 112, 136–138
  and social class, 112
  in the family, 78–82
Intestinal reactions to stress, 207
Intrauterine development, 27
Introjection, 239

Introspection, 142
Involutional melancholia, 279–280
Involutional psychosis, 279–280
Isolation, in old age, 180
  social, 200, 201

Joint Commission on Mental Illness
  and Health, 246, 339, 341
Juvenile delinquency, 5, 60

Kleptomania, 255

Leadership, 183
Learning, and emotions, 151, 152
  and stress tolerance, 218
  anxiety in, 213
  effects of aging on, 176–182
  emotional influences on, 178
  peak of, 177
Leucotomy, 305
Life cycle, 44, 58
Life expectancy, 171
Life span, 171
Lobotomy, 305
Loneliness in old age, 54
Lower classes, 107–114
Lysergic acid (LSD), 33, 38, 256, 303

Maladjusted behavior, degrees of, 12
Maladjustment, and social class, 112,
    113, 114
  degrees of, 13
  effects of mental hygiene programs
    on, 339
  extent of, 246–263
  inheritance of, 21–27
  origins of symptoms in, 256–257
  prevention of, 324, 328–330
  symptoms of, 247–257
  treatment of, 299–312
Male climacteric, 53
Manias, 255
Manic-depressive psychosis, 25, 279
Marriage, 101, 102
Masturbation, 261
Maternal deprivation, 70–72, 271
Maturation, 128
  defects in, 28, 29
Maturity, and behavior, 63, 65
  and learning, 177

Maturity (Continued)
  emotional, 162–167
  physical, 171–176
Mechanisms, of avoidance, 235–241
  of deception, 225–230
  of defense, 224–243
  of substitution, 230–235
Melancholia, involutional, 279–280
Memory and mental fatigue, 187
Memory loss, 177
Menopause, 53
Mental aberrations, 249–253
Mental ability, and aging, 176–182
  influence of education on, 180
  social influences on, 180
Mental activity, and emotions, 151, 152
  effects of age on, 176–182
  fatigue in, 187
Mental block, 188
Mental disorders and social class, 288,
    289
  primary prevention of, 328
Mental disturbance and social environ-
    ment, 38
Mental efficiency, 179, 187, 188
Mental energies, 124
Mental fatigue, 187, 188
Mental health education, 334, 335
Mental hospitals, 316
Mental hygiene, and the family, 325
  and the schools, 326
  consultation services in, 334
  influence of economic deprivation
    on, 325
  preventive services, 323–330
  research in, 341
Mental hygiene clinics, see clinics
Mental hygiene programs, effects of,
    339
  financing of, 341
  in communities, 336–338
  in school districts, 338
  of federal government, 330–334
  of states, 334–335
Mental hygiene services, by private
    organizations, 333
  for the culturally deprived, 336–
    337
  in metropolitan areas, 336
  of the federal government, 331–333

Mental illness, and social class status, 113, 114
  cost of, 4
  cure of, 316
  decrease of, 340
  prevalence of, 4, 5
  pseudotherapy in, 317
  public perception of, 340
  recovery from, 289, 290, 302, 317
  spontaneous remission of symptoms in, 316
  treatment of, 299–307
Mental institutions, changes in, 315
Mental mechanisms, 224
Mental retardation, genetic origins of, 26
  metabolic disorders in, 324
  prevention of, 324
Meprobamate, 300
Mescaline, 33
Mesomorphs, 22
Metabolic defects, 26
Metabolic disturbances, in mental retardation, 324
  in stress, 209
Metabolic influences, on behavior, 36
Metabolism, and endocrine activity, 36, 37
  in emotions, 150
  in psychotics, 284, 285
Metrazol shock, 305
Middle age, adjustments of, 53
  interests in, 53, 54
  physiological changes in, 53
Middle classes, 107–114
Migraine headaches, 208
Milbank Memorial Fund, 333
Milieu therapy, 315
Mind, 30
Minority groups, 138, 200
Mobility, in families, 98
Mongoloids, 26
Monozygotic twins, 24, 25
Moods, 154
Moral character, origins of, 125
Mother-child relations, 30
Mothers, effects on infants, 30, 70–72
  of neurotic children, 270, 271
  of schizophrenic children, 287

Mothers (Continued)
  role in home, 70, 71
  working, 100–101
Motivation, 59
  and mental fatigue, 187
  in learning, 178, 179
Motor development, 171–176
Motor performance, 174
Motor reactions in stress, 211
Multiple personality, 255
Music in psychotherapy, 314

Narcoanalysis, 312
Narcotherapy, 327
Narcotics addicts, 6
National Association for Mental Health, 333, 335
National Institute of Mental Health, 331
National Mental Health Act, 330
Need satisfactions, factors influencing, 62–64
  in personality development, 64, 65
Needs, 58–65
  biological, 59–60
  psychosocial, 60–62
Negativism, 237, 238
Nerve fatigue, 186
Nerve tonics, 268
Nerve weakness, 268, 272
Nervous breakdown, 268
Nervous system, autonomic, 153
  development of, 46
Nervousness, 211, 267, 268
Neurasthenic neurosis, 272, 273
Neurokinen, 211
Neurological development, 28, 29
Neurological impairment, 324
Neuroses, 13, 267–274
  anxiety in, 269
  forms of, 272–274
  nature of, 268, 269
  origins of, 269–272
  physiology of, 271, 272
Neurotic behavior in animals, 268, 269, 271
Neurotic breakdown, 270
Normalcy, 13
Normality and adjustment, 12
Nuclear family, 98, 99

Obsessions, 251
Obsessive-compulsive reactions, 254
Official culture, 107
Old age, 54, 55
Older child, 86–88
Older workers, 185
Only child, 91–93
Ordinal position in family, 85–93
Organic needs, 59–60
Organic psychoses, 274, 275
Ovarian hormones and stress, 206
Overcompensation, 232
Overindulgence, 81, 82
Overprotection, 79, 80
Oxygen deprivation, 27

Paramnesia, 252
Paranoia, 282
Paranoid person, 251, 281, 282
Paranoid schizophrenia, 275–277
Parental domination, 80, 81
Parent-child interactions, 78–82
Parents, influence on emotional growth, 166, 167
  of neurotic children, 270, 271
Parkinson's Disease, 303
Pedophilia, 261
Peptic ulcers, 37, 38
Perceptions, distortion of, 248, 249
  in emotion, 151
Permissiveness in lower class homes, 110
Personality, and adjustment, 8
  and development of self, 125–126
  antisocial, 259, 260
  central core of, 65, 134
  definition of, 64
  improvement of, 139–142
  origins of, 129
Personality change, 318
Personality characteristics, genetic transmission of, 21
Personality development, and need satisfactions, 64, 65
  psychoanalytic theories of, 125–127
Personality deviations, 257–263
Personality disorders, 12, 247, 262, 263
Peyote cactus, 32
Phenothiazine, 300
Phobia, school, 238, 239

Phobias, 253, 254
Physical ailments as adjustment devices, 238, 239
Physical deterioration, 171–176
Physical development, 171–176
Physical disorders, emotional bases of, 157–158
Physical efficiency, 173
Physical fatigue, 186–187
Physical growth, in adolescence, 47, 48
  in early and middle childhood, 46
  in preschool child, 45
  in puberty, 47, 48
Physical stress, 185–191
  effects of alcohol on, 188, 189
  effects of injuries and disease, 190, 191
  effects of sleep on, 189
  nutritional and vitamin deficiencies in, 189, 190
Physical therapy, 306
Physiological function in emotions, 150
Physique and temperament, 22, 23
Pituitary hormones in stress, 205
Placebo, 301, 302
Pleasure drive, 127
Post-partum psychosis, 263
Preadolescence, 47–49
Prejudice, 137, 155–157
Premenstrual tension, 206
Preschool child, 45, 46
Primary prevention, focus of, 323
  in prenatal and infancy periods, 324–325
  scope of, 328
Prime of life, 182
Principles of growth, 55–58
Progesterone, 206
Projection, 226, 227
Projective tests, 313
Pseudotherapy, 317
Psilocybin, 33, 256
Psychasthenia, 272
Psychic energies, 124
Psychoactive drugs, 300–304
Psychoanalysis, 309
Psychoanalytic concepts of self, 124–127
Psychodrama, 311

Psychogenic disorders, 157, 158
Psychogenic mechanisms, 238
Psychogenic psychoses, 275–282
Psychological disorders, incidence of, 4–7
Psychological escape, 235, 236
Psychological stress, and life style, 36
accommodation of body to, 204
gastrointestinal reactions in, 206–207
glandular reactions in, 205–206
somatic reactions in, 204–212
sources of, 199–203
Psychological therapy, effects of, 316
Psychomotor retardation, 254
Psychoneuroses, 13, 272
Psychopath, 280, 281
Psychopathology in general population, 5
Psychophysiological ailments, 157–158
Psychoses, and social class status, 113, 119, 288
classification of, 274, 275
cyclothymic, 279
family genesis of, 286–288
functional, 275–290
hereditary transmission of, 25
involutional, 279, 280
manic-depressive, 279
multiple causation of, 289
organic, 274–275
origins of, 282–289
post-partum, 263
recovery from, 289–290
symptoms of, 33
Psychosocial needs, 60–62
Psychosomatic ailments, 157–158
Psychosurgery, 305, 306
Psychotherapy, and class status, 309
aids to, 312–314
communication in, 309
effects of, 316
emergency treatment, 309
handicaps of, 308, 309
in groups, 140, 141
purpose of, 308
Psychotic depression, 279, 280
Psychotics, in general population, 274
Psychotogenic families, 286–288

Puberty, and ego development, 126
and mental growth, 49
emotional reactions of, 49
physical growth in, 47, 48
sex differences in, 48
Puerperal reaction, 263
Pyromania, 255

Rationalization, 226
Rauwolfia, 304
Reaction formation, 233
Readjustment, 323–341
Reality distortions, 248, 249
Reality structuring, 90
Regression, 161, 162, 237
Rejecting children, 79
Rejection, 11, 78, 79, 138, 143
of children in school, 11
of self, 138, 143
Re-identity, in adolescence, 129
Repression, 203, 227–228
Retrograde amnesia, 252
Ribonucleic acid (RNA), 34
Role experimentation, 133, 134
Role playing, 311
Rorschach test, 313
Rozenzweig Picture-Frustration Study, 313

Schizoid personality, 275
Schizophrenia, and social class status, 113, 288
catatonic, 277
childhood, 30
family influences on, 287
hebephrenic, 277, 278
hereditary transmission of, 25
metabolic changes in, 284, 285
paranoid, 276, 277
physiological processes in, 286
simple, 275
treatment of, 305
types of, 275
Schizophrenic behavior, 275–276
Schizophrenic reactions, 275
Scholastic failure, 6
School, and emotions of children, 166, 167
and social class, 110–113
development of interests in, 180, 181

School achievement and self-esteem, 138, 139
School phobia, 238, 239
School's influence on adjustment, 326
Secondary gain, 158
Secondary prevention, 328–330
Selective behavior, 64, 65
Self, 123–144
Self-acceptance and anxiety, 135, 136
    and insight, 135
    and interpersonal relations, 136-138
Self-actualization, 62, 133
Self-assessment, 141, 142
Self-attitudes, 131
Self-concept, and behavior, 134–144
    changes in, 139–144
    definition of, 123
    emergence of, 124–134
    genetic concepts of, 127–134
    in adults, 130
    influence of parents on, 131
    preservation of, 134
    psychoanalytic theories of, 124–127
Self-confidence, 130
Self-esteem and adjustment, 138, 139
Self-ideal, 132
Self-identity, 123–144
Self-image, 51, 131
Self-improvement, 139–142
Self-insight, 135
Self-other concept, 130
Self-perception in adjustment, 9
Self-realization, 62, 133
Self-recognition, 128
Self-regard, 137
Self-rejection, 138
Self-role, 133
Senile decline, 185
Senility, 54, 55
Sensory changes with age, 174–176
Sensory defects, 30
Sensory deprivation, 33–35, 256
Sensory fatigue, 186
Serotonin, 37
Sex reversal, 28
Sex typing, 74, 76
Sexual deviations, 261, 262
Shock therapies, 304, 305
Siblings, interaction of, 90, 91
Simple amnesia, 252

Simple schizophrenia, 275, 276
Sleep and depression, 189
Social change, 201
Social class, 105–114
    and maladjustment, 112, 113–114
    school influences on, 110–113
Social class stratification, 106, 107
Social classes, characteristics of, 107–114
    psychoses in, 288
Social environment and mental disturbance, 38
Social influences on biological functioning, 37, 38
Social interaction and emotional disorder, 38
Social isolation, 200, 201
Social pressure, 62
Social sensitivity, 11
Social stress, 199–201
Sociocultural influences on psychoses, 288, 289
Socioeconomic groups, 105–114
Sociopath, 281
Somatic stress reactions, 204–212
Somatic therapy, forms of, 300–307
    purpose of, 299
Somatotypes, 22, 23
Spoiled child, 81, 82
State mental hygiene agencies, 334
Stomach, reactions to stress, 206, 207
Stress, acute, 203, 204
    and discipline, 202
    and social class, 109
    chronic, 203, 204
    cumulative effects of, 257
    definition of, 185
    emotional, 3
    in child rearing, 201, 202
    in the home, 201, 202
    internal, 202, 203
    physical, 158, 185–191
    psychological, 199–219
    tolerance of, 218, 219
    unconscious, 202, 203
Sublimation, 233, 234
Substitution as a defense mechanism, 232, 233
Suicide, 6, 7

Superego, 124–127
  emergence of, 125
  in personality formation, 127
Suppression, 152, 228–229
Syndrome, 257

Taraxein, 284
Television, addiction to, 236
  in group therapy, 311
Tests, of intelligence, 176
  projective, 313
Temperament, and body build, 21
  and body humors, 22
  transmission of, 24
Tension, accumulation of, 204
  circulatory effects of, 208
  premenstrual, 206
  warnings of, 219
Thematic Apperception test, 313
Therapies, psychological, 307–312
  somatic, 299–307
Therapists, adequacy of, 340
  types of, 307, 308
Therapy, and social class, 114
  art and music in, 314
  environmental, 315
  group, 310–312
  milieu, 315
Thinking, disturbed, 249, 250, 251
Thyroid gland, 35, 205
Tolerance to stress, 218, 219
Tranquility and adjustment, 14
Tranquilizers, effects of, 303, 304
  major, 300
  minor, 300
Tranquilizing drugs, 15, 300–304
Transferred compensation, 232

Transient personality disorder, 262, 263
Transient rage, 253
Traveling clinics, 334
Tryptamine, 33
Twins, dizygotic, 24, 25
  maladjustment in, 24, 25
  monozygotic, 24, 25
  studies of, 24–26

Ulcerative colitis, 207, 217
Ulcers, peptic, 37, 38, 207
Unconscious mind, 227–229
Underachievement, 139
Undernourishment, 189, 190
Urbanization, 102

Values in adjustment, 9
Verbal dissociation, 250
Visual deterioration with age, 175
Vitamin deficiency, 36, 189, 190
Volunteer mental health associations, 335

Walk-in clinics, 338
Wasted talents, 5
Withdrawal as a stress response, 217, 218
Work experience programs, 339
Working mothers, 100, 101

Youngest child in family, 89–90
Youth, social stress in, 200
  wasted talents of, 5
Youth culture, 103, 104

Zoophobia, 254